Monetary union in Europe began in 1999. The fiscal policy implications are, in many ways, more complex than the monetary issues, yet very little has been written on them. This book contains eleven chapters and three discussion essays, which analyse a spectrum of empirical, theoretical, institutional and political aspects of the design and impact of fiscal policy in EMU. The contributors are some of the most experienced analysts in the field.

Topics covered include the need for the consequences of fiscal coordination, constraints on national deficits and debt levels (the Stability Pact) and the role of fiscal federalism and insurance. The importance of coordinating fiscal and monetary policies is also considered in depth. As long as these strategic and institutional aspects remain imperfectly understood, EMU will not be able to function to its full advantage and may suffer periods of instability or weakness.

ANDREW HUGHES HALLETT is Professor of Economics at the University of Strathclyde. He has previously been Professor of Economics at the University of Newcastle and Princeton University and has also worked as a consultant to the IMF, World Bank and European Commission.

MICHAEL M. HUTCHISON is Professor of Economics, University of California at Santa Cruz. He is also a Research Fellow at the Economic Policy Research Unit, University of Copenhagen, and a Visiting Scholar at the Federal Reserve Bank of San Francisco. He has previously worked at the Bank for International Settlements and been a Visiting Scholar at the Bank of Japan and the Reserve Bank of New Zealand.

SVEND E. HOUGAARD JENSEN is Head of Research in Economics, Ministry of Business and Industry, Denmark and a Research Fellow at the Economic Policy Research Unit, University of Copenhagen. His research interests include European integration, dynamic fiscal policy and productivity analysis.

T0328300

Fiscal aspects of European monetary integration

Edited by

Andrew Hughes Hallett
University of Strathclyde

Michael M. Hutchison
University of California, Santa Cruz

and Svend E. Hougaard Jensen
University of Copenhagen

CAMBRIDGE
UNIVERSITY PRESS

CAMBRIDGE UNIVERSITY PRESS
Cambridge, New York, Melbourne, Madrid, Cape Town, Singapore,
São Paulo, Delhi, Dubai, Tokyo, Mexico City

Cambridge University Press
The Edinburgh Building, Cambridge CB2 8RU, UK

Published in the United States of America by Cambridge University Press, New York

www.cambridge.org
Information on this title: www.cambridge.org/9780521178273

First published 1999
First paperback edition 2011

A catalogue record for this publication is available from the British Library

ISBN 978-0-521-65162-2 Hardback
ISBN 978-0-521-17827-3 Paperback

Contents

v

Preface

The chapters in this volume were inspired by the EPRU conference 'Fiscal Aspects of European Monetary Integration', held in Hornbaek, Denmark (15–16 August 1997). Revised papers from that conference, and several additional invited contributions (Andersen and Dogonowski, Artis and Winkler and DeGrauwe, respectively, chapters 4 and 7 and the discussion following part IV) cover the main topical issues in the debate over how fiscal policy and institutions should be designed in Europe against the background of the new monetary union. The conference was sponsored by the Economic Policy Research Unit (EPRU), University of Copenhagen, and organised by Michael M. Hutchison and Svend E. Hougaard Jensen.

Our principal debt is to the contributors and the conference participants, who have all helped make this project an exciting and worthwhile undertaking. For financial support we are grateful to the Danish National Research Foundation which provides the prime funding of EPRU. Grethe Mark, EPRU's administrative secretary, has handled the logistics of the conference and this manuscript with her usual professionalism. We also thank Barbara Docherty for the detailed and insightful editing of the manuscript. Finally, the assistance of Ashwin Rattan of Cambridge University Press has been essential to the book's swift publication.

Glasgow and Copenhagen   Andrew Hughes Hallett
July 1998   Michael M. Hutchison
                                    Svend E. Hougaard Jensen

Contributors

Christopher Allsopp, Professor, Department of Economics and Statistics, Oxford University, UK

Torben M. Andersen, Professor, Institute of Economics, University of Aarhus, Denmark, and Research Fellow, Centre for Economic Policy Research, London, UK

Michael J. Artis, Professor, Department of Economics, European University Institute, Italy, and Research Fellow, Centre for Economic Policy Research, London, UK

Roel M. W. J. Beetsma, Economist, Ministry of Economic Affairs, the Netherlands, and Research Fellow, Centre for Economic Policy Research, London, UK

U. Michael Bergman, Associate Professor, Department of Economics, University of Lund, Sweden

Giancarlo Corsetti, Assistant Professor, Department of Economics, Yale University, USA, and Assistant Professor, Department of Economics, University of Rome III, Italy

Paul De Grauwe, Professor, Centre for Economic Research, University of Leuven, Belgium, and Research Fellow, Centre for Economic Policy Research, London, UK

Robert R. Dogonowski, PhD student, Department of Economics, University of Aarhus, Denmark

Svend E. Hougaard Jensen, Head of Research, Division of Economic Analysis, Danish Ministry of Business and Industry, and Research Fellow, Economic Policy Research Unit, University of Copenhagen, Denmark

Andrew Hughes Hallett, Professor, Department of Economics, University of Strathclyde, and Research Fellow, Centre for Economic Policy Research, London, UK

Michael M. Hutchison, Professor, Department of Economics, University of California at Santa Cruz, USA, and Research Fellow, Economic Policy Research Unit, University of Copenhagen, Denmark

Kenneth M. Kletzer, Professor, Department of Economics, University of California at Santa Cruz, USA

Peter McAdam, Lecturer, Department of Economics, University of Kent, UK

Warwick McKibbin, Professor, Department of Economics, Australian National University, Australia, and Research Fellow, Brookings Institution, USA

Paolo Pesenti, Assistant Professor, Department of Economics, Princeton University, and Research Fellow, National Bureau of Economic Research, Boston, USA

Neil Rankin, Senior Lecturer, Department of Economics, University of Warwick, and Research Fellow, Centre for Economic Policy Research, London, UK

Niels Thygesen, Professor, Department of Economics, University of Copenhagen, and Research Fellow, Economic Policy Research Unit, University of Copenhagen, Denmark

David Vines, Professor, Department of Economics and Statistics, Oxford University; Department of Economics, Australian National University, Australia, and Research Fellow, Centre for Economic Policy Research, London, UK

Thomas D. Willett, Professor, Department of Economics, Claremont Graduate University, USA

Claas Wihlborg, Professor of Economics, University of Goteborg, Sweden

Bernhard Winkler, Economist, European Central Bank, Frankfurt, Germany

Acronyms and abbreviations

BHMT	Bryant–Henderson–McKibbin–Taylor rules (see chapter 11)
CAD	Capital Adequacy Directive
CAPM	capital asset-pricing model
CGE	computable general equilibrium
CPI	consumer price index
EC	European Community
ECB	European Central Bank
ECOFIN	Economic and Financial Council
ECU	European Currency Unit
EDP	Excessive Deficits Procedure
EIB	European Investment Bank
EMI	European Monetary Institute
EMS	European Monetary System
EMU	Economic and Monetary Union
EPRU	Economic Policy Research Unit, University of Copenhagen
ERM	Exchange Rate Mechanism
EU	European Union
FD	fiscal dominance
G7	Group of 7
GDP	gross domestic product
IMF	International Monetary Fund
LR	likelihood-ratio
MD	monetary dominance
MSG2	McKibbin–Sachs Global Economic Model (see chapter 11)
NAIRU	non-accelerating inflation rate of unemployment
NPV	net present value
OCA	optimum curency area
OECD	Organization for Economic Cooperation and Development
PPP	purchasing power parity
SCA	single currency area
SFA	supranational fiscal authority
SGP	Stability and Growth Pact
UIP	uncovered interest parity
VAR	vector autoregression
VMA	vector moving average

1 Fiscal aspects of European monetary integration: an introduction

*Andrew Hughes Hallett, Michael M. Hutchison and
Svend E. Hougaard Jensen*

Economic and Monetary Union began on 1 January 1999 with eleven
Member States of the European Union (EU). Control over national
monetary policies has been transferred to the European Central Bank
(ECB) in Frankfurt, an entity setting a common policy and interest rate
for all Economic and Monetary Union (EMU) participants. Having been
discussed intensively since at least 1969, when Pierre Werner received a
mandate to prepare a report (Werner *et al.*, 1970) on monetary integration
for the European Community (EC), monetary union in Europe has been
made a reality partly by economic calculus but mainly by the sheer force
of political and bureaucratic determination. In several respects, EMU
represents a unique historical experiment, not least because it combines
a centralized monetary union with largely independent national fiscal
policies and budgetary arrangements. Indeed, much of the debate over
the plans for the preparation and operation of EMU set out in the
Maastricht Treaty and the Stability and Growth Pact (SGP or 'Stability
Pact') focused *not* on the operation of a common monetary policy *per se*,
but on the appropriate convergence criteria, constraints and institutional
frameworks for the conduct of national fiscal policies.

The fiscal issues related to the operation of EMU are in many ways
more complex than the monetary issues, and continue to be an important
source of debate and contention in the European context. A host of questions remain unanswered – for example, those concerning the desirability,
and even necessity, of national fiscal policy coordination among EMU
participants, the need for constraints on national budget policies and
national debt levels and the role for European fiscal federalism and insurance. Other key issues concern the need for national fiscal policy coordination with the common monetary policy; pressures on national fiscal
policies to play a stabilization role in the absence of independent monetary
and exchange rate policies; the ability of a common monetary policy, with
constraints placed on budgetary policies, to counteract the next large

1

(asymmetric) cyclical downturn affecting only some of the European economies; and the political economy and technical aspects of fiscal consolidation in Europe within the new EMU institutional framework. Fiscal and budgetary policies and institutional arrangements, as long as these and related issues remain unresolved, will continue to evolve in EMU member nations and at the EU-wide level, in part as a conscious attempt to design policies and institutions to best reflect and correspond to the new monetary reality in Europe.

This volume focuses on these and other important unresolved issues concerning the operation of fiscal policy in the new EMU. We have a collection of eleven chapters, with three discussion essays, which focus on the fiscal aspects of European monetary integration. The chapters cover a spectrum of theoretical, empirical, institutional and political economy topics which permit insights into the formulation and design of fiscal policy in the EMU context. We have grouped the chapters into four parts, each with a particular focus: Institutions and political economy; Automatic stabilizers in a monetary union; The Stability and Growth Pact; and Asymmetric business cycles and fiscal linkages in Europe. Each part contains contributions focusing on a key fiscal issue and, except for part I (which introduces institutional and political economy aspects of fiscal policy in EMU), each is followed by a Discussion drawing out key elements from each contribution and identifying common themes and policy issues.

Institutions and political economy

The appropriate design and operation of fiscal institutions in the new EMU is the central topic addressed by Niels Thygesen in chapter 2. Thygesen begins by describing the way in which the Maastricht Treaty – and, more recently, the Stability Pact – have effectively circumscribed the principle of decentralized fiscal policies by placing rules and constraints on national debt levels and budgetary deficits. Thygesen presents a review of the arguments for budgetary 'guidelines' or imposed rules in EMU, arguing that some form of mandatory upper limit to public sector imbalances is warranted because of the strong incentives towards budgetary laxity provided by entry into EMU itself.

The question then becomes: how can budgetary guidelines be formulated in a sensible manner? Thygesen considers international experience with budgetary rules, and contrasts it with those set in the Stability Pact. He notes that the Stability Pact is really a compromise solution between the extremes found internationally – no federally imposed guidelines on state budgets, or strict quantitative limits (such as zero) on budgetary imbalances. He views the fiscal guidelines in the Stability Pact as a mix of a cooperative approach (between the centre and the member states) and a rules-based system, though more weight is placed on rules. Although Thygesen expresses some reservations about specific aspects of the EMU fiscal guidelines – mainly the focus on short-term budgetary flows as opposed to longer-term debt levels – his calculations suggest that the constraints on budgetary deficits will still leave room for substantial stabilization policy actions. Despite a positive reading of the new fiscal framework for EMU participants, Thygesen still sees an important gap: a need for supplementing the monitoring of rules by closer coordination on a voluntary basis. He does not believe that the argument for substantial fiscal transfers is strong, however, at least as a stabilization instrument at the central level, and argues that initially operating EMU without them in place is a reasonable strategy.

In chapter 3, Thomas Willett provides us with a survey of fiscal policy issues in Europe. His focus is on the *role* of fiscal policy institutions – and the Maastricht or Stability Pact criteria in particular – rather than on institutional design as such. This sets the tone and agenda for much of this volume. Willett is able to give a wide-ranging review of the political economy issues facing Europe's fiscal policy makers. A recurring theme is that monetary union may lead to fiscal interventions becoming a more important feature of economic policy. That provides some arguments that fiscal limitations may be needed to protect the other targets of the union. But Willett argues that this may in fact be less important than the need for limitations which can offset domestic political pressures – whether for increased stabilization in the face of increased cyclical dependence, or because the single monetary policy takes no account of local differences, or as an antidote to an 'excessively tight' monetary policy, or simply from the greater political competition for the benefits of the single currency.

In this context, the Stability Pact's provisions look far more sensible from a political economy than they do from a purely economic perspective. Nevertheless, the Maastricht convergence criteria were actually reached through a series of short-run expedients ('fiddles') rather than serious budgetary reform. In these circumstances, a rule-based system is likely to increase the political pressures against it, and is likely at the same time to reduce the room for fiscal manoeuvre and compliance in the name of stabilization. That, of course, makes the case for a more careful analysis of the likely impacts of the Stability Pact, and how it changes the incentives of national policy makers to act in a coordinated and responsible manner. If their incentives lie in the opposite direction, there is little reason to believe the other institutional structures – the independent central bank, the 'no-bail-out' clause – will prove effective, or that markets will provide their own discipline. Once the political economy of fiscal policy in the Union is taken into account, much of what has been written on these institutional arrangements may thus turn out to be wishful thinking in a low-growth, high-unemployment, politically-driven union. In such a world, Willett concludes, the Stability Pact may actually weaken the fiscal position of some countries and increase the pressure on monetary policy – rather as the attempt to increase exchange rate discipline by pegging exchange rates has so often resulted in exchange rate crises and instability.

Automatic stabilizers in a monetary union

The role of budgetary policy in output stabilization takes on a new dimension in EMU as presently designed. A more important role for national fiscal policy as a stabilization instrument could be envisaged, since a common monetary and exchange rate policy is now being followed. Alternatively, greater centralization of the fiscal function with an increased EU budget for stabilization purposes or a more extensive system of inter-regional fiscal transfers could be designed to smooth income fluctuations among EMU participants. Despite this economic rationale, there appears to be little political support at present to increase the stabilization role of national fiscal policy, to substantially increase the EU budget, or to expand the system of inter-regional transfers for stabilization purposes.

Will the lack of policy instruments for stabilization purposes pose a significant problem? Torben Andersen and Robert Dogonowski in chapter 4 take up the issue of the role of automatic stabilizers in smoothing the business cycle in a monetary union. They employ an intertemporal, non-Ricardian, model for the analysis and specify two alternative budgetary regimes – a balanced budget (roughly the Stability Pact rule) and a pro-cyclical budget policy. A key result of the Andersen–Dogonowski chapter is that the variability of (the present value of) output is smaller under the pro-cyclical budgetary regime. This result holds, however, only if the government faces a lower interest rate than private agents – a capital market imperfection likely to hold in practice. The comparative advantage of the pro-cyclical regime relative to the balanced budget regime is increasing in the variability of the underlying shocks, meaning that the role of the government budget as a shock absorber is more valuable the more volatility there is to absorb. Andersen and Dogonowski also report some empirical evidence for the EU countries, showing that the 3 per cent deficit norm will be a binding constraint in recessions, especially for countries with very cyclically sensitive budgets such as the Scandinavian countries with highly developed welfare systems. They also find that in the early stage of EMU – with continued high public debt levels – most countries will be in conflict with the deficit norm even under a mild recession.

Kenneth Kletzer takes up the issue of fiscal insurance in chapter 5, where he provides an analytical overview and critical discussion of the main points argued for an extended system of fiscal insurance among EMU member states. One view is that a extensive system of fiscal insurance – monetary transfers from states experiencing unexpected good economic conditions to those faring poorly – is necessary to replace the two main stabilization instruments lost in the transition to EMU – independent national monetary and exchange rate policies. To address these arguments, Kletzer considers a theoretical model economy in which production is subject to asymmetric national shocks – i.e. the conventional background against which fiscal insurance may play an income stabilization role. A key feature of the model, and the channel through which fiscal insurance may have tangible benefits, is that international markets are 'incomplete', in the sense that households cannot trade claims on future labour income. The point of comparison, for both allocative efficiency and welfare considerations, is the benefits of fiscal insurance under monetary union and under flexible exchange rates. On the basis of a variety of model specifications, Kletzer argues that there is surprisingly little to be gained by setting up an extensive system of fiscal insurance in the European context. His theory, taken together with the well known empirical evidence on the high degree of home bias in portfolio allocation, is that the benefits from fiscal insurance are only marginally greater in a monetary union than in a flexible rate system.

In chapter 6, Svend E. Hougaard Jensen also investigates the need for an inter-member fiscal transfer mechanism to provide insurance against asymmetric shocks. Fiscal transfers of this form may be helpful for output stabilization purposes and are becoming increasingly important in line with the growing concern about the behaviour of real variables – as witnessed by, for example, the 1997 Amsterdam Resolution on Employment and Growth, with its emphasis on coordination of economic policies. The background Jensen considers fits the stylized European economy: monetary union combined with constraints on national fiscal policy, relatively inflexible economic structures (at least during the early stages of EMU), and a small common EU budget. Using a standard two-country macroeconomic model, Jensen first identifies a number of effects in the absence of both monetary and fiscal activism. His analysis shows that although the transition towards EMU might induce a higher degree of wage/price flexibility, thereby raising the speed of adjustment, this might come at the cost of a substantial output divergence in the early stage of the adjustment period. This highlights an important point: a system with fiscal transfers helps to stabilize output and dampen asymmetric business cycles. But a very ambitious supranational fiscal intervention may also cause price instability – that is, there is a trade-off between output and price stabilization. Jensen concludes that while a fiscal transfer mechanism could be desirable during the early years of EMU, it also creates a moral hazard problem which is inherent in any system of risk-sharing.

The Stability and Growth Pact

The Stability and Growth Pact (SGP), agreed to at the Amsterdam European Council in June 1997, may have crucial implications for the conduct of fiscal policy in the EU. Indeed, the SGP has parallels with the Balanced Budget Amendment in the United States, since it invokes a commitment to produce a 'medium-term budgetary position of close to balance or in surplus' (European Council, 1997). Like the ECB in the area of monetary policy, the SGP may in the area of fiscal policy be seen as weighing discipline (credibility) too high relative to stabilization (flexibility). Even though there is an escape clause in situations where a member state is hit by a 'severe recession', the SGP is seen by many as a straitjacket limiting the ability of countries to use fiscal policy as a countercyclical stabilization instrument.

In chapter 7, Michael Artis and Bernhard Winkler ask if there really is a trade-off between flexibility and credibility as a consequence of the SGP. Artis and Winkler identify several dimensions to this problem. First, as sanctions may be waived in special circumstances, such as 'severe recession', it could be said that the SGP combines *ex ante* deterrence with a limited degree of *ex post* flexibility: too much of the former could undermine the latter, and vice versa. Second, there is evidence that in some countries with high debt ratios, market fears of further deterioration in public finances have already effectively curtailed both the advisability and effectiveness of allowing automatic stabilizers to operate fully. If so, the trade-off between discipline and flexibility clearly disappears, at least in the long run. Third, in view of the critical debt and deficit ratios currently faced by most EU member states, Artis and Winkler argue that the discipline–stabilization conflict is most likely to show up in the early stage of EMU. As the ECB would need at the same time to establish its reputation as being tough on inflation, the risk of extreme fiscal-cum-monetary conservatism should not be overlooked.

Artis and Winkler argue that the SGP is likely to provide incentives for discipline and, to this end, some numerical (and somewhat arbitrary) criteria are necessary. If governments choose the 'wrong' policies to meet those criteria, this is not a criticism that should fall back upon the

Maastricht Treaty or the SGP. They argue further that there need not be a discipline–stabilization conflict: if the SGP successfully contributes to ensuring more discipline in the conduct of fiscal policy, countries should be allowed to keep a safety margin large enough to allow for the automatic stabilizers to operate in response to 'normal-size' shocks and without violating the Maastricht numerical targets. However, there is a risk that the SGP might impose excessive constraints on fiscal stabilization. This could have been avoided, of course, had a 'strict' interpretation of the EMU entry conditions been imposed, reducing national debt levels further; this would have allowed larger safety margins for the conduct of fiscal policy in EMU, while at the same time ensuring fiscal solvency.

An important rationale for the SGP's constraints on national budget policy is that many countries generally have a bias towards running excessive deficits, and that this bias will increase after entry into a monetary union. Roel Beetsma, in chapter 8, develops a theoretical model where these considerations are made explicit. A deficit bias arises from 'political myopia' – i.e. there is some likelihood that the incumbent political party will not be re-elected and, as a consequence, does not fully take responsibility for the future adverse tax consequences of running current budget deficits. The bias is exacerbated by entry into a monetary union, since one member state's fiscal expansion will not have the (undesirable) inflationary consequences that would otherwise occur if it were following an independent monetary policy. The prospects of higher future inflationary consequences of deficits thus hold in check to some degree the deficit bias, and this mechanism will be much weaker in EMU since a common monetary policy is in place.

Why should other EMU participants worry about excessive deficits in other member states? Beetsma shows that excessive deficits in one or several member countries can induce the ECB to follow a somewhat more inflationary policy stance than would be socially optimal without a precommitment mechanism. This creates a negative linkage to other EMU members and provides a rationale for budgetary rules such as those incorporated in the Excessive Deficits Procedure (EDP) of the Stability Pact. Beetsma shows that imposing a fine which is increasing in the size of national government debt can, in fact, correct the deficit bias exacerbated by monetary union. The problem with this type of EDP, however, is that a recession in one member country can cause the debt level to increase – which, together with the EDP fines, may make the problem even worse. Designing a penalty mechanism which is conditional on the severity of recessions, however, can solve this problem, while preserving its role in reducing the debt bias. But the severity of the 'shocks' inducing downturns in economic activity must be observed to ensure that a fiscal insurance scheme operating at the central level does not induce 'moral hazard' – i.e. the fiscal insurance must be tied to the exogenous disturbances affecting the country and not influenced by policies under the national government's control.

Andrew Hughes Hallett and Peter McAdam study the likely long-run implications of the SGP in chapter 9. They do this with the aid of an empirical multicountry model which allows different fiscal transmission mechanisms and different debt stocks, but a uniform monetary policy. The difference here is the focus on the potential long-run costs (or benefits) of the SGP when not all countries have the same policy responses or initial conditions. This contrasts with previous work which has focused on the short-run output costs of fiscal consolidation, emphasizing that, while not negligible, they are neither large nor insurmountable.

Hughes Hallett and McAdam argue that an expansion in the *real* value of the money supply is necessary to avoid large costs of fiscal consolidation. In the absence of this change in policy mix, real interest rates are likely to rise – which, in the longer term, would hurt investment, output capacity and employment. This could be a far more serious cost than the transient losses in output itself, and reveals a potential conflict between deficit reductions and the debt criterion in conditions of slow growth and low inflation. The authors stress that monetary loosening is needed to avoid liquidity shortages and stop debt from growing more rapidly in the higher-debt countries. The SGP lacks any incentives to prevent this problem – any investment and output capacity will fall when one high-deficit or high-debt country has to adjust when union-wide monetary policy is set by others who do not have to adjust. Hughes Hallett and McAdam predict that, in practice, we are likely to observe less fiscal – monetary coordination, rather than more, because an independent central bank can do little to encourage those who do not need to consolidate to help those who do; the result will be a deflationary bias in the EMU area. By targeting structural rather than actual deficits, they argue, it would be possible to improve fiscal – monetary coordination with less distortionary taxation.

Asymmetric business cycles and fiscal linkages in Europe

One of the main costs of entering a monetary union is giving up an independent exchange rate policy – and, more broadly, losing the option of following an independent monetary policy. This cost is especially great if countries are expected to face largely different business cycles (or 'asymmetric shocks') in terms of timing, duration or magnitude. For this reason, losing national monetary independence would in principle place a greater burden on fiscal policy for stabilization purposes, arguing for greater flexibility in national fiscal policies (not less, as dictated by the EDP) or a more centralized (federal) system of fiscal insurance.

Michael Bergman and Michael Hutchison, in chapter 10, argue that the costs of joining a monetary union, and the pressures for more activist fiscal policies, may be exaggerated. A major objective of EU policy is to foster stronger economic integration in Europe, probably resulting in a more synchronous European business cycle with less need for macroeconomic stabilization policy at the national level. They argue that previous studies evaluating the symmetry of European business cycles, and drawing policy conclusions on this basis, are ignoring future integration of European economies and how this will be spurred by the creation of EMU. To illustrate their points, Bergman and Hutchison demonstrate – on the basis of time-series relationships in thirteen European nations – that the extent of 'common shocks' and dependence on the German economy has increased markedly over the past twenty years.

This combination of shocks and linkages implies that a more synchronous European business cycle has developed, and is likely to become stronger yet. Bergman and Hutchison identify a 'core' group of EMU countries on the basis of strong trade and financial linkages with Germany, which in turns leads to rapid and powerful transmission of German shocks. They argue that these linkages are likely to become stronger for countries currently on the 'periphery' – often relatively new EU members – and hence gradually reduce the costs for these countries from losing monetary independence and diminish the pressures to follow more activist national fiscal policies.

Focusing on the issue of fiscal linkages among member states, Christopher Allsopp, Warwick McKibbin and David Vines argue in chapter 11 that a coordinated approach to fiscal contraction is necessary. Using a simple algebraic model of the Mundell–Fleming type, as well as a sophisticated intertemporal macro model of the McKibbin–Sachs (MSG2) type, it is shown that fiscal consolidation in a monetary union has the feature of a prisoner's dilemma: if both countries cut expenditures, output losses would be small and consolidation will be pursued. If, however, an individual country cuts expenditures, and the others do not, then the output losses will be large and consolidation is unlikely to be pursued. The authors use this finding to offer an alternative explanation as to why European policy makers agreed to the Maastricht criteria and to the SGP – namely, because uncoordinated fiscal retrenchment would be more costly in terms of lost output than the coordinated measures implied by the Maastricht Treaty (in the run-up to EMU) and the SGP (during

EMU's operation). Their argument challenges the standard interpretation of the Maastricht criteria as (imperfect) means of excluding countries from EMU whose governments were unwilling to take steps to prevent their countries from becoming insolvent. Furthermore, the chapter suggests, as Paul De Grauwe points out in his Discussion, that the monetary context in which fiscal consolidation takes place is of crucial importance for its success, perhaps even more so than whether it is coordinated or not.

The key issue of spillover effects in fiscal policy is also taken up by Corsetti and Pesenti in chapter 12. They take a very different approach, analysing the long-run welfare consequences when budget cuts are introduced by some member states (the 'ins') but not others (the 'outs') in a monetary union. Their theoretical analysis focuses on the micro-foundations of different agents' welfare and the spillovers and interactions between markets of the 'ins', where the budget cuts originate, and the 'outs'. An important finding is that member states cutting deficits suffer a terms-of-trade loss, and this benefits consumers in the rest of the monetary union. If national goods are substitutes, this will also lead to increased consumption of goods from the deficit-cutting countries and help offset their welfare loss. But if goods are complements, the consumption of the 'out' country goods will rise – creating problems if this group of countries is producing at close to full capacity – and simultaneously causing a further welfare loss in the deficit-cutting group. Either way, it appears that national budget policies have greater welfare implications (losses and gains) for other member states in a highly integrated Europe where fiscal linkages are strongest.

Concluding comments

Not all the questions raised about the operation of fiscal policy in EMU in this volume are satisfactorily answered. But the value of identifying key issues, combined with bringing a number of important insights to light, is substantial in its own right. Moreover, many questions are empirical by nature. Only after some years of operation in EMU, and the experience brought by uneven business cycles and policy conflicts, will some of the issues involving policy coordination, fiscal federalism and inter-regional transfers be resolved. Fiscal institutions and structures in Europe will evolve to reflect these tensions, responding to both economic fundamentals and political reality. We believe the chapters in this volume provide some strong signals as to what to expect about the evolution of fiscal policy in the context of the new monetary reality in Europe.

References

European Council (1997). 'Presidency Conclusions', Amsterdam European Council (16 and 17 June) (reprinted in *European Economy*, 64)

Werner, P. *et al.* (1970). *Report to the Council and the Commission on the Realization by Steps of Economic and Monetary Union in the Community* (the Werner Report), Supplement to Bulletin II – 1970 of the European Communities, Brussels

Part I

Institutions and political economy

2 Fiscal institutions in EMU and the Stability Pact

Niels Thygesen

Introduction

Economic and Monetary Union (EMU), which started on 1 January 1999 among initially eleven member states of the European Union (EU), is a unique policy experiment in the sense that it will combine a high degree of centralization of monetary policy in the European Central Bank (ECB) with, in principle, decentralized policies in other areas of macroeconomic and structural policies, in particular with respect to public finances.[1] Such decentralization has been seen as a necessary application of the principle of subsidiarity, but also as justified in the light of the loss of monetary policy instruments at the national level, as exchange rates become locked permanently and interest rate decisions move to the ECB level.

However, in the Maastricht Treaty and in its subsequent introduction in the so-called Stability and Growth Pact (SGP) (hereafter, 'Stability Pact') the decentralized exercise of budgetary policies has become circumscribed. First, the convergence criteria to be applied for judging the readiness of countries for participation in EMU took up the suggestion in the Delors Report (1989) that there had to be upper binding limits on budget deficits by introducing the much-discussed reference values of 3 per cent for the deficit/GDP ratio and 60 per cent for the debt/GDP ratio. Second, and much later, an elaborate version of how these budgetary rules were to be applied more permanently after the start of EMU emerged in the form of the Stability Pact. Even more recently, the debate on desirable features of

Niels Thygesen was a member of the Delors Committee on EMU (1988–9). This chapter is a revised version of the paper presented at the EPRU conference (August 1997), and draws upon my contribution in Pochet and Vanhercke (1998), pp. 23–45 and in Gros and Thygesen (1998) ch. 8. The author is grateful to Daniel Gros for cooperation over more than a decade and to Tom Willett and Michael M. Hutchison for critical comments.

[1] This chapter uses the term 'budgetary policies', rather than 'fiscal policies', because the latter are sometimes interpreted as comprising not only macroeconomic stabilization efforts, but also tax and subsidy policies of a more microeconomic orientation which will not be addressed in this chapter.

15

policy coordination more generally among the EMU participants has resurfaced in recognition of the concern that mechanistic application of the budgetary rules of the Stability Pact, though in itself a daunting task, would not constitute an adequate agenda for the Finance Ministers.

The rest of this chapter is structured as follows: the next section examines three arguments which are traditionally put forward as a possible rationale for imposing upper limits to budget deficits for participants in EMU. The desirable features of budgetary rules are reviewed, and the crucial question of the feasibility of the implementation of the Stability Pact with its norms and sanctions is discussed. The chapter then turns to the question of possible gaps in the policy framework of EMU in two important respects: macroeconomic coordination proper and supplementary fiscal transfers at the EU level to insure participants better against national specific disturbances than can be done through what remains of room for manoeuvre for national budgetary policies. The final section offers some tentative conclusions.

Arguments for budgetary guidelines in EMU

We first turn to the more specific arguments that arise in favour of budgetary guidelines for the EMU participants while keeping in mind the general desirability of retaining some scope for national budgetary policies in stabilizing their economies.

From the start of the EMU debate, marked by the publication of the Delors Report in 1989, three basic arguments were advanced to support the imposition of binding guidelines in the form of upper limits to national public sector deficits in the specific economic environment of EMU: (1) the need to maintain an appropriate policy mix for participants in the aggregate; (2) the desirability of avoiding union-wide interest rate effects of the budgetary policies of individual member states; and (3) the need to offset additional incentives to fiscal laxity. All three types of arguments are reviewed in Lamfalussy (1989); they do not lead to identical recommendations as to the type of constraints that should be put on individual country behaviour, but they all three in different ways support the view that national budgetary policies should not simply be left to the discretion of the participants. Before embarking on a discussion of the strength of the three basic arguments, two simple points should be recalled.

The first is that the locking of exchange rates and the introduction of a common monetary policy definitely removes from national authorities some instruments of macroeconomic stabilization on which member states have in the past put reliance for correcting external and internal imbalances – even though this reliance has been sharply decreasing in recent years, hence making monetary unification look less dramatic. However, an *a priori* case remains that one should avoid, to the greatest extent possible, putting constraints also on the remaining, and largely budgetary, stabilization instruments in order to preserve some capacity to react to country-specific disturbances and structural features. The second point to note is that the Maastricht Treaty, though generally regarded as ambitious, does indeed reveal a more liberal attitude towards the role of national budgetary policies in macroeconomic stabilization than the two earlier attempts at formulating policy principles for a monetary union.[2] The Werner Plan of 1970 advocated a high degree of centralization of budgetary authority in a transformed Council of Finance Ministers (ECOFIN). The outline presented by the Commission President, Roy Jenkins, in 1977 saw the transfer to a European budget of important stabilization (as well as allocation) responsibilities as a prerequisite for a well functioning monetary union. The present state of thinking about the budgetary complements to monetary union is therefore a minimalist version by past standards of the European debate. Both political realism and a loss of confidence in the power and accuracy of macroeconomic instruments above have contributed to the lowering of ambitions. Still it is necessary to ask whether the residual elements of intended collective influence are warranted by three arguments advanced in defence of budgetary rules in EMU.

The first argument is that the *policy mix under EMU could become distorted*, if national budgetary policies were to be left unconstrained. The most likely example might be a situation in which several member states conduct strongly expansionary policies, forcing the European Central Bank (ECB) into increasingly tight monetary policies. A less likely example would be the opposite one in which the aggregate of national budgetary policies were to become so contractionary in their effects that even an expansionary monetary policy could not achieve a satisfactory outcome in terms of output and employment. There are several points to be made in relation to this argument.

An initial observation is that the task of assuring a satisfactory policy mix is one which has often remained unresolved within existing nation states. A high degree of federal authority (or at least influence) over budgetary policy did not prevent the United States from slipping into a very unbalanced policy mix in the first half of the 1980s. Tight monetary policy from late 1979 triggered a recession in 1980–2; when that had succeeded in reducing inflation a strong recovery took place from 1982 as structural budget deficits widened dramatically in the first Reagan administration.

[2] For a further discussion see Thygesen (1996). The two earlier EMU projects are outlined in Werner *et al.* (1970) and Jenkins (1977).

Though monetary policy was somewhat relaxed in 1982, the policy imbalance persisted for several years. Nor did it stop Germany from reliving a similar experience nearly a decade later, following German unification. In the latter case massive public sector deficits pushed the Bundesbank towards severely restrictive policies. In retrospect, both of these phases were recognized as having produced a clearly suboptimal policy mix. Yet this mix was not corrected, perhaps because of major errors of analysis and forecasting, but more likely because of shorter-term political preferences of the type explained by public choice economists. A degree of modesty in searching for an optimal policy mix in EMU is therefore appropriate. We should not expect more of the policy framework under EMU than can realistically be delivered in nation states.

A second important observation is that the extent to which the policy-mix argument should prevail depends on the strength of spillover effects between countries participating in EMU. In the absence of major spillover effects of national budgetary policies, the case for collective authority over the latter would be unable to rely on the policy mix argument.

The evidence for strong spillover effects is not convincing. Simulations with large-scale econometric models suggest that such effects have bordered on the insignificant and that there is even doubt about the direction of the impact. For example, the European Commission in its major study of the implications of the single currency (see CEC, 1990), found that a German fiscal expansion tended to have a very minor impact on the three other large European economies (France, Italy and the United Kingdom) – and actually in all three cases a slightly negative one. While this was based on average experience in the preceding decades, new and more potent evidence was obtained following the explosion of German public expenditures and deficits linked to unification after 1990. This event at first generated expansionary spillover effects on other countries through increased imports into Germany, but, after a while – the duration depending on the strength of trade links – these effects were largely offset, or even overtaken, by the impact of higher interest rates in all countries that had linked their currencies firmly to the D-mark and hence were obliged to match the Bundesbank's escalation of interest rates. Towards the end of the recession of 1991–3 the net impact was clearly seen as negative by Germany's partners.

This experience suggests that although demand and interest rate effects of budgetary changes operate in opposite directions, they do not necessarily cancel out. The timing of these effects may, in particular, be sufficiently different to give rise to major temporary effects in one direction or the other and in any case to justify concern over the composition of demand even when the net impact is modest. Larger public deficits in one country foster increases in exports from its partners, but decreases in interest-sensitive expenditures abroad – private investment, construction and consumer durables. This change in the composition of demand cannot be a matter of indifference.

In short, concern about the policy mix does offer some justification for constraining the full sovereignty of national states over their budgetary policies. But the constraints are difficult to formulate in terms of clear rules, notably binding upper limits to public sector deficits. What is acceptable in some phases of the EMU business cycle will need to be discouraged at other times. Achieving a better policy mix is an objective that can be addressed by better coordination of all macroeconomic policies, not by rigid constraints on individually deviant behaviour. However, given the uncertainties surrounding the international transmission of changes in national policy instruments and their generally weak impact it would appear sufficient to base such coordination on voluntary, rather than mandatory, actions. Art. 103 of the Maastricht Treaty provides for policy coordination in this form, since the ECOFIN Council can draft 'broad guidelines of the economic policies of the member states and the Community'. We return below (pp. 31ff.) to the implementation of this provision in the perspective of the Stability Pact which has specified the rules-based part of the budgetary policies.

The argument that *union-wide interest rate effects of national deficits* justify constraints on the latter is open to criticism. Undoubtedly some member states have experienced in the relatively recent past deficits sufficiently large to influence the overall savings/investment balance in EMU; a deficit of 8–10 per cent of national GDP in a large member state can absorb more than 5 per cent of EU net savings. Variations could thus influence interest rates throughout EMU, even in a situation with smaller deficits than in the past. However, this type of spillover is – in contrast to the direct demand effects of budgetary changes – a pecuniary externality (i.e. one that works solely through the market). There is no clear reason on economic efficiency grounds for imposing mandatory rules on deficits simply because market participants have a dislike for an increase in the market price for savings.[3] In any case, interest rate linkages via the aggregate savings/investment balance are caused by financial integration which is a global phenomenon; they are not confined to participants in a monetary union, though they may become stronger in EMU.

While the two first arguments seem on balance inadequate for justifying mandatory limits on deficits, the third argument is more persuasive. Launching EMU without such limits could well create a risk of an

---

[3.] For a further statement of this view, see Buiter, Corsetti and Roubini (1993).

excessively lax aggregate budgetary stance. Some national policy makers have favoured EMU, not least because the financing of external deficits becomes more predictable and the effects of budgetary policies become more powerful within the borders of the initiating country. This is obviously the counterpart to the argument discussed above: there will be less crowding-out through higher interest rates and, possibly, an external crisis as the public sector deficit widens. A policy adviser could find good arguments in this new environment for concluding that national ambitions in the budgetary area can be raised. And the policy maker, no longer confronted with pressures in financial markets, would be more likely to follow the advice.

If such a change of attitude were to become widespread, a bias towards laxity would indeed arise. If debt accumulation becomes so large as ultimately to generate a funding problem for the country (or countries) concerned, pressure on the ECB would build up to lower interest rates generally or to extend favourable treatment to the debt instruments issued by the deficit country in order to prevent a crisis in financial markets. Even a strongly independent ECB might in the end be obliged to cave in if such pressures were to become persistent.

Modern macroeconomic theory has provided arguments for society to select a leadership of the central bank with an aversion to inflation which is stronger than that of the median voter.[4] While such an arrangement can be shown to lower – in some situations, eliminate – the normal 'inflation bias', a related argument has recently been made in favour of formally restraining the capacity of governments to generate public sector deficits larger than expected (see notably Agell, Calmfors and Jonsson, 1996). This argument has particular relevance in an environment where the inflationary risks have initially been perceived to be minimal because of a country's participation in EMU.

The counterargument against budgetary limits, already discussed in Lamfalussy's (1989) overview, is that financial markets could still have a disciplinary role *vis-à-vis* governments as long as they are prepared to distinguish public sector debtors inside EMU by pricing credit risk correctly. Experience from existing national federal states such as Canada shows some systematic relationship between deficits or debt levels of component units and the interest rate they have to pay on their borrowings relative to the national debt. The premia are not large (up to about 80 basis points above federal borrowing costs), but this is hardly surprising, given that experiences with defaults have been extremely rare. The premia likely to develop on sovereign debt issued by EMU governments may be

---

4. Rogoff (1985) is the classic reference on the advantages of a 'conservative central banker'.

unable in themselves to trigger restraint in government behaviour – at least that was the expectation of the central bankers who largely shaped the initial ideas on monitoring budgetary limits. Financial markets appear so far to have interpreted the formation of EMU primarily as an upgrading of the creditworthiness of its weaker members: for example, the interest premium on Italian ten-year government bonds has recently narrowed to approx. 0.30 per cent above the benchmark rate on the German *Bund* ahead of any reduction of the debt ratio. If this is indeed an implicit assessment of credit risk, it offers evidence that financial markets are less than fully convinced by the provisions of the Maastricht Treaty (and elaborated in many official statements) that the European institutions – and the ECB, in particular – will not bail out a member state in financial difficulties. Mandatory budgetary rules may then be regarded as a necessary correction to 'free riding'.

An alternative and arguably superior way of ensuring that markets take the riskiness of public debt into account would have been to enforce a risk rating linked to the level of the debt ratio.[5] At present, public debt of all OECD governments is assumed to be risk-free for the purposes of prudential regulation, although private rating agencies do distinguish moderately between issuers in the light of relative macroeconomic indicators. Such complacency may be reasonable as long as national governments retain the option to print the money they need to service their debt. But in EMU they lose that option, making it logical to treat public debt in the same way as debt issued by private corporations. If so, that would have an important major impact on bank balance sheets; the EU Capital Adequacy Directive (CAD) requires banks to hold own funds corresponding to at least 8 per cent of risk-weighted assets, and an increase in the risk rating of government debt – say, from 0 to the 20 per cent which applies to regional public debt today – would oblige EMU governments to reduce their dependence on finding a market for their debt in the banks. There has, however, been no political readiness to apply these rules, or the more radical ones on large exposure, to government debt in EMU.

On balance, and having considered the alternatives, it is difficult to escape the conclusion that some form of mandatory upper limits to imbalances in public sector finances are warranted, primarily in the light of the third argument advanced – i.e. the additional incentives to budgetary laxity provided by entry into EMU. The other two arguments appear to carry relatively less weight, but they do give support to better coordination of non-monetary stabilization policies in the member states. With this in

---

[5.] This idea goes back to Bishop (1990).

mind the next section turns to the formulation of the guidelines and the efforts made in this direction by the Stability Pact.

How could budgetary guidelines be formulated?

If budgetary guidelines are indeed thought to be desirable, attention shifts to the most appropriate way of implementing them. Some compromise has to be found between rigid rules and excessive reliance on analytically satisfactory but vague notions which would defy effective monitoring. We first outline the two extremes before turning to the compromise solution embodied in the Stability Pact.

Some observers have pointed to the experience in the United States as particularly reassuring from the viewpoint of financial stability. No federal constraints are imposed on the budgetary policies of individual US states, but 49 out of the 50 states have on their own adopted some version of 'Balanced Budget Amendments' which, in principle, constrain them to keep current expenditures in line with revenues year by year; observed deficits and debt ratios are low everywhere. This framework may be appropriate in the United States where the federal government has taken over the responsibility for stabilization policy as well as a number of other tasks of public finance; it would not be appropriate in Europe where the ambition is – because of both political realism, embodied in the so-called 'subsidiarity principle', and economic efficiency – to maintain as many functions as possible, including stabilization, in national hands for the foreseeable future. Given the very different starting points for EMU members, one could in any case hardly have expected early commitment to a rigid rule in the form of balancing the budget year after year; something more flexible had to be aimed for.

The United States is unique in that sub-federal governments have themselves adopted budgetary rules – initially, incidentally, because of concern that they would otherwise lose the capacity to borrow in financial markets. Other federal countries – as well as unitary states - have adopted different methods for constraining the borrowing instincts of their subnational units. These practices have been surveyed in great detail in the literature on fiscal federalism (see, among others, CEC, 1993; Ter-Minassian, 1997); they range widely from main reliance on discipline through monitoring by financial markets in countries where the latter are particularly well developed (such as Canada) to outright administrative controls in most developing and transition economies.[6]

[6.] Ter-Minassian and Craig in their survey (Ter-Minassian, 1997) conveniently tabulate recent practices in 53 IMF member countries (pp. 158–62).

Given that financial market discipline was seen to be inadequate in the case of EMU participants, while outright administrative controls would obviously have been seen as too intrusive and politically unacceptable in the European context, the real choice in EMU lies between the two intermediate forms of federal interference in full national budgetary autonomy: a cooperative approach and rules. In practice, EMU will operate with a mixture of these two approaches, though with more reliance on rules than on cooperation, at least initially.

An example of the cooperative approach may be found in Australia, where a Loan Council with representatives of the federal government and all state governments has served as a multilateral forum for negotiations on global debt limits for individual states and monitoring of compliance. Since 1993 the focus has shifted towards *ex ante* discussions of financing requirements and *ex post* monitoring of deficits. Flow magnitudes were found to be less subject to manipulation than debt. Efforts have also been stepped up to provide financial markets with more timely information. The cooperative approach, as illustrated by the Australian example, has been valuable in promoting dialogue between the different government levels and in raising the awareness of policy makers at the subnational level of the macroeconomic implications of their decisions. But it may work only when the national or federal level is offering firm leadership in the process, a condition which is hardly met at the present stage of European political integration, despite the recent much greater convergence of views among the EMU participants. By a logic of excluding sole reliance on the other approaches it is understandable that the rule-based approach has become the main one in EMU. The difficulty has been to devise rules which can be applied to all participants.

To most economists, the idea that the financial position of governments should in some sense be 'sustainable' is appealing.[7] 'Sustainability' can be broadly defined as a situation in which – with current tax and expenditure policies – government debt will not grow without limit, possibly that the ratio of debt/GDP remains stable, if it is judged not to be excessive initially. Such a situation would keep to a minimum the likelihood of a financial crisis that can arise when markets develop doubts whether a government will be able to service its debts. But when can a particular debt/GDP ratio be judged to indicate sustainability?

The answer depends crucially on the projected difference between the rate of growth of real GDP and the real interest rate. If the latter clearly exceeds the former – as has been the case in the European economies since interest rates were increased sharply in 1979–80 to combat the inflationary

[7.] For an excellent survey of the issues, see AMUE (1998).

shock of the second jump in international energy prices – the debt ratio will rise without limit under the weight of increasing interest payments even if the imbalance in the rest of public finances (the primary deficit) stays small and stable and possibly even exhibits a primary surplus. Normally such a surplus will be required for stabilizing public debt accumulation. The general uncertainty over the relative size of the two main determinants of sustainability makes the application of criteria based on this concept very problematic.

The gap between the growth rate of GDP and the real interest rate has recently narrowed considerably relative to the gap of 4–5 per cent which had opened up in the early 1990s. With short-term interest rates in the benchmark countries of the euro area currently at $2\frac{1}{2}$ per cent, long rates below 4 per cent and inflation at less than 2 per cent, the gap between the two determinants of debt sustainability has narrowed to close to zero for both. Europe finally appears to be returning to the pre-1980 average experience which was marked by a near-zero gap between the two. In this perspective, many of the analyses of debt sustainability by international institutions and in academic studies over the 1990s now appear overly pessimistic. But this points to the first major difficulty of basing budgetary rules primarily on sustainability – the large room for divergent and inevitably often self-serving interpretations by national authorities of their feasible constallations of growth and interest rate prospects.

A second reason why sustainability cannot be left as the sole criterion is that it would appear to be too lax in some cases and too stringent in others. Why should the norm be to stabilize the debt/GDP ratio at any particular and necessarily arbitrary level? Countries with a low ratio must be permitted more leeway, because a moderate increase in their case could not be interpreted as an indicator of unsustainability in the longer run. Conversely, for countries with a relatively very high ratio, stabilization will not suffice to eliminate the risk of financial crisis; one could not condone any relaxations of policies to reduce the debt ratio in countries where the latter is above, say, 100 per cent of GDP.

In practice, the task of defining an objective indicator of sustainability which can eliminate the need for discretionary judgement and minimize the scope for political interference will prove to be an elusive one. This is wisely recognized in the Maastricht Treaty, which does refer to the notion of sustainability as a general principle, but soon thereafter introduces a practical definition: a country which has been taken out of the 'Excessive Deficits Procedure' (EDP) is *ipso facto* assumed to have sustainable public finances. Does this bring us back to the opposite danger to that of excessive flexibility – overly rigid and undifferentiated rules? Not necessarily, if one looks more closely at EDP and its more recent elaboration in the Stability Pact.

One thing is clear, however: the EDP and the Stability Pact represent an indirect approach to improving the sustainability of public finances. They focus on budget deficits – i.e. flows – rather than stocks and are hence directed towards short-term, rather than long-term sustainability, though compliance with tight budgetary rules will obviously over a longer horizon make the public finances of the EMU participants sustainable if they were not in such a state initially. Some concern over the dominance of a short-term perspective did become evident in the preparations for the final selection of the first group of EMU participants, during which the European Monetary Institute (EMU) and, in particular, the German authorities expressed concern over the very high debt levels in Belgium and Italy. Both countries have tried to supplement their impressive short-term budgetary efforts by plans for debt reduction over much longer horizons.

The convergence criteria and the Stability Pact

The Maastricht Treaty contains two safeguards against strongly deviant national budgetary policies and the financial instability which they might entail. One safeguard is the specification of entry conditions in the form of the budgetary components of the convergence criteria. The other is the enforcement procedure for countries participating in EMU which was considerably strengthened in the Stability Pact. Both safeguards are somewhat different from what is generally asserted in the public debate.

The application of the budgetary convergence criteria is now history and did not in the end involve the borderline cases which had long been foreseen. Due to a mixture of good luck – an economic upturn which automatically improved public budgets in 1996–7 – and continuing determined efforts by most countries with dangerously high deficits in the mid-1990s to bring their deficits below the 3 per cent upper limit and hence firmly establish their credentials for joining EMU, as many as 11 member states formed the first group of participants as of 1 January 1999. The provisions of art. 104c which introduce some flexibility in the decision to take a country out of the EDP were not really put to the test, though they remain of interest in future accessions to EMU.[8] Very briefly, the provisions say that for deficits small over-runs of the upper deficit limit are

---

[8.] The EMI Report on Convergence discussed critically the temporary nature of some of the budgetary improvements implemented in 1997 (notably in the case of France and Italy) but the continuing improvements foreseen for 1998 and 1999 clearly blunted these criticisms (see EMI, 1998).

permissible at entry, provided they look temporary or as a residue from 'substantial and continuous' progress towards the reference value; for the government debt ratio the entry requirement will be met if 'the ratio is sufficiently diminishing and approaching the reference value at a satisfactory pace'. Neither the Treaty, nor the Stability Pact, defines what could be regarded as 'satisfactory'. In practice, this vagueness has implications beyond the entry requirements, which is unfortunate from the viewpoint of the future application of budgetary rules in EMU. It would have been preferable to give a precise definition of the objective of reducing the debt ratio; Gros and Thygesen (1998) make an attempt in this direction.[9]

Interest must now centre on the second safeguard, the enforcement of budgetary rules after the start of EMU. Here it was recognized soon after the Maastricht Treaty was signed that the enforcement procedures outlined were too imprecise and long drawn out to give comfort. The basic principle was a very gradual escalation of sanctions, starting with peer pressure through statements by ECOFIN, followed by outright warnings to the European Investment Bank (EIB) and other lenders on a member state's policies and ultimately – presumably after several years – by financial sanctions in the form of imposing non-interest-bearing deposits on an offending and recalcitrant country, later to be converted into fines. The size of the financial sanctions – the only ones with real teeth – was not specified.

Recognition of these weaknesses prompted the German Finance Minister to propose in 1995 a so-called 'Stability Pact', later approved by the Amsterdam and Dublin European Councils under the name 'Stability and Growth Pact' (SGP). The Pact has three main elements: (1) a clarification of medium-term budgetary commitments; (2) a specification of the ultimate financial sanctions; (3) a detailed outline and speed-up of the EDP.

(1) is the most fundamental: EMU participants are committing themselves to maintain approximate balance or a small surplus on average over the business cycle, while confirming 3 per cent of GDP as an upper limit to budget deficits in unfavourable years. This is a version of 'Balanced Budget Amendments' consistent with some considerable role for national budgetary policies in stabilizing the economies participating in EMU, as discussed further below. It is a retreat from the arbitrariness of setting rigid limits to measured deficits in a particular year – the principle adopted for deciding on entry – to a more structural view of budgetary imbalances.

[9.] For a specific proposal to interpret the debt rule in art. 104c, see Gros and Thygesen (1998, p. 340).

When this analytically more satisfactory perspective was proposed as an alternative in the discussion leading up to Maastricht, officials – and particularly central bankers – rejected the idea that the structural budget position could be used in monitoring and ultimately deciding a country's preparedness for EMU. The concept was seen as excessively vague and open to intrepretation when compared to actual budget deficits which have to be financed in the market and are more readily measurable. The combination of retaining an upper limit at any time while reintroducing a medium-term objective brings better economic sense into the budgetary rules.

The ultimate financial sanctions (2) have now been stipulated. The required deposit with the EU – to be converted into a fine if the deviant country fails to correct its course within two years – will amount to 0.2 per cent of GDP for any transgression *plus* 0.1 per cent for each percentage point in which the deficit exceeds 3 per cent; the deposit will be capped at 0.5 per cent of GDP. Critics have argued that these sanctions are inappropriate since they will tend to worsen an already difficult position in public finances. Here it should be kept in mind that during the two-year period of deposit, only the interest income on the assets transferred is lost – with, say, a 8 per cent interest rate and a 0.4 per cent deposit, the addition to the deficit is a modest 0.012 per cent of GDP. In reality, the sanction schedule is finely graduated and hardly serious in strictly financial terms unless the deposit is ultimately converted into a fine. But the political embarrassment of being subjected to increasingly critical scrutiny by partner countries should not be under-rated during the build-up of sanctions. Furthermore, increasing peer pressure may interact with financial market concerns to widen interest rate premia.

A speed-up of the procedure of the EDP (3) was urgently required, and the Stability Pact has certainly achieved that by telescoping the early stages of the procedure into a year or less, whereas the wording of art. 104c could well imply a very much longer period, given the past record of clubbiness in ECOFIN with strong incentives constraining criticism of any member state. But the tightening goes beyond the simple calendar for the succession of steps to two further elements crucial to the credibility of any effective monitoring in the EDP: a definition of the circumstances in which the deficit may rise above 3 per cent without triggering sanctions, and a pre-commitment to voting in favour of the latter in all other cases.

On the former point the Stability Pact now defines what are the exceptional situations in which sanctions will not be considered appropriate – if real GDP of the country in question has declined by 2 per cent or more. Such events have been rare in the past; over the 1960–97 period fewer than 1 per cent of the more than 500 observations for the EU-15 countries fall in this category of major GDP contraction. If a country has experienced a decline of GDP of between 0.75 and 2 per cent there has to be a discussion in ECOFIN, and individual Finance Ministers retain full discretion in their voting. It is realistic to expect no sanctions to be imposed in this situation; looking at the same sample as before, close to 5 per cent of all observations fall in this intermediate category. With economic growth hopefully becoming smoother after the start of EMU than in the turbulent two decades that followed the oil price explosion of 1973–4 with many frustrating experiences of stop–go policies, it is surely an over-estimate to say that the exceptions in one or the other category could amount to 5 per cent of all yearly observations after the start of EMU. Remarkably, in the remaining 95 per cent of cases, if a deficit transgresses 3 per cent, EMU participants are now committed to not using the discretion they formally have and hence to imposing sanctions.

There are two types of outcome in which one could regard the disciplining provisions of the Stability Pact as 'successful'. The first is the better one: sanctions are never applied, because the threat of imposing them has effectively changed incentives to prevent the type of budgetary laxity that might otherwise have occurred after the formation of EMU. The second acceptable outcome, though less satisfactory, is one where sanctions are required in a particular situation and then applied and accepted, leading the offender's deficit onto a lower path. Determined application of sanctions will at least strengthen the incentive to comply in other countries, even if it has not worked *ex ante* in the first test case. A third outcome would be clearly less acceptable in both its potential variants: sanctions become required by the Stability Pact, but ECOFIN fails to apply them, hence breaking the precommitment undertaken; or the offending country refuses to follow the rules by not depositing or by failing to adjust policies. If either of these variants of the third outcome were to occur, confidence in the provisions of the Stability Pact would be severely shaken.

It is impossible to assess the prospects for the Pact being 'successful' in the sense of the first two outcomes mentioned. Recent cyclical developments – a stronger upturn in the economies of the EMU participants than earlier projected – and favourable constellations of internal price stability and historically low interest rates imply that the conditions for starting EMU at the moment long-planned have clearly become more propitious, not least for maintaining moderate budget deficits and in most cases for reducing them further in the early years of EMU. Germany and France, having just managed to squeeze their 1997 deficits within the 3 per cent limit, will have the greatest difficulties in observing the provisions of the Stability Pact, since they can hardly expect any major reductions in interest rates and face more limited prospects for growth than several other EMU participants. It could be a particularly dangerous test for the new procedures if one of the two largest participants were to get into a conflict with the others over the application of the rules early in the life of EMU.

In view of the incentives to increasing budgetary laxity in EMU, something like the Stability Pact was a desirable complement to monetary union. The question whether its design could have been improved further depends on the evaluation of the likely size of unfavourable disturbances that will affect the course of public deficits and on how well the EMU participants succeed in supplementing the rules of the Pact with co-operative interpretations of the speed with which deficits should be reduced to their longer-term levels during the initial phase (see p. 31 below).

The argument most commonly advanced against the provisions of the Stability Pact is that it may leave too little room for the automatic stabilizers in national budgets to operate. It has already been hinted that if EMU participants take the commitment to balance or a small surplus in the medium term seriously, then they should have assured themselves sufficient room for the normal operation of the stabilizers. Calculations of the sensitivity of budget deficits to fluctuations in GDP growth suggest that if real GDP declines by 1 per cent the budget balance worsens by between 0.5 and 0.9 per cent of GDP (see CEC, 1998); most of the effect comes through the revenue side, though variations in transfer payments (largely unemployment benefits) also contribute significantly in some countries. These figures imply that if an EMU participant starts from budget balance, it can tolerate a cumulative divergence of its GDP from a trend growth rate (of, say, $2\frac{1}{2}$ per cent) of almost 6 per cent before it transgresses the 3 per cent deficit/GDP ratio, if the country has a normal (or modest) budget sensitivity, or divergence of 3–4 per cent, if its budget sensitivity is high. Countries in the latter category have therefore to show more prudence and may be well advised to aim for a small surplus – as, for example, Denmark and Sweden are already doing (though not members of the first group to enter EMU). But the upshot of this is that all EMU participants – if starting from approximate budget balance – could live with zero growth for more than a year without infringing the limit set by the Stability Pact. If an economic downturn is a general phenomenon in EMU it should be recalled that the joint monetary policy will be used to assist in mitigating the contraction as long as inflationary risks remain low. A substantial role for national budgetary policies in macroeconomic stabilization can also be retained after the Stability Pact, as long as the medium-term commitments of the latter are observed.

Budget deficits are sensitive to disturbances not only in GDP growth but also in interest rates. Ideally, budget policies should be sufficiently cautious to allow room for not just shortfalls in GDP growth but also the impact of interest rate hikes. Here the sensitivity of a country's budget is determined primarily by the size of the outstanding government debt and its maturity structure. The nightmare scenario which has preoccupied some officials is one in which one or more of the countries with the highest debt ratio – Belgium and Italy are still at more than 115 per cent – is close to the deficit ceiling at a time when a need to raise EMU interest rates arises. A meeting in the ECB Council, where the central bank governors from the countries in a tight spot strongly oppose a rise in the short-term interest rate which is the ECB's main policy instrument with the argument that this will bring their respective deficits above the limit and hence trigger sanctions, could be deeply divisive. It should, however, be unlikely to arise. Interest rates are likely to be moving more slowly in EMU than they have done in the past in individual countries since inflation – the primary objective of the ECB – can be expected to change more sluggishly and the need to contain exchange market pressure will largely disappear. Changes in short-term interest rates are anyway (even in Italy) reflected in the cost of debt servicing only with some considerable delay and intensified efforts to lengthen maturities on public debt must be expected. The potential conflict is accordingly likely to be diluted, though it suggests an additional motive for staying well within the 3 per cent limit at all normal times.

Is there then no merit in the accusation that the Stability Pact is eroding sovereignty in national policy making outside the monetary area almost as completely as the installation of the ECB will do with respect to monetary policy? This accusation is largely unfounded, though the Stability Pact, if taken seriously, will eliminate one pervasive and pernicious feature of past budgetary policies – the tendency for them to become moderately procyclical in good times. Evidence on this type of behaviour by governments has been supplied by Mélitz (1997) and CEC (1998). Both studies show that in moderate upswings, when automatic stabilizers have been working to mitigate rising pressures on capacity, these effects have often been offset by simultaneous discretionary tax cuts or by increases in expenditures delayed from earlier periods. This experience, most vividly illustrated by the failure of EU countries to improve their overall budget positions in the later stages of the upswing in the late 1980s and the very beginning of the 1990s, is not one which should be repeated. The Stability Pact is well designed to achieve this in the current moderate upswing.

On balance, the Stability Pact, despite its apparently rigid rules and arcane procedures, can help to move budgetary policies closer to the kind of medium-term stable path which is already the aim of the joint monetary policy. It has already helped to put pressure on countries with a record of budgetary problems (e.g. Italy and Sweden) to improve their capacity to contain expenditures and plan the total outturn of the budget with more precision. To the extent it can help countries to achieve what is basically in their own long-term interest, this is already a major contribution (see also the discussion in von Hagen and Harden, 1994, of budgetary reforms in EU countries).

The question whether this still leaves some gaps to be filled in macroeconomic policies in EMU will be taken up in the next section.

Possible gaps in the policy framework after EMU

In reviewing the arguments advanced in favour of mandatory guidelines for national budgetary policies in EMU (pp. 16–22) the conclusion was that achieving a good policy mix between the joint monetary policy and the sum of national budgetary policies is a desirable objective, but hardly one that could justify mandatory rules; in view of relatively limited spillover effects of national efforts, better voluntary coordination of the latter should be encouraged. We now take up the question whether such coordination is likely to develop without further efforts. Art. 103 of the Treaty provides the formal authority for ECOFIN in this role and the emergence after May 1998 of a new body comprising only the eleven Finance Ministers from the countries participating in EMU – the so-called Euro-11 Council – suggests that coordination will be given a higher priority than in the past. There are both economic and political reasons for this.

In economic terms, it may appear that the Stability Pact has superseded anything that could be agreed under the heading of 'coordination'. The situation looks analogous to the position of the ECB, which is committed to price stability as a primary objective and cannot therefore also commit itself to output stabilization. But the analogy is more subtle than that; both the monetary and the budgetary authorities will need from time to time to decide upon the desirable speed at which economic disturbances that cause temporary departures from expected achievements should be eliminated. If, say, a negative output disturbance with potential inflationary consequence occurs for (most of) the EMU participants, the ECB will need to consider how rapidly future inflation can be brought back to its desired trajectory; in parallel, the ECOFIN Council, while continuing to insist on national budget deficits staying below 3 per cent of GDP, will need to show some leniency with respect to departures from previously submitted stability plans. In the opposite situation, where both inflation and budgetary targets are temporarily being under-shot, there could be a case for initiatives to shift the policy stance in a less contractionary direction. The simple rule-bound policies that have been given prominence in the Maastricht framework, useful as they are, can hardly be the full story of economic policy in EMU, nor would they be accepted as such in the European public debate. They will in practice be supplemented by efforts of a cooperative nature of the type discussed in the review of fiscal federalism on pp. 22–25 above following Ter-Minassian (1997) and CEC (1993). There is also the issue of the external position of EMU, in terms of both the current account balance and the strength of the euro which will require monitoring by the Euro-11 Council and reconsideration of the appropriateness of the aggregate budgetary stance and the policy mix.

There have recently been indications that extended coordination will be on the agenda of the Euro-11 Council (and hence of ECOFIN itself) in addition to the main responsibility of guarding against deviant behaviour through the Stability Pact. This would be sensible in economic terms, and it could have two political benefits: it would facilitate the role of EMU participants in fora for global policy coordination to have had prior discussions of the policy mix in EMU; and it could protect the ECB against the pressures on it which would arise more forcefully if the central bankers were perceived to be virtually alone on the EU policy stage. Some visible role for ECOFIN (or the Euro-11Council) in the coordination of non-monetary policies may tend to protect rather than endanger the independence of the ECB.

Many critics have foreseen that a joint monetary policy coupled with national budgetary policies which have retained most of their capacity to achieve some degree of automatic stabilization in the face of country-specific disturbances may still offer too limited an insurance mechanism against the impact of the latter upsets. This position implies either advocacy of a fiscal transfer mechanism at the European level or rejection of the whole EMU framework as inadequate prior to a much higher degree of political unification. Is the absence of a transfer mechanism a serious gap in EMU?

There are two main observations to be made, neither of which amounts to a clear answer to the question. The first is that is is extremely difficult to evaluate *a priori* whether country-specific disturbances could take on such proportions in EMU that they would relatively often pose insuperable challenges to national policies. Country-specific disturbances should become less important in EMU than in the past, for a double reason: the further deepening of economic integration will reduce their size, and the joint monetary policy and the Stability Pact will severely constrain the disturbances that have in the past come from divergent national policies. These arguments inspire some confidence that the proposed EMU framework will prove sufficiently robust without new provisions for budgetary transfers among the member states.

A second observation is that should it nevertheless be perceived to be desirable to develop a modest scheme for fiscal transfers, some useful groundwork has already been done. The European Commission, assisted by an expert group, developed some years ago a set of papers which suggested that a scheme of transfers targeted at reducing differences in the evolution of unemployment between EMU participants could be implemented at moderate budgetary cost (see CEC, 1993). Countries with a performance better than the average would transfer directly (or through the EU budget) to countries with below-average performance. Approximately the same degree of protection against asymmetries as between US states could be offered at the cost of increasing the EU budget by only 0.2 per cent of EU GDP – though the figures would be larger for individual countries in particular years. These costs are encouragingly small – until one recalls the great difficulties encountered in raising the present EU buget to 1.27 per cent of EU GDP – and contradict the impression in the public debate of vast amounts crossing borders once fiscal transfers are introduced.

The difficulty in gaining political acceptance for any scheme of this type is, however, only partly financial. Unemployment is recognized as the main problem for EU economic policies in the foreseeable future, but there is today a general distrust among member states that the others are doing their best to reduce it. A transfer scheme might ultimately gain acceptance if it were to address purely cyclical divergences in the evolution of national unemployment rates, but this component is not seen as the main source of existing recent differences in both the level and the direction of changes in unemployment. Structural factors, usually summarized under the general heading of 'labour market rigidities' are seen as the main source of differences in unemployment performance. This view clearly saps any enthusiasm for showing solidarity in this difficult area. This situation may gradually change over the next decade or so as EU member states intensify their exchange of experience in handling the unemployment problem. As a result of this process, launched at the November 1997 European Council in Luxembourg, mutual examinations of labour market policies have moved on to the regular agenda of ECOFIN. Confidence that other member states are also doing their best to reduce unemployment should improve, though it may take a long time before there will be any readiness to use differences in unemployment performance as the trigger for such transfers.

The case for a scheme of fiscal transfers as an essential complement to EMU is currently unproven. It does not seem hazardous to begin the final stage of EMU without them and judge, in the light of some years of experience with national budgetary policies in their stabilization role, whether transfers could indeed make an important further contribution to the robustness of EMU – and, if so, how they could most appropriately be designed keeping in mind the lessons from the experience with fiscal federalism in large federated states.

Conclusions

This chapter has looked critically at the proposed policy framework for EMU where the joint monetary policy will be supplemented by still decentralized national budgetary policies. Some tentative conclusions have emerged. There is some merit in the argument that the risks of increasing budgetary laxity in EMU could well have materalized in the absence of special rules to counter them. Financial market reactions to deficits were in themselves unlikely to have been sufficient. Other arguments for budgetary rules – achieving a proper policy mix and preventing generalized interest rate effects – were found to be less convincing, though they support more policy coordination on a voluntary basis.

The particular form of budgetary rules embodied in the Stability Pact are easy to criticize as somewhat arbitrary, though they are less subject to that criticism than the budgetary convergence criteria applicable at entry into EMU. It would have been appealing to give more weight to the concept of sustainability, but the concept lacks the necessary operationality. The Stability Pact will preserve some considerable room for budgetary stabilizers to continue to work – provided EMU participants take their commitment to medium-term budgetary balance seriously. Greater transparency of procedures and sanctions are other appealing features of the Pact.

In view of this rather positive view of the new framework it is not obvious whether serious gaps in economic policy making remain. Two such potential gaps are discussed. There is probably a need for supplementing the monitoring of rules by closer coordination on a voluntary basis and some examples for the agenda of ECOFIN and the Euro-11 Council are reviewed. Another potential gap which is less likely to be filled in the initial years of EMU is the development of a budgetary transfer scheme to provide additional insurance against country-specific disturbances. The case for such a scheme is currently unproven, but on the other hand it need not be as costly as most observers seem to believe. The basis for the solidarity which such a scheme would embody may develop a good deal further as EU member states intensify their monitoring of each other's employment policies.

References

Agell, J., Calmfors, L. and Jonsson, G. (1996). 'Fiscal Policy when Monetary Policy is "Tied to the Mast"', *European Economic Review*, 40: 1413–40

Association for the Monetary Union of Europe (AMUE) (1998). *The Sustainability Report*, Paris: AMUE

Bishop, G. (1990). 'Separating Fiscal from Monetary Sovereignty in EMU – A United States of Europe is not Necessary', London: Salomon Brothers International

Buiter, W., Corsetti G. and Roubini, N. (1993). 'Excessive Deficits: Sence and Nonsense in the Treaty of Maastricht', *Economic Policy*, 16: 57–101.

Commission of the European Communities (CEC) (1990). 'One Market, One Money', *European Economy*, 44, Brussels

(1993). 'Stable Money, Sound Finances', *European Economy*, 53

(1998). 'Economic Policy in EMU, Parts A and B', *Economic Papers*, 124 and 125, Brussels: Directorate-General for Economic and Financial Affairs

Committee for the Study of Economic and Monetary Union (1989). *Report on Economic and Monetary Union* (the Delors Report), Luxembourg: EC Publication Office

European Monetary Institute (EMI) (1998). 'Convergence Report: Report Required by Article 109 of the Treaty Establishing the European Community, Frankfurt (March)

Gros, D. and Thygesen, N. (1998). *European Monetary Integration – From the European Monetary System to Economic and Monetary Union*, London and New York: Addison-Wesley Longman

Jenkins, R. (1977). 'Europe's Present Challenge and Future Opportunity', First Jean Monnet Lecture, Florence, European University Institute

Lamfalussy, A. (1989). 'Macro-coordination of Fiscal Policies in an Economic and Monetary Union', in Committee for the Study of Economic and Monetary Union, *Report on Economic and Monetary Union* (the Delors Report), Luxembourg: EC Publications Office.

Mélitz, J, (1997). 'Some Cross-country Evidence about Debt, Deficits and the Behaviour of Monetary and Fiscal Authorities: A Progress Report', *CEPR Discussion Paper*, 1653, London: Centre for Economic Policy Research

Pochet, P. and Vanhercke, B. (1988). *Social Challenges of Economic and Monetary Union*, Brussels: European Interuniversity Press

Rogoff, K. (1985). 'The Optimal Degree of Commitment to an Intermediate Monetary Target', *Quarterly Journal of Economics*, 100: 1169–90.

Ter-Minassian, T. (ed.) (1997). *Fiscal Federalism in Theory and Practice*, Washington, DC: International Monetary Fund

Thygesen, N. (1996). 'Should Budgetary Policies be Coordinated Further in EMU – And is that Feasible?', *Banca Nazionale del Lavoro Quarterly Review*, 196, Special Issue: 5–32 von Hagen, J. and Harden, I. (1994). 'National Budget Processes and Fiscal Performance', *European Economy, Reports and Studies*, 3: 310–418

Werner, P. *et al.* (1970). *Report to the Council and the Commission on the Realization by Steps of Economic and Monetary Union in the Community* (the Werner Report), Supplement to Bulletin II-1970 of the European Communities, Brussels

3 A political economy analysis of the Maastricht and Stability Pact fiscal criteria

Thomas D. Willett

Introduction

The fiscal provisions of the Maastricht Treaty have proven to be highly controversial. Many economists have attacked the Treaty's convergence criteria provisions which limit the size of budget deficits to 3 per cent of GDP and debt/GDP ratios to 60 per cent as being arbitrary and likely to impose substantial costs in terms of unemployment and lost economic output owing to forced fiscal stringency at inappropriate times.[1] With monetary union removing the option of countercyclical monetary policy at the national level, one can argue that greater flexibility in fiscal policy is needed to compensate. The requirement to reduce deficits to Maastricht reference levels, however, has subjected many economies to self-imposed deflationary shocks and has robbed governments of the flexibility to respond to future shocks.[2] For better or worse, the role of the fiscal convergence criteria is now ended, but their spirit lives on in the Excessive Deficits Procedure (EDP) of the Stability and Growth Pact (SGP or 'Stability Pact'). These provide for penalties of up to 0.5 per cent of GDP per year for budget deficits in excess of 3 per cent of GDP.[3]

Helpful comments from Tom Borcherding, Richard Burdekin, Michael Hutchison, Craig Stubblebine, Neils Thygesen and an anonymous reviewer are gratefully acknowledged.
1. See, for example, Buiter, Corsetti and Roubini (1993); De Grauwe (1993, 1996, 1997); Eichengreen (1994, 1997); Eichengreen and von Hagen (1995); Glick and Hutchison (1993); Kenen (1995). The fiscal provisions of the Maastricht Treaty and the Stability Pact are summarized in the contribution by Niels Thygesen in this volume (chapter 2).
2. See, for example, von Hagen and Lutz (1996).
3. Procedurally, the EDP process will begin with a report from the European Commission of the existence of an excessive deficit. This will be studied by the Economic and Financial Committe (ECOFIN), which will issue an opinion. Taking this opinion into account, the Commission will make a recommendation to the Council. If the Council concludes that an excessive deficit exists, it will offer guidelines for policy adjustments in the offending countries. The member is then expected to take actions within four months that would bring its deficit back within bounds within a year. If no actions are taken, sanctions are to be imposed within ten months of the report of the violation.

Critics often explain the fiscal provisions of Maastricht, and the subsequent Stability Pact, in terms of German politics, reflecting government desires to prevent some countries, such as Italy, from participating in the initial membership of EMU and to assure German public opinion that the D-mark mark would be replaced with a hard, not a soft, euro.[4] These considerations probably did influence some German officials, but it should be recognized that the basic case for fiscal limitations was unanimously supported by the members of the Delors Commission; it was not just something imposed by Germany.

It is true that the Maastricht and Stability Pact fiscal criteria make little, if any, sense from the standpoint of traditional optimal policy analysis. They can be rationalized, however, on political economy grounds. Unfortunately, political economy considerations also suggest that the criteria may well not work as intended.

Much of the debate among economists about the Maastricht and Stability Pact fiscal provisions has focused on the extent to which monetary union itself presents a case for fiscal limitations. Other important topics concern the form of fiscal limitations and enforcement mechanisms adopted, and their inter-relations with central bank independence. The analysis of these issues cannot be limited to the type of optimal policy analysis which until recently dominated economists' thinking on such issues; a broader public choice or political economy perspective is required. In this broader framework optimal policy analysis continues to play a role, but it is not centre stage.

This chapter suggests that while monetary union *per se* provides some arguments for fiscal limitations, these are much weaker than the purely domestic arguments for fiscal limitations to offset political distortions (the nature of which will be discussed below). Indeed, in the absence of domestic distortion arguments, the case for monetary union increasing the need for group fiscal limitations virtually disappears. The purely economic spillover effects on interest rates and output that would remain are probably small and would call for policy coordination rather than the adoption of joint constraints.[5] From the standpoint of the subsidiary principle this suggests that collectively determined fiscal limitation is not the best approach; each country should adopt the form of limitation – if any – that it prefers.

Practical political economy considerations present a strong pragmatic argument in favour of the Maastricht Treaty and Stability Pact limitations, however. Some of the same types of political biases or distortions

---

[4] See, for example, DeGrauwe (1993, 1996, 1997).
[5] See Emerson *et al.* (1991); Eichengreen and Wyplosz (1998).

which create a case for monetary and fiscal limitations in the first place also make it difficult to get such limitations adopted. Thus it makes sense for advocates of limitations to seize whatever opportunities they may.

From this perspective, the Maastricht and Stability Pact negotiations are similar to IMF conditionality and the use of exchange rates as nominal anchors to constrain inflation.[6] They should be seen not so much as external limitations being imposed on unified national actors, but rather as processes which strengthen the hands of some actors – i.e. pro-stability monetary and fiscal officials, *vis-à-vis* others in the domestic political economy process.

Political economy considerations also help explain the forms taken by the Maastricht and Stability Pact fiscal limitations. If we limited our analysis to technical economic considerations, optimal fiscal limitations or constitutional rules would probably look quite different from those adopted; they would certainly be much more complicated. But for this very reason they would probably be far less effective. It is clear from the literature on constitutional political economy that simplicity and transparency are important desiderata of major institutional reforms.[7] Optimal contingency rules are unlikely to provide a potent political rallying cry and would make monitoring and enforcement more difficult.

There is considerable disagreement about the effectiveness of institutional reforms in actually modifying behaviour. Some critics fear that the fiscal criteria may generate severe economic hardships and impede rather than aid progress toward European integration; others suspect that they will have little effect. This chapter argues for an intermediate view of the effectiveness of institutions and suggests that this has important implications for the design of institutional arrangements. Such considerations will often make the best rules look quite different from what they would be if enforceability were not a problem. In particular, where one assumes that despite its high degree of formal institutional independence the European Central Bank (ECB) may still be subject to political pressures, then there is a case for fiscal restrictions which would be redundant if central bank independence and the 'no-bail-out' clause were expected to be fully effective.

Corsetti and Roubini (1993) discuss the trade-off between correcting biases toward budget deficits and facilitating tax smoothing in the face of shocks. They conclude (1993: 50) that

the optimal fiscal policy . . . would be one of full tax smoothing where fiscal deficits and surpluses are run in the face of transitory shocks. If such a first-best solution is

---

[6.] See Allsopp and Vines (1996); Buiter, Corsetti and Roubini (1993); Westbrook and Willett (1999); Willett (1998b).
[7.] See the analysis and references in Willett (1995, 1987).

not enforceable in a political equilibrium, a second-best equilibrium might take the form of a 'fiscal rule with an escape clause'. Such a flexible rule would impose a fiscal balance whenever the real output shock is below a certain threshold and would allow for tax smoothing fiscal deficits if the transitory disturbance is large enough.

This is indeed the form taken by the EDP of the Stability Pact where an automatic exemption to the 3 per cent budget deficit limit occurs if output falls by 2 per cent or more. (A drop between 2 and 0.75 per cent may qualify with the concurrence of the Council.)[8]

From a political perspective, the question is not whether the simple 3 per cent budget deficit limitations adopted in the Maastricht Treaty and Stability Pact can be derived from formal optimizing models, but rather whether they seem likely to produce a better ratio of benefits to costs than potentially feasible alternatives. The range of considerations relevant to such analysis is far too broad for us to be able to include all of them in a comprehensive formal model. Evaluations at this point must thus be judgemental and may be subject to differences in view among reasonable people. It is clear, however, that from the perspective of constitutional political economy analysis the Maastricht and Stability Pact provisions look far more sensible than from the optimal policy perspective adopted by many critics.

Still, a political economy perspective suggests a number of potentially serious problems with the Maastricht Treaty and Stability Pact criteria. While the 3 per cent deficit limits are not particularly severe for counties starting from a solid fiscal position,[9] they were quite stringent for the disequilibrium positions in which most European countries started, and this has been exacerbated by slow economic growth.[10] As a strategy for limiting the initial membership in EMU, such stringency had a rationale, but in the event this purpose of the Maastricht criteria did not work politically and EMU is starting with eleven participants.[11] To make this feasible, Germany's initial insistence on a strict interpretation of the criteria was abandoned in all but rhetoric. Attention to the debt criteria was dropped almost entirely, and the deficit criteria were subjected to numerous 'fiddles', including by Germany itself.

[8.] Corsetti and Roubini (1993: 50) are however, critical of the specific Maastricht formulation, arguing that 'such guidelines are...too rigid because they impose targets on the inflation-unadjusted and cyclically-unadjusted overall fiscal balances' but are also 'too loose because their implementation will be subject to a "political" evaluation'.

[9.] See, for erample, Masson (1996).

[10.] See Artis (1996).

[11.] For discussion of the evidence that the financial markets view the 'maxi EMU' as a source of monetary weakness, see Fratianni (1998).

The net result so far has been close to the worst of all possible worlds. The criteria proved to be of little effectiveness in limiting EMU membership (only Greece was screened out). Despite the 'fiddling', the deficit criteria did ensure considerable fiscal tightness, but it would have been hard for the timing of these adjustments to have been worse from the standpoint of standard stabilization policy. This could be worth the short-term costs if these adjustments yielded substantial improvements in the longer-run budget outlook, but sadly for most countries this has not been the case. Laudably the Maastricht Treaty called for countries to take action that would improve their medium-term fiscal positions and adopt domestic budget reforms which would make this easier to accomplish. The goal was to have budget balance or even a small surplus in normal times, giving plenty of room for automatic budget stabilizers to operate during mild recessions without violating the 3 per cent deficit limit. Maastricht represented a golden opportunity for countries to use the external clout of the European project to help implement reforms in domestic budget practices which would reduce the political biases toward budget deficits. Unfortunately, however, for many countries little productive use has been made of this opportunity. As Masson (1996: 997) notes

it is striking that the measures to reduce deficits since EU 'convergence programmes' were formulated (starting in 1992) are predominately tax increases rather than spending reductions

For most countries, little reform of budget procedures has taken place, and as Alesini and Perrotti (1995) have documented, tax increases tend to have much less permanency than spending cuts in reducing budget deficits.[12] While there is a good political economy case for Maastricht-type fiscal restrictions, the specific formulations of the criteria were sensible only if the convergence criteria were going to be used as a tight screen to limit initial EMU membership and/or if they were going to be used to spearhead domestic budget reforms. Neither of these has occurred.

In the following section the need for taking a political economy perspective to analyse these issues is discussed. Different views of the effectiveness of institutional reforms are then discussed and the case for an intermediate view of partial effectiveness is argued. The issue of whether EMU increases the need for fiscal restrictions is addressed, and a number of the specifics of the Maastricht and Stability Pact fiscal criteria are discussed and possibilities that the operation of the Excessive Deficits Procedure (EDP) of the

---

[12.] *The Economist* (1998: 9) argues that despite all of the fiscal fudging, the Maastricht criteria encouraged Italy and Spain 'to make genuine improvements in their public finances.' Ireland also made noticeable improvements.

Stability Pact could actually increase rather than reduce the pressures on the ECB are considered. The final section draws some conclusions

The need for a political economy perspective

In approaching the issue of imposing institutional limitations on the operation of the democratic political process in the area of economic policy, one needs to ask whether there are serious biases or distortions in the operation of the political process. If there are, then the first-best solution is to reform collective decision making procedures to remove these biases. If this does not appear feasible, then constitutional-type measures to limit the range of permissible policy actions and/or to cede authority to independent officials should be taken. In both cases one must consider whether there are feasible rules or other institutional reforms which would be likely to perform sufficiently well in practice that on average they would improve outcomes enough to justify the costs of institutional innovation. The possibilities for unintended negative side effects should also be carefully analysed.

In approaching this question, purely economic analysis can be tremendously useful because it can help predict the probable economic effects of alternative policy rules under different patterns of shocks and economic structures. The potential for a wide range of shocks, which will come in variable proportions, implies that optimal policy rules will typically be quite complicated. Further, the existence of uncertainty about the correct economic model and technical limitations on our ability to identify disturbances suggests that they can seldom be uniquely specified.[13] Thus as a practical matter there is often a strong case to leave scope for discretionary policy actions. This must be balanced against the benefits of constraints on political behaviour designed to offset the effects of political biases or distortions. Combined with the need to develop public support for institutional reforms, these considerations suggest that the best design will often be the delineation of a set of constraints on the allowable range of policy actions rather than a specific automatic rule.[14] Thus, for example, increased variability in the demand for money led some economists to advocate more complicated monetary rules which took velocity movements into account, but these proved to be too complicated to generate a substantial following.[15] On the other hand, inflation targeting has now become quite popular.[16]

[13] See the discussion and references in Byrant (1995) and Willett (1987).
[14] See Willett (1987, 1995).
[15] See, for example, the analysis and references in Willett (1987).
[16] See, for example, Mishkin and Posen (1997).

In undertaking such political economy analysis it is important to consider the effects that constraints will have on the incentives facing decision makers. Sometimes, the effects will be perverse, such as efforts to shift items off budget. In other cases, they may be favourable. For example, if officials paid no attention to constraints until they were hit, then constraint systems would probably produce costly instability in the setting of policy instruments. However, if farsighted policy makers are concerned with the costs of becoming constrained then, as Artis and Winkler discuss in their contribution to this volume (chapter 7), this lump-sum threat can provide graduated incentives to adjust prior to hitting the constraint.[17] The way that EDP constraints operate will make a huge difference to their desirability. Sadly, the continuous-pressures version is likely to operate more effectively on centralized than decentralized decision makers. Thus, as we shall discuss, the limitations and improved procedures approaches may be better seen as complements than as substitutes.

Inevitably there will be considerable subjectivity in the analysis of political biases or distortions. These distortions can occur because of a variety of real-world limitations on the efficiency of collective decision making structures and the information of participants in the political process.[18] Limited and costly information and the problems of free riding all suggest that unconstrained political processes will generate levels of government spending, budget deficits and inflation that will be excessive from the standpoint of what farsighted, well informed median voters would desire. This is accepted even by many economists who are critical of the Maastricht fiscal criteria. Thus, for example, Buiter, Corsetti and Roubini (1993: 84) conclude that 'the empirical evidence is consistent with the view that a bias toward excessive deficits exists in a number of countries'. Basic public choice analysis suggests that groups who benefit from government expenditures and tax breaks are likely to be more involved in the political process than the typical taxpayer, leading to incentives to over-expand government expenditures and under-finance them with tax revenues. Furthermore, the ability to finance expenditures from non-tax sources (such as deficits and regulatory fiat) further increases the bias toward excessive expenditures. Higher government expenditures and budget deficits in turn create pressure for monetary accommodation.

In principle the design of optimal constraint systems may depend on the specific nature of the biases to be corrected. As is stressed in the

---

[17.] See also Willett (1987).
[18.] See, for example, the contributions in Persson and Tabellini (1994), Wijnholds, Eijffinger and Hoogduin (1994) and Willett (1988).

contribution by Beetsma in this volume (chapter 8), the general theory of the second best applies to political economy as well as to economic analysis. In a distortion-ridden world, the correction of a single deficiency may worsen another.[19] This problem of unintended consequences needs to be taken very seriously in the analysis of proposed institutional reforms.

While formal modelling must necessarily consider the possible sources of bias, one – or, at most, a few – at a time, in reality a number of different processes may be at work simultaneously.[20] The theory of economic policy tells us that the first-best policy response to a distortion is to attack it directly; in this vein, the best solution to excessive budget deficits is to remove the bias in the operation of the political system. Where there are multiple sources of bias, the case for a second-best constraining rule is strengthened. Issues of political feasibility also often point in this direction. Especially where institutional reforms have only partial effectiveness, direct limitations on budget deficits and efforts to reform the budget process directly are better seen as complements than as substitutes. (This will be discussed further on pp. 54–55 below.)

In considering various types of political biases or distortions analyses it is important to distinguish clearly between the frequency with which they are modelled and their probable empirical importance. In the formal modelling literature in macroeconomics, issues of time-inconsistency and opportunism have understandably become highly popular.[21] These do describe some real-world problems, I believe, but far more important in my judgement are cases where biases result from the inability of often well intentioned officials to withstand political pressures for higher government spending and lower taxes.

The extent to which these different sources of bias may have different implications for the design of desirable institutional reforms is an issue which I believe deserves a great deal more attention. Thus, for example, in the model Beetsma presents in chapter 8, central bank independence increases budget deficits. However, when interest rate effects are included in the analysis central bank independence may induce governments to run lower deficits, for which there is some supporting empirical evidence.[22] In addition, Jensen (1996) concludes that firm monetary rules reduce the

---

[19.] For a more general discussion of this problem see Jervis (1997).

[20.] Corsetti and Roubini (1997) identify five classes of political models of fiscal deficits: the public choice approach (which they identify with James Buchanan) models of government weakness and decentralized government; distributional conflicts models; models of strategic public debt choice; political business cycle models.

[21.] For similar arguments that the formal literature on policy coordination over-emphasizes the problem of cheating relative to the problems of securing domestic political support for implementation, see Byrant (1995); Putnam and Henning (1989).

[22.] See Burdekin and Laney (1988); Parkin (1993).

likelihood that fiscal coordination will be counterproductive. We should thus not draw policy conclusions from Beetsma's model until more thorough analysis is undertaken.

Another illustration of how the effects of an economic change may depend on which of various political economy considerations dominates is given by Willett and Banaian (1996). They argue that while international currency competition will reduce optimal rates of inflation for efficiency- or revenue-maximizing governments since there is less revenue generated per unit of inflation, for this very reason it is likely to increase inflation for weak governments where deficits are the method of financing of last resort – i.e. a constant-sized deficit would generate more inflation in terms of the domestic currency. Thus without specifying the model of government, we cannot predict the effects on inflation.

Three views of the effects of institutions

Alternative views of the effectiveness of institutions have had a profound impact on the evaluations offered concerning the Maastricht and Stability Pact fiscal criteria. The two extreme views are that institutional provisions are virtually fully effective and alternatively that they have almost no effect. Ironically, both views have been used to criticize the fiscal criteria. The role played by the 'little effectiveness' view is straightforward. From its perspective the debate about fiscal criteria is largely irrelevant, as they will have little effect on actual behaviour. This view has been perhaps most consistently espoused by the realist school of international relations scholars: in this view underlying power relationships dominate international relations and institutional mechanisms and international agreements have little ability to alter the behaviour of contending nations.[23]

A number of critics of budget limitation proposals have also pointed to numerous channels through which the intent of various types of budget limitation measures can be circumvented.[24] Studies of the effects of the balanced budget requirements on states in the United States, for example, find effects on the composition but not the total amount of state debt. The direct government deficits were reduced, but debt issue by state authorities was increased by approximately the same amount.[25]

[23] For recent discussion of the realist view see Frieden and Lake (1995); Willett (1996).
[24] On ineffectiveness of particular fiscal limitations see Alesina and Perotti (1996a); Poterba (1996b): von Hagen (1990). Inman (1996) finds that the important requirements for budget rules to constrain fiscal behaviour are that they be constitutionally based – i.e. they require a super majority to be over-ridden; they focus on *ex post* accounting; they are enforced with penalties by an independent body.
[25] See von Hagen (1990).

At the US federal level, the Gramm–Rudman–Hollins deficit limitations are widely viewed to have been a failure.[26] As von Hagen (1998:140) stresses, 'numerical constraints induce substitution effects that work against the intended effect on aggregate discipline'. Not only does such circumvention reduce the effectiveness of the constraints, but in some cases it will actually increase the perverse economic effects of government activities – by, for example, increasing the incentives to put activities off-budget, which often increases their costs and reduces transparency.

At the other extreme are views that institutional reforms are typically highly effective. Such a view has underlain the beliefs not only of idealistic advocates of world government, but also of economists who have argued that the provisions for the independence of the ECB and the 'no-bail-out' rule are sufficient to ensure that the euro will enjoy low inflation and that, therefore, there is no need to worry on anti-inflation grounds about budget deficit limitations or convergence prior to monetary union.[27]

In my judgement both of these extreme views are fundamentally wrong. The critics are right that it would be naïve to assume that rules on the size of budget deficits will be effective, but De Grauwe (1997: 210) probably goes too far when he argues that 'the case for strict rules on the size of national government budget deficits is weak. There is no evidence that these rules are enforceable.' As Poterba (1994, 1996a) points out, the nature of the prohibitions on budget deficits vary widely across the states of the United States. Many apply to only a part of the budget, and most states have no explicit enforcement mechanism for their balanced budget mandates. The available studies suggest that weak commitments have little, if any, direct effects. However, in his review of the studies on the US states, Poterba (1996b: 398) concludes that

The studies surveyed . . . suggest that there are correlations between state balanced budget rules and state fiscal policy. Constitutional or legislative provisions that make it more costly to balance the budget in a given fashion, for example by raising taxes or issuing long-term debt, appear to discourage these fiscal actions.

Similar studies by von Hagen and others focusing on comparative institutional analysis across countries also find that 'institutions shaping the budget process of a country are an important factor in determining that country's level of public deficits and debts' (von Hagen, 1998: 1).[28]

Institutions do matter, but there can be considerable slippage in their effectiveness, and sometimes they have unintended consequences that are

---

[26.] See, for example, von Hagen (1998).
[27.] See, for example, De Grauwe (1993,1994); Dornbusch (1997).
[28.] For other recent analysis and references to the literature, see Weaver and Rockman (1993); Steinmo and Tolbert (1998).

more important than their direct effects. As a result, careful microanalysis is required of how institutions change actors' incentive structures and their relative influence. This 'partial effectiveness' view emphasizes issues of enforceability and implies the need for careful attention to the details of institutional designs and realistic appraisals of how much various institutional reforms can actually do to alter behaviour. As will be discussed on pp. 52–60 below, such analysis suggests that there are good reasons to be concerned about the effectiveness and possible perverse effects of the budget limitations imposed by the Stability Pact.

This approach also suggests that one cannot safely assume full effectiveness of the 'no-bail-out' and central bank independence provisions of the Maastricht Treaty. Analysis of central bank independence has become a major industry in recent years, this work illustrates both the difficulties and fruitfulness of the new institutional or public choice analysis. There has been considerable disagreement about the classification of specific central banks with regard to their degree of independence, about the relative importance of different types of institutional provisions and about the extent to which correlations between central bank institutions and inflation reflect causation or are themselves the result of third factors such as the public's aversion to inflation. Still, out of this controversy some consensus is emerging.[29]

In the industrial countries greater formal institutional independence does appear to give central banks greater, but far from complete, insulation from political pressures, and some aspects of institutional design have been found to be more effective than others. The need to distinguish between target and instrument independence has been stressed, with independence being seen as desirable for the latter and public accountability important for the former. In developing countries, where the rule of law typically has much less tradition, formal institutional independence appears to have offered central banks much less insulation from political pressures.

Despite having an institutional design that receives high marks from the standpoint of the literature on central bank independence, the ECB will be a new institution which will start with considerably less credibility than the Bundesbank, and the comments of the French government on the desirability of greater political supervision of the ECB have done little to help the Bank's initial stock of credibility. Nor has the agreement, forced by the French after considerable acrimonious bargaining, that Wim Duisenberg would step down half-way through his term as Governor of the ECB to be

[29.] See, for example, Banaian, Burkerin and Willett (1995); Cukierman (1992); Eijffinger and De Hann (1996); Fischer (1995); Grilli, Masciandaro and Tabellini (1991); Hutchison and Walsh (1998); Masciandaro (1995); Posen (1995); Willett (1995).

succeeded by the head of the French central bank, Jean-Claude Trichet.[30] If the new institutions of the EMU could be assumed to begin with full effectiveness and credibility, then the argument that there is no need for prior convergence would be quite powerful and there would be no need for the Stability Pact on anti-inflation grounds. On the partial effectiveness view, however, there is a strong case for such provisions to help the ECB have a successful launch.[31]

Does EMU increase the need for fiscal restrictions?

The effectiveness of institutions is also quite relevant to the debate about whether monetary union *per se* increases the case for fiscal limitation.[32] It has been argued that participation in monetary union will lower the interest rate cost of financing budget deficits, thus increasing the bias toward excessive deficits and imposing negative externalities on the other members of the monetary union.[33] In an intertemporal optimization model based on tax smoothing and re-election considerations, Corsetti and Roubini (1997: 44), for example, show that 'access to international capital markets, by reducing the financial constraint of the government, increase[s] the size of the [budget] deficit'. They stress that in their model (1997: 44) 'it is the slope of the supply schedule for capital, not the level of the interest rate, that produces this result'. In their simulations this effect of international borrowing is large, increasing deficits by as much as 2 per cent of GDP. They note, however, that if governments and the private sector have equal access to international borrowing, then a restraint on international borrowing by the government will have no effect on the bias toward excessive government borrowing.[34] Agell, Calmfors and Jonsson (1996) also present a model in which fixed exchange rates will increase budget deficits and argue (1996: 1414) their 'conclusions receive some empirical support from a comparison of the fiscal deficits in the [OECD] countries choosing monetary cooperation with Germany within the ERM... The average fiscal deficit [over 1980–7] rose by 2 per centage points more in countries that opted for exchange-rate cooperation with Germany.'

[30.] See, for example, Feldstein (1997).
[31.] See Andrews and Willett (1997); Corden (1993); Crockett (1993).
[32.] See, for example, Buiter, Corsetti and Roubini (1993); De Grauwe (1992), Glick and Hutchison (1991,1993); Gros and Thygesen (1998).
[33.] Note that the effect of deficits on other countries' interest rates is a pecuniary externality that does not generate economic inefficiency. See Buiter, Corsetti and Roubini (1993). Furthermore, it should be remembered that these effects would be spread over the whole global capital market, not just the EMU members.
[34.] See also Corsetti and Roubini (1995).

This argument provides an important qualification to the traditional discipline argument for fixed exchange rates. While external discipline over monetary policy will be increased, external discipline over fiscal policy may be reduced in the short term. Indeed, this appears to have been the case for Italy during the sticky pegged rate period of the EMS.[35]

There are several counters to such arguments. One is that as long as the 'no-bail-out' provisions of the Maastricht Treaty are observed, the private market will evaluate the risk of national government debt appropriately and penalize growing deficits with increasing risk premia.[36] The experience of state governments within the United States suggests that financial markets are relatively efficient in making these types of distinctions. Restoy (1996: 1630) concludes

The available empirical evidence is relatively supportive of the hypothesis that markets do discriminate among securities issued by regional governments with different degrees of financial and fiscal discipline.

If the 'no-bail-out' clause is not viewed as credible, however, the likelihood of group support in the case of a liquidity or solvency crisis with respect to a member country's debt provides an implicit subsidy. Many commentators have already questioned the credibility of the 'no-bail-out' clause, indicating that this particular institutional provision is likely to be of limited effectiveness. However, as De Grauwe (1997: 205) points out, 'keeping Italy outside the Union does not necessarily reduce the risk that EU members will have to engage in a future bail out operation.' The increased interest rate subsidy accruing to countries with budget deficits which would be due to joining the EMU *per se*, is thus likely to be small.

Furthermore, once one drops a unified-actor model of a government whose objective is to maximize economic efficiency, there is little reason to believe that modest variations in interest rates will have substantial effects on government behaviour. As von Hagen (1998:1) points out

the extent to which governments base their borrowing decisions on the level of real interest rates is much in doubt.

When one adopts more realistic political economy views of the operation of the political process, then unless interest rates reach sky-high levels, such as was the case in the 1994–5 Mexican crisis, it seems unlikely that the

---

[35] See, for example, Andrews and Willett (1997).

[36] While private financial markets can clearly provide useful discipline, recent experience ranging from the EMS crisis of the early 1990s to the Mexican crisis of the mid-1990s to the Thailand crisis of 1997 suggests that the private market typically provides graduated pressures in a much less continuous form than would be ideal. The early warning pressures are often too weak and the post-crisis pressures are sometimes too strong. See the analysis and references in Buiter, Corsetti and Roubini (1988); Willett (1998a).

level of interest rates will substantially influence unconstrained government tax and spending policies. As Corsetti and Roubini (1993: 74) suggest

the argument . . . that the discipline of the market will be enough to ensure fiscal discipline in the deviant countries, seems based more on wishful thinking than an assessment of the incentives faced by member countries. The market discipline in the form of higher interest rates did not prevent members of the Community from pursuing unsustainable fiscal policies throughout the 1980s.

Drawing on an analysis of unitary and federal states, Eichengreen and von Hagen (1995) find that budget limitations are not a general feature of federal states, and that in many of the cases where they are present these constraints were adopted unilaterally by the subgovernments rather than being imposed by the central government. Bayoumi, Eichengreen, and von Hagen (1997: 81) conclude that

The key to understanding the cross-country incidence of borrowing restrictions lies in the structure of the tax base . . . countries in which subcentral governments control a large share of the tax base are less likely to restrict borrowing by subcentral governments.

This is a useful finding which shows that there is no strong historical precedent for the Maastricht fiscal restrictions. But then there is no strong historical precedent for EMU, either. Small countries have at times adopted a larger nation's currency, and EMU is not the first example of a monetary union among countries of roughly equal size (see Cohen, 1994), but it is quite unusual. I believe that Bayoumi, Eichengreen and von Hagen thus go too far when they argue (1997: 81) that

the implications for EMU are clear. Taxes in the EU are controlled almost entirely by national governments . . . Given the scope for EMU members to use their own taxes to deal with financial difficulties, the EDP would appear to be redundant.

Another counter, offered by De Grauwe (1992: 175), is that

countries who join the union reduce their ability to finance budget deficits by money creation. As a result, the governments of member states of a monetary union face a 'harder' budget constraint than sovereign nations.[37]

As noted above, there is indeed some evidence that countries with more independent central banks tend to run lower budget deficits on average.[38] Furthermore, as De Grauwe shows, during the 1980s the budget deficits of

---

[37.] Of course, with strict budget deficit limitations the level of interest rates would matter as they would directly affect the amount of government interest expenses. In this regard credibility considerations had an important affect on the difficulty of meeting the Maastricht convergence criteria. See, for example, De Grauwe (1997).

[38.] See Burdekin and Laney (1988); Parkin (1993).

the states within federal systems – such as Australia, Canada, Germany, Switzerland and the United States – have tended to run deficits which are a much smaller proportion of their revenues than have their national governments or other member states of the EU. As De Grauwe notes (1992: 177), such evidence is not conclusive, but

at the very least, the results... suggest that the idea that in monetary unions members states have a strong incentive to create excessive levels of government debt is not corroborated by the facts of the 1980s.

In interpreting such results, however, we need to draw a sharp distinction between concerns that joining EMU would substantially increase the tendency for national governments to run budget deficits and concerns that in the absence of institutional reforms national budget deficits would probably continue to be a serious problem under EMU. I think that it is quite unlikely that on balance joining EMU would substantially increase problems on this score, but I think that for other (i.e. domestic) reasons, budget deficits would probably continue to be a major problem in the absence of institutional reforms.

Even with formal independence, the ECB will be subject to pressures. Buiter, Corsetti and Roubini (1993: 80) are probably correct that the

possibility seems remote that fiscal norms are necessary to render it impossible, or at any rate unlikely, that the new ECB will effectively be forced to monetize the budget deficits of countries without fiscal discipline.

The pressures are likely to be much more subtle than this. The danger may not be so much that the ECB will be forced, but that it will be induced, into partial monetary accommodation of budget deficits. As Gerlach (1998: 110) argues, there are likely to be differences of opinion among the members of the ECB board at times and

the fact that a tightening of [monetary] policy is likely to worsen the debt situation and increase the risk of financial instability may lead the average [ECB] council member to be marginally less willing to tighten or marginally more willing to relax monetary policy. Large public debts could therefore impart an inflation bias to the ECB's monetary policy. While it is difficult to speculate how large this inflation bias could be, a few per cent seems plausible.

If the independence of the ECB were firmly established, there would be less need for budget deficit limitations on monetary stability grounds. As a fledgling institution, however, the ECB will have to earn its credibility. We now have considerable evidence that the adoption of strong institutional arrangements, such as currency boards, does have immediate effects on credibility. But these initial effects are not complete, additional credibility has to be won by policy actions.[39] Good institutional arrangements can help full credibility be earned more quickly, but seldom, if ever, are they sufficient to generate instant full credibility. Efforts to limit budget deficits are thus especially important for the initial period of EMU and the ECB. It is not EMU *per se*, but the birth of the ECB, that presents the strongest international case for fiscal restrictions.

Evaluation of the specifics of the Stability Pact

A number of objections have been raised with regard to the specifics of the Stability Pact. The question of the consistency between the deficit and debt level provisions is addressed in contributions by Hughes Hallett and by Vines in this volume (chapters 9 and 11). As a long-run guide for fiscal policy the 3 per cent budget deficit rule appears quite reasonable. Allowing for the effects of normal cyclical fluctuations, this suggests that governments should shoot for full-employment balanced budgets or even a small surplus, and this goal is explicitly stated in the Stability Pact.[40] It is open to question whether a full-employment balanced budget formulation or the 3 per cent nominal deficit limitation could be explained more effectively to the general public, but either would seem to be a reasonable choice. Given the initial budget positions in many countries, however, the amount of budget adjustments required over a relatively short period of time to meet the letter of the Maastricht criteria has proven to be too great to be met without fudging.

In the initial German view this was to be expected, and would help the credibility of the monetary union by excluding the less disciplined countries from initial entry. However, as Artis (1996:1010) points out, 'barriers that one set too high may not be revealing'.[41] The German view misforecast both the strength of feelings of other members of the EU that the initial group of EMU members should be broad rather than narrow and also the problems that the two core members – France and Germany – would have in meeting the 3 per cent limit themselves. As a consequence, the specific Maastricht fiscal criteria adopted have proven to be quite

---

[39] See, for example, the analysis and references in Dubaskas, Wihlborg and Willett (1998); Westbrook and Willett (1999).

[40] The 3 per cent deficit limit also corresponds roughly to the Golden Rule of public finance that budget deficits equal capital expenditures.

[41] For a proposal to loosen the EDP by applying it to full employment rather than actual deficits, see Eichengreen (1997). Brander, Diebaler and Schuberth (1998) argue that for assessing short-term fiscal stances, focus on the cyclically adjusted balance would be preferable, while for evaluating the medium-term sustainability of budget deficits, structural primary gaps would give a better indicator.

unfortunate; with hindsight, adoption of a looser requirement of progress in fiscal restraint would have been more desirable.

A great deal of controversy has arisen over the degree of automaticity and structure of penalties for excessive deficits.[42] From the standpoint of the design of international institutional arrangements, the Stability Pact makes important innovations both in the adoption of fines to sanction wayward behaviour and in providing for graduated penalties. In the negotiations on international monetary reform following the breakdown of the Bretton Woods exchange rate system, a similar approach to dealing with sustained balance of payments disequilibrium was proposed, but never adopted.[43] The only sanction against persistent payments surpluses provided in the original Bretton Woods agreements – the scarce currency clause – was a very blunt instrument and was consequently never used. Having graduated penalties is clearly superior; it more closely approximates the increasing costs in terms of conditionality imposed on deficit countries' borrowing from the IMF.

Some have criticized the structure of the penalties of the Stability Pact for increasing the deficit when an excessive deficit is the problem in the first place. A second criticism is that the penalties are capped at 0.5 per cent of GDP per year of violation, whereas we would expect the externality costs imposed by the deficit to be an increasing function of its size. From the standpoint of the standard theory of optimal taxation and corrections of distortions, this objection is well taken. From the standpoint of practical political economy, however, it may be of little relevance. If the enforcement mechanisms have not been sufficient to keep the deficit from exceeding the level of maximum penalty, it seems extremely unlikely that additional penalties would help. Indeed, it is not clear that the offending country would be willing to pay or what would happen if they refused to pay. Most international sanctions are self-enforcing by those imposing them – for example, by increasing tariffs. The levying of fines under the Stability Pact is not self-enforcing in its present form. Perhaps a better structure of penalties would focus on exclusion of an offending country from participation and/or voting in some of the EU decision making bodies until its house was put in order (or substantial progress toward this was being made). Indeed, during the Maastricht negotiations Belgium proposed just such a suspension of voting rights as a sanction for excessive deficits.[44] Also superior on enforceability ground is the recommendation

---

[42.] On the importance of including a strong element of automaticity, see Gros (1996).

[43.] See, for example, Solomon (1982); Williamson (1977).

[44.] See Corsetti and Roubini (1993). This has also been proposed by Gros (1996). Note that this would not be appropriate for the ECB since the members of the decision making board are not supposed to act as national representatives.

made by the EU Monetary Committee that possible sanctions include suspension of payments from the EU budget. (Under the EDP the Council may also encourage the EIB to re-evaluate its lending to the wayward member.) In any event, I would suspect that moral suasion and the concerns of the harsh (if often belated) discipline which can be imposed by international financial markets will prove to be more important in practice than will be the use of formal penalties.[45] As *The Economist* (22 May 1998: 45) asked, 'In any case, who really believes that those penalty fines, if levied, would actually be paid?'

Eichengreen and Wyplosz (1998: 68) conclude that

the Stability Pact will have some effect. Governments will adjust their fiscal policies just enough to avoid incurring fines . . . Actually imposing fines would . . . lead to recrimination and deal a blow to EU solidarity. Actually incurring fines would subject a government to serious embarrassment and loss of political face.

They go on (1998:101)

Our assessment is that enforcement of the pact will be relatively loose, but still tight enough to affect some member states' deficits. EU officials will be reluctant to levy fines and lose goodwill. Member states will be reluctant to incur fines and suffer embarrassment . . . EU decision-makers . . . and governments will compromise, eliminating deficits that egregiously violate the Stability Pact, [governments] will modify their fiscal policies just enough to avoid forcing their neighbors to impose fines.

They further (1998: 106) argue that

The problem with the Pact as presently framed is that it is all stick and no carrot; rewarding good behavior in booms rather than, or in addition to, punishing bad behavior in slumps would surely make better sense. This could easily be done by relating payments to the EU budget or the distribution of euroseignirage to fiscal positions.

Much as the exchange rate provisions of the EMS were used over time by a number of national leaders as a way of strengthening their hands in the domestic battle to bring and keep inflation under control,[46] the fiscal provisions of Maastricht and the Stability Pact can be used as a powerful external force to help promote domestic budget discipline.[47] Unfortunately, to date this mechanism has not been utilized nearly as effectively as was the ERM in the 1980s. The 'partial effectiveness' view of institutions implies that neither the external exchange rate nor fiscal

---

45. As an anonymous reviewer pointed out, such forces will be much more powerful if there are only a few potential violators. If most countries are in this position, then the deficit criteria would probably go the way of debt criteria during the convergence period.

46. See the analysis and references in Andrews and Willett (1997).

47. See Agell Calmfors and Jonsson (1996); McKinnon (1997).

provisions should be viewed as an absolutely binding constraint, but rather as a valuable mechanism for helping to rally domestic political support in favour of discipline. This was done quite effectively by the Mitterrand government in France with respect to monetary and fiscal discipline. National leaders have put much less effort into explaining or selling the need for fiscal restraint to their voters. As a consequence there is considerable danger that the fiscal retrenchments of recent years – albeit in many cases probably insufficient to meet the strict letter of the Maastricht criteria-may generate a severe backlash among voters. Instead of the European project lending support to efforts at fiscal restraint, the fiscal restraints may be greatly damaging to support for the European project.

One of the greatest problems in designing institutions to constrain pressures on monetary and fiscal policies is that it is much easier to maintain sound economic policies once a stable situation has been achieved than to get to this point from a position of substantial disequilbrium. Such transitions can be quite painful and failures in the transition process can seriously damage the credibility of the new institutional arrangements. The Maastricht fiscal criteria unfortunately provide an excellent example of this point. They have been partially effective in bringing about greater fiscal restraint in a number of countries, but the process has been contaminated with considerable fudging, and the criteria for initial entry into EU were applied with considerable looseness. Furthermore, the criteria have been sharply criticized for forcing fiscal restraint at a time of high unemployment. All of these developments will serve to reduce the initial credibility of the Stability Pact.

The experiences with the convergence criteria of the Maastricht Treaty offer clear evidence, I believe, that such agreements can provide external help to the process of reducing budget deficits, but that the effectiveness of this help has its limits. Both the French and German governments have taken unpopular actions to reduce their budget deficits, but they also clearly indicated limits to how much domestic political pain they were willing to suffer to meet the strict letter of the Maastricht deficit criteria. As von Hagen (1998:18) notes,

The success of the Maastricht program...has been limited. A number of the smaller countries, Portugal and Ireland in particular, used the convergence process for a successful reduction of their deficits and debts. Yet, when the Maastricht process started in 1992, the average debt ratio of the European Union states was 60 per cent, today it is over 75 per cent.

An optimist might counter that at least the average budget deficit as a percentage of GDP had fallen over this period from over 6 to under

3 per cent. Still it is difficult to disagree with von Hagen's conclusion (1998: 18) that

In large countries . . . the role of external political constraints such as admonitions brought by the European Commission is simply too weak to coerce internal politics.

It is also interesting to note that von Hagen and Harden in their study of OECD countries (1995: 778) find that

the budget processes of all governments of large states that successfully limited spending and deficits in the 1970s and 1980s (France, Britain, and Germany) are based on a procedure-oriented approach. In contrast, the budget processes of all governments of smaller countries (Denmark, the Netherlands and Luxembourg) that successfully limited spending and deficits are based on a target-oriented one.[48]

Alesina and Perotti (1995) find that the composition of fiscal adjustments have a major impact on their durability.[49] The most persistent adjustments came from reducing social expenditures and the wage component of government consumption. The least durable adjustments come from raising taxes and cutting capital expenditures. Unfortunately, for most EU countries the sustainability of the recent fiscal retrenchments does not look secure on these criteria. Indeed, as Eichengreen and Wyplosz (1998: 76) argue,

while some progress has been made in curbing deficits in Stage II, the EDP [Excessive Deficits Procedure] has also encouraged fiscal fiddles like refundable 'euro taxes', sales of central bank gold reserves and one-off appropriations of public enterprise reserves.

Perhaps one of the most outrageous 'fiddles' was the receipt by the French government of a substantial one-time payment in exchange for taking over the pension liabilities of France Télécon. Vying with this was the Italian euro tax with its promise of a future refund. Both were certified by the EU statistical office as meeting the criteria of actions contributing to sustained reductions in deficits. Furthermore, by general consensus, the debt as opposed to deficit criteria were treated as non-relevant considerations for the purposes of meeting the convergence criteria.

Such acts are bound to hurt the credibility of the new EMU institutions. As a weapon to limit the size of the initial membership of the EMU the 'strict' convergence criteria had a strong, though admittedly controversial, rationale. However, as a mechanism for safeguarding monetary stability

---

[48]. von Hagen and Harden (1995: 775) describe a procedure-oriented approach to reforms in the budget process which 'vests the minister without portfolio with special strategic power . . . [in order to] strengthen the collective interests of the government over the individual incentives of the spending minister'.

[49]. See also Perotti (1996).

under the new-born ECB, it would have made much more sense to provide for transitional arrangements that started with looser targets, but which would be more effectively enforced. Indeed, there is considerable danger given that the way the criteria have been implemented to date they will not only not help the ECB in pursing monetary stability, but could even make its job more difficult by having reduced the credibility of the EMU process.

Bayoumi, Eichengreen and von Hagen (1997) point to a serious problem which the budget restrictions could create. In an ideal world member states would adjust their fiscal policies so that they would normally run balanced budgets or small surpluses, leaving plenty of room to allow automatic stabilizers and perhaps even some discretionary actions to help cushion negative macroeconomic shocks. If instead, however, budget deficits tend to average close to the 3 per cent limit, the scope for such cushioning at the national level will be sharply curtailed. This would probably stimulate pressure for Brussels to take on a larger fiscal role in the EU:

And because the member states will resist giving up their tax revenues as quickly as they demand additional services from the EU... restraints on the budgetary freedom of subcentral governments may thus increase the demand for central government borrowing, ultimately weakening the financial portion of the center. (1997: 83)

Furthermore, as De Grauwe argues (1997: 207)

as countries will be hindered in their desire to use the automatic stabilization in their budgets during recessions, they will increase their pressure on the ECB to relax monetary policies. Thus, paradoxically, the stability pact whose aim it was to protect the ECB from political pressure may in fact have increased the risk of such pressure.

Or as Artis and Winkler put it in their contribution in this volume (chapter 7) 'Tying the fiscal authorities' hands may well turn out to *increase* rather than decrease the burden on monetary policy with respect to stabilization policy'.

These are possibilities which clearly must be taken seriously. Efforts to impose discipline through fiscal constraints seem likely to have effects quite similar in many respects to the use of pegged exchange rates as a nominal anchor. Where there is a good deal of discipline anyway, the exchange rate constraint has often been effective in increasing it further, but where the domestic forces for discipline are weak, the adoption of pegged rates has typically proven to be only a short-term palliative, which has typically resulted in crises and undermined stabilization efforts.[50] While

[50] For evidence on this issue, see the analysis and references in Willett (1998b).

fiscal restrictions are not likely to be as prone to generating crises as exchange rate pegs, the danger of generating perverse reactions is similar.

This presents further support for our intermediate view that institutional arrangements are generally neither completely effective nor completely ineffective. It also clearly suggests that international agreements are not a substitute for domestic institutional reforms designed to reduce or harness the political pressures for large budget deficits. They can be useful complements, and indeed this was explicitly recognized in the Maastricht Treaty (art. 103d), but most EU governments have not yet put enough effort into taking advantage of this potential complementarity.[51] This is a source of considerable danger. As just discussed, if governments do not respond as the designers of the fiscal criteria intended and succeed in running balanced budgets or surpluses in normal period, then it is not just a question of the effectiveness of the fiscal criteria being reduced – the effects may be quite costly in terms not only of the ability to cushion the employment and output effects of shocks and cyclical fluctuations, but also in terms of contributing to rather than reducing pressures on the ECB.

Bayoumi, Eichengreen and von Hagen (1997: 84–5) suggest that

> an alternative to the numerical guidelines and politicized procedures of the EDP would ... be to encourage countries seeking to qualify for monetary union to reform their fiscal procedures and institutions ... This approach is consistent with that adopted to guide the policies of the European Central Bank. The framers of the Maastricht Treaty did not set numerical targets for money growth but gave the ECB a mandate to pursue price stability and specified the procedures it was to follow.

I am very sympathetic to the general thrust of this argument, but I do not think that the analogy holds fully. In one sense, the price stability and budget mandates are quite similar. The major difference is that a numerical target is specified for the budget deficit, 3 per cent of GDP or less, while the meaning of price stability is left (perhaps wisely) undefined. The procedures for giving the ECB independence were specified, but not the procedures by which it would adjust monetary policy in order to achieve price stability.

As Bayoumi, Eichengreen and von Hagen (1997: 84) discuss, there are a number of ways to reform national budgetary procedures to help promote fiscal discipline. One approach is greater centralization of budgeting –

> centralized procedures empower the prime minister, the finance minister or the treasury minister to overrule spending ministers, limit the scope for parliamentary amendments to the government's budget, and limit modifications of the budget law in the implementation stage

---

[51.] On the importance of domestic reforms of the budgetary process, see von Hagen and Harden (1994).

Other examples include requirements that all spending proposals be accompanied by specific proposals for how the spending would be financed, either through revenue increases or cuts in other programmes, and line item vetoes for the executive. As Bayoumi, Eichengreen and von Hagen (1997: 84) go on to discuss,

a still more ambitious approach would be to create independent agencies at the national level to monitor the budget and prevent spending ministers and legislative coalitions from engaging in creative budgeting. Still more drastic reform would establish in each country a national Debt Board with the power to set a binding ceiling on the annual increase in public debt[52]

Given the range of options, it is very unlikely that the EU member states would have agreed on a common one. Alternatively, it would be very difficult to judge equivalencies among the options of the type – pick any x of the following y options for reform. What mix of such reforms would be best is far from clear, and it seems likely that the answer would differ from one country to another. Conceptually, each country could present its own provisional mix for approval by some central body such as the Council of Ministers, but this would be a highly awkward and politicized process.

There is considerable technical attraction to an EU-level Debt Board, which would set periodic debt limits for member states, but it seems doubtful that such a centralized approach would have been politically feasible, especially since Debt Boards are not a well known concept. I thus think it quite unlikely that a procedures approach would have worked as a substitute for the fiscal limitations of the convergence and Stability Pact criteria, and serious efforts on the procedures front are likely to be a necessary condition for the fiscal limitations to work well. To date, there is little cause for optimism on this score.

A further danger, raised by Eichengreen and Wyplosz (1998: 69) is that

in the present climate, where electorates lack the appetite for further spending cuts... the danger is... that the Stability Pact will divert efforts from the fundamental reforms needed... In particular, without fundamental labor market reforms, Europe will fail to grow by at least $3-3\frac{1}{2}\%$ a year, and deficits will not decline... Our view is that leaders have a fixed amount of political capital that they allocate to politically costly fiscal reform or politically costly labor market reform... [T]he Stability Pact may have some slight benefits in terms of fiscal discipline, but may have significant costs, both in diverting political effort from more fundamental problems and indeed in making those fundamental problems worse than before.

---

[52] On the concept of a national Debt Board, see von Hagen and Harden (1994); von Hagen (1998). See also the proposal by Blinder (1997).

Masson (1996) reaches a similar conclusion.

> I would therefore argue that the fiscal criteria are not necessarily bad in themselves, but rather the difficulties have been with the measures taken to meet the criteria ... It has tended to swamp considerations of the problems ... such as inadequate labor flexibility (1998: 998)
>
> Given the strict time table ... the criteria may have produced a perverse focus on measures that could be implemented more easily – tax measure[s] – rather than the needed structural reforms on the spending side. (1996:1003)

Obstfeld and Peri (1998: 2091) agree that with an EMU with low labour mobility and limited scope for automatic fiscal stabilizers 'it will become hard to resist pressures for a more extensive "transfer union"' and argue that (1998: 246)

> if one views the prospect of a European transfer union with alarm ... the first option is to rethink and relax the excessive deficits procedure and the Stability Pact as soon as possible after the EMU starts.

Concluding remarks

The basic objective sought by the Maastricht and Stability Pact fiscal criteria is a desirable one, but the need for it comes primarily from domestic political biases and the infancy of the ECB, not from EMU *per se*. The basic form of the Stability Pact is not necessarily seriously deficient. What is clear, however, is that it is not sufficient by itself to meet its objectives. On the one hand, its enforceability is open to considerable question. On the other, its full enforceability at the EU level in the absence of national budgetary reforms could generate substantial costs in terms of reduced flexibility to cushion asymmetric shocks. Paradoxically, if countries do not achieve approximate budget balance during normal periods, then the limits on fiscal deficits designed to protect the ECB from pressures to accommodate fiscal deficits could generate even greater pressures for monetary expansion to counter unemployment. The loss of automatic fiscal stabilizers could also stimulate pressures for greater fiscal transfers at the EU level, which in the opinion of a number of economists could generate deficits and retard the incentives for adjustments to shocks.[53]

This is the worst case scenario, but is also perhaps the most unlikely. It is more probable that the Stability Pact will be viewed as a symbolic victory for the Germans, but one which will be given few teeth and have relatively little effect on the fiscal behaviour of EMU governments. This would also be unfortunate. The ideal solution

---

[53.] See, for example, Bayoumi, Eichengreen and von Hagen (1997), Obstfeld and Peri (1998).

would be a concerted political push to implement art. 103d of the Maastricht Treaty 'which instructs member states to make their budget procedures conducive to fiscal discipline' (Bayoumi, Eichengreen and von Hagen, 1997: 84).

Unfortunately, however, as with the need to promote greater labour market flexibility, little progress has been made during the run-up to EMU, and this bodes ill for progress afterwards. The problem is not that the Maastricht and Stability Pact fiscal criteria were wrongheaded, but rather that the opportunity to piggyback domestic budgetary reforms on the EMU project has borne so little fruit. It is still not too late to try, but time is short.

References

Agell, J., Calmfors, L. and Jonsson, G. (1996). 'Fiscal Policy when Monetary Policy is "Tied to the Mast"', *European Economic Review*, 40: 1413–40

Alesina, A. and Bayoumi, T. (1996)

Alesina, A. and Perotti, R. (1994). 'The Political Economy of Budget Deficits', *NBER Working Paper*, 4637

(1995). 'Fiscal Expansions and Fiscal Adjustments in OECD Countries', *Economic Palicy* (October): 205–48

(1996a). 'Fiscal Discipline and the Budget Process', *American Ecanomic Review* (May): 401–7

(1996b). 'Budget deficits and Budget Institutions', *NBER Working Paper*, 5556

Allsopp, C. and Vines, D. (1996). 'Fiscal Policy and Emu', *NIER WorkingPaper*, 158: 91–107

Artis, M. (1996). 'Alternative Transitions to EMU', *Economic Journal*, 106: 1005–15

Artis, M. and Marcellino, M. (1998). 'Fiscal Solvency and and Fiscal Forecasting in Europe', *EUI Working Paper*, ECO 98/2

Andrews, D. and Willett, T. D. (1997). 'Financial Interdependence and the State' , *International Organization* (Summer): 479–511

Banaian, K., Burdekin, R. and Willett, T. D. (1995). 'On the Political Economy of Central Bank Interdependence', in K.D. Hoover and S. M. Sheffrin (eds.), *Monetarism and the Methodology of Ecanamics*, Brookfield, Vt.: Edward Elgar: 178–97

Bayoumi, T. and Eichengreen, B. (1995). 'Restraining Yourself: The Implications of Fiscal Rules for Economic Stabilization', *IMF Staff Papers*, 42: 32–48

Bayoumi, T., Eichengreen, B. and von Hagen, J. (1997), 'European Monetary Unification', *Open Economies Review*, 8: 71–91

Bean, C. (1998). 'Discussion', *Economic Policy* (April): 104–7

Blinder, A. (1997). 'Is Government Too Political?', *Foreign Affairs* (November–December): 115–26

Brander, P., Diebalet, L. and Schuberth, H. (1998). 'Stuctural Budget Deficits and Sustainability of Fiscal Positions in the European Union', Österreichische National Bank, *Working Paper* (February)

Bryant, R. (1995). *International Coordination of National Stabilization*, Washington, DC: Brookings

Buchanan, J. M., Rowley, C. K. and Tollison, R. D. (1993)

Buiter, W., Corsetti, G. and Roubini, N. (1993). 'Excessive Deficits: Sense and Nonsense in the Treaty of Maastricht', *Economic Policy*, 16: 57–101

Burdekin, R. C. K. and Laney, L. O. (1988). 'Fiscal Policymaking and the Central Bank Institutional Constraint', *Kyklos*, 41: 647–62

Canzoneri, M. B. and Diba, B. T. (1991). 'Fiscal Deficits, Financial Integration and a Central Bank for Europe', *Journal of the Japanese and International Economies*, 5(4): 381–403

Cohen, B. J. (1994). 'Beyond EMU', in B. Eichengreen and J. Frieden (eds.), *The Political Economy of European Monetary Unification*, Boulder, Colo.: Westview Press: 149–66

Corden, W. M. (1993). 'Europoean Monetary Union: The Intellectual Prehistory', in A. Giovannini, M. Guitan and R. Portes (eds.), *The Monetary Future of Europe*, London: Centre for Economic Policy Research

Corsetti, G. and Roubini, N. (1993). 'The Design of Optimal Fiscal Rules for Europe after 1992', in F. Torres and F. Giavazzi (eds.), *Adjustment and Growth in the European Monetary System*, Cambridge: Cambridge University Press: 46–82

(1995). 'Political Biases in Fiscal Policy: Reconsidering the Case for the Maastricht Fiscal Criteria', in B. Eichengreen, J. Frieden and J. von Hagen (eds.), *Monetary and Fiscal Policy in an Integrated Europe*, Berlin: Springer: 118–37

(1996). 'European vs. American Perspectives on Balanced Budget Rules', *American Economic Review* (May): 408–13

(1997). 'Politically Motivated Fiscal Deficits', *Economics and Politics* (March): 27–54

Crockett, A. (1994). 'The Role of Convergence in the Process of EMU', in A. Steinherr (ed.), *30 Years of European Monetary Integration*, London: Longman

Cukierman, A. (1992). *Central Bank Strategy, Credibility, and Independence*, Cambridge, Mass.: MIT Press

De Grauwe, P. (1992). *The Economics of Monetary Integration*, 2nd edn., Oxford: Oxford University Press

(1993). 'The Political Economy of Monetary Union in Europe', *The World Economy*, 16: 653–62

(1994). 'Towards European Monetary Union without the EMS', *Economic Policy*, 18: 147–74

(1996). 'The Economics of Convergence: Towards Monetary Union in Europe', *Weltwirtschaftliches Archiv*, 132: 1–27

(1997). *The Economics of Monetary Integration*, 3rd edn., Oxford: Oxford University Press

Dornbusch, R. (1997). 'Fiscal Aspects of Monetary Integration', *American Economic Review* (May): 221–3.

Dubaskas, G., Wihlborg, C. and Willett, T. D. (1998). 'The Baltic States: Alternative Routes to Cedibility', in R. Sweeney, C. Wihlborg and T. D. Willett (eds.), *Exchange Rate Policies for Emerging Market Economies*, Boulder, Colo.: Westview Press

Eichengreen, B. (1994). 'Fiscal Policy and EMU', in B. Eichengreen and J. Frieden (eds.), *The Political Economy of European Monetary Unification*, Boulder, Colo.: Westview Press

(1997). 'Saving Europe's Automatic Stabilizers', *National Institute Economic Review*, 159: 92–8

Eichengreen, B. and Frieden, J. (eds.) (1994). *The Political Economy of European Monetary Unification*, Boulder, Colo.: Westview Press

Eichengreen, B. and von Hagen, J. (1995). 'Fiscal Policy and Monetary Union: Federalism, Fiscal Restrictions and the No-Bailout Rule', *CEPR Discussion Paper*, 1247

(1996a). 'Fiscal Policy and Monetary Union: Is There a Tradeoff between Federalism and Budgetary Restriction?', *NBER Working Paper*, 5517

(1996b). 'Fiscal Restrictions and Monetary Union: Rationales, Repercussion, Reforms', *Empirica*, 23: 2–23

Eichengreen, B. and Wyplosz, C. (1998). 'The Stability Pact: More than a Minor Nuisance?', *Economic Policy*, 26: 65–104

Eijfnger, S. C. W. and De Haan, J. (1996). 'The Political Economy of Central-bank Independence', *Special Papers in International Economics*, 19, International Finance Section, Princeton University

Emerson, M. *et al.* (1991). One Market, One Money, Oxford: Oxford University Press

Fatás, A. (1998). 'Does EMU Need a Fiscal Federalism?', *Economic Policy*, 26: 163–92

Feldstein, M. (1997). 'EMU and International Conflict', *Foreign Affairs* (November–December): 60–73

Fischer, S. (1995). 'The Unending Search for Monetary Salvation', in B. Bernanke and J. Rotenberg (eds.), *NBER Macroeconomics Annual*, 75–86, Cambridge, Mass.: MIT Press

Fratianni, M. (1998). 'Maxi Versus Mini EMU', *Columbia Journal of European Law* 4: 375–93

Frieden, J. and Lake, D. (eds.) (1995). *International Political Economy*, 3rd edn., New York: St Martin's Press

Gerlach, S. (1998). 'Discussion', *Economic Policy* (April): 107–10

Gros, D. (1996). 'Towards a Credible Excessive Deficits Procedure', in F. Torres / (ed.), *Monetary Reform in Europe*, Lisbon: Universidade Católica Editora

Gros, D. and Thygesen, N. (1998). 'The Relationship between Economic and Monetary Integration', in D. Gros and N. Thygesen, *European Monetary Integration*, rev. edn., New York: St Martin's Press

Glick, R. and Hutchison, M. (1991). 'Fiscal Constraints and Incentives with Monetary Coordination', in C. Wihlborg, M. Fratianni and T. D. Willett (eds.), *Financial Regulation and Monetary Arrangements After 1992*, Amsterdam: North-Holland

(1993). 'Fiscal Policy in Monetary Union: Implications for Europe', *Open Economies Review*, 4: 39–65

Hutchison, M. and Walsh, C. (1998). 'Credibility, Disinflation, and Central Bank Contracts: What Has the Reserve Bank of New Zealand Accomplished?', *Working Paper*, University of California at Santa Cruz

Inman, R. P. (1996). 'Do Balanced Budget Rules Work? – US Experience and Possible Lessons for the EMU', Wharton School, University of Pennsylvania (July), mimeo

Jensen, H. (1996). 'The Advantage of International Fiscal Cooperation under Alternative Monetary Regimes', *European Journal of Political Economy*, 12: 485–504

Jervis, R. (1997). *System Effects*, Princeton: Princeton University Press

Kenen, P. (1995). *Economic and Monetary Union in Europe: Moving Beyond Maastricht*, Cambridge: Cambridge University Press

Masciandaro, D. (1995). 'Review Essay: Designing a Central Bank: Social Player, Monetary Agent, or Banking Agent?', *Open Economies Review*, 6: 399–410

Masson, P. (1996). 'Fiscal Dimensions of EMU', *Economic Journal*, 106: 996–1004

McKinnon, R. (1997). 'EMU as a Device for Collective Fiscal Retrenchment', *American Economic Review, Papers and Proceedings*, 87: 227–9

Mishkin, F. and Posen, A. (1997). 'Inflation Targeting', Federal Reserve Bank of New York, *Economic Policy Review* (August): 9–11

Obstfeld, M. and Peri, G. (1998). 'Regional Non-adjustment and Fiscal Policy', *Economic Policy* (April): 207–47

Parkin, M. (1993). 'Domestic Monetary Institutions and Deficits', in J. M. Buchanan, C. K. Rowley and R. D. Tollison (eds.), Deficits, New York: Basil Blackwell: 310–37

Perotti, R. (1996). 'Fiscal Consolidation in Europe: Composition Matters', *American Economic Review* (May): 105–10

Persson, T. and Tabellini, G. (eds.) (1994). *Monetary and Fiscal Policy*, Cambridge, Mass.: MIT Press

Posen, A. (1995). 'Declarations are Not Enough', in B. Bernanke and J. Rotenberg (eds.), *NBER Macroeconomic Annual*, Cambridge, Mass.: MIT Press

Poterba, J. M. (1994). 'State Responses to Fiscal Crises: The Effects of Budgetary Institutions and Politics', *Journal of Political Economy*, 102: 799–821

(1996a). 'Do Budget Rules Work?', *NBER Working Paper*, 5550

(1996b). 'Budget Institutions and Fiscal Policy in the US States', *American Economic Review* (May): 395–400

Putnam, R. D. and Henning, C. R. (1989). 'The Bonn Summit of 1978: A Case Study in Coordination', in R. N. Cooper, B. Eichengreen, G. Holthan, R. Putnam and C. R. Henning (eds.), *Can Nations Agree? Issues in International Economic Cooperation*, Washington, DC: Brookings Institution: 12–140

Restoy, F. (1995). 'Interest rates and Fiscal Discipline in Monetary Union', *European Economic Review*, 40: 1624–46

Solomon, R. (1982). *The International Monetary System, 1945–1981: An Insider's View*, New York: Harper & Row

Steinmo, S. and Tolbert, C. (1998). 'Do Institutions Really Matter? Taxation in Industrialized Countries', *Comparative Political Studies*, 31: 165–87

von Hagen, J. (1990). 'A Note on the Empirical Effectiveness of Formal Fiscal Restraints', *Journal of Public Economics* (March): 199–210

—— (1998). 'Budgeting Institutions for Aggregate Fiscal Discipline', *ZEI Policy Paper*, B98-01, University of Bonn

von Hagen, J. and Eichengreen, B. (1996). 'Fiscal Restraints, Federalism and Monetary Union: Is the Excessive Deficit Procedure Counterproductive?', *American Economic Review*, 86: 134–8

von Hagen, J. and Harden, I. (1995). 'Budget Processes and Commitment to Fiscal Discipline', *European Economic Review*, 39: 771–9

von Hagen, J., and Lutz, S. (1996). 'Fiscal and Monetary Policies on the Way to EMU', *Open Economies Review*, 7: 299–326

Weaver, W. K. and Rockman, B. (eds.) (1993). *Do Institutions Matter?*, Washington, DC: Brookings Institution

Westbrook, J. and Willett, T. D. (1999) 'Exchange Rates as Normal Anchors: An Overview of the Issues' in R. J. Sweeney, C. Wihlborg and T. D. Willett (eds.), *Exchange Rate Policies for Emerging Market Economics*, Boulder: Westview Press

Wijnholds, J., Eijffinger, S. and Hoogduin, L. (eds.) (1994). *A Framework for Monetary Stability*, Amsterdam: Kluwer

Willett, T. D. (1987). 'A New Monetary Constitution?', in J. Dorn and A. Schwartz (eds.), *The Search for Stable Money*, Chicago: Chicago University Press

—— (1988). *Political Business Cycles: The Political Economy of Money, Inflation, and Unemployment*, Durham, NC: Duke University Press

—— (1995). 'Guidelines for Constructing Monetary Constitutions', in T. D. Willett, R. C. K. Burdekin, R. J. Sweeney and C. Wihlborg (eds.), *Establishing Monetary Stability in Emerging Market Economies*, Boulder, Colo.: Westview Press: 102–14

—— (1996). 'The Public Choice approach to International Economic Relations', *Lectures on Virginia Political Economy*, Farfax, Va.: Center for the Study of Public Choice, George Mason University

—— (1998a). International Financial Markets as Sources of Crisis or Discipline?' *Claremont Working Papers*, Claremont Graduate University

—— (1998b). 'Credibility and Discipline Effects of Exchange Rates as Nominal Anchors', *The World Economy* (August): 803–26

Willett, T. D. and Banaian, K. (1996). 'Currency Substitution, Seigniorage and the Choice of Currency Policies', in P. Mizen and E. J. Pentacost (eds.), *The Macroeconomics of International Currencies*, Cheltenham: Edward Elgar: 77–95

Willett, T. D., Burdekin, R. C. K., Sweeney, R. J. and Wihlborg, C. (eds.) (1995). *Establishing Monetary Stability in Emerging Market Economies*, Boulder, Colo.: Westview Press

Williamson, J. (1997). *The Failure of World Monetary Reform*, New York: New York University Press

Part II

Automatic stabilizers in a monetary union

4 EMU and budget norms

Torben M. Andersen and Robert R. Dogonowski

Introduction

European Economic and Monetary Union (EMU) implies a common centralized monetary policy conducted by the European Central Bank (ECB), but fiscal policy will remain decentralized at the level of member states. Although there is a common EU budget it amounts to less than 2 per cent of total GDP in the EU and hence it is not at its present level able to play any significant role – that is, EMU will not be accompanied by fiscal federalism. This raises the question of the role of fiscal policy in EMU.

The Maastricht Treaty takes the position that this decision structure necessitates a need for budgetary discipline, and it accordingly stipulates norms for fiscal policy which are also part of the convergence criteria. Specifically, the norms stipulate that the debt level must not exceed 60 per cent of GDP and that the public deficit must not exceed 3 per cent of GDP. These norms will apply after the establishment of EMU and they have recently been accompanied by the so-called Stability and Growth Pact (SGP, herafter Stability Pact). This specifies monitoring procedures as well as sanctions in cases where the deficit norm is violated. A country having a deficit exceeding the 3 per cent limit should make a non-interesting-bearing deposit of 0.2 per cent of GDP *plus* 1/10th of the excess deficit. There is a maximum deposit of 0.5 per cent of GDP. Additional deposits will be required as long as the deficit norm is violated, and the deposit is transformed into a fine if the problem is not solved within two years. The Stability Pact also includes an escape clause as countries having experienced a fall in real GDP of 2 per cent within the last four quarters will be allowed to exceed the deficit limit, and for countries experiencing a fall above 0.75 per cent it may be evaluated by

We thank participants at the AEA conference 'Public Deficits and Monetary Union', held in Rome (November 1997) and the anonymous referee for comments.

the European Council whether a deficit in excess of the norm can be justified.

Restraints on fiscal policy in a monetary union with decentralized fiscal authorities can be justified on two counts. First, a monetary union may have a free-rider problem to the extent that countries may pursue unsustainable policies in the belief that they will be bailed out either directly or indirectly via a more inflationary policy in the EU. The Treaty contains a 'no-bail-out' clause and the debt norm makes it unlikely that a bail-out situation is going to arise (Eichengreen and Wyplosz, 1997). Second there is an effect from fiscal policy to monetary policy via the effect public debt may have for the level of interest rates. There is thus a risk that lax fiscal policies will force a restrictive monetary policy and thus an undesirable policy mix. As higher public debt levels seem to be associated with higher levels of interest rates, there is an argument for restraining debt levels[1]. Hence the two most important channels through which fiscal policy may spill over on monetary policy are effectively dealt with by the debt norm, and the deficit norm does not seem directly relevant for addressing any of these problems. Of course, one could argue about the appropriate critical debt level, but the level stipulated in the Treaty seems to be on the safe side, at least judged from the fact that a number of countries have had stable macroeconomic development despite debt levels exceeding 60 per cent of GDP. The paradox is that the Stability Pact does not strengthen the interpretation of the debt norm, which actually is interpreted rather flexibly using the proviso in the Treaty that a debt level in excess of the 60 per cent norm can be accepted provided that it displays a satisfactory downward trend. Instead, the Stability Pact strengthens the interpretation of the deficit norm, with which countries have already had difficulty in complying as part of the entry requirement. While it is difficult to give the deficit norm a direct economic justification it can be given a political justification to the extent that the political system suffers from myopia and does not realize that systematic deficits accumulate to give an increasing debt level. Imposing deficit rules to deal with this problem may, however, interfere with other roles of public deficits.

A particularly important issue here is the ability to pursue an active stabilization policy. According to the standard literature on optimum currency areas (OCAs) it may be optimal to establish a currency area provided that there is sufficient flexibility in labour markets such that nominal exchange rates are not needed as a stabilization instrument (Kenen, 1969). It is hard to argue that Europe fulfils this condition, as

[1] See, for example, Andersen (1997) for a discussion and references.

labour markets are generally considered to be fairly inflexible. However, fiscal policy may be a substitute for the exchange rate instrument in its capacity as a macroeconomic stabilization instrument. Essential for a monetary union among countries which suffers from inflexible labour markets is thus the possibility of using fiscal policy to stabilize economic activity, and this requires discretionary power in fiscal policy at the level of single member states. It can be argued that this need is larger to the extent that the common monetary policy is more focused on price than output stability.[2] This brings forth the paradox that restraints are imposed on fiscal policy precisely in the situation where more fiscal activism may be called for.

The purpose of this chapter is to clarify the extent to which there is a conflict between these two concerns. The plan of the chapter is as follows. We start out by considering the role of public sector deficits. Based on this we turn to some empirical evidence on the cyclical behaviour of budget deficits and the implications for macroeconomic stability. Finally, some attempt is made to evaluate the extent to which the deficit norm of the EMU will be a binding constraint on national fiscal policy, and if so what the possible policy responses would be. The final section summarizes and concludes the chapter.

Why not balance the budget?

In a world with Ricardian equivalence there is no interesting role for budget deficits as changes in public savings will be matched one-to-one by changes in private savings. Although there is a voluminous theoretical and empirical literature addressing whether Ricardian equivalence holds (Seater, 1993), there is a surprisingly scant literature dealing with the role of public budget deficits when this equivalence result does not hold. This is particularly puzzling given that most observers would agree that Ricardian equivalence does not hold in practice.

Substantial interest has, of course, been devoted to analysing the consequences of budget deficits in the absence of Ricardian equivalence, addressing the effects on interest rates and so on. But this still leaves open the basic question why there is a case for not balancing the budget. One interpretation is that budget deficits are primarily driven by a bias in the political system causing a failure to finance all current expenditures, and the problem accordingly boils down to be a question of political

---

[2.] The 1997 report of the European Monetary Institute (EMI) leaves open the question whether monetary or inflation targets should be the preferred intermediate goal

conflicts over distributional issues. In an overview of the role of public deficits, Ball and Mankiw (1995: 108) take this view

Thus, the winners from budget deficits are current taxpayers and future owners of capital, while the losers are future taxpayers and future workers. Because the gains and losses balance, a policy of running budget deficits cannot be judged by appealing to the Pareto Criterion or other notions of economic efficiency.

If budget deficits play a role only in relation to political conflicts over distribution, a straightforward solution would be to impose a balanced budget norm. However, this may overlook the fact that budget deficits may improve efficiency in allocations precisely under the circumstances where Ricardian equivalence does not hold.

Tax smoothing

The Ricardian equivalence proposition assumes that lump-sum taxes can be levied so as to finance public expenses. In practice, policy makers have to resort to distortionary taxes. Under a balanced budget rule there will be variations in distortionary taxes if there are variations in public expenses or the tax base on which the taxes are levied. Distortionary taxes would accordingly be high in some periods, implying large efficiency losses, and low in other periods, implying small efficiency losses. Such variations in the distortionary costs of taxation would not in general be optimal under the plausible assumption that the distortionary costs are increasing in the tax rate. The distortionary costs of taxes can thus in some cases be lowered by keeping tax rates constant (Barro, 1979) or by having tax rates moving pro-cyclically (Andersen and Dogonowski, 1997b). In either case, the budget would move pro-cyclically and compared to a balanced budget rule there are clearly efficiency gains from such a policy

Shock absorption

The tax-smoothing argument relies on the distortionary effects of taxation in an otherwise frictionless economy. There may, however, also be cases where budget deficits can play a role in mitigating the consequences of imperfections in the market economy. This idea can be traced back to Keynes and has played an implicit role in many macroeconomic analyses. However, standard macro-models are not cast in an explicit intertemporal setting with a modelling of economic decision making and imperfections, and it is accordingly not possible to identify the precise route by which budget deficits may improve economic efficiency. To that end, an explicit intertemporal model is indispensable: it is not enough that budget deficit matters, one has to prove a case for using this actively in economic policy making.

We shall in the following present a stylized model in which to illustrate why budget deficits matter and why this can be used to design budget rules which enhance economic efficiency. The specific setting is a model with a capital market imperfection, implying that Ricardian equivalence does not hold. To simplify, we assume an exogenous but stochastic production level to illustrate how the public sector budget can be used to ensure a better adjustment to shocks impinging on the economy. Tax distortions are not essential to the argument.

We model capital market imperfections in a very simple way by assuming that public and the private agents face different interest rates in the capital market. Specifically, it is assumed that the public sector faces a lower interest rate than private agents. This could be due to uncertainty about the time of death (see Blanchard, 1985), but is also a convenient way of capturing the fact that problems of information, moral hazard and adverse selection pose a more binding constraint for private agents than the public sector in capital markets. Although some of this may result in credit rationing for private agents, one can always find a shadow interest rate which is equivalent to such a quantity constraint (Neary and Roberts, 1980). Even disregarding such quantity constraints, empirical evidence confirms that the public in general face lower interest rates than private agents.[3] We take the economy to have perfect capital mobility and to be perfectly integrated in the international capital market, implying that all agents including the public sector face an exogenously given interest rate and that there is a constant exogenous interest rate premium for private agents relative to the public sector.

Households

Consider a representative household maximizing the expected value of lifetime utility over an infinite horizon

$$\max_{\{c_t\}_{t=0}^{\infty}} E_0 \left\{ \sum_{t=0}^{\infty} \beta^t u(C_t) \right\}$$

where $0 < \beta < 1$ is the subjective discount factor, and instantaneous utility u depends only on the current-period consumption level C_t. E_0 is the expectation operator given the information available in the first period.

---

[3] In general a positive interest rate spread is observed between private and state bonds – see, for example, *International Financial Statistics*

The instantaneous utility function is assumed to be quadratic,[4] i.e.

$$u(C_t) = C_t - \frac{\alpha}{2}(C_t)^2, \qquad \alpha > 0.$$

The essential property of this utility function is the aversion to risk captured by the coefficient α.

The intertemporal budget constraint reads

$$E_0 \sum_{t=0}^{\infty} \left(\frac{1}{1+r}\right)^t C_t = E_0 \left\{(1+r)B_0^H + \sum_{t=0}^{\infty} \left(\frac{1}{1+r}\right)^t (Y_t - T_t)\right\}$$

(4.1)

where Y_t is production/income in period t and T_t is the tax collected by the government in period t. The household may borrow and lend in the capital market at a constant real interest rate, r. B_t^H is the value of the private net assets at the start of period t. We assume without loss of generality that $B_0^H \equiv 0$. The budget constraint (4.1) says that the expected net present value (NPV) of consumption has to equal the expected net present value of disposable income.

The first-order condition to the household decision problem is given by a stochastic Euler equation which may be written as

$$E_0 C_t = C_0 \qquad \forall t$$

given that marginal utility is linear in C and the assumption that the subjective discount rate equals the subjective discount rate – i.e. $\beta(1+r) = 1$. This relation says that consumption should follow a random walk.

When we substitute C_0 for $E_0 C_t$ in the budget constraint, we may write consumption in the first period as

$$C_0 = \frac{r}{1+r}\left[(1+r)B_0^H + \sum_{t=0}^{\infty}\left(\frac{1}{1+r}\right)^t E_0\{Y_y - T_t\}\right].$$

This consumption function says that the household wishes to consume the annuity value of its expected discounted net wealth (expected permanent income).

[4.] The linear-quadratic utility has been extensively applied in the empirical literatue. An attractive feature is that an explicit solution for consumption can be obtained. Unfortunately, we also have constant absolute risk aversion which is an unattractive description of behaviour toward risk and we have to assume an upper bound on consumption $C = 1/\alpha$ to ensure that marginal utility is positive (Blanchard and Fischer 1989).

Production

Output is exogenous but uncertain. Specifically, it is assumed that Y relative to its steady-state value $\bar{Y}$ follows a mean-reverting AR(1) process given as

$$(Y_{t+1} - \bar{Y}) = \rho(Y_t - \bar{Y}) + \varepsilon_t \tag{4.2}$$

where the disturbance term ε_t is assumed to be iid, $E(\varepsilon_t) = 0$, $E(\varepsilon_t^2) = \sigma_\varepsilon^3$ and $0 \leq \rho < 1$. The larger ρ, the more persistence there is in shocks to income. This process captures cyclical variations in activity with potentially high persistence matching stylized facts (see, for example, Christodoulakis, Dimelis and Kollintzas, 1995; Backus and Kehoe, 1992).

Government

The government expenditures are assumed exogenous and constant $(\bar{G})$, and the problem is under which budget regime these expenditures should be financed. We shall consider two different budget regimes:

(i) Balanced budget regime   This regime is defined by the requirement that the government in each period levies taxes precisely so as to finance public outlays, i.e.

$$T_t^B = \bar{G} \qquad \forall t.$$

(ii) Pro-cyclical budget regime   This regime is characterized by taxes being dependent on the state of nature. In the present setting with exogenous production, it does not matter whether taxes are levied as an income tax or a lump-sum tax.

A simple pro-cyclical budget regime consistent with debt sub-stainability[5] is one where taxes raised in period t are

$$T_t^C = \tau Y_t - (1 + i)\tau(Y_{t-1} - \bar{Y})$$

where the proportional income tax τ is

$$\tau = \frac{\bar{G}}{\bar{Y}}.$$

The total tax payment in period t is given as the sum of an income tax and the deficit *plus* interest incurred in the previous period.

In general, we have that public wealth B_t^G is given as

$$B_{t+1}^G = T_t - G_t + (1 + i)B_t^G$$

---

5. Regimes allowing a given positive debt level may also be sustainable. Restricting attention to sustainability at a zero-debt level ensures that the difference to the balanced budget regime does not arise owing to different debt levels.

where i is the real rate of interest at which the government can borrow/lend at the capital market ($i < r$). Assuming initial public wealth B_0^G to be zero such that

$$B_{t+1}^G = \tau(Y_t - \bar{Y}).$$

It is seen that this regime has a pro-cyclical public budget.

The specific requirement that debt including interest is always repaid next period is obviously a restrictive way in which to specify a pro-cyclical budget regime. It simplifies the analytics considerably by removing persistence in public deficits, despite persistence in output. It follows that we have not considered the optimal pro-cyclical budget regime, but only a suboptimal regime, implying that subsequent results are not biased in favour of pro-cyclical budget regimes.

Net assets

The dynamics of net asset holdings is not trivial since the household and government face different rates of interest.

Net foreign assets for the aggregate economy B_t may be written as

$$B_t \equiv B_t^H + B_t^G$$

where B_t^H is net assets of the household in period t given as

$$B_{t+1}^H = (1+r)B_t^H + Y_t - T_t - C_t$$

and similarly the net assets of the government B_t^G can be written as

$$B_{t+1}^G = (1+i)B_t^G + T_t - \bar{G}.$$

For later reference, we note that private net assets can be written (see appendix 4.1, p. 89)

$$B_t^H = (Y_{t-1} - \bar{Y})(1 - \tau) + \left(1 - \tau\left(1 - \frac{1+i}{1+r}\right)\right)$$

$$\times \left\{ \sum_{i=0}^{t-2}(Y_i - \bar{Y}) - \frac{r}{1+r}\sum_{j=0}^{\infty}\sum_{i=0}^{t-1} E_i(Y_{j-1} - \bar{Y}) \right\}.$$

Since, $B_t^G = \tau(Y_{t-1} - \bar{Y})$, it follows that net foreign assets are given as

$$B_t = B_t^H + B_t^G$$

$$= (Y_{t-1} - \bar{Y}) + \left(1 - \tau\left(1 - \frac{1+i}{1+r}\right)\right)$$

$$\times \left\{ \sum_{i=0}^{t-2} (Y_i - \bar{Y}) - \frac{t}{1+r} \sum_{j=0}^{\infty} \sum_{i=0}^{t-1} E_i(Y_{j+1} - \bar{Y}) \right\}.$$

Indirect utility

To compare the efficiency properties of the two budget regimes we need to solve for the utility of the household obtained under the two tax regimes. To this end we may express expected utility as

$$V_0 = E_0 \sum_{t=0}^{\infty} \left(\frac{1}{1+r}\right)^t u(C_t) = E_0 \sum_{t=0}^{\infty} \left(\frac{1}{1+r}\right)^t \left(C_t - \left(\frac{\alpha}{2}\right)C_t^2\right)$$

which can be rewritten as

$$V_0 = \frac{1+r}{r} C_0 - \frac{\alpha}{2} \sum_{t=0}^{\infty} \left(\frac{1}{1+r}\right)^t E_0 C_t^2.$$

The last term captures the aversion to uncertainty over future consumption.

To compare the two budget regimes note that they both imply the same expected tax burden, i.e.

$$E_0 T_t^B = E_0 T_t^C \qquad \forall t$$

and hence they yield the same expected level of consumption ($C_0^B = C_0^C$). They differ only in the variability of consumption.

We may write consumption (see appendix (4.1)) in the pro-cyclical regime as

$$C_t = (\bar{Y} - \bar{G}) + \left(1 - \tau\left(1 - \frac{1-i}{1+r}\right)\right)$$

$$\times \left\{ r \sum_{j=0}^{t-1} (Y_j - \bar{Y}) + \frac{r}{1+r} \left\{ \sum_{j=0}^{\infty} \left(\frac{1}{1+r}\right)^t \right. \right.$$

$$\left. \left. \times \left\{ E_t(Y_{t+j} - \bar{Y}) - r \sum_{i=0}^{t-1} E_t(Y_{j+i} - \bar{Y}) \right\} \right\} \right\}$$

and given the process specified in (4.2) we find that consumption is given as

$$C_t = (\bar{Y} - \bar{G}) + \left(1 - \tau\left(1 - \frac{1+i}{1+r}\right)\right)\left(\frac{r}{1+r-\rho}\right)\sum_{j=0}^{t}\varepsilon_j.$$

The balanced budget regime appears as a special case where $\tau = 0$. Consumption is then given as

$$C_t = (\bar{Y} - \bar{G}) + \frac{r}{1+r-\rho}\sum_{j=0}^{t}\varepsilon_j.$$

The variability of consumption enters the indirect utility function through the term

$$-\frac{1}{2}\alpha E_0\left\{\sum_{t=0}^{\infty}\beta^t(C_t - C_0)^2\right\}.$$

Since var$[C_t]$ may be written as

$$\text{var}[C_t] = \left(\left(1 - \tau\left(1 - \frac{1+i}{1+r}\right)\right)\left(\frac{r}{1+r-\rho}\right)\right)^2(t+1)\sigma_\varepsilon^2$$

it follows using $EX_t^2 = \text{var}[X_t] - (EX_t)^2$ that only the variance term in the expected utility calculation is different between the two regimes (see appendix 4.2, p. 92)

$$-\frac{1}{2}\alpha E_0\left\{\sum_{t=0}^{\infty}\beta^t(C_t - C_0)^2\right\}$$

$$= -\frac{1}{2}\alpha\left(\left(1 - \tau\left(1 - \frac{1+i}{1+r}\right)\right)\frac{r}{(1+r-\rho)(1-\beta)}\right)^2\sigma_\varepsilon^2.$$

Comparing the variability of the present value of income under the two regimes, we find that the pro-cyclical budget regime ($\tau > 0$) delivers the lowest variability if

$$1 - \tau\left(1 - \frac{1+i}{1+r}\right) < 1$$

or

$$i < r.$$

That is, when the capital market is imperfect in such a way that the public sector faces a lower effective interest rate than the private sector it is possible to pursue a pro-cyclical budget regime which Pareto-dominates the balanced budget regime since they both deliver the same expected level of consumption but the former has lower variability.

Obviously the gain from the pro-cyclical budget regime relative to the balanced budget regime is increasing in the variability of the underlying shocks. This is just another way of saying that shock absorption via the public budget is more valuable the more volatility there is to absorb.

Note that the condition under which the pro-cyclical budget regime dominates the balance budget regime does not depend on the persistency parameter (ρ) in the process for the underlying shock variable. Although it might be conjectured that shock absorption is not possible for permanent shocks we find that this intuition is not justified,[6] the reason being that the public sector caused by the capital market imperfection can spread out even permanent shocks over time at better terms than can the private agents themselves

In the model considered above, production was exogenous, implying that there are no distortionary effects of taxation. This is of course an implausible assumption and it is necessary to question how the possibilities for shock absorption via the public budget are affected by allowing for endogenous production. This question is analysed in Andersen and Dogonowski (1997a) using an overlapping-generations model for a small open economy with liberalized capital movements. In this setting, Ricardian equivalence is broken because of the finite horizon of private agents and the consequences of different budget regimes are considered when the available tax instrument is a distortionary income tax. It is found that there is scope for shock absorption which provides social insurance and reduces macroeconomic volatility. It would actually be possible via the public budget to ensure full insurance to temporary productivity shocks, but this will not in general be the optimal policy owing to the distortionary effects of taxation. The optimal policy has a pro-cyclical budget and a progressive taxation system.

The effects discussed here relate to the discussion of the stabilizing effects of automatic stabilizers. This problem has, as noted, been subject to much interest in the standard macro-models and it is generally found that there is a stabilization gain in terms of lower output variability from such automatic budget effects. However, these models are not explicitly intertemporal, which is problematic when the mechanism studied is the importance of intertemporal substitution via the public budget. In modern intertemporal macroeconomics there are examples of how it is possible to design rules for fiscal policy which contribute to stabilizing economic

[6.] This disproves the claim by Fátas (1998) that intertemporal risk-sharing is not able to deal with shocks to permanent income.

Table 4.1. *Cyclical sensitivity of budget revenues and expenditures in the EU, 1995[a],*
1 per cent change in GDP

	Impact on revenue GDP ratio	Impact on expenditure GDP ratio	Impact on budget GDP ratio
BEL	0.5	−0.1	0.6
DEN	0.5	−0.3	0.7
GER	0.4	−0.1	0.5
GRE	0.3	−0.1	0.4
SPA	0.5	−0.2	0.6
FRA	0.5	−0.1	0.5
IRL	0.4	−0.2	0.5
ITA	0.3	−0.1	0.5
LUX	0.4	−0.2	0.6
NL	0.5	−0.2	0.8
AUT	0.4	−0.1	0.5
POR	0.4	−0.1	0.5
FIN	0.5	−0.2	0.6
SWE	0.6	−0.2	0.9
UK	0.5	−0.2	0.6
EUR	0.4	−0.1	0.5

Note: [a] Figures are rounded off.
Source: Commission of the European Communities (1997).

activity and therefore potentially creating welfare gains (see Andersen and
Holden 1997).

Cyclical properties of public budgets

Turning to the empirical evidence on the public budget deficit raises two
issues which have to be addressed – on the one hand whether there is a
systematic tendency to run budget deficits and accumulate debt, and on
the other the cyclical properties of budget deficits. For the present discussion it is the latter which is relevant.[7]

Looking at this issue is complicated by the problem of defining and
measuring the cyclical component of aggregate activity, as well as the
need to distinguish between discretionary and automatic budget effects.
It is a generally observed phenomenon that the budget balance moves

[7] For an analysis of the systematic deficit level, see Alesina and Perotti (1995).

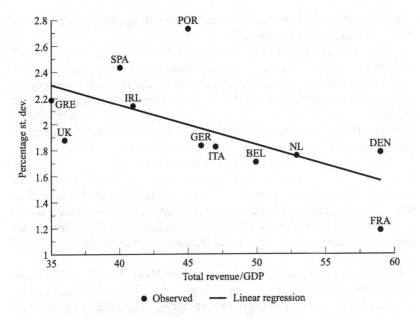

Figure 4.1   Output volatility and size of the public sector[a]

Note: [a]The percentage standard deviation of the HP-detrended output series is a measure of the volatility of the cyclical component relative to that of the pertinent output variable in percentage terms. As a measure of the size of the public sector we use tax revenue/GDP. The estimated relation presented in figure 4.1 is

$$\text{st. dev. of GDP(HP)} = 3.38 - 0.03 \cdot (\text{Total revenue/GDP})$$
$$(0.34) \quad (0.012)$$

with $R^2 = 0.38$.

pro-cyclically reflecting the fact that the revenue from different sources of taxes goes up and certain types of expenditures (such as unemployment benefits) are reduced in upturns. This is brought out by table 4.1, giving information on budget sensitivity for the EU countries. All countries included have a very cyclically sensitive budget and the revenue side accounts for most of this sensitivity. As can be seen, there is also a clear positive relationship between budget sensitivity and the size of the public sector such that the larger the public sector the more sensitive is the budget.

Is there any evidence that this actually works so as to absorb shocks and thus reduce macroeconomic volatility? A very crude indication of this is given by figure 4.1, showing that there is a negative relationship between aggregate volatility measured by the standard deviation of a cyclical measure of output and the size of the public sector as a proxy for the automatic budget reactions.[8]

Although suggestive, this evidence cannot be taken as a strict test of the effects of cyclical budgets for macroeconomic stability. That requires a consideration of the shocks which have affected the economy as well as the underlying structure, and for that a structural model is needed.

Some attempt have been made to assess the macroeconomic effects of budget regimes. In a study of the single states of the United States, Bayoumi and Eichengreen (1995) find that institutional restraints on the budget position limit the cyclical responsiveness of public finances and therefore potentially the automatic stabilizers. Building on US as well as international evidence, Bayoumi and Eichengreen (1995) conclude, based on simulations with the MULTIMOD model, that fiscal restraints may have severe consequences for macroeconomic volatility in the case of demand shocks.

In OECD (1993) simulations based on the INTERLINK model show that automatic stabilizers reduce the amplitude of cyclical fluctuations by one-quarter in the major European countries. The effect of automatic stabilizers turned out to be very different among the economies; in the smaller European economies the stabilizers were less effective than in the major European countries, the United States and Japan, indicating that openness may reduce their effectiveness.

The results of a more detailed study for Denmark for the period 1980–95 is reported in table 4.2. Using a large-scale macroeconomic model (SMEC) the counterfactual experiment of calculating aggregate output in the case of a passive fiscal policy (defined as unchanged real expenditures, tax revenues, etc.) has been constructed so as to evaluate the consequences of fiscal activism (see table 4.2). As can be seen, fiscal policy has contributed to a smoother path for aggregate activity. Splitting up the effects of fiscal policy into those arising from discretionary policy changes and those from automatic stabilizers, it is found that the latter accounts for most of the stability gain and that they always have worked in the right direction. Discretionary policy change have contributed less to smooth activity and has in some cases even been destabilizing.

It seems safe to conclude that automatic stabilizers are of quantitative importance and contribute to reducing the volatility of aggregate activity – that is, the public budget works as a shock absorber.

[8.] See Andersen and Schmidt (1997) for an attempt to identify the channels through which this stability effect arises.

Table 4.2. *Output growth in Denmark, effects on fiscal policy, 1980–1995, per cent*

Year	Actual growth	Growth with passive policy	Growth effect of discretionary fiscal policy	Growth effect of automatic stabilizers
1980	−0.4	−1.6	−0.3	1.5
1981	−0.9	−2.3	−0.2	1.6
1982	3.0	1.5	0.6	0.9
1983	2.5	4.1	−0.7	−0.9
1984	4.4	8.0	−0.6	−3.0
1985	4.2	5.4	0.1	−1.3
1986	3.6	7.8	−0.6	−3.6
1987	0.3	−2.2	0.3	2.2
1988	1.2	0.2	0.1	0.9
1989	0.6	−1.7	0.5	1.8
1990	1.4	0.8	0.4	0.2
1991	1.3	0.6	0.3	0.4
1992	0.2	−0.7	0.1	0.8
1993	1.5	0.7	0.5	0.3
1994	4.4	5.3	0.1	0.1
1995	2.6	6.9	−0.2	4.1

Source: Economic Council (Spring 1996).

Will the deficit norm be a binding constraint?

Next we have to assess whether the 3 per cent deficit norm of EMU will actually constrain national fiscal policies. One way of trying to address this problem is to look at past experience and see if there are episodes where a 3 per cent deficit/GDP norm would have been binding. Figure 4.2 reports the frequencies of observed budget changes on a year-to-year basis over the period 1970–96 for all current EU countries. In about 10 per cent of cases the budget deteriorated by more than 3 percentage points, and in 13 per cent of cases the budget worsened by 2–3 percentage points. That means that if countries start out with a balanced budget they would in about 23 per cent of the cases be brought into a situation where either the budget norm is violated or is very close to being violated, calling for policy action.[9]

[9] Poterba (1994) examines the effects of balanced budget rules on US states' response to income shocks. He finds that in the presence of stringent balanced budget rules spending fall by $44/resident and state taxes by $23/resident for an unexpected deficit of $100/ resident. If a state has a weak balanced budget rule spending will fall only by $17/resident while the tax rate will be unchanged.

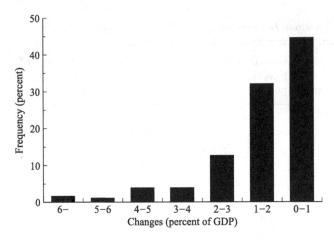

Figure 4.2   Frequencies of budget changes[a]

Note: [a]Our calculations are based on data from OECD (1997a, 1989); data for Austria, Luxembourg and Portugal (1970–9) are missing.

This way of reasoning suffers from the problem that it does not allow a separation of budget deteriorations caused by cyclical variations from other reasons for budget deteriorations.

Another way of judging the potential importance of the deficit norm is to consider actual cyclical fluctuations in EU countries, as given in table 4.3, and compare them to the minimum output gap which is feasible given the 3 per cent deficit norm and the observed budget sensitivity given in table 4.2. Two countries – Italy and Finland – have experienced downturns in which the budget caused by the automatic budget reaction would deteriorate by more than 3 percentage points. For three countries – France, Portugal and Sweden – the worst downturns would have brought them very close to the limit. This type of calculation has the problem that it considers only the effects of already built-in automatic budget reactions, leaving out discretionary fiscal policy. Hence, even if the automatic budget reactions do not by themselves violate the deficit norm, it may still be the case that the freedom left for discretionary fiscal policy is severely reduced. This may imply that discretionary policies which may be particularly efficient in relation to output stabilization cannot be used in a situation where they are greatly needed or that automatic stabilizers have to be weakened so as to create room for discretionary policy making. In this respect, it should be noted that the observed tendency to run systematic budget deficits was not caused by lax policies in recessions. Buti *et al.* (1997) find that the build-up of public debt in EU countries over the

Table 4.4. *Size of the negative output gaps in the EC and their critical values*[a] *1970–1995*

| Country | Split time-trend method | | Smoothing GDP using a HP filter | | Critical output gaps subject to 3 per cent deficit criteria |
	Value	Year	Value	Year	Critical value
BEL	2.7	1987	1.9	1987	5.0
DEN	4.1	1993	3.2	1975	4.3
GER	3.6	1975	3.5	1975	7.5
GRE	4.7	1974	3.6	1974	7.5
SPA	3.7	1995	2.3	1986	5.0
FRA	6.0	1994	2.3	1993	6.0
IRL	5.1	1976	4.3	1976	6.0
ITA	5.0	1994	3.5	1975	6.0
NL	3.2	1975	2.6	1982	3.7
AUT	2.6	1993	2.0	1987	6.0
POR	5.7	1975	5.8	1975	6.0
FIN	7.0	1993	6.4	1993	5.0
SWE	3.2	1993	2.9	1993	3.3
UK	4.2	1993	3.9	1982	5.0

Note: [a]The critical values are subject to the 3 per cent deficit criteria and are based on the elasticity of the budget/GDP with respect to GDP from the Commission's *Annual Economic Report 1997*
Source: Giorno *et al.* (1995).

past few years did not take place during recessions, but resulted rather from lax fiscal policies in non-recession periods. It follows that an eventual deficit bias is not targeted very well by the deficit norm, but it may reduce the room for an active stabilization policy.

Retrospective studies of this type all suffer from the problem that the business cycle may change owing to EMU. It can be argued that output volatility may increase due to the loss of the exchange rate instrument for short-term stabilization and the fact that monetary policy will be more strongly geared to maintaining price stability than has been the case generally for European countries. On the other hand, it is possible that EMU reinforces the process of international integration, which in turn may lower output volatility. The effectiveness of fiscal policy may also change, but the net effect is uncertain. On one hand, it is possible that EMU increases the effectiveness of fiscal policy by removing crowding-out

Table 4.4. *Critical growth rates,[a] 1970–1996*

Budget sensitivity to GDP growth (γ)		0.4	0.5	0.8
Structural deficit of GDP (d^s) (%)	0	−4.8	−3.4	−1.1
	1	−2.3	−1.3	0.2
	2	0.2	0.7	1.4
	3	2.7	2.7	2.7

Note: [a] The trend growth rate is $\bar{g}$ set equal to 2.7 which is the average growth rate for EU countries over the period 1970–96, based on data from OECD (1997b).

effects (see, for example, the Mundell–Fleming model with fixed exchange rates), but on the other does tighter international product market integration reduce fiscal multipliers.

To consider the inter-relationship between the structural budget deficit, budget sensitivity and the budget norms, it is useful to consider the following stylized illustration of the budget position. Let the budget deficit be denoted d and the structural budget deficit d^S, both measured relative to GDP, then

$$d_t = d_t^S + \gamma(\bar{g} - g_t) \tag{4.5}$$

where γ is the budget sensitivity to activity, $\bar{g}$ is the trend growth rate and g is the actual growth rate. Equation (4.5) implies that the budget position equals the structural budget deficit if growth is at its trend level.

For the budget deficit not to exceed 3 per cent of GDP, it is required that the growth rate exceeds a critical level $\hat{g}$ given by

$$g_t \geq \hat{g} \equiv \bar{g} + \frac{1}{\gamma} [d_t^S - 0.03].$$

Table 4.4 reports the critical growth level under various assumptions concerning budget sensitivity and the structural budget deficit.

Consider first the case with a structural deficit equal to zero. This situation will be in accordance with the Stability Pact. In this case, negative growth rates are required to bring the deficit in conflict with the 3 per cent norm. With low or average budget sensitivity ($\gamma = 0.4$ or 0.5) this situation arises only if output falls by more than 2 per cent, in which case the escape clause of the Stability Pact applies. However, for countries with a high budget sensitivity, a conflict with the 3 per cent norm can arise even if output does not fall by enough to make the escape clause applicable. Hence, even with 'sound' public finances, countries with high budget

Table 4.5. *Structure budget deficits EU countries, 1995–1998, per cent of GDP*

	Level				Change		
	1995	1996	1997	1998	1996	1997	1998
BEL	−3.7	−2.7	−2.4	−2.5	1.0	0.3	−0.1
DEN	−1.5	−1.2	−0.6	−1.1	0.3	0.6	−0.5
GER	−3.5	−3.5	−2.3	−2.0	0.0	1.2	0.3
GRE	−8.3	−7.5	−6.4	−5.7	0.0	1.1	0.7
SPA	−5.8	−3.5	−2.2	−2.3	2.3	1.3	−0.3
FRA	−4.8	−3.5	−2.6	−2.9	1.2	0.8	−0.3
IRL	−3.2	−3.9	−3.1	−2.4	−0.7	0.8	0.7
ITA	−7.1	−6.1	−2.7	−2.8	1.0	3.4	−0.1
LUX	1.7	1.3	−0.9	0.6	−0.4	−0.4	−0.3
NL	−3.7	−2.3	−2.3	−2.1	1.4	0.0	−0.2
AUT	−6.1	−4.1	−2.3	−2.5	2.0	1.8	−0.2
POR	−4.6	−3.5	−2.5	−2.9	1.1	1.0	−0.4
FIN	−3.8	−2.2	−2.2	−2.1	1.6	0.0	0.1
SWE	−6.8	−3.0	−2.5	−1.3	3.8	0.5	1.2
UK	−5.1	−4.0	−3.3	−2.2	1.1	0.7	1.1
EUR	−4.7	−3.8	−2.5	−2.4	0.9	1.3	0.1

Source: Commission of the European Communities (1997).

sensitivity may find the 3 per cent budget norm a binding constraint in the sense that a recession may bring the deficit above the 3 per cent norm, even though output did not fall enough to reach the escape clause applying for decreases in output above 2 per cent. This situation can be avoided only either by reducing the budget sensitivity or by creating a structural surplus to have enough room for manoeuvre in case of a recession. Obviously, the situation is more problematic if countries have a structural deficit.

The current situation for EU countries is far from a situation with a structural deficit equal to zero (see table 4.5). Actually, structural deficits are on average close to 3 per cent and even though fiscal consolidation may improve on this, it remains the case that this makes the fulfilment of 3 per cent a knife-edge exercise; even small reductions in the growth rate below its trend rate with the current level of structural deficits will cause problems. This is, of course, reflected in the current difficulties most EU countries have in fulfilling the deficit norm. Given the initial budget situation in all EU countries, it can be concluded that the deficit norm will be a binding constraint in a transition period of non-trivial length.

Conclusions

Contrary to widespread belief, the role of the public deficit is not confined only to political conflicts over distributional issues. The possibility of being able to run a pro-cyclical budget has efficiency implications by providing social insurance where market imperfections prevail. Imposing budget norms does restrain the ability of the public sector to cushion the economy to shocks.

Most countries have very sensitive public budgets, and there is indication that these automatic budget reactions work to stabilize the economy. Evaluated in this perspective, we find that there are realistic recessions which will bring countries into problems with the 3 per cent budget norm, even if they have a structurally balanced budget, and in which the escape clause defined in the Stability Pact will not apply. Moreover, in a probable long transition period, most countries will have a structural deficit and thus be very vulnerable to even mild recessions.

The preceding discussion has taken the deficit norm and the Stability Pact literally. Obviously, there is the possibility that it will be interpreted more softly in practice, precisely because it is a too binding constraint. It is also possible that it may be redefined to exclude cyclical variations from the norm. One possibility would be to define the norm relative to the structural budget deficit (see, for example Buiter, Corsetti and Roubini (1993); Eichengreen (1996)). Although this will create room for an active stabilization policy, it leaves fundamental problems concerning definition and implementation. The government could also create room for an active stabilization policy by improving the structural budget surplus. This may be costly if the government then has to leave a regime with sustainable positive debt, and start accumulating wealth. A fourth possibility would be to move towards fiscal federalism so as to have operational intra-regional insurance. However, this is politically unlikely within a foreseeable future.

One paradox in relation to fiscal norms is that while there are arguments why debt levels may exert negative externalities and thus have to be restrained, the Maastricht Treaty, and especially the Stability Pact, reinforces the deficit norm. The primary justification for this may be that the political system is perceived to be myopic and therefore tends to neglect the fact that systematic deficit accumulates in a rising debt level, the deficit norm can be interpreted as a rule intended to deal with this problem. However, this brings forth a conflict with the rules-based stabilization policy running via automatic and pro-cyclical budget reactions. In terms of informational requirements and implementation problems, this rules-based part of fiscal policy is to be strictly preferred to more discretion in fiscal policy. Very sensitive budgets will, however, easily cause a violation of the 3 per cent norm and a consequence of this may be that policy makers are forced to reduce budget sensitivity. It is not obvious that the redirection of rules implied by EMU is conducive to dealing with problems in the political system.

Appendix 4.1 *Consumption and net assets*

The tax system in the pro-cyclical budget regime is

$$T_t^c = \tau Y_t - (1+i)\tau(Y_{t-1} - \bar{Y})$$

and we may write net assets of the household in period t as

$$B_{t+1}^H = (1+r)B_t^H + Y_t - T_t - C_t.$$

Consumption in period t is

$$C_t = \frac{r}{1+r}\left\{(1+r)B_t^H + \sum_{j=0}^{\infty}\left(\frac{1}{1+r}\right)^j E_t(Y_{t+j} - T_{t+j})\right\}.$$

If we substitute in the tax function, consumption can be written as

$$C_t = rB_t^H + \frac{r}{1+r}\sum_{j=0}^{\infty}\left(\frac{1}{1+r}\right)^j E_t(Y_{t+j}(1-\tau)$$

$$+ (1+i)\tau(Y_{t+j-1} - \bar{Y})).$$

This can be simplified further to

$$C_t = rB_t^H + (\bar{Y} - \bar{G})$$

$$+ \frac{t}{1+r}\left(\sum_{j=0}^{\infty}\left(\frac{1}{1+r}\right)^j E_t(Y_{t+j} - \bar{Y})\left(1-\tau\right)\left(1 - \frac{1+i}{1+r}\right)\right)$$

$$- (1+i)\tau(Y_{t-1} - \bar{Y}).$$

We can also write net assets of the household as

$$B_{t+1}^H = (1+r)B_t^H + (Y_t - \bar{Y})(1-\tau) + (\bar{Y} - \bar{G})$$

$$+ (1+i)\tau(Y_{t-1} - \bar{Y}) - C_t.$$

If we consider period $t = 0$ where $B_0^H = 0$ and $Y_{-1} = \bar{Y}$, we get

$$C_0 = (\bar{Y} - \bar{G}) + \left(\frac{r}{1+r}\right)\left(1 - \tau\left(1 - \frac{1+i}{1+r}\right)\right)$$

$$\times \sum_{j=0}^{\infty} \left(\frac{1}{1+r}\right)^j E_0(Y_j - \bar{Y})$$

and

$$B_1^H = (Y_0 - \bar{Y})(1 - \tau) + \left(1 - \tau\left(1 - \frac{1+i}{1+r}\right)\right)\left(\frac{r}{1+r}\right)$$

$$\times \sum_{j=0}^{\infty} \left(\frac{1}{1+r}\right)^j E_0(Y_j - \bar{Y}).$$

We can use B_1^H and C_0 when solving for C_1 and B_2^H. When solving for C_1, we get

$$C_1 = rB_1^H + \frac{r}{1+r}\sum_{j=0}^{\infty}\left(\frac{1}{1+r}\right)^j E_1(Y_{j+1} - \bar{Y})\left(1 - \tau\left(1 - \frac{1+i}{1+r}\right)\right)$$

$$+ (\bar{Y} - \bar{G}) + r\frac{(1+i)}{(1+r)}\tau(Y_0 - \bar{Y}).$$

When substituting in B_1^H we get

$$C_1 = r(Y_0 - \bar{Y})\left(1 - \tau\left(1 - \frac{1+i}{1+r}\right)\right) + (\bar{Y} - \bar{G})$$

$$+ \left(1 - \tau\left(1 - \frac{1+i}{1+r}\right)\right)\frac{r}{1+r}\sum_{j=0}^{\infty}\left(\frac{1}{1+r}\right)^j$$

$$\{E_1\{Y_{j+1} - \bar{Y}\} - rE_0\{Y_j - \bar{Y}\}\}.$$

When solving for B_2^H we get

$$B_2^H = B_1^H + (Y_1 - \bar{Y})(1 - \tau)$$

$$+ (1+i)\tau(Y_0 - \bar{Y}) - r\frac{(1-i)}{(1+r)}\tau(Y_0 - \bar{Y})$$

$$- \left(1 - \tau\left(1 - \frac{1+i}{1+r}\right)\right)\left(\frac{r}{1+r}\right)$$

$$\times \sum_{j=0}^{\infty}\left(\frac{1}{1+r}\right)^j E_1\{Y_{j+1} - \bar{Y}\}.$$

When we use the derived expression for B_1^H we get

$$
B_2^H = (Y_1 - \bar{Y})(1 - \tau) - \left(1 - \tau\left(1 - \frac{1+i}{1+r}\right)\right)\left(\frac{r}{1+r}\right)
$$

$$
\times \sum_{j=0}^{\infty} \left(\frac{1}{1+r}\right)^j E_0(Y_j - \bar{Y})
$$

$$
+ (Y_0 - \bar{Y})\left(1 - \tau\left(1 - \frac{1+i}{1+r}\right)\right)
$$

$$
- \frac{r}{1+r}\left(1 - \tau\left(1 - \frac{1+i}{1+r}\right)\right) \sum_{j=0}^{\infty} \left(\frac{1}{1+r}\right)^j E_1(Y_{j+1} - \bar{Y}).
$$

In more general terms we may write consumption as

$$
C_t = (\bar{Y} - \bar{G}) + \left(1 - \tau\left(1 - \frac{1+i}{1+r}\right)\right)
$$

$$
\times \left\{ r \sum_{j=0}^{t-1}(Y_j - \bar{Y}) + \frac{r}{1+r}\left\{\sum_{j=0}^{\infty}\left(\frac{1}{1+r}\right)^t\right.\right.
$$

$$
\times \left.\left.\left\{ E_t(Y_{t+j} - \bar{Y}) - r \sum_{i=0}^{t-1} E_i(Y_{j+1} - \bar{Y})\right\}\right\}\right\}
$$

and B_t^H may be written as

$$
B_t^H = (Y_{t-1} - \bar{Y})(1 - \tau) + \left(1 - \tau\left(1 - \frac{1+i}{1+r}\right)\right)
$$

$$
\times \left\{ \sum_{i=0}^{t-2}(Y_i - \bar{Y}) - \frac{r}{1+r} \sum_{j=0}^{\infty}\sum_{i=0}^{t-1} E_i(Y_{j-1} - \bar{Y})\right\}.
$$

Since $B_t^G = \tau(Y_{t-1} - \bar{Y})$, it is easy to find net foreign assets for the economy:

$$
B_t = B_t^H + B_t^G
$$

$$
= (Y_{t-1} - \bar{Y}) + \left(1 - \tau\left(1 - \frac{1+i}{1+r}\right)\right)
$$

$$
\times \left\{ \sum_{i=0}^{t-2}(Y_i - \bar{Y}) - \frac{r}{1+r} \sum_{j=0}^{\infty}\sum_{i=0}^{t-1} E_i(Y_{j+1} - \bar{Y})\right\}.
$$

Appendix 4.2 *The variance of C_t*

We will by an iterative argument solve for the variance of C_t.

We know that income is given by the following AR(1) process

$$(Y_{t-1} - \bar{Y}) = \rho(Y_{t-1} - \bar{Y}) + \varepsilon_t \qquad t = 0, 1, 2, \ldots.$$

If we substitute this in the expression for C_0, we get

$$C_0 = (\bar{Y} - \bar{G}) + \left(\frac{r}{1+r}\right)\left(1 - \tau\left(1 - \frac{1+i}{1+r}\right)\right) \sum_{j=0}^{\infty} \left(\frac{\rho}{1+r}\right)^j \varepsilon_0$$

$$C_0 = (\bar{Y} - \bar{G}) + \left(1 - \tau\left(1 - \frac{1+i}{1+r}\right)\right) \frac{r}{1+t-\rho} \varepsilon_0$$

$$\mathrm{var}[C_0] = \left(\frac{r}{1+t-\rho}\left(1 - \tau\left(1 - \frac{1+i}{1+r}\right)\right)\right)^2 \sigma_\varepsilon^2.$$

If we focus on C_1, we may write C_1 as

$$C_1 = (\bar{Y} - \bar{G}) + \left(r\varepsilon_0 + \frac{r\rho\varepsilon_0}{1+r} \sum_{j=0}^{\infty} \left(\frac{\rho}{1+r}\right)^j + \frac{\varepsilon_1 r}{1+r} \sum_{j=0}^{\infty} \left(\frac{\rho}{1+r}\right)^j \right.$$

$$\left. - \frac{r^2}{1+r} \varepsilon_0 \sum_{j=0}^{\infty} \left(\frac{\rho}{1+r}\right)^j\right)\left(1 - \tau\left(1 - \frac{1+i}{1+r}\right)\right)$$

$$C_1 = (\bar{Y} - \bar{G}) + \left(r\varepsilon_0 + \frac{r\rho\varepsilon_0}{1+r-\rho} + \frac{r\varepsilon_1}{1+r-\rho} - \frac{r^2\varepsilon_0}{1+r-\rho}\right)$$

$$\times \left(1 - \tau\left(1 - \frac{1+i}{1+r}\right)\right).$$

If we collect these terms, we get

$$C_1 = (\bar{Y} - \bar{G}) + \left(\frac{r\varepsilon_0}{1+r-\rho} + \frac{r\varepsilon_1}{1+r-\rho}\right)\left(1 - \tau\left(1 - \frac{1+i}{1+r}\right)\right)$$

and

$$\mathrm{var}[C_1] = \left(\frac{r}{1+t-\rho}\left(1 - \tau\left(1 - \frac{1+i}{1+r}\right)\right)\right)^2 2\sigma_\varepsilon^2.$$

It is straightforward to continue on these iterations, and we find that

$$C_t = (\bar{Y} - \bar{G}) + \left(1 - \tau\left(1 - \frac{1+i}{1+r}\right)\right)\left(\frac{r}{1+r-\rho}\right)\sum_{j=0}^{t}\varepsilon_j$$

$$(A4.1)$$

and

$$\text{var}[C_t] = \left(\left(1 - \tau\left(1 - \frac{1+i}{1+r}\right)\right)\left(\frac{r}{1+r-\rho}\right)\right)^2 (t+1)\sigma_\varepsilon^2.$$

$$(A4.2)$$

The variance term in the expected utility calculation looks like

$$-\frac{1}{2}\alpha E_0\left\{\sum_{t=0}^{\infty}\beta^t(C_t - C_0)^2\right\}$$

$$= -\frac{1}{2}\alpha\sum_{t=0}^{\infty}\beta^t\,\text{var}[C_t] \qquad\qquad (A4.3)$$

$$= -\frac{1}{2}\alpha\left(\left(1 - \tau\left(1 - \frac{1+i}{1+r}\right)\right)\left(\frac{r}{1+r-\rho}\right)\right)^2\sum_{t=0}^{\infty}\beta^t(t+1)\sigma_\varepsilon^2$$

$$= -\frac{1}{2}\alpha\left(\left(1 - \tau\left(1 - \frac{1+i}{1+r}\right)\right)\frac{r}{(1+r-\rho)(1-\beta)}\right)^2\sigma_\varepsilon^2.$$

$$(A4.4)$$

The balanced budget case is when $\tau = 0$, and we will observe a smaller variance in the pro-cyclical budget regime if

$$1 - \tau\left(1 - \frac{1+i}{1+r}\right) < 1.$$

Since $\tau > 0$, the pro-cyclical budget regime has a smaller variance than the balanced budget regime ($\tau = 0$) if $r > i$.

References

Alesina, A. and Perotti, R. (1995). 'The Political Economy of Budget Deficits', *IMF Staff Papers*, 42: 1–31.

Andersen, T. M. (1997). 'Fiscal Policy in the EMU and Outside', *Swedish Economic Policy Review*, 4: 235–75.

Andersen, T. M. and Dogonowski, R. R. (1997a). 'Social Insurance and the Public Budget', University of Aarhus, mimeo

(1997b). 'What Should Optimal Income Taxes Smooth?', University of Aarhus, mimeo.

Andersen, T. M and Holden, S. (1997). 'Business Cycles and Fiscal Policy in an Open Economy', *Working Paper*, University of Aarhus

Andersen, T. M. and Schmidt, T. D. (1997). 'The Macroeconomics of the Welfare State', in T. M. Andersen, S. E. H. Jensen and O. Risager (eds.), *Macroeconomic Perspectives on the Danish Economy*, London: Macmillan.

Backus, D. and Kehoe, P. (1992). 'International Evidence on the Historical Properties of Business Cycles', *American Economic Review*, 82: 864–88

Ball, L. and Mankiw, G. N. (1995). 'What do Budget Deficits Do?', in *Budget Deficits and Debt: Issues and Options*, The Federal Reserve Bank of Kansas City

Barro, R. J. (1979). 'On the Determination of Public Debt', *Journal of Political Economy*, 87: 940–71

Bayoumi, T. and Eichengreen, B. (1995). 'Restraining Yourself: The Implications of Fiscal Rules for Economic Stabilization', *IMF Staff Papers* 42: 32–48

Blanchard. O. (1985). 'Debt, Deficits and Finite Horizons', *Journal of Political Economy*, 93: 223–47

Blanchard, O. and Fischer, S. (1989). *Lectures on Macroeconomics*, Cambridge, Mass.: MIT Press

Buiter, W., Corsetti, G. and Roubini, N. (1993). 'Excessive Deficits: Sense and Nonsense in the Treaty of Maastricht', *Economic Policy*, 16, 57–101.

Buti, M. *et al.* (1997). 'Budgetary Policies during Recessions', European Commission, *Economic Papers,* 121

Christodoulakis, N., Dimelis, S. and Kollintzas, T. (1995). Comparison of Business Cycles in the EC: Idiosyncrasies and Regularities', *Economica*, 62: 1–27

Commission of the European Communities (CEC) (1997) *Annual Economic Report: Growth, Employment and Convergence on the Road to EMU*, Brussels: Commission of the European Communities.

Economic Council (1996). *Danish Economy* (Spring)

Eichengreen, B. (1996). 'Saving Europe's Automatic Stabilizers', *National Institute Economic Review*, 159: 92–8

Eichengreen, B. and Wyplosz, C. (1997). 'The Stability Pact: More than a Minor Nuisance', *Economic Policy*, 26: 65–104

European Monetary Institute (EMI) (1997). 'The Single Monetary Policy in Stage Three', Frankfurt: European Monetary Institute

Fatás, A. (1998). Does EMU Need a Fiscal Federation?', *Economic Policy*, 26: 163–92

Giorno, C. *et al.* (1995). 'Potential Output, Output Gaps and Structural Budget Balances', *OECD Economics Studies*, 24/I

Kenen, P. B. (1969). 'The Theory of Optimum Currency Areas: An Eclectic View', in R. A. Mundell and A. K. Swoboda (eds), *Monetary Problems in the International Economy*, Chicago: University of Chicago Press

Neary, J. P. and Roberts, K. W. (1980). 'The Theory of Household Behaviour under Rationing', *European Economic Review*, 13: 25–42.

OECD (1989). *OECD Economic Outlook*, 46, Paris: OECD

(1993) *Economic Outlook,* 53, Paris: OECD

(1995). *OECD Economic Survey – Sweden*, Paris: OECD

(1997a). *OECD Economic Outlook*, 61, Paris: OECD

(1997b). *OECD Statistical Compendium*, 1997 #1, CD-ROM, Paris: OECD

Poterba, J. (1994). 'State Responses to Fiscal Crisis: The Effects of Budgetary Institutions and Politics', *Journal of Political Economy*, 102: 799–821

Seater, J. J. (1993). 'Ricardian Equivalence', *Journal of Economic Literature*, 31: 142–90

5 Monetary union, asymmetric productivity stocks and fiscal insurance: an analytical discussion of welfare issues

Kenneth M. Kletzer

Introduction

Discussions of the economic case for or against European monetary unification inevitably concern the concept of an optimum currency area (OCA). By Mundell's classic definition (1961), a group of states form an OCA if the permanent fixing of nominal rates of exchange between them has no effect on real economic variables. This is the case if all prices and wages are perfectly flexible or, as pointed out by Mundell, all factors are perfectly mobile even if there are nominal price or wage rigidities. If labour market adjustment is sluggish, then nominal exchange rate movements can be a stabilizing tool in the presence of asymmetric national productivity or demand disturbances.[1]

Eichengreen (1992b), Bayoumi and Eichengreen (1993) and others have focused the analysis of the macroeconomic effects of the monetary unification of Europe on comparisons between the European Union (EU) and the United States.[2] These studies compare the degree of inter-regional labour mobility and the incidence of idiosyncratic regional aggregate supply and demand disturbances between the United States (and Canada) and the EU. A conclusion is that Europe may be a more problematic candidate for monetary unification, although it is difficult to compare

I have benefited from comments and suggestions made by the Andrew Hughes Hallett, Michael Hutchison, Svend E. Hougaard Jensen, Neil Rankin and Carl Walsh. This chapter also reflects conversations over time with Willem Buiter and Charles Engel on these and related issues.

[1.] The theory of optimum currency areas (OCAs) is further elaborated by McKinnon (1963); Kenen (1969); Ingram (1973); Ishiyama (1975).
[2.] These include Bayoumi and Masson (1994); Bayoumi and Thomas (1995); De Grauwe and Vanhaverbeke (1991); Dehesa and Krugman (1993); Eichengreen (1992a); Eichengreen and Wyplosz (1993); Kenen (1992); Krugman (1993); Melitz (1991); von Hagen and Hammond (1995). Most recently, Obstfeld (1997a, 1997b) and Obstfeld and Peri (1998) have reviewed the empirical evidence for and against European monetary unification.

regional real disturbances for an established monetary union with those experienced under a flexible exchange regime with separate national monetary policies.

Nominal exchange rate flexibility allows autonomous monetary policy responses to idiosyncratic aggregate fluctuations, and allows nations to pursue different goals of stabilization policy. By adopting a common currency, the EU appears to be placing a greater burden on fiscal policies for achieving differential responses to productivity and demand disturbances, whether these are common or region-specific. Economists differ widely in their views on the justification and prospects for success of a European monetary union. McKinnon (1997a, 1997b), for example, argues that fiscal discipline imposed by the disestablishment of national central banks on national governments provides a strong justification for monetary union.[3] Feldstein (1997) argues that a system of floating exchange rates is desirable for Europe because of differing political goals and sluggish labour market adjustment.

The recent policy debate on monetary unification also notes that the United States supplements a single monetary policy with a system of fiscal federalism. Inter-state transfers through the federal tax system and transfer payments automatically stabilize spending power against idiosyncratic regional shocks, as observed by Ingram (1959).[4] Many authors therefore suggest that successful European monetary unification may require fiscal consolidation as well.[5] In this chapter, I use a formal general equilibrium model to discuss the potential role for fiscal insurance between member states of a monetary union to act as a replacement for nominal exchange rate flexibility for short-run stabilization in the presence of asymmetric real shocks.

An analytical model of an international economy in which financial asset markets are integrated but labour markets are not is used to compare the welfare benefits of a system of state-contingent fiscal transfers with and without monetary union. Temporary nominal wage rigidities provide a role for monetary policies to alleviate short-run labour market disequilibrium caused by productivity shocks that can differ across countries. The

---

[3.] McKinnon (1997a, 1997b) is supportive of limitations on public sector debts and deficits as set forth in the Treaty of Maastricht and subsequently tightened in the Stability Pact. Criticisms of these restrictions are given by Buiter and Kletzer (1991); Buiter, Corsetti and Roubini (1993); Eichengreen and von Hagen (1995). An overview is given by Hutchison and Kletzer (1995).

[4] Sachs and Sala-i-Martin (1992) estimate inter-state fiscal transfers in response to aggregate income shocks for the United States. von Hagen (1990) argues that these over-estimate the role of fiscal federalism in stabilization by including permanent interstate income transfers.

[5.] Examples in the economics literature include van Rompuy, Abraham and Heremans (1991); Eichengreen (1992a); Courchene (1993), Bayoumi and Masson (1994).

elimination of nominal exchange rate flexibility with monetary union reduces the capacity of monetary authorities to influence resource allocation in the model economy. The model is analysed in stages, adding structure as needed to discuss possible rationale for the argument that fiscal insurance is needed to replace independent monetary policies after monetary unification.

Fiscal insurance is first discussed in a standard model of international portfolio diversification under perfect price and wage flexibility and idiosyncratic national productivity shocks. Asset markets are incomplete because assets capitalizing future labour earnings are not tradeable. The flexible price allocation of resources can be replicated when nominal rigidities are added to the economy under independent national monetary policies. This provides a benchmark case for discussing the gains from fiscal insurance with monetary union. It is argued that empirical evidence suggests that fiscal insurance schemes are unlikely to generate significant welfare benefits in the benchmark economy. Fiscal insurance schemes are most important when monetary policies are effective for reducing short-run labour market disequilibrium and prices in national markets for goods and services are arbitraged across borders. Empirical evidence shows that goods and services are priced-to-market, so that these markets are segmented across member states of the EU. The model reveals that the failure of the law of one price greatly reduces both the welfare benefits of fiscal insurance under monetary union and the welfare costs of monetary unification with nominal rigidities and asymmetric productivity disturbances.

In the model, consumption, saving, labour supply, money demand and portfolio allocation decisions are made by households optimizing over time. Investment and employment decisions are made by firms seeking to maximize their value. Nominal wage and price rigidities are introduced in a simple and, necessarily, ad hoc fashion following the literature on overlapping nominal wage contracts. The next section presents the basic model of international asset trade with asymmetric productivity risk and discusses state-contingent fiscal transfers under flexible prices. We then introduce nominal rigidities and discuss the comparison benchmark of resource allocation with nominal exchange rate flexibility. The welfare gains and losses from fiscal insurance with integrated goods markets and with segmented goods markets are discussed and the final section concludes.

Fiscal transfers with nominal flexibility

Behind arguments in favour of a system of fiscal transfers between members of a monetary union is the incompleteness of markets to share the risk of idiosyncratic disturbances to national productivities. Even with the highly integrated international financial markets of the EU, labour income risk is largely uninsurable across borders, aggregate labour income risk is the focus of concerns about asymmetric disturbances to real economic performance in the EU. A natural starting point for a welfare analysis of fiscal insurance schemes is a model of incomplete international asset markets without nominal wage or price rigidities. A simple model is used in this section to show how the uninsurability of national labour income risk can lead to a welfare argument for inter-governmental fiscal insurance schemes. It is also used to argue, on the basis of empirical evidence, that the welfare benefits of fiscal federalism in Europe may be minor.

The basic model is a variant of the Lucas (1982) model of international portfolio diversification. A two-country model is used for illustration. In each country, there is a representative resident household. A single trade-able good is produced using capital and labour under constrant returns to scale in each country. Factor productivity is subject to stochastic distur-bances that are independent across countries. Households can trade equity claims to the earnings of capital and riskless bonds, but there is no asset market on which to trade claims to future wage income. Households there-fore diversify their portfolios through purchases of internationally traded equities and bonds to reduce their exposure to productivity risk. They may be unable to share fully idiosyncratic productivity risks internationally because labour income is not capitalized by tradeable assets.[6]

The equations of the model are shown only for the home country when-ever the equations for the foreign country are analogous. Home variables do not carry superscripts and foreign variables are indicated by an aster-isk. The home-country household supplies labour at each date t in the amount ℓ_t earning a real wage given by $w_t \equiv W_t/P_t$, where W_t and P_t are the nominal wage and price, respectively. It can hold bonds denominated in units of the single good, nominally-indexed bonds, money and equity claims. The single-period budget identity for the home-country household at time t is given by

$$\frac{W_t}{P_t}\ell_t + (1+r_t)b_t + (1+i_t)\frac{B_t}{P_t} + \frac{M_{t-1}}{P_t}$$

$$+ [\gamma_t(V_t + d_t) + \gamma_t^*(V_t^* + d_t^*)]$$

$$= c_t + b_{t+1} + \frac{B_{t+1}}{P_t} + \frac{M_t}{P_t} + [\gamma_{t+1}V_t + \gamma_{t+1}^* V_t^*]. \tag{5.1}$$

[6.] Neumeyer (1998) considers the effects of monetary unification in a general equilibrium model with incomplete markets adopting a special specification for household utilities and incorporating the transactions demand for money differently.

Here, b_t and B_t are the household's holdings of single-period bonds at the beginning of period t denominated in units of output and currency, respectively. M_{t-1} denotes the nominal money balances it carries forward from period $t-1$. V_t is the total market value of equities issued by home-country firms, ex dividend, at time t, and d_t is the corresponding dividend paid at the beginning of period t. The share of outstanding home-country equities held by the home household at the beginning of period t equals γ_t, and its share of foreign equities equals γ_t^*, where $0 \le \gamma_t, \gamma_t^* \le 1$. Purchases of home and foreign equities in period t equal $\gamma_{t+1} V_t$ and $\gamma_{t+1}^* V_t^*$, respectively. The household's consumption is c_t, and M_t equals the money balances held in period t.

The household makes its consumption, labour supply, saving and portfolio-allocation decisions seeking to maximize expected utility,

$$U_t = E_t \sum_{s=t}^{\infty} \beta^{s-t} \left[u(c_s) + v \left(\frac{M_s}{P_s} \right) + v(\bar{\ell} - \ell_s) \right], \tag{5.2}$$

which is assumed for convenience to be additively separable in consumption, real balances and leisure, subject to the budget identity and the solvency constraint,

$$\lim_{T \to \infty} \left[\prod_{s=t}^{T} (1 + r_s)^{-1} \right] \left(b_{T+1} + \frac{B_{T+1}}{P_T} + \frac{M_T}{P_T} \right) \ge 0. \tag{5.3}$$

The subjective discount rate, $(1 - \beta)/\beta$, is assumed to be the same for home and foreign residents, although preferences can otherwise differ across borders.

Household utility maximization with respect to holdings of real-indexed bonds gives the standard Euler condition for riskless bonds,

$$u'(c_t) = (1 + r_{t+1}) E_t \beta u'(c_{t+1}). \tag{5.4}$$

The choice of holdings of nominally-indexed bonds leads to another Euler condition,

$$u'(c_t) = P_t (1 + i_{t+1}) E_t \frac{\beta u'(c_{t+1})}{P_{t+1}}. \tag{5.5}$$

Combining these gives the consumption-based Fisher interest parity condition,

$$(1 + r_{t+1}) E_t \beta u'(c_{t+1}) = (1 + i_{t+1}) E_t \left(\frac{\beta u'(c_{t+1})}{P_{t+1}/P_t} \right). \tag{5.6}$$

The household's holdings of nominal balances satifies the first-order condition,

$$u'(c_t) = v'\left(\frac{M_t}{P_t}\right) + P_t E_t \frac{\beta u'(c_{t+1})}{P_{t+1}}. \tag{5.7}$$

Optimal portfolio diversification leads to the necessary conditions,

$$V_{t+1} = E_t\left[\frac{\beta u'(c_{t+1})}{u'(c_t)}(V_{t+1} + d_{t+1})\right], \qquad \text{for } 0 < \gamma_{t+1} < 1, \tag{5.8}$$

for home equities and

$$V^*_{t+1} = E_t\left[\frac{\beta u'(c_{t+1})}{u'(c_t)}(V^*_{t+1} + d^*_{t+1})\right], \qquad \text{for } 0 < \gamma^*_{t+1} < 1, \tag{5.9}$$

for foreign equities. Similar conditions hold for the optimal portfolio allocations for foreign country residents, so that

$$V_{t+1} = E_t\left[\frac{\beta u^{*'}(c^*_{t+1})}{u'(c^*_t)}(V_{t+1} + d_{t+1})\right], \qquad \text{for } 0 < \gamma_{t+1} < 1, \tag{5.10}$$

for example.

It is possible that all home equity is held by domestic residents, in which case $\gamma_{t+1} = 1$ and

$$E_t\left[\frac{\beta u^{*'}(c^*_{t+1})}{u'(c^*_t)}(V^*_{t+1} + d_{t+1})\right] \leq V_t$$

$$\leq E_t\left[\frac{\beta u'(c_{t+1})}{u'(c_t)}(V_{t+1} + d_{t+1})\right], \tag{5.11}$$

or by foreign residents, in which case $\gamma_{t+1} = 0$ and

$$E_t\left[\frac{\beta u^{*'}(c^*_{t+1})}{u'(c^*_t)}(V_{t+1} + d_{t+1})\right] \geq V_t$$

$$\geq E_t\left[\frac{\beta u'(c_{t+1})}{u'(c_t)}(V_{t+1} + d_{t+1})\right]. \tag{5.12}$$

The household makes its labour supply decision so that the marginal rate of substitution between leisure and goods consumption equals the real wage rate,

$$v'(\bar{\ell} - \ell_t) = w_t u'(c_t). \tag{5.13}$$

The household optimum also satisfies the transversality condition, so that the solvency condition for the household sector holds with equality.

The home country aggregate production function is given by

$$Y_t = \theta_t F(\kappa_t, \ell_t) = \ell_t \theta_t f(k_t) \tag{5.14}$$

where κ_t is the capital stock, ℓ_t is employment and θ_t is a stochastic productivity disturbance. The capital/labour ratio is $k_t \equiv \kappa_t/\ell_t$. Under perfect competition in the domestic labour market, labour demand is determined by marginal productivity,

$$w_t = \theta_t(f(k_t) - k_t f'(k_t)). \tag{5.15}$$

Firms choose their investment levels to maximize shareholder value net of the cost of capital. Along with the equilibrium conditions for asset demands (5.8) and (5.10) this implies that

$$u'(c_t) = E_t[\beta u'(c_{t+1})(1 + \theta_{t+1} f'(k_{t+1}))), \tag{5.16}$$

if home residents hold home equities and

$$u'(c_t^*) = E_t[\beta u'(c_{t+1}^*)(1 + \theta_{t+1} f'(k_{t+1}))], \tag{5.17}$$

if foreign residents do. With perfect international financial capital mobility, the expected marginal productivity of capital will be equal across borders,

$$E_t\theta_t f'(k_t) = E_t\theta_t^* f'(k_t^*). \tag{5.18}$$

In equilibrium, the equities are valued according to the standard capital asset-pricing model (CAPM) equations.

It is useful to begin with the (well known) efficient allocation for this model economy. A welfare optimum can be implemented by a market equilibrium if tradeable equities capitalize all of gross domestic product. In the case that $u(c)$ displays constant relative risk aversion, home-country residents will hold claims to the same share of GDP in each country. This share is equal to the home country's initial share of total financial wealth. In this case, there is no net trade in either real-indexed or nominally-indexed bonds in equilibrium. If the two countries begin with equal wealth, then the residents of each hold exactly half of the claims on GDP for each country.

Under the assumption that only claims to the share of GDP paid to non-human factors are tradeable, the efficient allocation can be supported in a market equilibrium only if the share of labour payments in national product is less than the share of national wealth in total wealth. This must hold for each country. If this is the case, then the residents of each country can select portfolios that give them equal proportionate shares of the output of each country. To do this, the portfolio shares, γ_t and γ_t^*, must satisfy the equalities,

$$\gamma_t \alpha_t + (1 - \alpha_t) = \gamma_t^* \alpha_t^*, \tag{5.19}$$

and

$$(1 - \gamma_t^*)\alpha_t^* + (1 - \alpha_t^*) = (1 - \gamma_t)\alpha_t, \tag{5.20}$$

for $0 \leq \gamma_t \leq 1$ and $0 \leq \gamma_t^* \leq 1$, where $\alpha_t = \kappa_t f'(k_t)/f(k_t)$ and $\alpha_t^* = \kappa_t^* f'(k_t^*)/f(k_t^*)$ are capital's share in national income for the home and foreign countries, respectively. Here, $(\gamma_t \alpha_t + (1 - \alpha_t))$ is the fraction of home output that is paid to home residents, and $\gamma_t^* \alpha_t^*$ is the fraction of foreign output paid to home residents. For an efficient allocation, these are equal to the home share in total initial wealth. If factor shares are the same in the two countries, an efficient allocation of risk implies that households will hold a larger share of foreign capital than of home capital equity. This follows because households already hold claims to domestic output via labour income shares. Equation (5.19) requires that home residents hold a larger share of claims to the output of each country than labour earns in national output. Equation (5.20) states that this must also hold for the foreign country.

For trade in capital equities and bonds to implement the efficient allocation, labour's share in each country must be less than that country's share of total wealth of the monetary union. For N countries with equal initial wealth, this means that labour's share in national product must be less than $1/N$. Efficient diversification of idiosyncratic national productivity risk is not possible without tradeable claims to future labour income for actual values of labour's share around 70 per cent.

For realistic factor shares, the model implies that diversification goes as far as it can with the assets available to households. Using (5.19) and (5.20), the share of labour for the home country exceeds home-residents' share of foreign output, $(1 - \alpha_t) > \gamma_t^* \alpha_t^*$, so that $\gamma_t = 0$ in the solution for equilibrium. For the foreign country, we have that $(1 - \alpha_t^*) > (1 - \gamma_t)\alpha_t$ and $\gamma_t^* = 0$. This means that home residents receive a higher share of income from home production than from foreign production in equilibrium. All home earnings for home residents, however, will be in the form of labour income for a constrained equilibrium. This is implied by the Euler equations for capital assets, (5.11) and (5.12), with dividends calculated as capital earnings – home residents would like to trade away more of the claims to national GDP they hold than they can by trading claims to capital alone.

When the constraint on international risk-sharing imposed by the absence of assets in future labour income binds, the marginal rate of substitution between date t and date $t + 1$ consumption is not perfectly correlated across countries (as it would be for efficiency with constant relative risk aversion). In particular, the marginal productivity of home-country capital will have a higher covariance with home-country consumption than with foreign-country consumption. The general model of international portfolio diversification therefore predicts that domestic residents would hold only claims to foreign capital and that all claims to domestic capital would be held by foreigners. This prediction is in sharp contrast with what we observe for the member states of the EU. Also, note that in equilibrium with incomplete risk-sharing, net holdings of internationally traded riskless bonds will not necessarily be zero as in the efficient allocation.

An international transfer scheme that promotes allocative efficiency can be designed to replicate the consumption path for each household in equilibrium with assets based on total national income. In such a scheme, the home country makes a gross transfer to the foreign country equal to the difference between the share of home output foreign residents would be paid under efficient risk-sharing and the capital income they actually receive with incomplete asset markets. The foreign country makes a similar gross transfer to the home country. The net transfers give the residents of each country the same share of output for the monetary union as they would receive in the efficient allocation – that is, all asymmetric risk is shared. The returns to capital and levels of investment will therefore be the same under this transfer scheme as in the efficient equilibrium. Algebraically, the equilibrium lump-sum transfer net of tax to the home household under this scheme at each date is given by the difference between the gross transfer received and that paid as

$$\tau_t = [\mu - \gamma_t^* \alpha_t^*] Y_t^* - [(1 - \alpha_t) - \mu] Y_t, \qquad (5.21)$$

where μ is the share of home initial wealth in total wealth. Output and factor inputs are evaluated in equilibrium. This is a balanced budget scheme, as $\tau_t = \tau_t^*$ for all dates t.

The portfolio-diversification model with the realistic assumption that financial claims to future labour income cannot be traded provides a welfare argument for fiscal insurance schemes between countries. So far, all prices and wages are assumed to be perfectly flexible, and the equilibrium is Walrasian. The nominal exchange regime does not affect the welfare analysis until nominal price or wage rigidity is introduced. Monetary unification thus does not affect these benchmark welfare gains from international fiscal insurance schemes. Before introducing nominal price or wage rigidity to the model, it is useful to consider how strong this welfare case is.

The model shows that international fiscal insurance can yield welfare benefits in competitive equilibrium when international asset markets are incomplete. Potential Pareto-benefits arise if residents seek to share more idiosyncratic national productivity risk than they can by trading equities to capital only. International fiscal insurance is welfare-improving only when the residents of at least one country hold equities only in foreign capital income and foreigners hold all the equities in home capital income. Because fiscal insurance replaces trade in equities based on labour's share in GDP, the gains from fiscal insurance are the same as the gains from trading additional claims to GDP. If we observe that domestic residents hold net claims to domestic capital in internationally integrated financial capital markets, then we should conclude that the gains from fiscal insurance schemes are nil.

Many authors (for example, Tesar, 1995, among others) have noted the strong home bias in asset-holding patterns for the advanced industrialized countries. This observation contradicts the model prediction that is necessary under perfect capital mobility for fiscal insurance to be desirable. Cole and Obstfeld (1991) and Backus, Kehoe and Kydland (1992) have estimated the gains from international risk-sharing among the advanced industrialized countries to be very small. The diversification of productivity risk with fully flexible prices and wages does not therefore appear to provide a substantial basis for implementing fiscal insurance schemes to make up for the absence of complete markets for sharing asymmetric labour income risk between member states of the EU.

Nominal rigidities and the role of exchange rate flexibility

In the model so far, the labour market clears every period in each country. Productivity shocks, however, can have a larger impact on output if real wages do not adjust to clear the labour market each period. With nominal wage or price stickiness, monetary policy has real effects and can be used actively to influence the output response to idiosyncratic national productivity disturbances. Nominal rigidities also mean that the exchange rate regime matters. The capacity of monetary policies to promote labour market equilibrium with imperfect international labour mobility and idiosyncratic productivity disturbances is reduced by the adoption of a common currency. By permanently fixing nominal exchange rates, monetary unification eliminates the role of nominal exchange rates between member states as automatic stabilizers of employment and incomes against asymmetric national productivity shocks. National monetary authorities lose the ability to influence national employment, consumption and investment independently of other member states. This suggests that the welfare case for international fiscal insurance may be increased by the creation of a monetary union.

To assess how monetary unification affects the gains from fiscal transfer schemes, nominal wage rigidities are added to the model of international portfolio diversification with asymmetric productivity shocks. I then discuss resource allocation under nominal exchange rate flexibility. This provides the comparison case for discussing the argument that fiscal insurance is needed to compensate for the loss of nominal exchange rate flexibility with monetary union.

A simple way to introduce nominal rigidities is to assume that nominal wages are set one period in advance of employment. This could be extended to allow for infinitely forward- and backward-looking nominal wage contracts, as explored in Jensen (1998). Eliminating immediate real wage adjustment to shocks to the marginal productivity of labour leads to labour market disequilibrium. Some assumption must therefore be made about how employment and output are determined. Adding nominal wage rigidity to the model of the previous section, it is assumed that employment is demand-determined each period, as is done in the monopolistic general equilibrium model used by Obstfeld and Rogoff (1995) and Corsetti and Pesenti (1998). A significant amount of algebra is avoided by sticking with the perfectly competitive market structure for producers.

The home nominal wage rate is set by firms at date $t - 1$ so that

$$W_t = E_{t-1}\left[p_t\theta_t(f(k_t) - k_tf'(k_t))\right], \tag{5.22}$$

where W_t is the nominal wage rate and p_t equals the nominal price of output. The capital-labour ratio, $k_t = \kappa_t/\ell_t^d$, depends on employment, ℓ_t^d, chosen at time t and on the capital stock, κ_t, chosen in period $t - 1$. k_t thefore depends on the state of nature, θ_t. Employment demand, ℓ_t^d, at date t is chosen by firms *ex post* for each realization of $p_t\theta_t$ so that the predetermined nominal wage rate equals the nominal value marginal product of labour,

$$W_t = p_t\theta_t(f(k_t) - k_tf'(k_t)). \tag{5.23}$$

With separate national currencies, home money demand satisfies the first-order condition,

$$\frac{v'(M_t/P_t)}{u'(c_t)} = \frac{i_{t+1}}{1 + i_{t+1}}, \tag{5.24}$$

that the opportunity cost of money in terms of consumption equals the marginal rate of substitution of consumption for real balances. Consumption-based uncovered interest parity (UIP) also holds,

$$(1 + i^*_{t+1})E_t\left(\frac{(s_{t+1}/s_t)\beta u'(c_{t+1})}{P_{t+1}/P_t}\right) = (1 + i_{t+1})E_t\left(\frac{\beta u'(c_{t+1})}{P_{t+1}/P_t}\right)$$

$$(5.25)$$

where s denotes the spot exchange rate. Equation (5.25) is derived by adding bonds nominally-indexed to each currency to the household budget constraint, (5.1). This leads to two versions of the bond Euler condition, equation (5.5), one in terms of each currency. Combining these conditions yields this arbitrage condition, which holds with equality because asset markets are assumed to allow trade in bonds denominated in either currency. Counterparts to (5.22), (5.23), (5.24) and (5.25) for the foreign country are similar. With a single good, p_t and P_t are identical, and both are expressed in units of the home currency. With several goods, P_t is the consumption-based price index for the home country and p_t is the price of a home output. The price level is determined by requiring saddle-path stability and ruling out speculative bubbles.

It is first assumed that exchange rate pass-through is complete, so that the law of one price holds for each tradeable commodity individually,

$$p_t = s_t p^*_t. \qquad (5.26)$$

Consider an adverse output realization (θ_t less than its mean) for the home country and a positive one for the foreign country. In equilibrium, current home income falls so that home real consumption falls (relative to its value for a mean output realization). Consumption-smoothing, implied by household optimization over time, implies that consumption is lower in both periods t and $t + 1$. In a stable equilibrium for the model, the home price level and the exchange rate rise to their expected future levels if both the home and foreign money supplies are held constant. The foreign price level falls. With nominal wage adjustment in one period, over-shooting or under-shooting of the exchange rate does not occur in a saddle-stable equilibrium. Because nominal wages are preset, the adverse productivity shock for the home country leads to an insufficiency of labour demand relative to labour supply at a constant nominal output price. The opposite occurs in the foreign country for p^* constant. Nominal rigidities exacerbate the output effects of productivity shocks. The adjustment of nominal prices, p and p^*, can at least partially offset these additional fluctuations to output. These changes are in opposing directions, so that nominal exchange rate flexibility is essential for this automatic stabilizing effect to work. The nominal exchange rate is also an automatic stabilizer under longer-term nominal contracting regimes.

Independent monetary policies can be used to exploit this adjustment process. With pre-determined nominal wages, but flexible goods prices, independent expansions or contractions of national money supplies lower or raise the real wage rate faced by each firm in the current period. Nominal exchange rate flexibility allows the two monetary authorities (before monetary union) to expand employment and output separately in the two countries to satisfy, *ex post*, the two equilibrium conditions for labor-market clearing necessary for a Walrasian equilibrium:

$$\frac{v'(\bar{\ell} - \ell_t)}{u'(c_t)} = w_t = \theta_t \left(f\left(\frac{\kappa_t}{\ell_t}\right) - \frac{\kappa_t}{\ell_t} f'\left(\frac{\kappa_t}{\ell_t}\right) \right) \tag{5.27}$$

and

$$\frac{v^{*'}(\bar{\ell}^* - \ell_t^*)}{u^{*'}(c_t^*)} = w_t^* = \theta_t^* \left(f\left(\frac{\kappa_t^*}{\ell_t^*}\right) - \frac{\kappa_t^*}{\ell_t^*} f'\left(\frac{\kappa_t^*}{\ell_t^*}\right) \right). \tag{5.28}$$

Along with all the other equilibrium conditions, these choices of endogenous money supply responses to productivity shocks yield a, possibly constrained, efficient equilibrium allocation of risks and resources. The constraint that may be binding is that household portfolio diversification is limited by the absence of international trade in assets based on labour income, exactly as in the previous section. International monetary coordination that seeks to maintain labour market equilibrium in each country in every period achieves all the same equilibrium conditions for the model under perfectly flexible prices and wages. The equilibrium allocation and relative prices under trade in capital income securities and in riskless real-indexed and nominally-indexed bonds are the same. That is, nominal exchange rate flexibility allows endogenous money supply reaction functions to implement the flexible price equilibrium despite nominal wage rigidity. This implies that the welfare benefits of a fiscal insurance scheme are the same in this flexible exchange rate regime as in the Walrasian equilibrium.

This gives a benchmark for discussing how the welfare benefits of fiscal insurance are increased by monetary unification. The empirical results that actual asset portfolios are not diversified internationally to the extent predicted by a competitive equilibrium model also implies that fiscal insurance schemes would not provide notable welfare improvements under flexible exchange rates.

The efficacy of monetary policy in this model derives from the result that nominal but not real wages are rigid in the short run. When nominal wages are *de facto* indexed to nominal prices, monetary policies are in-effective for adjusting employment demand to clear the labour market in response to productivity shocks. Therefore, the larger is the proportion of goods prices that are preset along with wages, the less important and useful is nominal exchange rate flexibility for aiding short-run output stabilization. With short-run real wage rigidity, monetary policy affects only resource allocation through its impact on nominal and real interest rates – and hence investment – as implied by (5.24) and (5.25). In this case, the benefits from sharing national productivity risk internationally through fiscal insurance schemes would be greater than in the Walrasian equilibrium. But real wage rigidity also implies that the exchange rate regime has little to do with the welfare benefits of intro-ducing a fiscal insurance scheme.

Monetary union and fiscal insurance

The adoption of a common currency reduces the capacity of monetary authorities to influence labour market clearing in each country separately. Under the assumptions made so far, nominal exchange rate flexibility plays a key role for monetary stabilization with nominal wage rigidities. It allows coordinated monetary policies to implement the same equili-brium as would be achieved under perfectly flexible prices. The elimina-tion of nominal exchange rate flexibility and adoption of a common monetary policy can increase the benefits of a system of international fiscal insurance between member states of the EU. This section continues to use the basic portfolio-diversification model with idiosyncratic productivity shocks with the assumption that nominal output prices are flexible while nominal wages are predetermined.

Under a common currency, the demands for money by home and foreign residents satisfy the equilibrium conditions,

$$\frac{v'(M_t/P_t)}{u'(c_t)} = \frac{i_{t+1}}{1 + i_{t+1}} \quad \text{and} \quad \frac{v'(M_t^*/P_t^*)}{u'(c_t^*)} = \frac{i_{t+1}}{1 + i_{t+1}}.$$

$$(5.29)$$

Financial market integratation implies that the nominal rate of interest faced by the residents of different countries is the same. The money equi-librium condition becomes

$$M_t + M_t^* = M_t^s,$$

where M_t is home money demand, M_t^* is foreign money demand and M_t^s is the common supply of nominal balances. Equation (5.29) is written to allow for differences in consumer price levels, P_t and P_t^*, respectively. Under the assumptions of the previous section (a single good and fully integrated goods markets), these price levels are identical. The rest of the equations for the household equilibrium are unchanged.

With predetermined nominal wages, an increase in the money supply affects employment in each country by raising the nominal price of output for each. The response of labour demand to an increase in the nominal price level is given by differentiating the labour demand equation for each country as

$$\frac{d\ell_t}{\ell_t} = \frac{(f(k_t) - k_t f'(k_t))}{-k_t^2 f''(k_t)} \frac{dP_t}{P_t}$$

and

$$\frac{d\ell_t^*}{\ell_t^*} = \frac{(f(k_t^*) - k_t^* f'(k_t^*))}{-k_t^{*2} f''(k_t^*)} \frac{dP_t}{P_t}$$

where ℓ_t and ℓ_t^* satisfy the labour demand equations for predetermined capital stocks. The output of one country cannot be increased in response to an adverse asymmetric national productivity shock without raising the output of every member state of the monetary union. Monetary expansions and contractions can be used to stabilize output against common productivity shocks. Using the common monetary policy to stabilize employment in one country in the presence of asymmetric productivity shocks will destabilize employment for the other member states.

As a realistic objective for monetary policy under the euro, let the money supply respond to common aggregate shocks but not to idiosyncratic regional productivity disturbances. This allows a comparison of the impact of asymmetric shocks on national output under monetary union with that under a system of national monetary policies with flexible nominal exchange rates that seeks to stabilize employment. Under the flexible exchange rate regime, the national money supply reaction function satisfies the two relationships by raising or lowering P_t,

$$\frac{v'(\bar{\ell} - \ell_t)}{u'(c_t)} = \frac{W_t}{P_t} = \theta_t \left(f\left(\frac{\kappa_t}{\ell_t} \right) - \frac{\kappa_t}{\ell_t} f'\left(\frac{\kappa_t}{\ell_t} \right) \right). \tag{5.30}$$

Under monetary union, an idiosyncratic shock does not lead to a change in the price level and only the second equality holds.

For an adverse asymmetric productivity shock, output falls by more under monetary union than under national currencies with monetary policy coordination. How much more determines the increase in the welfare benefits of fiscal insurance. It also depends on the elasticity of labour supply with respect to real wages,

$$\eta = \frac{v'(\bar{\ell} - \ell_t)}{(\bar{\ell} - \ell_t)v''(\bar{\ell} - \ell_t)}.$$

If labour is perfectly elastic, there is no difference between the effect of asymmetric shocks on output with or without monetary union. Therefore, if labour supplies are fairly elastic in the short run, monetary unification will have a small impact on the capacity of governments to stabilize output against temporary asymmetric productivity disturbances.

Upper bounds on the costs of monetary unification for stabilization with idiosyncratic shocks can be characterized by assuming that increases in output volatility do not lead to responsive changes in the structure of production through the allocation of investment. A simple calculation can be done by letting the aggregate national production function be given by

$$y_t = \theta_t \kappa_t^\alpha \ell_t^{1-\alpha}$$

and assuming that productivity shocks are distributed log-normally. The approximation also assumes that under monetary union the common monetary policy does not respond to asymmetric output shocks, while with separate national currencies monetary policies are perfectly coordinated to take advantage of nominal exchange rate flexibility in stabilizing output.

When separate money supplies are used to maintain labour market equilibrium, differentiation of (5.30) for the Cobb–Douglas production function gives the response of equilibrium employment to a productivity shock as

$$\frac{d\ell_t}{\ell_t} = \left(\frac{1}{\eta_t} + \alpha\right)^{-1} \frac{d\theta_t}{\theta_t},$$

and the response of output as

$$\frac{dy_t}{y_t} = \frac{d\theta_t}{\theta_t} + (1-\alpha)\frac{d\ell_t}{\ell_t} = \left(\frac{1+\eta_t}{1+\alpha\eta_t}\right)\frac{d\theta_t}{\theta_t}.$$

Under monetary union, labour demand is determined by the equality of the real wage facing producers and marginal productivity of labor,

$$\frac{W_t}{P_t} = \theta_t(1-\alpha)\kappa_t^\alpha \ell_t^{-\alpha},$$

with both the price level P_t and the nominal wage rate, W_t remaining constant as θ_t varies. This implies that the quantity $\theta_t \ell_t^{-\alpha}$ remains constant, and labour demand and output vary with productivity shocks according to

$$\frac{d\ell_t}{\ell_t} = \frac{1}{\alpha} \frac{d\theta_t}{\theta_t} \quad \text{and} \quad \frac{dy_t}{y_t} = \frac{1}{\alpha} \frac{d\theta_t}{\theta_t}.$$

If labour supply is perfectly elastic, then monetary union does not affect short-run output volatility. The other extreme is achieved if households supply labour perfectly inelastically. When monetary policy responds to regional shocks, as in a constrained-efficient equilibrium with nominal exchange rate flexibility, ℓ_t always equals the fixed supply of labour desired by households, and output varies proportionately to θ_t. In that case, money supply increases and decreases have the greatest impact on output when they are chosen to achieve labour market equilibrium. Under monetary union without monetary accommodation of asymmetric shocks, labour demand varies with productivity and output varies in proportion to $\theta_t^{1/\alpha}$. For a share of labour in GDP equal to two-thirds, the percentage standard deviation of output is three times greater with monetary unification than without if the labour supply elasticity equals zero and twice if the elasticity is one.

Monetary union should increase the variability of output under asymmetric productivity shocks. The real returns to financial claims to shares of national output should consequently increase. If the residents of each country held the optimal portfolio before the elimination of national currencies and intra-union exchange rates, then no further risk-sharing opportunities arise. Each household would already be exposed only to aggregate risk and not to idiosyncratic risk. This does not mean to say that the equilibrium without independent monetary policies is efficient. Full diversification with perfectly flexible relative prices or the equivalent of perfectly coordinated output-stabilizing national monetary policies achieves a first-best allocation. With monetary union, the labour market distortions caused by nominal wage rigidity remain. This is because monetary policies under a common currency cannot be used to clear all national labour markets simultaneously.

A system of fiscal insurance cannot achieve the first-best either. Redistributing spending power between the residents of different countries does not have an asymmetric effect on employment across borders with a single good. State-contingent redistribution policies therefore cannot raise employment and output for one member state suffering an adverse productivity shock without also raising it for another country that is not.

Fiscal transfers can have differential effects on employment across countries in a monetary union with more than one good if consumption demands vary with residence. State-contingent redistributions of income change relative expenditures on different commodities. When the home country experiences an adverse productivity shock and receives a fiscal transfer from the foreign country, the relative price of home products generally rises in response to an increase in demand if there is a home consumption-spending bias. This can cause domestic employment to rise and foreign employment to decrease. The common monetary policy can be used to balance the effect on foreign employment. However, households smooth their consumption intertemporally. A fiscal transfer to the home country made contingent on a low realization of θ_t represents an increase in the permanent income of the home country, so that demand for the home country's consumption bundle rises in period t and in expectation for future periods. This shifts investment during period t toward the home country because the expected future price of home relative to foreign goods rises. The investment effects of the policy can be welfare reducing. For example, suppose that productivity shocks are serially correlated; a fiscal insurance scheme in a monetary union will then tend to destabilize output.

This contrasts with how a monetary transfer to home residents under a flexible exchange rate serves to raise home output to clear the home labour market. In that case, a money transfer leads to an increase in the home-currency price level, raising the nominal producer price and labour demand. The increase in the value of output produced in the home country raises real income for both countries equiproportionately with unconstrained asset trade. Output-stabilizing monetary policies therefore increase the relative supply of home goods without changing the distribution of real income across households with heterogeneous tastes. For homothetic preferences, the relative price of home goods falls; that is, a monetary expansion causes a nominal and real depreciation. If risk-sharing is incomplete due to the inability of households to sell claims to labour income, then aggregate spending patterns are affected by national monetary policies. But in this case, the constrained optimum can be achieved using monetary policies.

Fiscal insurance schemes under monetary union do not replicate the allocation of resources that can be implemented under flexible exchange rates. As already noted these schemes introduce a distortion to capital accumulation because they affect employment by changing the pattern of consumer spending across tradeable commodities and over time. If household portfolios are fully diversified internationally *a priori*, then the welfare benefit of increased employment is reduced – possibly reversed – by the welfare costs of investment distortions.

It was demonstrated that fiscal insurance is a first-best policy instrument if the constraint on international portfolio diversification (caused by the absence of trade in labour income-based assets) was *a priori* binding. With each labour market clearing in every period, fiscal insurance exactly filled the role of the missing market in claims to labour earnings – that is, fiscal transfers are equivalent to dividend payments on GDP-based assets. To attain an efficient allocation, if the constraint on asset trade is binding in a market equilibrium, these transfers simply match the shares of labour income that would be paid to the residents of each country by the other country in a fully diversified Pareto-optimum. The introduction of a state-contingent transfer scheme does affect the pattern of consumption spending and investment with more than one good and home consumption bias; these these effects, however, are consistent with full portfolio diversification and efficient equilibrium investment in each sector for each country.

With nominal wage rigidities and monetary union, a fiscal insurance scheme can provide the benefits of increased risk-sharing if the constraint on diversification by households binds; can also reduce labour market disequilibrium. In this case, it is one policy instrument seeking to address two distortions. This suggests that the benefits of fiscal insurance in the absence of trade in claims to future labour earnings are increased by monetary union – that is, support is found here for the argument that monetary union raises the incentives to introduce inter-regional fiscal insurance. The importance of these welfare benefits depends on the how responsive relative prices are to fiscal redistribution, the elasticity of output supplies and marginal propensity to consume from permanent income.

The empirical observations that international risk-sharing is much less extensive than feasible with existing markets contradicts this line of thinking. Suppose that the portfolio diversification observed is optimal subject to transactions costs (for exactness, assume these to be convex); the marginal benefit of increasing the holding of shares in the foreign country's capital stock just equals the marginal cost of doing so for home-country residents. As shown above, the variance of share returns rises with monetary union. Households will therefore diversify their portfolios more after monetary union than before, and the same marginal condition for optimal household portfolio selection will hold. So, what happens if a fiscal insurance scheme is added? It distorts investment decisions relative to what they are under the optimal portfolio selection of households facing transactions costs. Taking the degree of diversification of savings in international asset markets as revealed to be preferred by households given unobserved transactions or similar costs (assuming these are convex) implies that fiscal insurance has a negative welfare effect through investment that could offset the benefits of stabilizing current output against asymmetric regional shocks.

Monetary union and the need for fiscal insurance with market segmentation

Deviations from purchasing power parity (PPP) and the law of one price for many individual tradable goods are well documented. Goldberg and Knetter (1997) survey the empirical evidence that goods are priced-to-market, and there are many models of pricing with market segmentation that rationalize failures of the law of one price for traded goods (see Feenstra, 1995). Most recently, Engel (1998) finds that relative prices are more volatile across borders within the EU than within each country, controlling for transport and other transactions costs using distance.[7] Essentially, the domestic currency prices of consumer goods in the EU respond slowly to exchange rate changes and are much less volatile than nominal exchange rates.

Adding incomplete exchange rate pass-through turns out to reduce the welfare costs of monetary unification with nominal rigidities. With commodity market segmentation, nominal exchange rate flexibility becomes less important for enabling short-run monetary stabilization of national outputs in the presence of idiosyncratic productivity disturbances. By explaining these claims, this section shows that the case for a system of fiscal insurance as a replacement for separate monetary policies under monetary union is further reduced. It also shows that the extent to which goods and services markets are integrated across borders is an important concern for assessing the welfare case against monetary union.

In the model, the failure of exchange rate pass-through means that (5.26) no longer holds. Again, nominal rigidities are represented by assuming that nominal wages are set one-period in advance of employment and that nominal goods prices are flexible so that real wages can respond to changes in the supply of money. All the other equilibrium conditions of the basic model with nominal wage rigidities hold for either a flexible exchange rate regime or monetary union, as appropriate. Resource allocation under flexible exchange rates is discussed first.

In the absence of exchange rate pass-through, exchange rate fluctuations do not directly change consumer relative prices, but they can affect national income through the return to equities calculated in terms of the appropriate consumption price index for shareholders. Let wages be set in domestic currency and consumption take place at domestic currency prices. The value of a claim on a firm's capital depends on the proportions of output that are sold at home and abroad. The total revenue in domestic

---

[7.] Engel (1998) also discusses the usefulness of nominal exchange rate flexibility in an IS-LM version of the Mundell–Fleming model.

currency units of home production if firms do not hedge against exchange rate risk is given by

$$p_t^p Y_t = (p_t(1 - x_t) + s_t p_t^* x_t)\theta_t \ell_t f(k_t) \tag{5.31}$$

where p_t^p indicates the producer price index for period t and x_t equals gross exports. Nominal wages are given by

$$W_t = E_t[(p_t(1 - x_t) + s_t p_t^* x_t)\theta_t(f(k_t) - k_t f'(k_t))]), \tag{5.32}$$

and the net returns to capital equal $(p_t(1 - x_t) + s_t p_t^* x_t)\theta_t f'(k_t)$. The earnings of foreign capital denominated in units of foreign currency equal

$$\left(p_t^*(1 - x_t^*) + x_t^* \frac{p_t}{s_t}\right)\theta_t^* f^{*'}(k_t^*).$$

Imperfect competition and market segmentation could be used to model pricing behaviour in each national market, but it would unnecessarily complicate the exposition. Assume that imports and exports are imperfect substitutes, so that $c_t = \phi(c_{1t}, c_{2t})$ is the home country's consumption index defined over home and foreign goods, respectively. With prices set in each market, adverse productivity shocks will tend to be associated with domestic currency depreciation with separate currencies (this depends on the endogenous monetary policy response). If this correlation holds, the variability of firm earnings can be reduced by international goods market segmentation. With currency-adjusted producer prices unequal across borders, nominal and other financial shocks can create significant exchange rate risk for firms so that they have an incentive to hedge against exchange risk in financial markets. Hedging does not affect the arguments made here.

Under these additional assumptions, the asset-pricing relationship implies that investment in home capital satisfies

$$1 = E_t\left[\frac{\beta u'(c_{t+1})}{u'(c_t)}\left(\frac{p_{t+1}^p}{P_{t+1}}\right)(1 + \theta_{t+1}f'(k_{t+1}))\right], \tag{5.33}$$

and foreign investment satisfies

$$\frac{s_t P_t^*}{P_t} = E_t\left[\frac{\beta u'(c_{t+1})}{u'(c_t)}\left(\frac{s_{t+1}p_{t+1}^{*p}}{P_{t+1}}\right)(1 + \theta_{t+1}^* f^{*'}(k_{t+1}^*))\right], \tag{5.34}$$

if home-country residents hold claims on capital in each country. The term,

$$\left(\frac{p_{t+1}^p}{P_{t+1}}\right)(1 + \theta_{t+1}f'(k_{t+1})),$$

is the return to home-country capital in terms of home consumption. Capital goods can be taken as identical composites of the two commodities for each country. Equations (5.33) and (5.34) imply that exchange rate flexibility reduces the variance of the returns to households' holdings of equity claims in terms of their consumption bundle with respect to productivity shocks.

The labour market equilibrium conditions for the home and foreign countries are given by

$$\frac{v'(\bar{\ell}-\ell_t)}{u'(c_t)} = \frac{W_t}{P_t}, \qquad \frac{W_t}{p_t^p} = \theta_t\left(f\left(\frac{\kappa_t}{\ell_t}\right) - \frac{\kappa_t}{\ell_t}f'\left(\frac{\kappa_t}{\ell_t}\right)\right) \qquad (5.35)$$

and

$$\frac{v'(\bar{\ell}^*-\ell_t^*)}{u'(c_t^*)} = \frac{W_t^*}{P_t^*}, \qquad \frac{W_t^*}{p_t^{p*}} = \theta_t^*\left(f\left(\frac{\kappa_t^*}{\ell_t^*}\right) - \frac{\kappa_t^*}{\ell_t^*}f'\left(\frac{\kappa_t^*}{\ell_t^*}\right)\right),$$

$$(5.36)$$

respectively.

Equilibrium for the money market requires

$$\frac{v'(M_t/P_t)}{u'(c_t)} = \frac{i_{t+1}}{1+i_{t+1}}, \qquad \frac{v'(M_t^*/P_t^*)}{u'(c_t^*)} = \frac{i_{t+1}^*}{1+i_{t+1}^*}, \qquad (5.37)$$

and uncovered interest parity (UIP) (5.25).

The consumer price indices, P_t and P_t^*, for each country depend on the domestic prices of the two goods as

$$P_t = P(p_{1t}, p_{2t}) \qquad \text{and} \qquad P_t^* = P^*(p_{1t}^*, p_{2t}^*),$$

respectively. With goods market segmentation, nominal wage rigidity and nominal goods prices flexible, the real wage rates in each country can adjust independently of each other even if the exchange rate is permanently fixed – that is, with the exchange rate constant, nominal interest rates, i_{t+1}^* and i_{t+1}, are equal, but P_t and P_t^* can move separately and p_{1t} and p_{2t} do not have to equal $s_t p_{1t}^*$ and $s_t p_{2t}^*$, respectively, through continuous goods market arbitrage. With a permanently fixed nominal exchange rate, the real exchange rate defined in terms of consumer price indices, P_t/P_t^*, can still change with the common money supply to clear both labour markets simultaneously.

Two essential assumptions are being made here. The first is that nominal wages are preset in each country but nominal goods prices are not. A monetary expansion immediately increases the nominal price level through money market clearing, which in turn translates into a rise in the nominal producer price of output lowering the real wage rate for the firm. The second is pricing-to-market. The relative prices p_{1t}/p_{1t}^* and p_{2t}/p_{2t}^* are endogenous. The addition of pricing-to-market leads to the conclusion that monetary union does not affect the capacity of monetary authorities to influence resource allocation in the presence of asymmetric national productivity shocks. Under these conditions, the welfare benefits of fiscal insurance are identical with or without monetary union. Asymmetric productivity shocks provide the same basis for introducing state-contingent international fiscal transfers before the elimination of national currencies as after. The observed absence of exchange rate pass-through argues against the claim that fiscal insurance is needed to compensate for the loss of nominal exchange rate flexibility under monetary union.

For the United States, the evidence suggests there are nominal rigidities but that nominal prices and wages are not highly correlated. Nominal wage and price movements are more highly correlated within each member state of the EU. Real wages are more rigid in Europe than in North America.[8] Movements in the prices of consumer goods and services are imperfectly correlated across regions of the United States and between European countries.

Introducing correlations between nominal wages and nominal prices allows nominal exchange rate flexibility to serve an essential role for the efficacy of monetary policy in short-run adjustment under pricing-to-market. With real wage flexibility and pricing-to-market, the nominal producer prices in one country can move independently of producer prices in the other through uncorrelated movements in national consumer price levels under a common currency. In this case, nominal exchange rate flexibility is an additional way to achieve the same adjustment in real wage rates but a redundant instrument of policy. If real wages are indexed to national consumer prices, then producer prices can adjust independently of each other through international trade receipts expressed in domestic currency. The second term in the expression,

$$p_t^p = p_{1t}(1 - x_t) + s_t p_{1t}^* x_t,$$

rather than the first allows producer real wages to adjust, although (5.35) and (5.36) show that the labour market does not clear because household real wages are rigid. Flexible exchange rates and separate currency are a partial substitute for real wage flexibility when there is pricing-to-market. Their usefulness in this regard rises with the openness of national economies conditional on the degree of goods market integration.

8. See, for example, Eichengreen (1992a) for typical comparisons of wage–price correlations.

This suggests that nominal exchange rate flexibility reduces the cost of real wage rigidity for allocative efficiency. The adoption of a common currency should raise the welfare costs of indexing nominal wages to the price level. If the result of monetary union for Europe is a significant reduction in the extent of real indexation, then monetary policy could end up being more effective as a tool of short-run stabilization. With nominal goods prices flexible and markets in similar goods incompletely arbitraged across regions, regional asymmetries will yield asymmetric short-run real wage movements in response to a common monetary policy. On the other hand, if real wage rigidity persists under monetary union, then the benefits of a fiscal insurance scheme appear along with the intertemporal welfare costs discussed in the previous section.

Conclusions

The general equilibrium model allows an analysis of the argument that monetary union raises the welfare benefits of introducing a system of fiscal insurance between member states. Progressive changes in the model structure enable us to understand how fiscal insurance and monetary unification affect resource allocation in the presence of real productivity disturbances. This helps to identify a possible rationale for the idea that fiscal insurance is needed to compensate for independent monetary policies as an instrument for short-run output stabilization with aymmetric national productivity shocks.

The monetary economy with perfectly flexible prices provides a benchmark for understanding the welfare gains from international fiscal insurance for diversifying the idiosyncratic share of production risk. In the model, international asset markets are incomplete in the sense that households cannot trade claims to future labour income. The benefits of introducing fiscal insurance in this case are the same as the benefits from further international diversification of household asset portfolios, so that these arise only if the constraint on asset trade is binding. Introducing nominal rigidities with separate national currencies and flexible exchange rates did not change the welfare economics of fiscal insurance. By comparing the implications of the model with the empirical observation of a strong home bias in the portfolio allocation of national saving, the analysis predicts no incentive to introduce fiscal insurance with independent monetary policies.

Monetary union can raise the benefits for allocative efficiency that can be gained from a system of inter-regional fiscal insurance. This follows from the well understood point that a common monetary policy cannot achieve labour market equilibrium in each member country with asymmetric productivity shocks. However, fiscal insurance does not replace coordinated separate monetary policies; it brings additional distortions to the allocation of resources intertemporally that must be counted against the potential gains. The strongest case for fiscal insurance arises when markets for goods and services are internationally integrated and real wages are responsive to money supplies.

The next embellishment of the model allows goods markets not to be arbitraged continuously across member states of the monetary union. This is an empirically important case, as many studies of exchange rate pass-through have demonstrated. Monetary union does not increase the welfare case for fiscal insurance with pricing-to-market in the absence of indexation of nominal wages to nominal price levels. The model also implies that market segmentation within the European Community may enable the current flexible exchange rate regime to aid labour market equilibrium in a restricted way despite rigid real wages in terms of domestic consumer prices. However, wage indexation does not provide a convincing argument that monetary union will raise the benefits of fiscal insurance under consumer market segmentation.

This chapter concentrates on the role of fiscal insurance schemes in replacement of nominal exchange rate flexibility in the presence of asymmetric productivity disturbances. Others have considered the macroeconomic benefits of monetary union for providing fiscal and monetary discipline (see McKinnon, 1997a, 1997b, for example) or eliminating the adverse effects of nominal and financial market disturbances for allocative efficiency (see Buiter, 1997, for example). Another argument that fiscal insurance schemes may be inessential for promoting allocative efficiency with nominal rigidities and asymmetric real shocks is given by Kletzer (1997) and Buiter and Kletzer (1997). In an overlapping-generations framework, they show that fiscal insurance may add little if anything to the capacity of policy instruments already available to national fiscal authorities for alleviating short-run disequilibrium caused by temporary nominal rigidities. Eichengreen (1997) provides a political economy perspective that fiscal federalism may not be necessary under EMU.

References

Backus, D., Kehoe, P. and Kydland, F. (1992). 'International Real Business Cycles', *Journal of Political Economy*, 100: 745–75
Bayoumi, T. and Eichengreen, B. (1993). 'Shocking Aspects of European Monetary Unification', in F. Giavazzi and F. Torres, (eds.), *Adjustment and Growth in the European Monetary Union*, Cambridge, Cambridge University Press: 153–229

Bayoumi, T. and Masson, P. (1994). 'Fiscal flows in the United States and Canada: Lessons for Monetary Union in Europe', *CEPR Discussion Paper*, 1057

Bayoumi, T. and Thomas, A. (1995). 'Relative Prices and Economic Adjustment in the United States and the European Union: A Real Story about EMU,' *IMF Staff Papers*, 42: 108–133

Buiter, W. (1997). 'The Economic Case for Monetary Union in the European Union', in C. Deissenberg, R. F. Owen and D. Olph (eds.), *European Economic Integration*, Supplement to the *Review of International Economics*, 5: 10–35.

Buiter, W., Corsetti, G. and Roubini, N (1993). 'Excessive Deficits: Sense and Nonsense in the Treaty of Maastricht', *Economic Policy*, 16: 57–100

Buiter, W. and Kletzer, K. (1991). 'Fiscal Implications of a Common Currency', in A. Giovannini and C. Mayer, (eds.), *European Financial Integration*, New York: Cambridge University Press, 221–44

Cole, H. and Obstfeld, M. (1991). 'Commodity Trade and International Risk Sharing: How Much do Financial Markets Matter?', *Journal of Monetary Economics*, 28: 3–24

Corsetti, G. and Pesenti, P. (1998). 'Welfare and Macroeconomic Interdependence', Department of Economics, Princeton University, mimeo

Courchêne, T. (1993). 'Reflections on Canadian Federalism: Are There Implications for the European Economic and Monetary Union?' in 'The Economics of Community Public Finance', *European Economy*, Special Issue, 4: 23–166

De Grauwe, P. and Vanhaverbeke, W. (1991). 'Is Europe an Optimum currency Area? Evidence from Regional Data', *CEPR Discussion Paper*, 555

Dehesa, G. de la and Krugman, P. (1993). 'Monetary Union, Regional Cohesion and Regional Shocks', in G. de la Dehesa, A. Giovannini, M. Guitian and R. Portes, (eds.), *The Monetary Future of Europe*, Cambridge: Cambridge University Press

Eichengreen, B. (1992a), 'Should the Maastricht Treaty be Saved?', *Princeton, Studies in International Finance*, 74

(1992b). 'Is Europe an Optimum Currency Area?', in S. Borner, and H. Gruble, eds., *The European Community after 1992: The View from the Outside*, London: Macmillan

(1997). *European Monetary Unification: Theory, Practice and Analysis*. Cambridge. Mass. MIT Press.

Eichengreen, B. and von Hagen, J. (1995). 'Fiscal Policy and Monetary Union: Federalism, Fiscal Restrictions and the No-bailout Rule', Kiel Institute of World Economics, conference paper

Eichengreen, B. and Wyplosz, C. (1993). 'The Unstable EMS', *Brookings Papers on Economic Activity*, 1: 51–124

Engel, C. (1998). 'A Retrial in the Case against the EMU', Department of Economics, University of Washington, mimeo

Feenstra, R. (1995). 'Estimating the Effects of Trade Policy', in G. Grossman and K. Rogoff, (eds.), *Handbook of International Economics*, 3, Amsterdam: North-Holland

Feldstein, M. (1997). 'The Political Economy of the European Economic and Monetary Union: Political Sources of an Economic Liability', *Journal of Economic Perspectives*, 11: 23–42

Goldberg, P. and Knetter, M. (1997). 'Goods Prices and Exchange Rates: What have we Learned?', *Journal of Economic Literature*, 35: 1243–72

Hutchison, M. and Kletzer, K. (1995). 'Fiscal Convergence Criteria, Factor Mobility and Credibility in Transition to Monetary Union in Europe', in B. Eichengreen, J. Frieden and von Hagen, J. (eds.), *Monetary and Fiscal Policy in an Integrated Europe*, Berlin: Springer-Verlag

Ingram, J. (1959). 'State and Regional Payments Mechanisms', *Quarterly Journal of Economics*, 73: 619–32

(1973). 'The Case for European Monetary Integration', *Princeton Essays in International Finance*, 98

Ishiyama, Y. (1975). 'The Theory of Optimum Currency Areas: A Survey', *IMF Staff Papers*, 22

Jensen, S. E. H. (1998). 'Nominal Stability, Real Convergence, and Fiscal Transfers in a Monetary Union', in chapter 6 in this volume

Kenen, P. B. (1969). 'The Theory of Optimum Currency Areas: An Eclectic View', in R. A. Mundell and A. K. Swoboda, (eds.), *Monetary Problems in the International Economy*, Chicago: University of Chicago Press

(1992), *EMU After Maastricht*, Washington, DC: Group of Thirty

Kletzer, K. (1997). 'Macroeconomic Stabilization with a Common Currency: Does European Monetary Unification Create a Need for Fiscal Insurance or Federalism?', in B. Eichengreen and J. Frieden, (eds.), *The Political Economy of European Integration: The Challenges Ahead*, Ann Arbor: University of Michigan Press

Kletzer, K. and Buiter, W. (1997). 'Monetary Union and the Role of Automatic Stabilizers', in J.-O. Hairault, P.-Y. Hénin and F. Portier, (eds.), *Business Cycles and Macroeconomic Stability: Should We Rebuild Built-in Stabilizers?*, Dordrecht: Kluwer: 109–47

Krugman, P. (1993). 'Lessons of Massachusetts for EMU', in F. Torres and F. Giavazzi, (eds.), *Adjustment and Growth in the European Monetary Union*, Cambridge: Cambridge University Press

Lucas, R. E., Jr. (1982). 'Interest Rates and Currency Prices in a Two-Country World', *Journal of Monetary Economics*, 10: 335–60

McKinnon, R. (1963). 'Optimum Currency Areas', *American Economic Review*, 53: 717-25

(1997a). 'Monetary Regimes, Government Borrowing Constraints, and Market-preserving Federalism: Implications for EMU', in T. Courchêne, (ed.), *The Nation State in a Global/Information Era: Policy Challenges*, Kingston, Ontario: Queen's University: 101–41

(1997b). 'EMU as a Device for Collective Fiscal Retrenchment', *American Economic Review Papers and Proceedings*, 87: 227–9

Mélitz, J. (1991). 'A Suggested Reformulation of the Theory of Optimal Currency Areas', *CEPR Discussion Paper*, 590

Mundell, R. A. (1961). 'A theory of Optimum Currency Areas', *American Economic Review*, 51: 657–75

Neumeyer, P. (1998). 'Currencies and the Allocation of Risk: The Welfare Economics of a Monetary Union', *American Economic Review*, 88: 246–59

Obstfeld, M. (1997a). 'Europe's Gamble', *Brookings Papers on Economic Activity*, 2: 241–317

　(1997b). 'Open-economy Macroeconomics: Developments in Theory and Policy', Institute for Economic Research, Queen's University, Kingston, Ontario, *Discussion Paper*, 958

Obstfeld, M. and Peri, G. (1998). 'Regional Non-adjustment and Fiscal Policy: Lessons for EMU', *NEBR Working Paper*, 6431

Obstfeld, M. and Rogoff, K. (1995). 'Exchange Rate Dynamics Redux', *Journal of Political Economy*, 103: 624–60

Sachs, J. and Sala-i-Martin, X. (1992). 'Fiscal Federalism and Optimum Currency Areas: Evidence for Europe from the United States', *CEPR Discussion Paper*, 632

Tesar, L. (1995). 'Evaluating the Gains from International Risk Sharing', *Carnegie–Rochester Conference Series on Public Policy*, 42: 95–143

van Rompuy, P., Abraham, F. and Heremans, D. (1991). 'Economic Federalism and the EMU', *European Economy*, Special Edition, 1: 109–35

von Hagen, J. (1992). 'Fiscal Arrangements in a Monetary Union: Evidence from the US', in D. Fair and C. de Boissieu, (eds.), *Fiscal Policy, Taxes and the Financial System in an Increasingly Integrated* Europe, Boston: Kluwer Academic

von Hagen, J. and Hammond G. (1995). 'Regional Insurance against Asymmetric Shocks: An Empirical Study for the European Community', *CEPR Discussion Paper*, 1170.

6 Nominal stability, real convergence and fiscal transfers in a monetary union

Svend E. Hougaard Jensen

The issues

The annual efficiency gains from European Economic and Monetary Union (EMU) have been estimated to amount to between 1.4 per cent and 1.7 per cent of GDP (EC Commission, 1990). These gains would result from lower transactions costs for firms and consumers, reduction (and, eventually, elimination) of information costs and price discrimination between countries and dynamic effects on trade and investment according to comparative advantage and scale economies. While certainly worthwhile, these benefits seem rather small and, for countries being particularly exposed to shocks, the costs of giving up the exchange rate as a shock absorber might well exceed the benefits.

The presence of shocks may thus be of critical importance for the economic success of EMU. Against this background, a number of questions arise. First, since many think of EMU as a regime shift, would the formation of EMU diminish the frequency and magnitude of shocks, and would they become more symmetric? Second, if shocks are likely also to remain important after EMU, and if no tendency for these shocks to become more symmetric can be observed, would policy makers then be allowed to respond to them? Third, if restrictions are imposed on both fiscal and monetary policy, would there be enough wage/price flexibility and/or labour mobility to act as alternative shock absorbers?

The answers to these questions seem, in view of recent evidence, less promising for the prospects of EMU. Indeed, a number of studies suggest

The research underlying this chapter was initiated when I visited the Economics Department at the University of California, Santa Cruz (Spring 1997). I thank Michael Hutchison, Kenneth Kletzer, David Vines and, in particular, Andrew Hughes Hallett and Neil Rankin, for helpful discussion. Martin Nielsen provided valuable research assistance. Financial support from the Danish National Research Foundation is gratefully acknowledged. The opinions expressed in this chapter are those of the author and are not necessarily shared by the Ministry of Business and Industry.

that asymmetric shocks are fairly important and likely to remain so in most countries of the European Union (EU) (Bayoumi and Eichengreen, 1993; Bayoumi and Prassad, 1995; Christodoulakis, Dimelis and Kollintzas, 1995). Similarly, factor mobility is relatively low, and labour mobility especially is considerably smaller in the EU than in the United States (Boltho, 1989; Begg, 1995). And even if shocks became more symmetric, there is evidence of significant asymmetries in economic structures (Demertzis, Hughes Hallett and Rummel, 1997), indicating that macroeconomic performances would diverge even in the presence of symmetric shocks. Moreover, the adjustment of real wages in Europe appears to be rather rigid (Bruno and Sachs, 1985; Manasse, 1991; OECD, 1994). Economic structures in Europe thus seem insufficiently geared to easily cope with shocks, whether symmetric or asymmetric.

Monetary policy à la Maastricht would be directed at price stability rather than output stabilization. Irrespective of what the target of monetary policy is, however, a *common* monetary policy cannot ensure against asymmetric shocks. The obvious question then is what fiscal policy can do to counter such shocks. Several scholars have analysed the extent to which existing federal budgets serve to stabilize individual parts of the economy (Sachs and Sala-i-Martin, 1992; Bayoumi and Masson, 1995). The general finding is that while automatic regional stabilization is considerable in mature federations (such as the United States, Canada, or Australia), it is currently fairly small in the EU. So little stabilization can be expected from the central EU budget.[1] The burden of output stabilization in a European monetary union will thus primarily rest with the *national* fiscal authorities.

The scope for national fiscal policies may be limited, however. Since public finances of only very few EU countries actually respect the Maastricht fiscal criteria, most member states would have to modify their fiscal policy considerably if they wanted to participate in the final stage of EMU. Indeed, if fiscal reductions in line with the Maastricht criteria were undertaken, recent empirical evidence shows that Europe might well be forced into deflation and recession (Hughes Hallett and McAdam, 1998; von Hagen and Lutz, 1996). Moreover, even if countries managed to bring their debt and deficits down sufficiently to qualify for entrance into EMU, the debt overhang might still restrict the room of

---

[1] Indeed, with the common EU budget constituting only little more than 1 per cent of total GDP in the EU, it is difficult to envisage that it would have the capacity to exercise any significant redistribution across member states. For example, the MacDougall Report (MacDougall, 1977) found that an EC budget of at least 5 per cent of EC GDP would be required in order for a monetary union to provide enough redistributive capacity to make it viable.

manoeuvre. It could therefore take quite some time for these countries before they were in a position which would allow them to respond to asymmetric shocks through fiscal policy (Allsopp *et al.* 1997; Jensen, 1997).

Motivated by a concern for macroeconomic stabilization and convergence of real economic variables such as output and employment, this chapter examines an alternative framework for the conduct of fiscal policy in an EMU where (1) the size of the common EU budget is likely to remain small, (2) fiscal policy is prevented from fulfilling its stabilization function at the level of the member state, and (3) the economic structure remains relatively inflexible. Provided that asymmetric shocks also remain significant, it seems fair to assume that there will be a need for some kind of shock absorber. Indeed, several scholars have emphasized the importance of the business cycle for the stability of fixed exchange rate systems (Eichengreen and Wyplosz, 1993; De Grauwe, 1994), an insight which may carry over to monetary union. In any case, while most of the EMU debate has so far focused on nominal convergence, there is a growing concern about real convergence. In this context, the design of fiscal policy is crucial. Moreover, economic theory suggests that the case for international fiscal cooperation is much stronger than the one for monetary cooperation (Sheen, 1992; Hughes Hallett and Ma, 1996).

Inspired by recent proposals, I shall consider the macroeconomics of an inter-member fiscal redistribution mechanism (Williamson, 1990; van der Ploeg, 1991; Eichengreen, 1992; Italianer and Vanheukelen, 1993; von Hagen and Hammond, 1997). The basic idea of such a scheme is to stabilize the effects of asymmetric shocks through a kind of international risk-sharing: whenever the monetary union is hit by a shock which causes divergence in real economic performance, international transfer payments are triggered with the aim of restoring convergence. It should be stressed that the transfer scheme discussed here is relevant only for short-term stabilization (or insurance) purposes and should be kept sharply distinct from schemes aiming at structural development of, say, poor regions (Bayoumi and Masson, 1995).

The chapter is organized as follows. The next section introduces a stylized model of a monetary union; I then explore how the business cycle may be affected by asymmetric shocks and discuss the design and performance of an international fiscal transfer system; the final section concludes.

The model

I model a monetary union of two countries. Think of country 1 as Germany (the core) and country 2 as the rest of the union (the periphery).

Apart from being subject to asymmetric shocks, the two countries are otherwise completely symmetric. There are international linkages through markets for money, bonds and goods, whereas labour is internationally immobile.

Monetary policy is managed by a common central bank (ECB) which issues a single currency. The ECB is assumed to operate a flexible exchange rate *vis-à-vis* the rest of the world.[2] Hence its stock of foreign exchange reserves is constant and may, for simplicity, be set equal to zero. In the long-run, the ECB's domestic credit expansion is also assumed constant and equal to zero. This allows for a stationary long-run equilibrium with price stability. In the short run, however, the money supply may respond to variations in some domestic target variable. Given the absence of risk and uncertainty, there can only be one interest rate, and the demand for the single currency can be expressed as a function of the average level of nominal income and the common nominal interest rate

$$d = p_a + y_a - \lambda i \tag{6.1}$$

where d is the money supply, p_a is the average price level, y_a is the average output level and i is the common nominal interest rate.[3]

There are two tradeable goods in the model, one produced by each country. The two goods are imperfect substitutes, reflecting the fact that the goods markets are not fully integrated internationally. Output is determined by aggregate demand

$$y_i = \pm \alpha(p_2 - p_1) - \gamma(i - \dot{p}_i) + \sigma y_j \pm \eta n + v_i; \quad i,j = 1,2; \quad i \neq j. \tag{6.2}$$

Specifically, each country's demand is, in the usual way, a function of relative output prices, the real interest rate (the nominal interest rate deflated by the expected rate of inflation of the domestic price level) and foreign output. In addition, aggregate demand is influenced by an international fiscal transfer, n, and a demand shock, v. Since this chapter is mainly about 'shocks' and fiscal policy, let me be more detailed here.

I restrict attention to shocks in savings and investment behaviour. Indeed, much of the turmoil in the EMS in the early 1990s has been caused by 'IS' shocks: German unification and huge swings in the UK savings

---

[2] The (real and financial) interactions with the world outside the union are not modelled. This simplification may be justified by the fact that intra-EU trade by far dominates EU trade with the rest of the world.

[3] All variables other than interest rates are in natural logarithms and expressed as deviations from a steady-state growth path.

rate are relevant examples.[4] In any case, one would expect monetary union to provide insulation against financial disturbances, and it is doubtful whether fiscal policy should at all be activated in response to supply shocks.[5] Since the analysis is limited to asymmetric shocks, I also ignore shocks to world inflation and interest rates which typically would be common to members of the union.

I shall further assume that the shocks are previously unanticipated by all agents in both countries. The expected (net) contribution rate to the fiscal transfer scheme would therefore be zero. This assumption also reduces the system's exposure to moral hazard. For example, it could be argued that if fiscal transfers were to be paid also if shocks were foreseen, the incentives for governments to take (possibly painful) remedies to overcome the underlying structural weaknesses would be too weak. A similar criticism could be raised if the system also applies to permanent shocks. Hence I assume that, after having hit the economy at $t = 0$, the shock dies away exponentially – that is, $v(t) = v(0) \exp(-\rho t)$, where ρ measures the persistence of the shock: if ρ equals zero, it is permanent, and if ρ goes to infinity it will be felt only as a 'blip'.

Broadly in line with the empirical evidence, I abstract from the possibility that the private sector can borrow against the prospect of future adjustment and thereby smooth the adjustment (Campbell and Mankiw, 1989; Deaton, 1992). Similarly, I assume that there is no flexibility for fiscal policy at the national level. This is a rigid – and, admittedly, an extreme but still possible – Maastricht interpretation. In fact, it is what the European Monetary Institute (EMI) intends to insist on (Duisenberg, 1997).

While the domestic automatic fiscal stabilizers have been switched off, an international fiscal transfer scheme is operated. The design of this rule is discussed in greater detail below. Since I assume that the two countries have identical structures, size and initial conditions, any difference in economic performance must be attributed to asymmetric shocks. This assumption is indeed helpful to avoid confusion over transfers designed

4. I do not distinguish between 'private' and 'public' demand shocks. That might be a relevant distinction, however, since many would find it inappropriate if a country, as a result of 'bad' behaviour on the part of its government, were eligible to receive transfers from abroad.

5. The point is that if supply shocks are permanent, fiscal responses can merely be a temporary buffer. What is in fact required to provide a complete solution in such circumstances is a real wage adjustment. This point tells us that if the model is extended to include a richer menu of shocks, the claims made about the effectiveness of fiscal policy should be limited to temporary shocks. From an economic policy perspective, a labour market reform is most probably a better response if permanent supply shocks are predominant. If, however, monetary policy has changed after a supply shock, it might indeed be desirable to trigger fiscal policy.

to offset long-standing inter-member differences in GDP *per capita* and transfers extended for cyclical reasons.

While both the absence of private sector co-insurance behaviour and the national fiscal rigidities are critical assumptions, the need for an international fiscal transfer system can also be motivated by the presence of wage/price rigidities. This feature of reality I introduce by assuming a continuous-time model of staggered contracts (Calvo, 1984; Ambler, 1988). The idea of this approach may be sketched as follows. There is a large number (continuum) of identical unions, acting as wage-setters, and there is a large number of identical firms, acting as price-setters by marking up over the average wage. Today's price level is thus a weighted average of wages set in the past, but each individual contract wage is set in a forward-looking manner. Technically, it is assumed that a new wage contract is 'born' at each instant in time and, once settled, there is a probability, δ, that it will be changed again at any time. The probability of 'survival' is independent of the length of the current contract, so the expected 'lifetime' (or 'time until next change') of a newly formed wage contract is the same as for an existing one. Since the model is cast in continuous time, δ can take any value between 0 and infinity.

The 'lifetime', T, of a contract is assumed to have an exponential (Poisson) distribution. A wage contract settled at *any* point in time will thus last for h more periods according to the density function $f_T(t) = \delta \exp(-\delta h)$. The expected remaining lifetime of a contract therefore equals

$$E(T) = \int_0^\infty t\delta \exp(-\delta t)dt = \delta^{-1}.$$

Obviously, the higher is the probability that the wage will be changed, the smaller is the expected length of the contract. A higher value of δ thus means a higher degree of wage/price flexibility. When the union sets the contract wage at time t, $w(t)$, it takes into account both the (expected) price level, p^e, and the (expected) level of aggregate demand, y^e, prevailing until the contract wage is changed again. Put formally

$$w_i(t) = \delta \int_t^\infty [p_i^e(\tau) + \nu y_i^e(\tau)] \exp(-\delta(\tau - t))d\tau; \quad i = 1, 2 \quad (6.3)$$

where 'e' denotes an expectation. Assuming that changes are uncorrelated across unions,[6] the proportion of wages at time t that were set at time $t - s$

---

6. This may not be a very realistic assumption – for example, the German 'wage round' is a fact of life.

is equal to $\delta \exp[\delta(t - s)]$. By defining the price level as a weighted average of wages currently in existence, we get

$$p_i = \delta \int_{-\infty}^{t} w_i(\tau) \exp(-\delta(t - \tau))d\tau; \quad i = 1, 2. \tag{6.4}$$

The long-run stance of the real economy is completely invariant to the absence or presence of international fiscal transfers as well as to whether the shocks are temporary or permanent. Since the model thus offers no long-run trade-off between inflation and unemployment, the transfer scheme would not involve permanent income redistribution. The long-run wage and price effects depend on the structural parameters of the model, including the longevity of the shocks

$$w_{i,\infty} = p_{i,\infty} = \left(\frac{2\alpha \pm \gamma\lambda^{-1}}{4\alpha\gamma\lambda^{-1}}\right) v_1(0) \exp(-\rho\infty) + d_i; \quad i = 1, 2. \tag{6.5}$$

A (negative) permanent shock to country 1's output would lead to lower wage and price levels in country 1, but not necessarily in country 2.[7] In the long run there is no impact of the fiscal transfer system, and money is strictly neutral.

The dynamics of the model may, upon differentiation of (6.3) and (6.4) with respect to time[8] – and upon elimination of the non-dynamic variables – be written as a four-dimensional simultaneous linear differential equation system. As an aid to both algebra and intuition, I utilize the well-known technique of 'averages' and 'differences' (Aoki, 1981).[9] Not only will this greatly simplify the dynamics, it will also be helpful given our focus on aggregate stability and nominal convergence. The

---

[7] Whether the foreign price level also falls will depend on the relative strength of international competitiveness and the real interest rate as determinants of aggregate demand. If the former dominates (α 'high'), the foreign price level must fall to partly offset the home country's gain in competitiveness.

[8] Upon differentiation with respect to time, we get

$$\dot{w}_i = \delta(w_i - p_i - \nu y_i); \quad i = 1, 2$$
$$\dot{p}_i = \delta(w_i - p_i); \quad i = 1, 2.$$

[9] Specifically, any average, difference and single-country variable, respectively, can be written

$$x_a = \frac{1}{2}(x_1 + x_2); \qquad x_d = x_1 - x_2; \qquad x_i = x_a \pm \frac{1}{2}x_d; \quad i = 1, 2.$$

average system may be written as follows

$$
\begin{pmatrix} \dot{p}_a \\ \dot{w}_a \end{pmatrix} = \frac{1}{\Omega} \left\{ \begin{pmatrix} -\delta\Omega & \delta\Omega \\ -\delta[\Omega - \nu\gamma(\delta + 1/\lambda)] & \delta(\Omega - \nu\gamma\delta) \end{pmatrix} \begin{pmatrix} p_a \\ w_a \end{pmatrix} \right.
$$

$$
\left. + \begin{pmatrix} 0 \\ -\gamma\delta\nu/\lambda \end{pmatrix} d + \begin{pmatrix} 0 \\ -\delta\nu \end{pmatrix} v_a \right\} \tag{6.6}
$$

where $\Omega = 1 + \gamma/\lambda - \sigma$ and $v_a = v_a(0)\exp(-\rho t)$. Similarly, the state–space form of the difference system reads

$$
\begin{pmatrix} \dot{p}_d \\ \dot{w}_d \end{pmatrix} = \frac{1}{\Phi} \left\{ \begin{pmatrix} -\delta\Phi & \delta\Phi \\ -\delta[\Phi - \nu(2\alpha + \gamma\delta)] & \delta(\Phi - \nu\gamma\delta) \end{pmatrix} \begin{pmatrix} p_d \\ w_d \end{pmatrix} \right.
$$

$$
\left. + \begin{pmatrix} 0 \\ -2\nu\delta\eta \end{pmatrix} n + \begin{pmatrix} 0 \\ -\delta\nu \end{pmatrix} v_d \right\} \tag{6.7}
$$

where $\Phi = 1 + \sigma$ and $v_d = v_d(0)\exp(-\rho t)$. Since p is a predetermined state variable and w is a non-predetermined one, existence and uniqueness of an equilibrium require that (6.6) and (6.7) be characterized by saddle-path stability. For there to exist a unique converging equilibrium path in both subsystems, it is necessary and sufficient that the determinant of the state matrix in the average system, $\Delta_a = -\delta^2\nu(\gamma/\lambda\Omega)$, and the determinant of the state matrix in the difference system, $\Delta_d = -2\delta^2\nu(\alpha/\Phi)$, be both negative. For most relevant cases, the two subsystems (and hence the model in general) would be saddle-path stable.

I have so far constructed a model of a monetary union in which there is enough endogenous flexibility for shocks to have no lasting effects on the real economy. However, owing to various rigidities in both policy making and private sector behaviour, shocks may cause much temporary distress. Since the role of monetary and fiscal policy is effectively a question about how much stabilization the economy can deliver in the absence of policy, it would be useful to start by examining some properties of the model in the absence of policy activism. This is the topic of the next section.

Monetary union without policy activism

The analysis in this section assumes a very rigid policy framework. Monetary policy is based on a strict monetarist rule ($d = 0$), and no fiscal transfers are triggered in response to asymmetric shocks ($n = 0$). In view of the high priority paid to aggregate price stability and nominal convergence in the Maastricht Treaty, I first examine how the average price level and the price difference behave following a negative IS shock in country 1

$$p_a(t) = \frac{1}{2} \frac{\delta^2 \nu}{\rho^2 \Omega - \delta^2 \nu \gamma (\rho + 1/\lambda)} (e^{h_a t} - e^{-\rho t}) v_1(0) \qquad (6.8)$$

$$p_d(t) = \frac{\delta^2 \nu}{\rho^2 \Phi - \delta^2 \nu (\rho \gamma + 2\alpha)} (e^{h_d t} - e^{-\rho t}) v_1(0) \qquad (6.9)$$

where h_a and h_d are the two stable eigenvalues

$$h_a = -\frac{1}{2\Omega} (\nu \gamma \delta^2 + \sqrt{(\nu \gamma \delta^2)^2 + 4 \nu \gamma \delta^2 \Omega/\lambda})$$

$$h_d = -\frac{1}{2\Phi} (\nu \gamma \delta^2 + \sqrt{(\nu \gamma \delta^2)^2 + 8 \Phi \delta^2 \gamma \alpha}).$$

By assumption, prices do not move at $t = 0$ $(p_a(0) = p_d(0) = 0)$. However, as it can readily be established that

$$\frac{\delta^2 \nu}{\rho^2 \Omega - \delta^2 \nu \gamma (\rho + 1/\lambda)} \lessgtr 0 \Rightarrow h_a \lessgtr -\rho \Rightarrow e^{h_a t} - e^{-\rho t} \lessgtr 0 \qquad (6.10)$$

and

$$\frac{\delta^2 \nu}{\rho^2 \Phi - \delta^2 \nu (\rho \gamma + 2\alpha)} \lessgtr 0 \Rightarrow h_d \lessgtr -\rho \Rightarrow e^{h_d t} - e^{-\rho t} \lessgtr 0,$$

$$(6.11)$$

the average price level will immediately start falling and the two price levels will diverge, no matter the duration of the shock. If the shock is a temporary one, the adjustment trajectory is non-monotonic: as the shock dies away, the average price level returns to its initial value, and the price difference will gradually be eliminated. In the case of a permanent shock, the adjustment path will be monotonic, and country 1's price level will be lower than country 2's even across steady states.

As monetary and economic integration progresses, the degree of nominal rigidity, as captured by δ, may actually diminish. The point is that if shocks cannot be absorbed through monetary and fiscal policy adjustments, the wage/price adjustments may become more flexible (Layard, 1990; Andersen and Sørensen, 1997). For example, a union striving to achieve a certain employment target would realize the need for more flexible wage responses if policies are non-accommodative. While certainly a limitation, the absence of learning and adaptation in the model may be justified by the fact that there is no clear-cut evidence of such endogenous responses to a regime shift *ad modum* EMU.

A negative demand shock causes an impact jump fall in the nominal wage set by unions – in anticipation of a lower price level and a fall in aggregate demand. If the adjustment is slow, which may correspond to an early stage of EMU, the nominal wage would undertake a relatively small initial fall, but the subsequent wage/price dynamics may be drawn out. If, conversely, there is a high degree of nominal wage flexibility, possibly corresponding to a later stage of EMU, there may be a significant initial divergence between nominal wages in the two regions, but this will be followed by a relatively short adjustment period. In the absence of nominal rigidities, the adjustment is clearly immediate ($\lim_{\delta \to \infty} h_d \to \infty$).

It could similarly be argued that α, the degree of differentiation (or substitutability) of the two goods, varies over time.[10] Think of α as a measure of the degree of integration of the two goods markets: the more closely integrated are the home and foreign goods markets, the higher is α. At an early stage, including the run-up to EMU, α may be fairly low. As monetary and economic integration progresses, α gradually becomes higher, and we would thus expect the home and foreign price levels to move in the same direction, irrespective of where the shock originates (Frankel and Rose, 1997). A high value of α would guarantee a high degree of nominal convergence, with the law of one price holding in the special case of perfectly integrated goods markets ($\lim_{\alpha \to \infty} P^d = 0$).

I now turn to the issues of real output stabilization and convergence, the main concerns in relation to fiscal policy. For the two subsystems, the behaviour of output reads

$$
y_a(t) = \frac{1}{2\Omega} \frac{\delta^2 \nu}{\rho^2 \Omega - \delta^2 \nu \gamma (\rho + 1/\lambda)}
$$

$$
\times \left(\gamma (h_a - 1/\lambda) e^{h_a t} + \frac{\rho^2 \Omega}{\delta^2 \nu} e^{-\rho t} \right) \upsilon_1(0) \tag{6.12}
$$

$$
y_d(t) = \frac{1}{\Phi} \frac{\delta^2 \nu}{\rho^2 \Phi - \delta^2 \nu (\rho \gamma + 2\alpha)} \left((h_d \gamma - 2\alpha) e^{h_d t} + \frac{\rho^2 \Phi}{\delta^2 \nu} e^{-\rho t} \right) \upsilon_1(0). \tag{6.13}
$$

[10]. More specifically, the sign of α answers the question of whether a relative price increase is contractionary ($\alpha < 0$) or expansionary ($\alpha > 0$). In the former case, there would be two stable roots (their product, $\Delta_d = -2\delta^2 \nu (\alpha/\Phi)$, is positive, and their sum, $T_d = -\delta^2 \nu \gamma / \Phi$, is negative). Hence the dynamic system would *always* converge to the steady state – that is, be locally stable. Though an interesting special case, referred to as 'embarrassment of riches' (Calvo, 1984), this situation would hardly be empirically relevant.

Since deviations of output and employment from their natural rate-levels are strictly temporary, regardless of the duration of the shock, only the impact and short-run effects are relevant. To see how these effects are distributed on the two countries, I write down explicitly both the domestic and the international transmission effects of a demand shock in country 1

$$
y_i(t) = \frac{1}{2}\left\{ \frac{1}{\Omega} \frac{\delta^2 \nu\left(\left(\gamma h_a - \frac{\gamma}{\lambda}\right)e^{h_a t} + \left(\frac{\rho^2 \Omega}{\delta^2 \nu}\right)e^{-\rho t}\right)}{\rho^2 \Omega - \delta^2 \nu \gamma(\rho + 1/\lambda)} \right.
$$

$$
\left. \pm \frac{1}{\Phi} \frac{\delta^2 \nu\left((h_d \gamma - 2\alpha)e^{h_d t} + \left(\frac{\rho^2 \Phi}{\delta^2 \nu}\right)e^{-\rho t}\right)}{\rho^2 \Phi - \delta^2 \nu(\rho\gamma + 2\alpha)} \right\} v_1(0); \quad i = 1,2.
$$

(6.14)

Since country 1's output is simply the sum of outputs in the two sub-systems, it unambiguously falls on impact, but may well exceed its steady-state level during the period of adjustment. Country 2's output, on the other hand, depends on the relative strength of the average and the difference component. In theory, therefore, the sign of the international transmission effect is ambiguous, a result similar to that predicted by the conventional wisdom (Mundell, 1968). If the difference component dominates the average component, y_2 would actually rise on impact following a fall in country 1's demand. In order for this outcome to be empirically relevant, the 'divergence-producing' effect of variations in the real interest rate (as captured by the value of γ) must be strong relative to the 'convergence-producing' effects stemming from the marginal propensity to import (as captured by the value of σ) and the degree of goods markets integration (as captured by the value of α). While as EMU matures, α and σ could be expected to grow, thereby reducing the 'divergence-producing' effect, they are in early years more likely to be low and thus likely to aggravate the divergence in real output when asymmetric shocks hit the EMU.

The presence of asymmetric shocks may thus not only jeopardize the objective of nominal convergence but also lead to a significant divergence in real variables. Given this chapter's emphasis on the latter, let me now be more specific about its magnitude. I shall assume the following overall loss function (on the part of some supranational authority)

$$L(0) = \int_0^\infty z(t) \exp(-\mu t)dt; \quad z(t) = y_d^2(t) \tag{6.15}$$

where $z(t)$ is the instantaneous (quadratic) loss function, thus penalizing differences between the two countries' output levels, and μ is the instantaneous rate of discount. To provide an analytically tractable indicator, I use a linear approximation of L, L'.[11] This can be found by observing that along the equilibrium path, $z(t)$ can be approximated by

$$z(t) = \tilde{z} + (z(0) - \tilde{z}) \exp(h_d t) \tag{6.16}$$

where $\tilde{z}$ is the steady-state impact, and $z(0)$ is the initial impact of the shock. Substitution of (6.16) into (6.15), and integrating, yields

$$L'(0) = \frac{\tilde{z}}{\mu} + \frac{z(0) - \tilde{z}}{\mu - h_d}$$
$$= \left[\frac{1}{\Phi} \frac{\rho^2 \Phi - \delta^2 \nu (-h_d \gamma + 2\alpha)}{\rho^2 \Phi - \delta^2 \nu (\rho \gamma + 2\alpha)} \right]^2 \bigg/ (\mu - h_d); \quad \tilde{z} = 0 \tag{6.17}$$

(6.17) may be more easily interpreted by assuming that the shock is permanent:

$$\lim_{\rho \to 0} L'(0) = \lim_{\rho \to 0} L(0) = \frac{1}{\Phi^2} \left[1 - \frac{1}{2} \frac{h_d \gamma}{\alpha} \right]^2 \bigg/ (\mu - h_d); \quad \Phi \equiv 1 + \sigma. \tag{6.18}$$

It can easily be established that the impact of asymmetric shocks on real output divergence is higher the lower is the degree of substitutability between the two countries' outputs (as captured by a 'low' value of α) and the smaller is the marginal propensity to import (as captured by a 'low' value of Φ). I have argued that both α and Φ would tend to be relatively low in an early stage of EMU. Moreover, the higher is the weight attached to output divergences occurring in the future, as captured by a 'low' value of the discount rate, μ, the higher will be the losses caused by asymmetric shocks.

[11] The welfare loss can be found to be equal to

$$L(0) = \tilde{A}^2 \left\{ \frac{(h_d \gamma - 2\alpha)^2}{\mu - 2h_d} + 2 \frac{(h_d \gamma - 2\alpha)(\rho^2 \Phi / \delta^2 \nu)}{\mu + \rho - h_d} + \frac{(\rho^2 \Phi / \delta^2 \nu)^2}{\mu + 2\rho} \right\}$$

where

$$\tilde{A} \equiv \frac{\delta^2 \nu}{\Phi(\rho^2 \Phi - \delta^2 \nu (\rho \gamma + 2\alpha))} \nu_1(0).$$

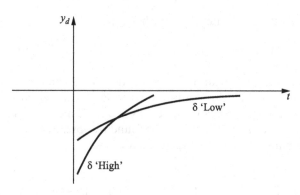

Figure 6.1   Increase in the degree of nominal flexibility

Since the adoption of less accommodative policies might reduce the degree of nominal rigidities, it would be of interest to examine how this would influence the overall loss. It can readily be established that a rise in h_d, as obtained through a rise in δ, does not necessarily reduce $L'(0)$. On the one hand, the higher is the degree of nominal flexibility (as captured by a 'high' value of δ), the higher is the speed of adjustment and the smaller would be the loss (as captured by h_d in the denominator). On the other hand, an increase in the degree of nominal flexibility means that a substantial output divergence might be observed in the early phase of the adjustment period (as captured by h_d in the numerator). Figure 6.1 shows this dilemma.

Why is it that an increase in the degree of nominal flexibility does not *both* enhance the speed of adjustment *and* limit the divergence in real output on impact? When country 1 is hit by a negative demand shock, the contract wage undergoes a jump fall, and – although the price *level* is predetermined – domestic price *inflation* also jumps downwards. Clearly, the higher is δ the higher is this effect and the more likely is it that the real interest rate in country 1 actually increases, thus exacerbating the impact of the shock. Country 2 may simultaneously see the common nominal interest rate fall and the price inflation go up, so the real interest rate may turn very low. Indeed, if the two price levels start moving in different directions, a considerable divergence in real interest rates may be observed. The point is that an increase in the degree of nominal flexibility would widen the gap between the two countries' outputs in the early stage of the adjustment period, but outputs would rapidly return to their (identical) steady-state levels.

The process by which country 1 gets a rise in real interest rates, and country 2 a fall following an asymmetric shock has been highlighted as the main adjustment channel (and cost) in EMU (Hughes Hallett and Vines, 1993), and it can be seen as a version of the so-called Walters' Critique of monetary integration (Walters, 1990).[12] This finding may have some important implications for how wage- and price-setters could be expected to react in EMU. It could be argued, for example, that wage flexibility is not what is needed to absorb shocks in EMU because it makes the transition so much worse, even if the final state is a return to equilibrium. Indeed, if the transition is bad enough, it may be that we never go through it and hence never get to the final equilibrium. Because of convex preferences, as in the present model, agents might think that the cure was worse than the illness - the transition sufficiently bad that it is not worth trying to re-establish equilibrium - so they would not allow δ to rise.

Flexible rules of monetary and fiscal policy

We have seen that if the nominal rigidities currently prevailing could be reduced the real effects of asymmetric shocks would be less persistent and a regime shift such as EMU might well become a success. In the absence of such changes, however, the built-in stabilization of shocks will remain weak, and the question arises as to what a more flexible monetary and fiscal response could do to smooth the adjustment.

The institutional framework I have in mind for the following analysis is one where not only monetary policy but also fiscal policy is governed by a supranational authority. As to monetary policy, the common central bank (ECB) is assumed, in accord with its constitution, to follow a rule aiming at aggregate price stability

$$d = -\beta p_a. \tag{6.19}$$

The ECB thus exercises control over (the domestic part of) the money supply, leaving the nominal interest rate and the value of its currency *vis-à-vis* outside currencies to be determined endogenously in financial

---

12. The basic claim of the Walters Critique is that it will not be possible to produce inflation convergence under fixed exchange rates: in the absence of expected exchange rate changes, there will be no interest differential and this will cause inflation rates to diverge. Walters himself has stated the Critique as follows:

   If Italy is inflating at a rate of 7 per cent and Germany at a rate of 2 per cent (both over the relevant period of exchange rate fixing), then there is a problem of perversity. With the same interest rate at 5 per cent, the real interest rate for Italy is minus 2 per cent and for Germany plus 3 per cent. Thus Italy will have an expansionary monetary policy, while Germany will pursue one of restraint. But this will exacerbate inflation in Italy and yet restrain further the already low inflation in Germany. This is the opposite of 'convergence', namely it induces divergence. (Walters, 1990: 79–80)

   For a critical appraisal of the Walters Critique, see Miller and Sutherland (1991).

markets. If a member state is hit by a demand shock, causing a fall in the average price level, the ECB would ease monetary policy, thereby mitigating the average effect on output without necessarily limiting the divergence between output levels.

As to fiscal policy, I introduce an inter-member fiscal transfer scheme, taking the form of an institutional amendment of EMU to include a supranational fiscal authority, (SFA, for short). This new institution would be granted the right to levy taxes and pay transfer payments with the aim of limiting real divergence when the union is hit by asymmetric shocks, in accord with the rule

$$n = -\xi y_d. \qquad (6.20)$$

(6.20) simply says that whenever country 1's output increases relative to country 2's output, the former will have to transfer resources to the latter. Transfers are thus paid to the country with the *relatively* weakest economic performance. The scheme is assumed to work regardless of the *absolute* output levels.[13] I assume that the SFA is not allowed to intervene through debt creation, so payments into the system continuously equal payments out of it. Within this balanced budget constraint the value of ξ measures the strength of the supranational stabilization efforts: the greater is ξ, the greater is the resistance offered by the SFA to real output divergence. Irrespective of the value of ξ, the policy rule is a very simple one, reflecting the presumption that a fiscal transfer system must be both intelligible and feasible in order to be accepted by decision makers.

At this stage, it is worth recalling my assumption that the shocks relevant for triggering tax and transfer payments are previously unexpected by all agents in both countries. Hence there should be no *ex ante* asymmetry in terms of the incentives offered to join the insurance scheme. In practice, however, it would typically be the case that both the frequency and the magnitude of the shocks differed for the countries involved. Moreover, the system might well be perceived as a *de facto* increase in the community-wide budget. Despite these (and other) obstacles to the introduction of a fiscal transfer mechanism, it would be of interest to examine in further detail the stabilizing properties it might possess.

The desirability of operating the simple proportional rules (6.19) and (6.20) may again be assessed in terms of the integrated loss, as calculated by the loss function (6.17). If the fiscal rule (6.20) is substituted into (6.7),

---

[13.] For example, a negative demand shock to one country may often show up as a positive shock elsewhere in the union. If so, the redistribution would be from an over-heated economy to one operating below its natural rate level.

and if it assumed, again for expositional convenience, that the shock is permanent, we get

$$\tilde{L}'(0) = \frac{1}{\tilde{\Phi}^2}\left[1 - \frac{1}{2}\frac{\tilde{h}_d\gamma}{\alpha}\right]^2 \bigg/ (\mu - \tilde{h}_d) \tag{6.21}$$

where

$$\tilde{h}_d = -\frac{1}{2\tilde{\Phi}}\left(\nu\gamma\delta^2 + \sqrt{(\nu\gamma\delta^2)^2 + 8\tilde{\Phi}\delta^2\gamma\alpha}\right) \quad \text{and} \quad \tilde{\Phi} = 1 + \sigma + 2\eta\xi.$$

Equation (6.21) suggests a very strong fiscal feedback: $\lim_{\xi\to\infty} \tilde{L}'(0) = 0$. The reason why the scheme should be operated so strongly in order to avoid divergencies in output is that the stabilization rule conditions the fiscal transfer on y_d – that is, only *indirectly* on the exogenous shock to aggregate demand. An efficient, exactly offsetting policy would make the fiscal transfer respond *directly* to the disturbance, not 'wait' until the thing we seek to stabilize has already been affected.

Another important point should be noted here: as the degree of fiscal feedback increases, the speed of adjustment falls. In economic terms this means that fiscal transfers will slow down the p_d part of the process, but remove the y_d earlier on. This (perhaps counterintuitive) finding may be explained by first assuming that there is no fiscal feedback. In this case, a negative demand shock would cause a fall in y_d, which would lead to a fall in p_d, in turn raising the difference between the real money supplies in the two countries, and y_d would begin to rise. The proportional feedback rule works to offset this automatic stabilization: as y_d rises, the SFA would transfer resources from country 1 to country 2, thereby slowing down the automatic stabilization being made.

There is also a limit as to how strongly the SFA can be involved in preventing the two outputs from diverging. An extremely ambitious fiscal intervention – such as one striving to fully offset the output effects of asymmetric shocks – would lead to the price indeterminacy problem ($\lim_{\xi\to\infty} h'_d(0) = 0$). This point shows that (complete) stabilization in terms of one objective may involve destabilization in terms of other dimensions.

Furthermore, there is an interesting intertemporal trade-off between 'endogenous' stabilization (as captured by a high value of δ) and 'exogenous' stabilization (as captured by a high value of ξ). While a high degree of the former would tend to cause a high degree of output divergence as an initial impact, the subsequent speed of adjustment would be very fast. This contrasts with the effects of the latter which guarantees only little output

Table 6.1 *Alternative stabilization policies*

	I		II[a]		III[b]	
	A	D	A	D	A	D
Stable eigenvalue	−1.054	−1.185	−1.137	−0.828	−8.154	−0.099
Stable eigenvector[c]	0.649	0.605	0.543	0.724	−1.718	0.967
Initial impact on output	−0.433	−3.471	−0.349	−3.201	−0.260	−2.442
Integrated loss						
y	0.735	7.058	0.478	2.452	0.269	2.225
p	25.703	43.566	0.731	44.472	0.003	72048

Notes:
[a] $\beta = \xi = 1.0$
[b] $\beta = \xi = 100.$
[c] Gives the ratio of w to p on the stable manifold.

Parameter values:
$\lambda = 0.75$; $\alpha = 0.5$; $\gamma = 1.0$; $\sigma = 0.4$; $\eta = 0.5$; $\varrho = 0.9$; $\delta = 2.0$; $\nu = 0.1$; $\mu = 0.06$.

deviation, but this takes place at the expense of a slow adjustment towards the steady state.

While the question about how strongly the the SFA should be engaged in limiting real divergence is thus tricky, it is more obvious how strongly the ECB should operate the monetary rule (6.19). Indeed, it would be possible to maintain the aggregate price level constant without sacrificing the overall stability of the average economy. As witnessed by the determinant of the relevant transition matrix,

$$\Delta_a = -\delta^2 \nu \gamma (1 + \beta)/(\lambda \Omega),$$

the average economy would exhibit saddle-path stability for *any* positive value of β.

The stabilising properties of, respectively, the rigid and flexible policy rules may be summarized with the aid of table 6.1, which shows numerical values for (1) the stable eigenvalue, (2) the stable eigenvector, (3) the initial impact on output and (4) the integrated loss, as calculated using (6.15). Results are reported for the average (*A*) and difference (*D*) systems, as well as for the paths under, respectively, (*I*) no stabilization, (*II*) 'weak' stabilization, and (*III*) 'strong' stabilization.

It turns out that, first, the ECB should be allowed to respond firmly to demand shocks. This would not only lead to aggregate price stability but would also stabilize aggregate output. Second, while fiscal feedback would limit the initial output deviation, it would prolong the adjustment towards the new steady state. The desirability of (strong) fiscal feedback in response to demand shocks would thus depend on the weight attached to nominal relative to real convergence.

Conclusions and qualifications

In view of the current shape of public finances in Europe, restrictions on fiscal actions are likely to be imposed when EMU begins. As long as the endogenous stabilizers in the economy are insufficiently geared to smooth the adjustment promptly, there may be a case for an inter-member fiscal transfer mechanism. Using a simple macroeconomic framework, this chapter has demonstrated some properties of a specific scheme designed so as to dampen the real output divergence resulting from asymmetric shocks in a monetary union.

While of potential interest, particularly in an early stage of EMU where both the economic structures and the policy responses may be most rigid, a number of reservations should be pointed out:

- First, while asymmetric shocks would be relevant to all members of the union, the risks of being hit by them would typically be different for 'core' and 'periphery' countries. For example, it is doubtful whether a 'core' country less likely to face adverse shocks would have incentives to transfer tax money to a 'periphery' country more (or even very) likely to face such shocks. For this reason, a major problem with a fiscal transfer mechanism is that it may be quite unrealistic for political reasons, however desirable.
- Second, the insurance system considered here operates by channelling income from a country in a boom – relative to the union average – to a country in relative bust. However, a country's willingness to contribute might not so much depend on its cyclical stance relative to the *union* average as it would depend on its cyclical stance relative to its *domestic* output gap. The general point here is that in an EMU with fiscal transfers disagreements between the SFA and national authorities over the economy's cyclical stance are likely to arise very often.
- Third, the success of a fiscal transfer scheme will critically depend on whether the contributors think that the shocks hitting the recipients were bad luck or due to bad management. In reality, it would be almost impossible to draw a sharp distinction between those two sources of bad performance.

In sum, the presence of moral hazard problems may undermine the functioning of a fiscal transfer scheme. This seems to provide a strong case for simply decentralizing the decisions about fiscal stabilization to each member state. Effectively, this means that one should adopt a relatively 'soft' interpretation of the fiscal convergence criteria. In any case, while it is clear that the Maastricht Treaty favours nominal over real convergence, this may not be enough to settle the issue for most voting publics. The Maastricht Treaty imposed that outcome without reference to the political conflict.

References

Allsopp, C., Davies, D., McKibbin, W., and Vines, D. (1997). 'Monetary and Fiscal Stabilisation of Demand Shocks Within Europe', *Review of International Economics*, 5: 55–77

Ambler, S., (1988). 'Fiscal and Monetary Policy in an Open Economy with Staggered Wages', *Weltwirtschaftliches Archiv* 124: 58–73

Andersen, T. M. and Sørensen, J. R., (1997). 'Product Market Integration and Labour Market Flexibility', University of Aarhus, mimeo

Aoki, M. (1981). *Dynamic Analysis of Open Economies*, New York: Academic Press

Bayoumi, T. and Eichengreen, B. (1993). 'Shocking Aspects of European Monetary Unification', in F. Torres and F. Giavazzi (eds.), *Adjustment and Growth in the European Monetary Union*, Cambridge: University Press: 153–229

Bayoumi, T. and Masson, P., (1995). 'Fiscal Flows in the United States and Canada: Lessons for Monetary Union in Europe', *European Economic Review*, 39: 253–274

Bayoumi, T. and Prassad, E. (1995). 'Currency Unions, Economic Fluctuations and Adjustment: Some Empirical Evidence', *CEPR Discussion Paper*, 1172

Begg, I. (1995), 'Factor Mobility and Regional Disparities in the European Union', *Oxford Review of Economic Policy*, 11: 96–112

Boltho, A. (1989). 'European and United States Regional Differentials: A Note', *Oxford Review of Economic Policy*. 5: 105–115

Bruno, M. and Sachs, J. (1985). *The Economics of Worldwide Stagflation*, Oxford: Blackwell

Calvo, G. (1984). 'Staggered Contracts and Exchange Rate Policy', in J. Frenkel, (ed.), *Exchange Rates and International Economics*, Chicago: Chicago University Press

Campbell, J. Y. and Mankiw, N. G. (1989). 'Consumption, Income, and Interest Rates: Reinterpreting the Time Series Evidence', in Blanchard, O. and Fischer, S. (eds.), *NBER Macroeconomics Annual*, Cambridge, Mass.: MIT Press

Christodoulakis, N., Dimelis, S. and Kollintzas, T. (1995). 'Comparisons of Business Cycles in the EC: Idiosyncracies and Regularities', *Economica* 62: 1–27

Deaton, A. (1992). *Understanding Consumption*, Oxford University Press

De Grauwe, P. (1994). 'Towards European Monetary Union without the EMS', *Economic Policy*, 18: 147–174

Demertzis, M., Hughes Hallett, A. and Rummel, O. (1997). 'Is a Two-Speed System in Europe the Answer to the Conflict between the German and the Anglo-Saxon Models of Monetary Control?', in S. Black, and M. Moersch, M. (eds.), *Which Way Forward for European Financial Markets?*, Cambridge: Cambridge University Press

Duisenberg, W. (1977). 'Monetary Policy and Competitiveness', speech to the European Meeting of the Trilateral Commission, The Hague, (25 October)

(1990). 'One Market, One Money', *European Economy*, 44

Eichengreen, B. (1992). 'Should the Maastricht Treaty be Saved?, *Princeton Studies in International Finance*, 74

(1997). 'Saving Europe's Automatic Stabilisers', *National Institute Economic Review*, 159: 92–98

Eichengreen, B. and Wyplotz, C. (1993). 'The Unstable EMS', *Brookings Papers on Economic Activity*, 1: 51–124

Frankel, J. A. and Rose, A. K. (1997). 'Economic Structure and the Decision to Adopt a Common Currency', University of California at Berkeley, mimeo

Hughes Hallett, A. and Ma, Y. (1996). 'Changing Partners: The Importance of Coordinating Fiscal and Monetary Policy Within a Monetary Union', *Manchester School*, 64: 115–34

Hughes Hallett, A. and McAdam, P. (1998). 'Fiscal Deficit Reduction in Line with the Maastricht Criteria for Monetary Union: An Empirical Analysis', in J. Frieden, D. Gros, and E. Jones, (eds.), *Towards European Monetary Union: Problems and Prospects*, Denver, Colorad.: Rowman & Littlefield

Hughes Hallett, A. and Vines, D. (1993). 'On the Possible Costs of European Monetary Union', *Manchester School*, 61: 35–64

Italianer, A. and Vanheukelen, M. (1993). 'Proposals for Community Stabilization Mechanisms', in 'The Economics of Community Public Finances', European Economy, Special Issue

Jeanne, O. (1997). 'The Dynamics of Unemployment in a Fixed-exchange Rate System: Theory and Application to the "Franc Fort" Policy', University of California at Berkeley, mimeo

Jensen, S. H. (1997). 'Wage Rigidity, Monetary Integration, and Fiscal Stabilization in Europe', *Review of International Economics*, 5: 36–54

Layard, R. (1990). 'Wage Bargaining and EMU', in R. Dornbusch, C. Goodhart and R. Layard, (eds.), *Britain and EMU*, London: London School of Economics

MacDougall, D. *et al.* (1977). *Report of the Study Group on the Role of Public Finance in European Integration* (MacDougall Report), I–II, Commission of the European Communities, Brussels

Manasse, P. (1991). 'Fiscal Policy in Europe: The Credibility Implications of real Wage Rigidity', *Oxford Economic Papers*, 32: 1031–1054

Miller, M. and Sutherland, A. (1991). 'The Walters Crique of the EMS: A Case of Inconsistent Expectations', *Manchester School*, 59: 23–37

Mundell, R. A. (1968). *International Economics*, London: Macmillan

OECD (1994). *The OECD Jobs Study: Facts, Analyses, Strategies*, Paris: OECD

Sachs, J. and Sala-i-Martin, X. (1992). 'Fiscal Federalism and Optimum Currency Areas: Evidence for Europe from the United States', in M. Canzoneri, V. Grilli and P. Masson (eds.), *Establishing a Central Bank: Issues in Europe and Lessons from the United States*, Cambridge: Cambridge University Press

Sheen, J. (1992). 'International Monetary and Fiscal Policy Cooperation in the Presence of Wage Inflexibilities', *Journal of Economic Dynamics and Control*, 16: 359–387

van der Ploeg, F. (1991). 'Macroeconomic Policy Coordination during the Various Phases of Economic and Monetary Integration in Europe', *European Economy*, Special Issue

von Hagen, J. and Hammond, G. (1997). 'Insurance Against Asymmetric Shocks in a European Monetary Union', in J.-O. Hairault, P.-Y. Hénin, and F. Portier, (eds.), *Business Cycles and Macroeconomic Stability: Should We Rebuild Built-in Stabilizers?* Dordrecht: Kluwer

Walters, A. (1990). *Sterling in Danger*, London: Fontana

Williamson, J. (1990). 'Britain's Role in EMU', Institute for International Economics, mimeo

Discussion

Neil Rankin

There is a natural development of the argument amongst the three chapters in part II dealing with fiscal mechanisms for stabilizing the real economy in the face of asymmetric shocks. Andersen and Dogonowski's chapter 4 is concerned with reminding us of the value of allowing the government deficit to follow its natural countercyclical path, and with demonstrating that, based on recent experience, the 3 per cent deficit limit set by the Stability Pact will probably come into conflict with the operation of the normal automatic fiscal stabilizers. Kletzer's and Jensen's chapters 5 and 6, respectively, move the argument on, by examining a mechanism which might compensate for the loss of stabilization instruments by national governments under a single currency – namely, a fiscal transfer scheme. Although in recent years increasing European economic integration has inspired numerous papers on international fiscal insurance, most of them have been within the 'public economics' tradition. This is one in which classical Walrasian markets are typically assumed, and there is no scope for demand to affect short-run real output. The usefulness of fiscal transfers in such a world is to smooth countries' consumption levels, but not to smooth their *outputs*. Fiscal transfers can *compensate* residents for output fluctuations, but they cannot affect the fluctuations themselves (this is also true in the simple economy presented in Andersen and Dogonowski's chapter, for example). Kletzer's and Jensen's contributions, on the other hand, set fiscal transfer schemes in a genuinely 'macroeconomic' environment where transfers are able to smooth outputs. They therefore bring a novel and welcome feature to the analysis of such schemes. Kletzer analyses international fiscal insurance in a fundamental theoretical way, by examining its potential effects on resource allocation and economic welfare, and asking whether it is a close substitute for exchange rate flexibility. Jensen, on the other hand, asks whether, given the sacrifice of both monetary autonomy and of deficit financing which EMU countries will soon – rightly or wrongly – have

145

imposed upon themselves, a fiscal transfer scheme would have any benefits as a stabilization mechanism for real output in the face of asymmetric shocks. Jensen therefore brings the argument the furthest up to date in relation to political decisions already taken about how EMU will operate.

Turning first to Andersen and Dogonowski's chapter 4, a specific theme in their critique of the 'Stability Pact' budgetary rules is the emphasis placed on deficit as compared to debt limits. Relative to the fiscal 'convergence' criteria in the Maastricht Treaty, the Stability Pact has shifted nearly all the weight onto deficit limits. Andersen and Dogonowski argue, however, that insofar as standard economic reasoning provides any justification for fiscal restraints on EMU members, the case for such restraints applies more obviously to the 'stock' measure of a country's fiscal position than to the 'flow' measure. This point is surely correct, and bears repeating. Standard models such as the overlapping-generations model, for example, predict that what matters for the determination of the real interest rate is not the size of the current government deficit, but the stock of outstanding government debt. Moreover, the incentive which a country has to default on its debt – and thus its incentive to pressure the European Central Bank (ECB) to bail it out by printing money – depends on the total size that the debt has attained, not on the rate at which it happens presently to be growing. By applying the fiscal limits to deficits rather than to debt, the Stability Pact prevents debt from performing its main economic function, which is to enable governments to smooth out their financing requirements over time. Andersen and Dogonowski's suggested explanation for the emphasis placed on deficits in the Stability Pact is a political one: a perceived tendency for governments to be myopic, which means that they cannot be 'trusted' to reverse a temporarily rising debt level when circumstances become favourable. However, as they point out, if it is generally true that weaknesses in political institutions favour the use of rules over discretion for the running of fiscal policy, then account should be taken of the fact that, in order to satisfy the deficit rules, governments are likely to have to *suspend* the operation of other, longer-established, fiscal rules – namely the automatic fiscal stabilizers which cause tax revenue to fall and benefit spending to rise in a recession. In order to satisfy the deficit rules, governments are likely to have to take discretionary action to cut spending or raise taxes in a recession; the amount of discretionary action may thus be increased, not reduced, by the deficit limits.

A significant part of Andersen and Dogonowski's chapter is devoted to a demonstration of how allowing the government to run a deficit can raise a country's welfare. The example they provide is quite a neat one, consisting of a small open economy with expected utility-maximizing agents, and stochastically varying income. Since agents are infinitely lived, Ricardian Equivalence would hold in this economy in the absence of a capital market imperfection, and there would be no useful role for government debt. Andersen and Dogonowski give government debt a purpose by the trick of assuming that the world interest rate at which private agents can borrow is greater than the rate at which the government can borrow. Such a device has also been used, for example, by van Wijnbergen (1987), and it roughly captures the idea that private agents may be perceived as worse risks than governments by international lenders, because of greater informational problems, so that they have to pay an interest premium. Andersen and Dogonowski proceed to show formally that, under a fiscal rule in which taxation is increasing in income, lifetime expected utility of agents is higher – because variability of consumption is lower – than under a rule in which the government is forced to balance the budget period by period. They do not, however, offer an intuitive explanation for this result. The explanation would appear to be something like the following. When there is a bad income shock, households would like to borrow in order to smooth their consumption. If the government uses the deficit-financing rule, it lowers taxation and runs a deficit this period, but raises taxation next period in order to pay back the debt. It therefore effectively borrows on households' behalf. Since it can borrow at a lower rate of interest than households, this clearly makes the latter better off, and avoids them having to cut consumption by as much as they otherwise would. Conversely, when there is a good income shock households would like to lend. This time, the deficit-financing rule means that the government lends on their behalf, but it gets a worse interest rate than households could, which makes households worse off, so that their consumption goes up by less than it otherwise would. Thus, in both directions, the interest rate differential works to dampen the fluctuations in consumption. This story is elegant, though it has, perhaps, two weaknesses. First, the case for assuming that the government can lend out less profitably than private agents is less convincing than the case for assuming that it can borrow more cheaply – it seems likely that governments would be more effective lenders, too. If this were incorporated it would break the symmetry and make the results less clear cut. Second, and more importantly, although this is a story about how deficits can be used for 'stabilization', it is – as noted earlier – not stabilization in the usual macroeconomists' sense of stabilizing output, but rather just of consumption. To incorporate output stabilization a less 'classical' model is required. Such models are what Kletzer and Jensen provide.

   Kletzer's chapter 5, as its title indicates, attempts to evaluate the case for a fiscal insurance scheme on deep-seated, welfare grounds. This is an undertaking which is admirable in its ambition, though whether it is possible to complete it thoroughly within such a confined space may be doubted. The framework which Kletzer uses is a two-country dynamic general equilibrium model with temporary nominal rigidities. This is an analytical framework of the type strongly advocated in recent work by Obstfeld and Rogoff (1995, 1996). Compared to 'classical' dynamic general equilibrium models (cf. the example in Andersen and Dogonowski), it derives relevance for short-run output determination from the inclusion of a constraint that money wages must be set one period in advance. Compared to 'conventional' macro-models (cf. that in Jensen's chapter 6), it has the advantage of a consistent general equilibrium structure with full intertemporal optimization by agents. Kletzer's framework is in fact one which extends the baseline Obstfeld–Rogoff model in numerous ways: it makes it stochastic; it introduces a capital market imperfection; it incorporates physical capital accumulation; and – in a final section – it extends it to the case of goods market segmentation. Potentially, the full version of such a model is a seriously complicated construction. Hence, perhaps wisely, Kletzer does not attempt to work out the model's full solution.

The starting point for his argument is a version of the model with fully flexible nominal wages and prices, but with a capital market imperfection in the form of the absence of a market in claims to risky future labour income. The latter potentially creates a role for a fiscal insurance scheme even when there are no nominal rigidities, to the extent that such a scheme can be used to substitute for the missing asset market and thus enable residents of the two countries to achieve full sharing of consumption risks. Later on, it also interacts with the case of nominal rigidities in an interesting way, because if nominal rigidities cause outputs to be more volatile, this increases the value of a scheme for achieving full consumption-risk sharing, even ignoring any effect the scheme may have in stabilizing outputs themselves. Kletzer's conclusion, however, is that empirically an international fiscal insurance scheme is unlikely to be of value under full nominal flexibility, because the missing market constraint is unlikely to be binding. He arrives at this conclusion by arguing that, if the constraint were binding, we ought to observe domestic residents holding no domestic equity in their portfolios and instead holding only foreign equity; yet empirically we observe the opposite of this – i.e. a high proportion of domestic, and a very low proportion of foreign, equity ('home bias'). This is an ingenious argument, but I cannot say that I am persuaded by it. In most of the literature on international portfolios, home bias is taken as a puzzle to be explained, and the absence of a market in claims to risky labour income is often appealed to as one explanation for it (see, for example, Bottazzi, Pesenti and van Wincoop, 1996). Thus, elsewhere in the literature, home bias is presented as evidence that the absence of a market in labour income claims *is* important for resource allocation, whereas Kletzer presents it as evidence for the opposite. One feature of Kletzer's theoretical model which lies behind this difference is that wages and profits are perfectly correlated in his model, and the capital market imperfection just takes the form of an unexplained no-short-sales constraint on equity. Elsewhere, one more commonly finds that wage and profit income streams are modelled as imperfectly correlated, so that claims to them are imperfect substitutes.

In the central version of Kletzer's model, the money wage is set one period in advance. Random productivity shocks in each country now cause output and employment to fluctuate more than under flexible wages. With separate currencies and a floating exchange rate, the monetary authorities in each country can act to stabilize outputs, restoring them to their full-employment levels. However, with a single currency, unless the shocks happen to be perfectly symmetric, monetary policy cannot be used for this. Kletzer points out that here, a fiscal insurance scheme potentially has increased value through two roles: a 'consumption-stabilizing' and an 'output-stabilizing' role. The former arises to the extent that the missing market constraint is preventing full risk sharing between the countries, and because output fluctuations are now bigger than before; and the latter arises because the scheme may be able to damp down the fluctuations in output themselves. The latter is the truly 'macroeconomic', Keynesian demand-management role. However, Kletzer is sceptical about whether this role is possible or desirable. First, it may not be possible: a fiscal transfer just redistributes wealth from the foreign to the home country (say); but if there is only one good in the world, produced at home and abroad, and if propensities to consume out of wealth are equal, then such a transfer has no effect on the demands for home and foreign outputs – it just changes where the demands come from. To obtain an effect, and moreover a differential effect, the countries need to produce differentiated goods and to have 'home bias' in goods preferences, so that the fiscal transfer has an expenditure-switching effect. Second, Kletzer claims that fiscal output stabilization may not be desirable, because it 'distorts' capital accumulation. By increasing home wealth permanently, the transfer permanently increases relative demand for home goods and thus their relative price, which raises the long-run level of capital that is devoted to their production, and hence the long-run level of home output. I am unconvinced that this is a true distortion, or that the net effect is destabilizing for output. A lump-sum redistribution of wealth is not 'distorting', surely. Moreover the argument ignores a counteracting negative effect on long-run home goods output, which will occur through a reduction in home labour supply, as wealth increases.

In the last section of his chapter, Kletzer deploys another argument to cement his negative verdict on fiscal insurance. He drops the assumption of perfect goods price arbitrage, arguing that empirical evidence suggests the prevalence of market segmentation and pricing-to-market. This means that the currency-adjusted prices of a particular good no longer have to be the same at home and abroad, so that – viewing a single currency as like a fixed exchange rate – the exchange rate no longer ties them together. It is then claimed that nominal rigidity in wages and the inability to devalue pose no problem for full employment under a single currency, because home and foreign prices can adjust independently; and from this it follows that a fiscal insurance scheme for output stabilization is unnecessary. Although I agree that to look at market segmentation is interesting, Kletzer's claim seems to me unproven. True, the 'restriction' represented by the law of one price goes away, but there ought to be another relationship between home and foreign prices to replace it. This relationship must derive from the way in which firms set their home and foreign prices. Kletzer does not provide an explicit model of price-setting, which would require the setting up of an imperfectly competitive market structure, and his lightly-sketched substitute for it is a bit too vague for comfort. Moreover, whatever this relationship may be, there is still the problem that, with a single currency, the authorities have only one policy instrument (the common money supply), yet two policy targets (full employment in each country).

Jensen's analysis of the fiscal transfer scheme uses a fairly conventional macro-model, in which the potential for demand shocks to affect short-run output stems from nominal rigidities modelled à la Calvo (1983) – that is, preset prices which firms can change only at random intervals. Compared to Kletzer's framework, the 'propagation mechanism' for shocks is different: there is no capital or foreign asset accumulation, but the use of staggered rather than one-period prices provides an alternative channel for perpetuating the effects of shocks over time. Jensen is particularly careful to relate his policy analysis to the strict rules which have already been enshrined in the Maastricht and Amsterdam Treaties. A common monetary policy, operated by an independent central bank whose sole objective is price stability, is represented by making the money supply feed back negatively on the average price level (and on nothing else); while the tight limits on deficits are represented by imposing that national governments must operate balanced budgets. The question posed by Jensen therefore is: given the straitjacket into which the EMU now appears to have strapped itself with regard to real output stabilization, is a fiscal transfer mechanism the solution?

From the technical viewpoint, a clever feature of Jensen's approach is the use of the 'Aoki method' (Aoki, 1981) for decomposing a quite complicated dynamic two-country model into two independent subsystems: one in the averages of country variables, and one in the differences. This is helpful not just because it reduces a fourth-order dynamic system to two much more tractable second-order ones, but more especially because – given that the focus of the chapter is on the issue of real divergence between countries – we have a direct interest in the 'difference' variables for their own sake. Jensen exploits this advantage of the Aoki decomposition very effectively, by centring the discussion on conveniently explicit solutions for the output divergence $y_d (\equiv y_1 - y_2)$.

Jensen first analyses the effect of a temporary negative shock to the demand for country 1's output on the time path of the output divergence, in the absence of any active stabilization rules. Since Jensen's model can be seen as a modern generalization of the classic two-country Mundell (1968) IS-LM model, it is to be expected that the results would be similar. This indeed proves to be the case: the spillover effect on country 2's output may be of the opposite sign to the own-country effect, if the 'convergence-producing' effects which work through goods markets (lower country 1 income, and a lower country 1 price level, reduce the demand for country 2 exports) are outweighed by the 'divergence-producing' effect which works through asset markets (a lower country 1, and thus world, interest rate stimulates country 2 output). Jensen plausibly argues that such a situation is likely during the early stages of monetary union, since fuller goods market integration, and a consequent strengthening of the convergence-producing effects, take time to develop. A less expected result is that a higher degree of price flexibility, although it speeds up the return to full employment after a shock, increases the size of the initial output divergence. Jensen provides an interesting explanation for this in terms of the 'Walters Critique' effect. Greater price flexibility increases the initial response of the inflation rate in each country. If the response is negative in country 1 but positive in country 2 (owing to the net spillover effect being negative), then since, under a single currency, there is a single nominal interest rate, the real interest rate in country 1 rises more while that in country 2 falls, which exacerbates the divergence in outputs.

The main contribution of Jensen's chapter concerns how the response to the shock is modified when an automatic fiscal transfer scheme is put in place. As in Kletzer's case, the scheme is envisaged as a tax on the residents of the country with the higher output, which is immediately distributed as a subsidy to the residents of the country with the lower output. The amount of the tax is assumed to be increasing in the size of the output divergence, with a sensitivity parameter ξ. Jensen shows that an increase in ξ reduces the magnitude of the initial output divergence; therefore the fiscal transfer scheme does have an effect in the desired direction. However, it is by no means a perfect stabilization tool, for two reasons. First, it is not possible to stabilize initial output perfectly except by setting ξ to infinity. Second, although a higher ξ dampens down the initial fluctuations, it also reduces the speed of return to full employment.

The last-mentioned finding means that it is not immediately obvious that, taking the time path as a whole, the fiscal transfer scheme reduces the amount of divergence. To assess whether this is so we need a measure of the cumulated divergence. Jensen provides this by introducing a loss function in the form of the discounted sum of the squared output divergence over the interval from impact to infinity. In fact, in order to obtain an algebraic solution for the loss, he drops the squaring and assumes the shock is permanent. From the resulting formula (6.21) it is then clear that the loss is, after all, minimized when ξ is pushed to infinity. However, it is less clear from the formula whether the loss is *monotonically* decreasing in ξ. Since in practice the feasible range for ξ would clearly be bounded above, the empirically relevant question is whether the loss is decreasing in ξ over this range. Doubts about this are brought to mind by the fact that, as Jensen points out, the qualitative effect of an increase in ξ on the time path of y_d is similar to the effect of a reduction in the degree of price flexibility – i.e. in δ; and he has earlier shown that δ has an ambiguous effect on the loss. One way to obtain reassurance is to compute some numerical examples. In table 6.1 Jensen does exactly this. If we look at the numbers for the integrated loss for the output divergence, they clearly fall as the degree of stabilization is increased, and thus appear to support the conclusions from the algebra. Nevertheless in the table the picture is slightly confused by the fact that the monetary feedback parameter (β) is increased simultaneously with ξ. More importantly, it would be useful to have some feeling for whether the values of 1.0 and 100 chosen for ξ lie in the likely feasible range. On the evidence presented, what we can say is that a fiscal transfer scheme at least holds out some promise of achieving a degree of stabilization; the next step is to try to quantify this more precisely.

Overall, this discussant takes away two lessons from these three chapters. First, the Maastricht and Amsterdam Treaties leave worryingly little scope for policies to stabilize real output in the face of asymmetric goods demand shocks. Second, taking the treaties as they stand, the possibility of using a fiscal transfer scheme as an instrument of short-run macroeconomic stabilization policy, and not just as an instrument of long-run structural adjustment, is one which deserves to be taken seriously. An issue which is not addressed in Kletzer's and Jensen's chapters – the chapters dealing with fiscal transfers – is the issue of how a fiscal transfer scheme might operate in practice. This needs to be addressed if such a scheme is to become reality. It would seem desirable to make transfers automatic – i.e. rule-based. If they are discretionary, subject to case-by-case political negotiation, they are unlikely to operate fast enough to be of use in short-run output stabilization. One way in which they would become automatic would be if there were full fiscal federalism – i.e. pooled taxation and benefit arrangements; but Kletzer and Jensen are clear that this is not what they intended to analyse. Jensen's model contains a rule which makes transfers a function of the output divergence between countries, but how this would be implemented in reality is not so obvious. It is straightforward to devise a tax or subsidy whose total value depends automatically on output in the country where it is levied – an income or sales tax or subsidy does this – but to make it also depend automatically on output in a *different* country is another matter. The rate of tax or subsidy would have to be determined by a formula linking it to the lagged value of some measure of activity in the other country. The fact that GDP data is available only quarterly then suggests using an alternative measure such as unemployment. Unemployment, indeed, is the basis of the scheme proposed by Italianer and Vanheukelen (1993). Further research of this nature, which includes quantitative estimates of how well any proposed scheme might succeed in stabilizing asymmetric shocks, would seem to be the next important step.

References

Aoki, M. (1981). *Dynamic Analysis of Open Economies*, New York: Academic Press

Bottazzi, L., Pesenti, P. and van Wincoop, E. (1996). 'Wages, Profits and the International Portfolio Puzzle', *European Economic Review*, 40: 219–54

Calvo, G. (1983). 'Staggered Prices in a Utility-maximising Framework', *Journal of Monetary Economics* 12: 383–98

Ingram, J. (1959). 'State and Regional Payments Mechanisms', *Quarterly Journal of Economics,* 73: 619–32

Italianer, A. and Vanheukelen, M. (1993). 'Proposals for the Community Stabilization Mechanisms: Some Historical Applications', *European Economy,* 5

Mundell, R. A. (1968). *International Economics*, London: Macmillan

Obstfeld, M. and Rogoff, K. (1995). 'Exchange Rate Dynamics Redux', *Journal of Political Economy*, 103: 624–60

(1996). *Foundations of International Macroeconomics*, Cambridge, Mass. MIT Press

Van Wijnbergen, S. (1987). 'Government Deficits, Private Investment and the Current Account: An Intertemporal Disequilibrium Analysis', *Economic Journal*, 97: 596–615

Part III

The Stability and Growth Pact

7 The Stability Pact: trading off flexibility for credibility?

Michael J. Artis and Bernhard Winkler

Introduction

At the Amsterdam Summit on 16 June 1997, the member states of the European Union (EU) agreed to a 'Stability and Growth Pact' (SGP, hereafter Stability Pact), to come into force when European Monetary Union (EMU) begins. The Stability Pact comprises two Council regulations and a European Council resolution (European Council 1997). The latter is a declaration of intent and self-commitment regarding the application of the revised excessive deficit procedure. It invokes an important commitment from the member states to conduct their fiscal affairs so as to produce a 'medium-term budgetary position of close to balance or in surplus', and a statement of intent on their part not to invoke the benefit of a waiver of the procedure unless a position of severe recession has been identified and to effect corrective action, if need be, promptly and with a view to completing correction within a year.

The two regulations relate to the surveillance and coordination of economic policies and to the elaboration and clarification of how the excessive deficit procedure – that was primarily set out as part of the process governing qualification for entry into EMU – should be adapted to the circumstances of Stage Three. Here, the key feature is that, whereas under the aegis of the Maastricht Treaty a member state found to have 'excessive deficits' could not qualify for entry into EMU, this penalty is substituted, under the Stability Pact, by a system of non-interest-bearing

We should like to acknowledge the fact that the National Institute of Economic and Social Research published a complementary version of this chapter, with which it partly overlaps, in its *Review* (January 1998) under the title 'The Stability Pact: Safeguarding the Credibility of the European Central Bank'. This chapter reflects research undertaken when Bernhard Winkler was affiliated to the European University Institute, Florence. Any views expressed are those of the authors and do not necessarily correspond to those of the European Central Bank.

deposits, ultimately capable of becoming outright 'fines' on a scale which is limited by a ceiling placed at the value of 0.5 per cent of GDP. It seems clear also that a member state which became subject to such fines would also be exposed to massive market penalties in the form of added interest rate premia. Whilst the penalties set out in the Stability Pact for persistence in a state of 'excessive deficits' are, on paper, large and carry the multiplier of the market's punishment, the finding of 'excessive deficits' can be waived in certain cases even when the recorded figure exceeds the 3 per cent reference value: if there is an accompanying annual fall in output of 2 per cent or more the waiver is automatic; between 0.75 and 2 per cent, the waiver is discretionary and depends on a decision of the Council of Ministers. In this latter case evidence that a downturn is abrupt – or, in succeeding previous downturns has led to a cumulative decline in output – can be used to deflect a finding of 'excessive deficits' and the sanctions procedures.

It is not our primary purpose here to elaborate on the procedures set out in the Stability Pact (such an elaboration can be found in Artis and Winkler, 1998), although we do provide an analytical account of the Stability Pact as an incentive device in the penultimate section, rather, the main issues addressed here are based on an assumption that – to some significant extent at least – the Stability Pact offers a genuine constraint on the fiscal policy of member states operating within the EMU. It is this feature that requires explanation.

Such an explanation could be sought strictly within the confines of fiscal policy considerations themselves, without reference to wider implications. We discuss explanations of this kind in the following section. An alternative – or, perhaps, complementary – approach is centred on the relationship of fiscal to monetary policy discussed in the subsequent section. We then lay out an analytical account of the Stability Pact as an incentive device. The final section provides some broad conclusions.

The Stability Pact and fiscal policy

Constraints on fiscal policy, such as the deficit ceiling of the Stability Pact, can be useful if in their absence deficits would tend to be excessive from the national or the international (here: European) point of view. In the first case inefficiency arises from domestic deficit biases, in the second from policy spillovers across different countries. In both cases the benefits of commitment to rules or deficit ceilings must be weighed against the potential losses from reduced flexibility of fiscal policy in stabilizing economic shocks.

Countering domestic deficit bias

There are several possible stories to tell here. The simplest one, put forward most forcefully by public choice theorists (Buchanan, 1977; Olson, 1965), draws on the observation that special interests pushing for public expenditure programmes are generally well organized, unlike taxpayers. Moreover, future taxpayers are not represented at all in the democratic process, which favours the build-up of public debt to be repaid by future generations and may also lead politicians to ignore the negative long-run growth effects of deficits via the crowding-out of productive private investment. Government instability and a host of other political and institutional factors can be used to explain why the public finance performance of political systems has differed widely across countries (Alesina and Perotti 1995, Roubini and Sachs, 1989; Grilli, Masciandaro and Tabellini, 1991; Corsetti and Roubini, 1993). The fact remains that the last two decades have produced a debt build-up in European countries, unprecedented in peacetime, where fiscal policies in several countries have become unsustainable, in particular in view of demographic trends and unfunded pay-as-you-go pension systems (Masson, 1996). Artis and Marcellino (1998) find that most EU countries fail to satisfy the solvency condition on the basis of their revealed behaviour in the past twenty years. This suggests that neither the political process nor the discipline of financial markets appears to have been sufficient to induce governments always to take heed of long-run budget constraints.

Furthermore, even if neither governments nor voters nor interest groups suffered from myopia but all agreed on the need to reduce deficits and debts, this remains a difficult goal to achieve. Each group will try to minimize its own contribution to deficit reduction, whose benefits have public good characteristics for all of society and future generations. The Maastricht 3 per cent deficit ceiling backed by an external enforcement mechanism can then be seen as a blunt device to impose an upper limit on the domestic deficit bias, which – depending on the stock of initial debt and the assumptions on nominal growth rates – may (or may not) suffice to guarantee a sustainable budget position. In this context the 3 per cent deficit criterion is internally consistent with the 60 per cent debt criterion, leading to a stable debt/GDP ratio under the assumption of 5 per cent nominal growth. Clearly more sophisticated rules could be derived from public finance considerations (Buiter, Corsetti and Roubini, 1993). Equally clearly it would be preferable to address the (political) distortion of budget policy at source, if possible, instead of imposing arbitrary numbers. However, the Maastricht criteria are best understood as a simple commitment device in a second-best world of incomplete contracts.

The fact remains that the Maastricht criteria have been welcomed by many policy makers as an external commitment device to enhance the domestic consolidation of public finances that was seen as necessary independently of EMU. However, it is not clear why countries could not have adopted unilateral self-commitment – e.g. in analogy to the constitutional 'Balanced Budget Amendments' long under frequent discussion in the United States and in widespread use at the state level, or reformed their budget processes. Unless international multilateral commitment is more credible than unilateral reforms the inclusion of the fiscal criteria in the Maastricht Treaty and now in the Stability Pact must derive from a fear that monetary union could increase the domestic deficit bias or render its effects more damaging.

The effects of monetary union and a single capital market on the incentives for fiscal policy-makers can go in both directions. On the one hand, the long-run budget constraint facing governments is hardened to the extent that the Maastricht Treaty's 'no-bail-out' clause is credible and monetary financing of government debt by the European Central Bank (ECB) is ruled out (Glick and Hutchison, 1993). On the other, access to financing will be easier in the unified European capital market and (presumably) cheaper for high debt and deficit countries no longer suffering national interest rate premia for devaluation and inflation risk. Abolishing national currencies removes the disciplining effect of international currency markets on national fiscal policies (Thygesen, 1996), even though bond markets may be expected to correctly price the remaining default risk (again if the 'no-bail out' clause is perceived as credible).

There are two main arguments against the need to impose additional fiscal constraints in monetary unions. One holds that bond markets price default risk correctly and that this would act as an adequate deterrent. The second line is to argue, on the contrary, that with sufficient taxing powers and control of the tax base countries will always be able to service their debt and there is little to worry about (Eichengreen and von Hagen, 1996). From this the probability of default should be very small for sovereign states with sufficient taxing powers (i.e. as long as tax bases are not too mobile) and large stocks of assets, even if the recourse to the printing press is ruled out. Default premia are therefore unlikely to be sizeable enough to act as an effective deterrent *ex ante*.

Moreover, market reactions and political crises in response to fiscal problems tend to be discontinuous – i.e. to provoke a sudden and abrupt withdrawal of confidence which is difficult and costly to deal with ex post and thus may render an explicit or implicit bail-out inevitable. This will at least be the case if financial market instability threatens to spill over and affect partner countries or the common monetary policy, as discussed below. For these reasons it remains doubtful that market discipline is effective, let alone efficient, in offsetting a domestic political deficit bias. Even if the 'no-bail-out' clause were credible, there are additional conditions for market discipline to be effective such as the timely availability of information – and, most importantly, that borrowers respond to market signals (Lane, 1993).

Empirically, the fact remains that governments have been seen to follow irresponsible budget policies in a wide variety of exchange rate regimes and in spite of market discipline. Fiscal constraints can therefore make sense in order to offset domestic deficit biases. Moreover, most federal states have restrictions on borrowing at the state level (Masson, 1996), even if introduced for different reasons as argued by Eichengreen and von Hagen (1996), or they form a political union with sufficient power to dissuade deviant behaviour. The additional case for fiscal restrictions under EMU and in the absence of political union then rests on the presence of (EMU-specific) fiscal policy spillovers across participating countries.

In the case of EMU there is, however, an additional point to be made – that in this case, countries are moving from a position in which they have both money-creating and taxing powers to one in which they are stripped of the former. Moreover, it is arguable that EU member states' taxing powers are becoming increasingly confined as integration promotes tax base mobility. McKinnon (1994), in particular, has drawn attention to the danger that may be implicit in this transition: that debt/GDP ratios which were sustainable in conditions where investors could be sure of the security of their assets, at least in the domestic currency of the issuing country, may not be sustainable when the countries concerned enter a monetary union and abandon their money-creating power to the ECB. The spectre of debt runs is thereby invoked – and, with it, the risk of breakdown in Europe's financial institutions. Eichengreen and Wyplosz (1998) also regard this as the most serious reason for fiscal constraints – even though they consider alternative approaches, such as strengthening prudential measures to govern financial institutions' exposure to public debt, to be more appropriate responses.[1] If this were the most important reason for the Stability Pact, though, it might be expected that it would refer explicitly to debt and debt ratios. In fact, these terms do not appear

---

[1] Eichengreen and Wyplosz note – as does McKinnon – that US State debt ratios (state debt/state product, including in the state debt totals in McKinnon's case the debt of local government and city units) are well below the levels of most EU member states. The US State figures are in the order of 9–16 per cent, depending how state debt is defined, as compared with figures around 60 per cent for the majority of EU countries (Italy and Belgium at twice this figure).

in the Stability Pact and it is significant that discussions of debt-reduction programmes are taking place outside it. Rightly or wrongly, the Stability Pact seems to be aimed primarily at other issues.[2]

Coordinating fiscal policies

From a standard Mundell–Fleming model we know that the effectiveness of fiscal policy is enhanced in a fixed exchange rate regime such as monetary union (Agell, Calmfors and Jonsson, 1996), because expansionary effects on output are no longer countered by an exchange rate appreciation, except via the common external exchange rate. The effect on foreign output, however, is ambiguous since the stimulation via greater import demand may be offset by the dampening effect from higher interest rates (Eichengreen, 1997). Under open global (and European) capital markets the effect on interest rates should be very small, however. Still, net spillovers are ambiguous, in principle, and not likely to be very sizeable, even though with increased economic integration the size of fiscal leakages increases and therefore the a priori case for coordinated policy responses to shocks (Masson, 1996).

The second aspect of fiscal spillovers concerns the crowding-out of investment from deficits raising the common interest rate in an integrated (European) capital market. Indeed one justification for formulating the criterion in terms of actual rather than primary or structural deficits is that actual deficits are an 'expression of the burden on financial markets' (Thygesen, 1996) as the relevant spillover. However, it has been argued that a member state will give rise to an externality only if it runs a current account deficit – i.e. if the sum of national investment and the deficit exceeds national savings (Pisani-Ferry, 1996). Again, to the extent that world capital markets are integrated the effect from any individual EMU member country on the common real interest rate should be small. Yet, as discussed in the next section, the conduct of fiscal policy, both deficits and debt, may affect both the short-run and the long-run credibility of the common monetary policy and thereby nominal interest rates, inflation expectations and actual inflation.

A third externality arises from effects on the common external exchange rate, which should appreciate in response to fiscal expansion and rising interest rates, crowding-out partner countries' net exports. A fourth possible channel of fiscal spillovers has already been mentioned in the context of the 'no-bail-out' clause. This channel arises if an increase in default risk

---

[2.] Although it does call for medium-term deficits to be zero, implying large primary surpluses and a reduction in debt/GDP ratios.

Table 7.1. *The fiscal prisoner's dilemma*

		Country *B*	
		Tight policy	Lax policy
Country *A*	Tight policy	1, 1	−1, 2
	Lax policy	2, −1	0, 0

in a member country or a subsequent financial crisis cannot be confined to the country in question but leads to expectations of an explicit or implicit bail-out or a systemic financial crisis across the common capital market.

Most of the spillovers of fiscal policies are not directly related to monetary union *per se* but rather rest on the degree of trade or financial market integration (Eichengreen and von Hagen, 1996). Moreover the issue of active policy coordination, addressed only slightly by the Maastricht Treaty in art. 103 that regards economic policy as 'of common interest', needs to be distinguished from the problem of a systematic deficit bias that might be addressed by imposing constraints on deficits. In the latter case, the deficit ceiling in the Stability Pact can serve as a blunt coordination device to the extent that undisciplined fiscal policy in any member state country has negative effects on partner countries' economic variables, by crowding-out investment or net exports, or by undermining the stability of the common financial system or the credibility of the common monetary policy. In the words of Giovannini (1994: 190) the role of the fiscal criteria is to 'prevent countries from trying to exploit monetary union to export their domestic fiscal problems', as a second-best safeguard against free riding in the absence of a set of rules on financial relations (as common in federal states).

Consider the pay-off matrix depicted in table 7.1 for a simple illustration of the coordination problem, where two countries can choose between tight and lax fiscal policy, with both preferring to free ride on the other country's fiscal discipline. Arbitrary pay-offs are chosen for illustration, but most of the above spillover stories, with negative externalities from lax policies, can be used to underpin table 7.1. Here, lax fiscal policies reduce the other country's utility by two pay-off units. All else being equal, governments prefer lax policies – i.e. implementing discipline carries economic and political costs (one pay-off unit). Fiscal discipline has public good features for both countries, but its provision is costly. Conversely, each country would like to reap the benefits of fiscal expansion (higher output and employment) for itself, while its negative effects via higher interest rates, the crowding-out of investment or exports and the risk of financial instability are shared throughout the union.

Countries get stuck in the inefficient Nash equilibrium (bottom right), where both pursue lax budget policies. The Pareto-superior cooperative solution (top left) is not sustainable, because each country has an incentive to deviate, given that the other country provides fiscal discipline. The same pay-off structure can be used to illustrate the domestic deficit bias discussed previously. In that case, the players are different economic interest groups who are interested in overall budget consolidation but try to avoid cuts hitting their own clientele. Dynamic versions of debt- or deficit-reduction games can be modelled as 'wars of attrition', where each side holds out in the hope that the other side gives in and contributes first to the public good (Bliss and Nalebuff, 1984; Alesina and Drazen, 1991). In this perspective the Maastricht criteria appear as a commitment device for coordinated fiscal adjustment (Allsopp and Vines 1996).

Fiscal stabilization

Whatever the rationale for the Stability Pact, there is a potential price to be paid for satisfying its rigid numerical limits. This price comes in the form of lost flexibility in the use of active fiscal policy or in the operation of the built-in automatic stabilizers of national budgets and has been the major source of criticism of the Stability Pact. There are two main questions with respect to EMU first, on the need for a federal European stabilization scheme and, second, on the implications of the Stability Pact for the functioning of national stabilization. It is useful to distinguish two aspects of stabilization here: *intra-union* stabilization in response to asymmetric shocks and *pan-European* responses to common shocks.

The debate over fiscal federalism examines the question where stabilization mechanisms should be located – i.e. at the European or at the national level (for example, Mélitz and Vori, 1992; von Hagen and Hammond, 1995). It is obvious that a European-wide stabilization scheme is superior in principle since it provides insurance across countries at any point in time, whereas national stabilization has to rely on debt build-up (with its concomitant negative side effects) for consumption smoothing over time. If there are significant Ricardian effects, fiscal stabilization may be less powerful to the extent that consumption is reduced in the expectation of a higher future tax burden (Bayoumi and Masson, 1996). However, empirically Ricardian effects are likely to be small, especially if deficits are perceived to be strictly temporary. The issue then hinges on the question to what extent capital market imperfections impede private agents and national governments from lending and borrowing in order to achieve consumption-smoothing over time (Gros, 1996). Here it is germane to note the evidence provided by Sørenson and Yosha (1998) indicating that capital market integration within the EU is less than that within the United States. Since this in itself inhibits private agents from risk-sharing behaviour, there is an added case for freeing national governments to engage in stabilization policies. Of course, it can be expected that the initiation of EMU will itself lead to greater capital market integration.

However, a European-wide scheme could be attractive for another reason since it may be able to stabilize intra-union shocks automatically and in a way that leaves the aggregate fiscal stance unaltered. In this way an unbalanced policy mix from uncoordinated national fiscal policies could be avoided. Unfortunately, there are serious design problems in a centralized insurance scheme; these relate to the difficulty of separating out temporary and permanent shocks (and therefore insurance and redistribution issues) and to problems of moral hazard. In any case, unlike in the discussions of monetary union in the 1970s the Werner and McDougall Reports, Werner, *et al.*, 1970 and Commission, 1977, respectively, the Maastricht construction does not call for an expansion of the central European budget nor the installation of a European-wide fiscal co-insurance mechanism.

Empirical research on fiscal federalism has looked at the experience of federal states such as the United States, where the federal budget does perform a sizeable stabilization function in the order of 20 per cent of income shocks (for example, Bayoumi and Masson, 1995). This does not necessarily imply that the same stabilization function could not be performed equally effectively at the state level. Kletzer (1997) argues that fiscal federalist arrangements in effect *substitute* stabilization through the federal budget for stabilization through the budgets of individual states or countries. The opportunity to stabilize through accession to a federal system is not a substitute for national monetary policy but for national fiscal policy. In the United States state budget policies are both less important for stabilization and more severely constrained (in the choice of tax instruments and in many cases by balanced budget provisions) compared to European countries. Moreover, the size of the state sector and the volume of welfare and unemployment benefits is generally much greater in Europe and therefore national automatic stabilizers should be more powerful (Allsopp and Vines, 1996). Bayoumi and Eichengreen (1995) have estimated the elasticity of the central government revenue/GDP ratio with respect to output in the order of 0.3–0.5 for a number of European countries, as a measure of the fraction of changes in disposable income that is offset by changes in government revenues. Buti, Franco and Ongena (1997) find that the elasticity of the budget balance (the percentage-point increase in the deficit ratio associated with a percentage-point increase in output growth) for Europe as a whole is around 0.5 per cent; the IMF's estimates of the same elasticities (IMF, 1997) are of the same order of magnitude.

The second issue, therefore, is to examine how well equipped national fiscal policy would be to perform stabilization within EMU. There are really two questions concerning how necessary and how effective national fiscal stabilization will be. The first point, addressed by the empirical optimum currency area (OCA) literature (see Bayoumi and Eichengreen, 1996) regards the incidence of asymmetric shocks. These could well be less important compared to the United States, given that European economies appear to be more diversified than US regional economies. Moreover, compared to historical data, the part of asymmetric shocks that is due to or amplified by divergent policy responses should be much reduced in EMU. On the other hand, OCA theory stresses the importance of fiscal policy when national monetary and exchange rate policy are forsaken in EMU and as long as prices/wages are rigid and labour mobility remains low.

The effectiveness of national fiscal policy has already been discussed. Again, in a simple Mundell–Fleming world fixed exchange rates make fiscal interventions more powerful, where the presence of cross-border leakages (even though of ambiguous sign) could provide a case for policy coordination. The main concern from the stabilization and OCA perspective is that the Stability Pact could hamper the operation of automatic stabilizers at the national level, just when they are most needed. In particular the fear is that in a recession countries will be induced to undertake 'perverse' pro-cyclical measures in order to avoid hitting the 3 per cent deficit ceiling. The main recommendation from this line of argument is to formulate any deficit targets in terms of structural deficits or 'constant-employment budget balance' (Eichengreen, 1997) rather than actual deficits. The problem with the NAIRU-adjusted deficit targets, besides disputes about measurement, is that they provide no reassurance at all about the long-run sustainability of public finances, unlike the combination of 60 per cent debt and 3 per cent deficit targets in the Treaty.

How much of a constraint on fiscal stabilization the Stability Pact turns out to be depends, of course, on the average, structural deficits that countries aim for, on the size of shocks and whether or not countries will decide to honour the 3 per cent ceiling in a recession. We will examine the incentive effects of the Stability Pact in more detail in the penultimate section of this chapter, where we argue that a rational government should be induced to aim for a structural deficit much below 3 per cent in order to reduce the *ex ante* probability of incurring fines under the Stability Pact. A constraint on actual deficits in practice may thus not operate much differently from targets for structural deficits, where the size of the 'cushion' depends on the distribution of shocks, the probability and size of fines and the costs of fiscal discipline. Moreover, in the event of large shocks, the Stability Pact does foresee the possibility of sanctions being waived, thus combining *ex ante* deterrence with a limited degree of *ex post* flexibility.

Indeed the Stability Pact calls on countries to keep their structural deficits close to balance or in surplus and if 'the structural deficit is close to zero...the operation of automatic stabilizers should still be available' (Lamfalussy, 1997). Over the course of normal business-cycle fluctuations the difference between actual and structural deficits is unlikely very frequently to exceed 3 per cent. Masson (1996) has calculated a standard deviation of c. 2 per cent, suggesting that aiming for 1 per cent deficits or below might be sufficient. Eichengreen (1997) reports cases where European countries have experienced shifts in their fiscal positions exceeding 3 per cent – i.e. implying a violation of the Maastricht ceiling under the assumption that countries start out in fiscal balance for four EU countries in the mid-1970s, one country in the early 1980s and five countries in the early 1990s. This inspires reasonable confidence that the Stability Pact need not be unduly restrictive in the face of 'normal' size business cycles. Buti, Franco and Ongena (1997) provide a retrospective application of the Stability Pact assuming starting points of either a balanced budget or a 2 per cent deficit for prerecession years. Since prerecession years tend to have a higher than average capacity utilization their results should make the Stability Pact look more restrictive than it really is, provided that its medium-term aim of budgets 'close to balance or in surplus' is taken seriously.

What does evidence from the past say about the incidence of large shocks, where the Stability Pact allows for the possibility of waiving sanctions on deficit ratios exceeding 3 per cent – automatically if there is an annual output decline of 2 per cent or more, by discretion if the output decline is between 0.75 per cent and 2 per cent?

It is not clear from the wording of the Stability Pact whether the 'decline in output' refers to annual data (as for the deficit figures) or to twelve-month comparisons of quarterly data throughout the year. Only in the latter case would recessions be treated the same independently of when they occurred, but the problem would then arise of how to match them with the deficit data. Considering annual changes Buti, Franco and Ongena (1997) have counted seven cases (five distinct episodes) of real GDP declines exceeding 2 per cent in the 1961–96 period for all fifteen EU countries, and thirty cases (twenty-five separate episodes) exceeding 0.75 per cent.

Clearly, output declines of more than 2 per cent have been comparatively rare events. But breaches of the 3 per cent deficit ratio ceiling have been relatively common: Eichengreen and Wyplosz (1998, table 7) count 186 breaches among the 15 EU countries in the forty years to 1996 – that is, in about 40 per cent of cases, deficits have exceeded 3 per cent of GDP.

What would have been the output effects of imposing a 3 per cent cap on deficits in the historical period? Eichengreen and Wyplosz venture to answer this question by estimating a small structural model for the EU 'Big Four' economies (Germany, France, Italy and the United Kingdom) and simulating it under the constraint of a limit of 3 per cent on the allowable deficit ratio. This is an extreme case scenario in the sense that it assumes the numerical limit to be strictly binding, with none of the Stability Pact's flexibility allowed for. Even so, they conclude from the exercise that 'fair characterization is that Stability-Pact ceilings on deficits would have mattered for output but not dramatically so'.

The real question, however, is what happens in the early days of EMU; whether countries will enter with deficits right up against the 3 per cent ceiling and even without their economies being in the trough of a recession. The European Commission's November 1997 forecasts for the 'broad-based EMU' eleven countries (that is, all EU countries except Greece, Denmark, Sweden and the United Kingdom) showed six countries with predicted deficit ratios at 2.2 per cent or above in 1999, a further two with deficits above $1\frac{1}{2}$ per cent and three (of the smaller countries) in surplus. These predictions may provide some ground for optimism, but they are of course prone to error.

It can be argued that a reduction in structural deficits and debt is required independently of EMU, particularly in view of demographic trends in Europe (Masson, 1996). From this reasoning prudent governments would be well advised to perhaps even aim for budget surpluses on average in the coming decades; in this perspective, the 3 per cent deficit ceiling does not appear to be excessively ambitious at all. Moreover, turning the critics' argument on its head, fiscal consolidation might be necessary precisely in order to regain the room for manoeuvre that allows automatic stabilizers to operate effectively. In the pre-EMU situation of a number of countries (e.g. Italy with deficits close to 10 per cent of GDP for much of the 1980s) market fears of further deterioration in public finances already effectively curtailed both the advisability and the effectiveness of letting automatic stabilizers operate fully. According to Buti, Franco and Ongena (1997: 13) EU countries with above average pre-recession debt and deficits have actually pursued pro-cyclical policies in the past, reducing structural primary deficits in recessions on average by 1.2 per cent of GDP.

Put in this perspective the trade-off between discipline and flexibility disappears, at least in the long run, and the debate really is one about the transition period in the run-up to EMU and in the early years of Stage Three. Even here it has been argued that fiscal retrenchment need not always compromise output, especially if it restores confidence in public finances over the longer term (Giavazzi and Pagano, 1991; Bertola and Drazen, 1993), even though the empirical evidence for 'anti-Keynesian' effects appears to be mixed at best (Cour et al. 1996, Hughes Hallett and McAdam, 1996). For high-debt countries EMU entry by itself should improve the fiscal outlook even in the short term via a reduction in the interest burden. The obvious way to reduce the risk of the Stability Pact imposing excessive constraints on fiscal stabilization in the early years of EMU is, of course, to insist on strict entry conditions and large enough safety margins for EMU participants from the start. It is important to recall that the Treaty not only establishes numerical reference values for the fiscal criteria but emphasizes the need for the sustainability of budgetary positions. The same point has been emphasized in the resolution of the German parliament (2 December), stating that compliance with the criteria must not only be statistical, but 'durable' and 'credible' (Deutscher, Bundestag 1992). This could be read as being much like a condition on structural deficits which should prevent countries with a high risk of violating the 3 per cent ceiling subsequently from joining in the first place.

The Stability Pact and monetary policy

The considerations reviewed in the previous section may all be relevant for the cost–benefit analysis of the Stability Pact, but in our view they do not reflect the principal motive of the insertion of the fiscal criteria in the Maastricht Treaty, which was to facilitate the ECB's primary task of achieving low and stable inflation. The relevant spillovers in this perspective concern the negative effects of undisciplined fiscal policy on the incentives, credibility and performance of the common monetary policy. As is stated in para. 18 of annex 1 of the Presidency conclusions of the Dublin summit (ECOFIN Report, 1996):

Sound government finances are crucial to preserving stable economic conditions in the Member States and in the Community. They lessen the burden on monetary policy and contribute to low and stable inflationary expectations such that interest rates can be expected to be low.

The primary task of the Stability Pact is to safeguard the credibility of monetary policy in both the long term (by preventing excessive public debt build-up) and the short run by keeping deficits in check and thereby reducing the risk of imbalances in the macroeconomic policy mix. However, the extensive literature on the credibility of monetary policy has little to say about the effect of fiscal policy on central bank behaviour and the inflation process. It proposes the delegation of policy to an independent central bank which is either more conservative than the population at large (Rogoff, 1985a) or subject to an inflation-performance contract (Walsh, 1995) as a solution to time-inconsistency problems of monetary policy in isolation. The first of these solutions, just like commitment to fixed rules on monetary growth suggested by Milton Friedman, gives rise to a trade-off between credibility and flexibility – i.e. the benefit of reduced inflation at a cost of suboptimal stabilization. This is much like the trade-off between fiscal rules and stabilization that was explored earlier under the assumption of a (political) deficit bias. The optimal-contract solution, by contrast, appears to make monetary credibility a 'free lunch' by exactly offsetting the underlying distortion. Again, the equivalent for the previous section would be a reform of the political system that induces politicians to maximize long-run social welfare.

In terms of policy implications for EMU, both of the above 'commitment by delegation' solutions can be misleading, in two main ways. First, as pointed out by McCallum (1995) and formalized by Jensen (1997), the commitment itself must be made credible. One possible enforcement mechanism suggested by Lohmann (1996) can be provided by reputational forces. For example, the reason why the Bundesbank has been successful is seen to be the reputational backing it received from the inflation averse German public. The second main shortcoming of the credibility literature is that it looks at a single policy area in isolation. In practice, the credibility of monetary policy depends on the help it receives from fiscal and wage policies in particular, as well as public support (Eijffinger and De Haan, 1996) and a country's overall 'stability culture'. In both dimensions – the credibility of commitment and the interdependence of policies – even a central bank which is independent does not operate in a vacuum but must continually earn its credibility. The ECB does not, initially, have its own stock of history and reputation nor can it be taken for granted that it will always enjoy sufficient legitimacy and support in the eyes of the European public. Moreover, fiscal policies and wage-setting remain decentralized, with the necessary degree of stability culture not assured and not uniform across Europe.

In this perspective the Stability Pact appears as a surrogate discipline and coordination device in the absence of a sufficiently strong common

Table 7.2. *A game of chicken*

		Fiscal authorities	
		Tight policy	Lax policy
ECB	Tight policy	4, 2	−1, −1
	Lax policy	0, 0	1, 3

stability culture, public support or common institutions to back up the 'empty shell' of central bank independence. Consider the simple illustration of monetary–fiscal policy interaction in table 7.2. Again pay-offs are arbitrary and chosen to capture the value of fiscal and monetary policy paths to be 'mutually consistent'. Conversely, if policy makers are on a collision course pay-offs are much lower. For example a 'lax' fiscal policy combined with 'tight' money leads to an unbalanced policy mix, high interest rates, currency appreciation and output losses in the short run. Note that both sides have an incentive to fall in line. Faced with persistently lax fiscal policy monetary authorities will in the end be forced to accommodate and, likewise, when facing a tough ECB fiscal authorities will 'chicken out' and accept discipline.

There are two Nash equilibria in the game in table 7.2. The central bank prefers the 'tight' equilibrium (top left) with tight monetary and fiscal policies, whereas fiscal authorities prefer the 'lax' outcome (bottom right) with relaxed policies. The pay-offs are as in the standard 'game of chicken' (except here we make the 'tight' equilibrium the socially more attractive one), where players have an incentive to coordinate their actions but differ over the preferred outcome and therefore each side would like to precommit in advance. Depending on which side gains strategic leadership in this way, we can distinguish two regimes – 'monetary dominance' and 'fiscal dominance' in the terminology of Canzoneri and Diba (1996).

The game can be given economic interpretations with respect to both the long-run or the short-run strategic interaction between monetary and fiscal policy makers, as discussed in the following subsections. The long-run interpretation focuses on the intertemporal government budget constraint and the credibility of low inflation and 'no-bail-out' promises. The short-run interpretation looks at the issue of the appropriate policy mix for macroeconomic stabilization. The Maastricht criteria can be seen as an attempt to secure precommitment to the monetary dominance regime – i.e. select the better of the two possible equilibria and in particular to avoid costly conflict (leadership battles) between monetary and fiscal policy.

Long-run credibility

A first link between fiscal and monetary variables can be established even in a simple Barro–Gordon (1983) framework. As stressed by De Grauwe (1996) the presence of nominal (long-term) debt undermines the central bank's anti-inflation incentives, because of the temptation to inflate away the stock of debt. De Grauwe's policy recommendations are either to suspend the voting rights of the representatives of high debt countries on the ECB board or to issue short-term debt. The former solution runs against the spirit of the ECB as being an independent and collegiate European institution, the latter has the drawback of undermining ECB credibility in the short run, as public finances become more vulnerable to variations in short-term interest rates.

More generally, monetary and fiscal policy are linked via the inter-temporal government budget constraint, which says that a stream of expenditures can be financed via taxes, issuing bonds or printing money. Here a regime of 'fiscal dominance' would mean that the government can precommit to a path of net deficits and thus ultimately force the central bank to inflate in order to avoid insolvency as in the 'unpleasant monetarist arithmetic' of Sargent and Wallace (1981). Under 'monetary dominance' the central bank can commit not to inflate (no explicit or implicit bailout) and thus force the government to adjust its path of spending and taxes as in the 'unpleasant fiscal arithmetic' of Winckler, Hochreiter and Brandner (1997).

There are a few papers which have explored the fiscal–monetary policy interaction that could be interpreted to underpin the situation in table 7.2 in more detail. Mourmouras and Su (1995) present a differential policy game between the central bank and the government in the context of debt stabilization. Under the assumption that central bank independence implies the precommitment of ruling out the inflation tax it will be able to discipline fiscal policy also – i.e. ensure 'monetary dominance'. Alesina and Tabellini (1987) have three players – the central bank, fiscal authorities and wage-setters. In the presence of distortionary taxation monetary commitment is not necessarily welfare-improving, if fiscal and monetary policy are not coordinated. The fiscal–monetary interaction in Beetsma and Bovenberg (1995a, 1995b) and Beetsma and Uhlig (1997), as in the Alesina–Tabellini paper, centres on the incentive for surprise inflation and seigniorage revenues in the presence of distortionary taxa-tion. If the central bank lacks the ability to precommit, then government financing requirements – debt, in particular – embody the stock of credibility problems faced by the central bank, leading to higher inflation. An independent central bank that can credibly ignore the government budget constraint can serve as a substitute for the Maastricht restrictions. Beetsma and Bovenberg (1995b) also have debt build-up undermine the credibility of the central bank, which can be seen as a public good. Here the solution of an independent conservative central bank will not be sufficient in the presence of additional fiscal distortions (say) from government myopia. In this case, debt targets as in the Maastricht criteria are required on top of central bank independence.

The model by Canzoneri and Diba (1996) in the new tradition of the 'fiscal theory of money' specifies a regime of fiscal dominance (FD) as one in which the fiscal authorities do not adjust the primary surplus in response to debt levels, which leads, as a consequence, to current inflation *irrespective* of the central bank's monetary policy. Solvency as such is assured here and the likelihood of default is discounted; the question is only *how* solvency comes to be assured. If it is not guaranteed by the appropriate path of primary surpluses a price-level jump, or inflation, will do the job, government debt being nominal-fixed. Under monetary dominance (MD) the fiscal authorities adjust primary surpluses to repay debt and the central bank is undisturbed in achieving its inflation target and enjoys 'functional independence'. The fiscal policy makers must follow a 'Ricardian fiscal policy rule' (Woodford, 1995, 1996), that offsets any change in debt exactly by a compensating change in the present value of future government surpluses if monetary dominance is to be preserved.

Whether an economy finds itself in a MD or FD regime depends on financial markets' beliefs about whether primary surpluses will respond fast enough to rising government debt. The statistical evidence in Canzoneri, Cumby and Diba (1997) suggests that the United States has been in an MD regime during the post-war period, contrary to the conjecture of Sargent and Wallace (1981), while it also appears that, tentatively, other OECD countries have likewise been in an MD regime (Canzoneri, Cumby and Diba 1997: 19). However, the issue that concerns us here is that a deficit rule, like the one endorsed by Maastricht and the Stability Pact, can be shown to ensure this responsiveness and thus establish MD and the 'functional' as opposed to 'legal' independence of the ECB. From this perspective the Stability Pact seems right in focusing on deficits rather than debt. However, large stocks of debt may reduce the credibility of the deficit rule if the required primary surpluses become too large.

The picture is complicated in models that introduce fiscal policy co-ordination issues on top of the fiscal–monetary interaction, as in Jensen

(1996). Using a two-country general equilibrium model he finds that fiscal coordination may be bad if the common monetary policy lacks credibility with the private sector. This mirrors an earlier result by Rogoff (1985b) showing that coordination of a subset of players can be counterproductive. In other words, in a second-best world, removing one distortion in the presence of another may make matters worse. If the central bank cannot precommit, fiscal coordination will reduce the credibility of the central bank further, supporting the Stability Pact's choice of fiscal constraints rather than fully fledged fiscal coordination, also in line with the conclusions of Bryson, Jensen and van Hoose (1993). Similar results are obtained by Levine and Pearlman (1992), who highlight fiscal policy spillovers via the crowding-out of investment and terms of trade effects. They compare cooperative and non-cooperative equilibria under different assumptions about ECB credibility. Again, in regimes where the ECB would accommodate public debt build-up, fiscal coordination will be counterproductive, unlike the case where the ECB can commit to credible inflation targets.

Agell, Calmfors and Jonsson (1996) have a version of the coordination-cum-commitment story with a more Keynesian flavour – i.e. not based on the inflation tax as the link between fiscal and monetary policy (which arguably is of scant empirical relevance). The government faces an *ex ante* trade-off between stimulating economic activity and containing budget deficits. It may or may not heed the intertemporal budget constraint, while for the monetary authorities both discretion and commitment via permanently fixed exchange rates (monetary union) is considered. Under discretion both inflation and deficits will be high – i.e. the situation of a wage-devaluation cycle with debt build-up. Under monetary union inflation will be low, but the deficit bias is worsened, which provides a case for introducing fiscal constraints when moving to EMU.

In the models discussed usually two regimes can be distinguished, depending on the assumption about precommitment abilities and corresponding to the two equilibria in table 7.2. In what ways can the Stability Pact help the ECB to acquire strategic leadership and why is central bank independence not enough to ensure this? On the face of it, the ECB seems in an extremely strong strategic position, enjoying legal independence, an explicit commitment to price stability and facing a fiscal player that is fragmented among national governments (Masson, 1996). However, recall our concerns about central bank independence being an empty shell, the experience that even the most independent central banks like the Bundesbank occasionally have to fight hard to reassure their leadership against the fiscal authorities and that they need to draw on widespread public support to be able to succeed. The fragmented fiscal policy landscape means that it may be difficult to always ensure that aggregate fiscal outcomes are compatible with a monetary leadership regime, let alone an optimal policy mix in either the short or the long run. Furthermore doubts about the pan-European legitimacy of the ECB and lack of public support may weaken its resistance to political and economic pressures to ease monetary policy. The fiscal rules and the Stability Pact try to prevent such pressures from building up (Masson, 1996).

Short-term credibility and policy mix

Critics of the Stability Pact have argued that 'discipline is a long-term issue' and that, if anything, restrictions should be placed on the debt stock rather than on current deficits (Pisani-Ferry, 1996). From the Canzoneri–Diba (1996) perspective of the previous subsection, by contrast, what matters is the *responsiveness* of current deficits to a debt build-up and therefore a deficit rule would be needed. Discipline becomes a short-term issue because the long-run deficit–debt dynamics can affect inflation expectations and current inflation directly. However, the stock of debt can also affect the *short-term* credibility of monetary policy by making public finances more vulnerable to variations in short-term interest rates.

In addition to the long-run compatibility of fiscal and monetary policy paths, as reflected in interaction via the intertemporal government budget constraint, the choice of policy mix also becomes important in short-term macroeconomic management. Conflicts between fiscal and monetary authorities can be very costly, as the episodes of Reagonomics in the early 1980s and in the wake of German unification demonstrate. In both cases an expansionary fiscal policy collided with tight monetary policy, and the real economy paid a high price for the re-establishment of the monetary authorities' strategic leadership. In normal times, when monetary leadership is uncontested, it is very helpful in coordinating economic agents' responses to shocks and expectations (especially for wage-bargaining and financial markets) and in reducing economic uncertainty if agents can rely on the central bank to maintain price stability over the medium term. European countries' differing responses to the oil price shocks in the 1970s neatly illustrate the virtue of MD with respect to FD. The long but unbalanced struggle of European economies to regain stability over the course of the 1980s also illustrates the costs of an unbalanced policy mix (Allsopp and Vines, 1996: 97), resulting from a credibility bias towards monetary policy (perhaps excessively constrained by the EMS) but too lax fiscal regimes. The story here applies both to the medium-to-longer-term disinflation effort as well as the short run.

In the case of EMU the short-run concern over an unbalanced policy mix mainly relates to the fear that undisciplined fiscal policies (in the aggregate) will force the ECB to keep short-term interest rates higher than desirable in order to offset inflationary pressures, on top of any upward pressure large public deficits might exert on real interest rates. More generally, if other economic players affecting the determinants of inflation (fiscal authorities and wage-setters in particular) do not play their part the ECB will either be induced to accommodate (i.e. accept the FD outcome) or impose great real economic costs in an attempt to reassert its leadership. The Stability Pact is designed as a (blunt) safeguard to limit the extent to which the ECB will be confronted with this dilemma. Again the criteria are an (imperfect) substitute for explicit or implicit coordination mechanisms via credible common institutions or a shared stability culture. They try to limit the risk that the ECB's independence is tested or contested too severely.

The deficit ceiling, to the extent that it is credible, can also perform an important coordination function simply by providing information – both to the ECB and to the markets – on the likely future evolution of fiscal policy. However, the Maastricht deficit limit represents an asymmetric constraint and is therefore informative for short-term macroeconomic management only when countries are close to the ceiling – i.e. generally in recessions not in booms; again, the Maastricht limits are an imperfect substitute for full coordination. The main risk with the Stability Pact is that it could actually achieve the exact opposite of what it sets out to do, as long as fiscal–fiscal and monetary–fiscal coordination remains rudimentary. Tying the fiscal authorities' hands may well turn out to *increase* rather than decrease the burden on monetary policy with respect to stabilization policy. In particular, the macroeconomic policy mix may become unbalanced in the opposite direction, if unduly tight fiscal policy in a recession forces monetary authorities into a much laxer monetary stance.

The Stability Pact attempts to preempt any potential leadership battles between fiscal and monetary policy in favour of the ECB and to prevent an unbalanced policy mix of a lax fiscal stance and tight money. Here, it is not quite clear how the European Council Resolution on Growth and Employment, adopted at French insistence in Amsterdam, will play out. It calls for 'developing the economic pillar' and 'enhancing policy co-ordination' under arts. 102a and 103 of the Maastricht Treaty (European Council 1997). This could be harmful for stability if it undermines the strategic leadership of the ECB, but it could also be helpful if policy coordination serves to provide support for the ECB's objectives and contributes to finding an appropriate policy mix.

The process of institution-building in the euro zone is also as yet far from complete. The new Euro-X Council has yet to impress its capacity on the European policy making scene. It was first conceived by French policy makers as a 'political counterweight' to the ECB, and although this description of its role was subsequently withdrawn the impression remains that the setting up of the Council might be a way of diluting ECB leadership, although it could also be a productive means of providing coordination and support for stability-oriented policies.

The Euro-X Council will almost certainly have a key role to play in relation to exchange rate policy, a 'grey area' where the Maastricht Treaty in art. 109 balances the operational independence of the ECB with the right of the European Council to determine the euro's participation in international exchange rate systems (where unanimity is required), to formulate general orientations for exchange rate policy and conclude international agreements on monetary and exchange rate matters (both by qualified majority vote), where the ECB and Commission are consulted. In fact, the Amsterdam Conclusions of the Presidency (European Council, 1997) 'invite the Council and the Commission, in cooperation with the EMI, to study effective ways of implementing all provisions of Article 109', which could be read as an indication that (some) governments are keen to exert direct influence over the euro exchange rate policy.

The implications of the Stability Pact, taken by itself, for the euro exchange rate can go in two directions. By reducing the risk of conflicts between fiscal and monetary policy (in particular, the risk of a lax fiscal-cum-tight money policy mix) the Pact may help avoid exchange rate mis-alignment and over-valuation in particular. On the other hand, the constraints on fiscal policy and the lack of coordinated macroeconomic responses may place an additional burden on the euro exchange rate to stabilize (common) shocks. This may increase pressures to call for an exchange rate policy as a discretionary policy instrument or as a check on the ECB's monetary policy. Exchange rate policy is likely to be the decisive testing ground for the *de facto* independence of the ECB and an indicator for the degree of *de facto* coordination across macroeconomic policy actors in Europe in the absence of a unified 'economic government'.

Finally, on top of intra-European problems of policy coordination strategic interaction with the rest of the world complicates the picture further. Drawing on a three-country Mundell–Fleming model Eichengreen and Ghironi (1997) examine the impact of EMU (i.e. intra-European monetary policy coordination) and the question of whether intra-European fiscal policy coordination would also be desirable given that both monetary and fiscal policies remain uncoordinated with the rest of the world. Their (simulation) results depend on the output effects of fiscal contraction, which could be negative or positive (in the 'anti-Keynesian' case). Again the general conclusion emerges that coordination between a subset of players or across a subset of policy areas is not necessarily welfare-improving. This could mean that moves towards co-ordinating intra-European fiscal policies beyond the Stability Pact should be resisted; but it could also mean that monetary and/or fiscal policy ought to be better coordinated globally, in the G7 context and in parti-cular with Japan and the United States. By fostering greater symmetry in the global financial and commercial system EMU by itself may facilitate efforts in this direction.

The Stability Pact as an incentive device

What incentives does the Stability Pact give to EMU participants to mod-ify their behaviour? Here we explore how a stylized version with a fixed penalty for breach of the 3 per cent deficit criterion would operate. The presentation draws on the analysis presented in Winkler (1997a) in the context of the Maastricht entrance conditions.[3]

In the utility function (7.1) the 3 per cent deficit criterion can be seen to determine $p(E)$, which is the probability of *avoiding* fines under the Stability Pact as an increasing function of consolidation effort (E). E concerns only the extra adjustment effort induced by the Stability Pact – i.e. neglecting that part of the adjustment that policy makers would find it in their *own interest* to undertake in the absence of the 3 per cent constraint. For the fiscal authorities, this *extra* convergence is costly, with increasing marginal costs. The higher β, the more (economic-ally and politically) painful it is for a government to pursue fiscal rigour or unpopular budget reforms in compliance with the fiscal criteria. The (dis-counted) penalty – i.e. the 'fine' imposed by the Stability Pact – is denoted by T. It could include both pecuniary as well as political costs of breaching the criteria.

$$U = p(E)T - \frac{\beta}{2}E^2. \tag{7.1}$$

In the absence of uncertainty $p(E)$ will be a two-valued function; it will be equal to one if the 3 per cent limit is satisfied and zero if not. In this

---

[3.] The framework is as in Dornbusch's (1991) model of exchange rate-based stabilization in developing countries.

case, a country will undertake the required minimum level of fiscal adjustment if the benefit of avoiding the fine exceeds the costs of convergence.
However, uncertainty in relation to the operation of the Stability Pact
arises from two principal sources. First, given that a vote in the Council
of Ministers is required, it is unclear *ex ante* how strictly the fines of the
Stability Pact will be applied and whether exceptions may be granted.
Second, there is forecasting uncertainty concerning the economic conditions which affect the success of fiscal adjustment and there is instrument
uncertainty regarding how the budgetary measures adopted will impact on
the actual deficit. On both counts, uncertainty can be seen to intervene
between adjustment effort and the actual deficit.

Therefore, more specifically, a fine under the Stability Pact will be
avoided if fiscal adjustment exceeds some threshold value, M, the 3 per
cent criterion. In (7.2) fulfilment F of the deficit criterion depends on
adjustment effort E, but also on a random term θ. The marginal 'productivity' of effort with respect to deficit reduction – i.e. its effectiveness – is
measured by α. From this we can derive an expression for the probability
of success $p(E)$ for some distribution function $f(\theta)$, in (7.3).

$$F = \begin{cases} 0 & \text{if} \quad \alpha E + \theta < M \\ 1 & \text{if} \quad \alpha E + \theta \geq M \end{cases} \tag{7.2}$$

$$p(E) = p(\theta \geq \phi) = \int_{\phi}^{\infty} f(\theta)\, d\theta \qquad \text{where } \psi \equiv M - \alpha E. \tag{7.3}$$

A country faced with the 3 per cent deficit threshold, M, and a
prospective fine of size T maximizes (7.1) with respect to E, which yields
the first-order condition for optimal effort E^*.

$$E^* = \frac{\partial p}{\partial E}\frac{T}{\beta} \equiv -f(\psi)\frac{\partial \psi}{\partial E}\frac{T}{\beta} \equiv f(\psi)\frac{\alpha T}{\beta}. \tag{7.4}$$

With adjustment costly and reward uncertain, the optimal convergence
effort will not guarantee that a fine can be avoided. The probability of
success can be obtained by substituting the optimal adjustment effort into
(7.3). Optimal convergence effort, E^*, is increasing in the size of the fine,
T, decreasing in β. A higher M (more ambitious deficit target) increases
effort for $f'(\psi) > 0$, otherwise it reduces effort. The effect of changing α is
negative for $f'(\psi) > 0$, positive otherwise. The corresponding equilibrium
probability p^* is always increasing in T and α, decreasing in β and M.

A (credible) *tightening of the deficit limit*, all else being equal, leads to
increased convergence effort (as long as $f'(\psi) > 0$), but always a lower
probability of success. For the designer of the criterion this gives rise to
a potential trade-off, if she is interested in keeping the probability and

frequency of violations of the Stability Pact low as well as in fiscal discipline *per se*. The targets should not be overly ambitious if frequent violations would undermine their credibility and hence their effectiveness as incentive devices.

The *impact of a recession* on adjustment incentives can operate through three channels in our model. If it makes the deficit target look further away it is equivalent to raising M. If recession makes any given level of effort more painful (e.g. unpopular or economically costly) it increases β; if it makes convergence results harder to obtain, for given effort, it lowers α. An increase in the size of the fine T increases adjustment effort and the probability of success. Note that for different countries parameter values will differ. In particular, the Maastricht numerical targets are the same for all countries, but the implied *extra* discipline that is required varies considerably. The uniformity of the numerical criteria for all countries (a 'non-discrimination constraint') means that they cannot be designed as a tailor-made incentive device for each country.

The above analysis has interpreted the deficit criterion as a simple threshold incentive contract. Under uncertainty governments will equate the marginal cost of undertaking fiscal adjustment with the marginal benefit of reducing the risk of incurring penalties under the Stability Pact. Rational governments optimizing *ex ante* will aim for a deficit much below the 3 per cent as a 'cushion' against subsequent unfavourable shocks. This cushion will be even greater in the presence of self-fulfilling credibility feedbacks. If countries react to the Stability Pact in this way automatic stabilizers need not necessarily be compromised, as feared by Eichengreen (1997), in particular in view of exceptions in the event of unusually large shocks.

In our *ex ante* interpretation the 3 per cent ceiling on the actual deficit induces behaviour not much different from a target on structural deficits. The main difference is that countries can choose their target structural deficit for themselves – i.e. the optimal size of their 'cushion' depending on their own preferences. Likewise, the choice of the nature and instruments of fiscal adjustment is left to the individual countries. The criticism of the 3 per cent target as arbitrary and 'one-size-fits-all' (Eichengreen, 1997) is therefore only partially justified. Moreover, the same criticism would apply equally to the alternative suggestions of NAIRU-adjusted deficit targets or a centrally imposed reform of national budget procedures proposed by von Hagen and Harden (1994). It is also difficult to imagine that the latter would be politically feasible, contractible and enforceable in an international treaty. Both the alternatives suffer from the additional drawback of not giving any assurance on the stabilization of the deficit–debt dynamics.

The justified concern, however, is that governments, because they behave myopically or find it expedient, will not optimize *ex ante* but will delay their deficit reduction measures until 'the last minute' after the realization of shocks. In the extreme, governments would cling close to the 3 per cent ceiling throughout the cycle and adopt *ad hoc* budget measures only whenever the deficit limit was about to be violated. Such a behaviour would of course be exactly pro-cyclical and extremely damaging, but its prospect cannot entirely be discarded in light of the experience of countries trying to meet the EMU entry conditions. Here the incentive structure was very similar, except that the reward for convergence, i.e. – EMU entry – is perceived to be much greater than the (avoidance of the) fines of the Stability Pact. Why then, even with so much more at stake, did countries wait so long after the signing of the Treaty to undertake serious fiscal adjustment and then were forced to do so under very unfavourable cyclical conditions? Winkler (1997b) points to some possible answers: these include the political uncertainty surrounding the *if* and *when* of the EMU launch, which reduced the expected reward from convergence effort. Moreover, the application of the convergence criteria in the entry decision, just like the decision on the launch of EMU itself, was uncertain and seen to depend on relative convergence performance, not only on compliance with absolute numbers. Both features made it rational for countries to sit and wait until late in the game.

The clarification of procedures in the Stability Pact should be helpful in addressing some of these problems, but it is entirely possible that countries allowed to enter EMU with high structural deficits might indeed respond to perverse pro-cyclical incentives initially. This distortion of economic stabilization – or, alternatively, paying the fines – may however be a price well worth paying for low-stability entrants, and perhaps even worth tolerating for high-stability members, if the Stability Pact succeeds in limiting negative spillovers in particular on the common monetary policy, at least in the longer term. In the terminology of the previous section, the Stability Pact's primary task is to ensure an MD regime, which largely hinges on the credibility of medium- to longer-term fiscal adjustment paths, not on the precise initial conditions.

Conclusion

In the opinions of some, the Stability Pact promises to be an unduly restrictive framework, a straitjacket for fiscal policy; others view its dependence on declared self-commitment and the room that it gives to discretion as signs that it is no more than a 'paper tiger'. Much like central bank independence, the Stability Pact appears to be an 'empty shell', but this does not mean that it is necessarily ineffective. The framework and procedures that are created together with the numerical benchmarks may well by themselves influence incentives in the desired direction, but 'soft' factors such as peer pressure and the degree of shared 'stability culture' are likely to be at least as important as the legal force and details of the Stability Pact's provisions.

The focus on the numerical values of the Maastricht fiscal criteria and in the Stability Pact, even more pronounced in the public debate than in the actual wording of the provisions, runs the risk of diverting attention to ways of fiddling with the numbers, of taking token measures and manipulating budget forecasts. Yet, some such measure of actual performance had to be chosen, however imperfect, in order to provide incentives for discipline. Moreover, the reference values have to be seen together with the emphasis – in both the Treaty and the Stability Pact – on the sustainability of medium-term budget policies. As argued by Masson (1996), the Maastricht criteria may be sensible, even if the measures taken to fulfil them are not. An increased emphasis on structural reforms of national budgetary procedures may well be called for (von Hagen and Harden, 1994; Eichengreen and Wyplosz, 1998), but this does not obviate the need for providing a numerical target for the outcomes of any such reforms. Indeed, it may be that the provision of the target is necessary to instigate the reform process.

Nor need there be a contradiction between the 3 per cent numerical target and longer-run reforms and sustainability, nor between discipline (credibility) and stabilization (flexibility). If the Stability Pact operates as an effective (*ex ante*) incentive device, countries should be induced to keep a safety margin that would allow automatic stabilizers to deal with normal-size shocks without breach of the 3 per cent ceiling. Moreover, the degree of flexibility and the procedures of the Stability Pact make it quite possible that countries can get by with repeated violations of the numerical target without incurring any sanctions. This could be welcomed for the increased *ex post* flexibility, but it undermines Stability Pact's the *ex ante* deterrence. The problem here is that there is an ambitious, declared numerical norm (the 3 per cent deficit ceiling throughout a normal economic cycle), while sanctions for violations of this norm are likely to bite only in cases of persistent or outright defiance. Here there is room for a potential conflict between those who might come to view sanction-free behaviour as an acceptable standard, leaning towards a state-contingent reading of the 3 per cent rule, and those defending the 3 per cent rule at face value. A further negative side effect of the Stability Pact could be that planned and actual deficits will diverge even more than at present, especially with respect to medium-term projections, since by holding out the promise of successful stabilization a country can postpone the imposition of sanctions under the excessive deficit procedure.

Trade-offs between discipline and stabilization seem most likely to arise in the early phase of EMU if countries join Stage Three with deficits right up against the 3 per cent ceiling or with deficit ratios which benefit unduly from one-off acts of creative accounting. The provisions of the Stability Pact would then face an early test just at the same time as the new ECB will be keen to establish its reputation. The seriousness of the problem (the strain on the ECB and the Stability Pact) will depend on the cyclical position of the European economies and on how strictly the Maastricht entry criteria have been applied. The scope for a trade-off between the Stability Pact and the entry criteria therefore appears to be limited. On the one hand the Stability Pact should give reassurance on the longer-run stability orientation of EMU and could therefore allow a more relaxed attitude to the entry conditions and a larger initial membership (Artis, 1996). However, in the short run, if cyclical conditions and budget figures remain weak, the Stability Pact could prove counter-productive by either inducing pro-cyclical behaviour or by being shown as ineffective (if overshoots of the 3 per cent are allowed) right from the start. We share the view that Eichengreen and Wyplosz (1998) have also expressed, that the risks with the Stability Pact are front-endloaded: but these risks are also two-sided – on the one hand that in the early years of its operation the Stability Pact may prove unduly restrictive and, on the other, that it may be exposed almost from the beginning as a 'paper tiger'.

While there is some reason to doubt the effectiveness of the technical provisions of the Stability Pact in guaranteeing the desired discipline and flexibility in practice, the mere fact that member states have agreed to subject national budget policies to a concerted European joint discipline is of great significance on two counts. First, conceding concerted fiscal discipline in order to safeguard the leadership and credibility of the ECB may be a first significant step towards further implicit or explicit coordination among economic policy makers. Second, the conclusion of the Stability Pact also represents a small, but important, transfer of national sovereignty in the budgetary field. Unlike Gros (1996) and Thygesen (1996) we believe that there is a nexus between political union and monetary union. In the final analysis EMU will be successful only if all the main policy actors are sufficiently ready to subordinate national or special interests to common objectives, the stability of the common currency in particular, and if the ECB enjoys solid public support across Europe.

It is fashionable to describe policy institutions and arrangements as being located somewhere along a spectrum that prizes flexibility at one end and credibility at the other. In the wider perspective suggested here, the Stability Pact may mean something more than simply a choice to locate at the 'credibility' end of the spectrum. It may promise an improvement in the trade-off between these two desirable characteristics of policy and imply a promise of better economic government in Europe.

References

Agell, J., Calmfors, L. and Jonsson, G. (1996). 'Fiscal Policy When Monetary Policy is "Tied to the Mast"'. *European Economic Review*, 40: 1413–40

Alesina, A. and Drazen, A. (1991). 'Why are Stabilizations Delayed?', *American Economic Review*, 81: 1170–88

Alesina, A. and Perotti, R. (1995). 'The Political Economy of Budget Deficits'. *IMF Staff Papers*, 42: 1–32

Alesina, A. and Tabellini, G.(1987). 'Rules and Discretion with Non-coordinated Monetary and Fiscal Policies', *Economic Inquiry*, 25: 619–30

Allsopp, C. and Vines, D. (1996). 'Fiscal Policy and EMU', *NIER Working Paper*, 158: 91–107

Artis, M. (1996). 'Alternative Transitions to EMU'. *Economic Journal*, 106: 1005–15

Artis, M. and Marcellino, M. (1998). 'Fiscal Solvency and Fiscal Forecasting in Europe', *EUI Working Paper*, ECO 98/2

Artis, M. and Winkler, B. (1998). 'The Stability Pact: Safeguarding the Credibility of the European Central Bank', *National Institute Economic Review* (January): 87–98

Barro, R. and Gordon, D. (1983). 'A Positive Theory of Monetary Policy in a Natural Rate Model'. *Journal of Political Economy*, 91: 585–610

Bayoumi, T. and Eichengreen, B. (1995). 'Restraining Yourself: The Implications of Fiscal Rules for Economic Stabilization'. *IMF Staff Papers*, 42: 32–48

(1996). 'Operationalizing the Theory of Optimum Currency Areas'. *CEPR Discussion Paper*, 1484

Bayoumi, T. and Masson, P. (1995). 'Fiscal Flows in the United States and Canada: Lessons for Monetary Union in Europe', *European Economic Review*, 39: 253–274

(1996). 'Debt-creating versus Non-debt-creating Fiscal Stabilization Policies: Ricardian Equivalence, Fiscal Stabilization, and EMU', International Monetary Fund (March), mimeo

Beetsma, R. and Bovenberg, L. (1995a). 'Does Monetary Unification Lead to Excessive Debt Accumulation?', *CEPR Discussion Paper*, 1299

(1995b). 'Designing Fiscal and Monetary Institutions for a European Monetary Union', *CEPR Discussion Paper*, 1303

Beetsma, R. and Uhlig, H. (1997). 'An Analysis of the "Stability Pact"', *CEPR Discussion Paper*, 1669

Bertola, G. and Drazen, A. (1993). 'Trigger Points and Budget Cuts: Explaining the Effects of Fiscal Austerity', *American Economic Review*, 83: 11–26

Bliss, C. and Nalebuff, B. (1984). 'Dragon-slaying and Ballroom Dancing: The Private Supply of a Public Good,' *Journal of Public Economics*, 25: 1–12

Bryson, J., Jensen, H. and van Hoose, D. (1993). 'Rules, Discretion, and International Monetary and Fiscal Policy Coordination', *Open Economies Review*, 4: 117–32

Buchanan, J. (1977). 'Democracy in Deficit,' in J. Buchanan, *The Political Legacy of Lord Keynes*, New York: Academic Press

Buiter, W., Corsetti, G. and Roubini, N. (1993). 'Excessive Deficits: Sense and Nonsense in the Treaty of Maastricht', *Economic Policy*, 16: 57–100

Buti, M., Franco, D. and Ongena, H. (1997). 'Budgetary Policies during Recession – Retrospective Application of the "Stability and Growth Pact" to the Post-war Period', European Commission, DGII, *Economic Papers*, 121 (May)

Canzoneri, M. and B. T. Diba (1996). 'Fiscal Constraints on Central Bank Independence and Price Stability'. *CEPR Discussion Paper*, 1463

Canzoneri, M., Cumby, R. E. and Diba, B. T. (1997), 'Is the Price Level Determined by the Needs of Fiscal Solvency?', *CEPR Discussion Paper*, 1772

Commission of the European Communities (1977) *Report of the Study Group of the Role of Public Finance in European Integration* (the McDougall Report)

Corsetti, G. and Roubini, N. (1993). 'The Design of Optimal Fiscal Rules for Europe after 1992', in F. Torres and F. Giavazzi (eds.), *Adjustment and Growth in the European Monetary System*, Cambridge: Cambridge University Press 46–82

Cour, P., Dubois, E., Mahfouz, S. and Pisani-Ferry, J. (1996). 'The Cost of Fiscal Retrenchment Revisited: How Strong is the Evidence?', *CEPII Document de Travail*, 96–116, Paris: CEPII

De Grauwe, P. (1996). 'The Economics of Convergence: Towards Monetary Union in Europe', *Weltwirtschaftliches Archiv*, 132: 1–27

Deutscher Bundestag (1992). *Bundestagsdrucksache*, 12/3906 (2 December)

Dornbusch, R. (1991). 'Credibility and Stabilization'. *Quarterly Journal of Economics*, 106: 837–50

ECOFIN Report (1996). 'Report by the ECOFIN Council to the European Council'. Annex 1 of Presidency Conclusions of the Dublin European Council, *Europe Documents*, Agence Internationale d'Information pour la Presse, Luxembourg, 2015/16 (18 December)

Eichengreen, B. (1997). 'Saving Europe's Automatic Stabilizers'. *National Institute Economic Review*, 159: 92–8

Eichengreen, B. and Ghironi, F. (1997). 'How will Transatlantic Policy Interaction Change with the Advent of EMU?', *CEPR Dicussion Paper*, 1643

Eichengreen, B. and von Hagen, J. (1996). 'Fiscal Policy and Monetary Union: Federalism, Fiscal Restrictions, and the No-bailout Rule,' in H. Siebert (ed.), *Monetary Policy in an Integrated World Economy*, Tübingen: Mohr (Paul Siebeck): 211–31

Eichengreen, B. and Wyplosz, C. (1998). 'The Stability Pact: More than a Minor Nuisance?', *Economic Policy*, 26: 65–104

Eijffinger, S. and De Haan, J. (1996). 'The Political Economy of Central-bank Independence'. *Special Papers in International Economics*, 19, International Finance Section, Princeton University

European Council (1997). 'Presidency Conclusions', Amsterdam European Council (16 and 17 June) (reprinted in *European Economy*, 64)

Giavazzi, F. and Pagano, M. (1990). 'Can Severe Fiscal Contractions Be Expansionary? Tales of Two Small European Countries', *NBER Macroeconomics Annual*; Cambridge, Mass. and London: MIT Press: 75–116

Giovannini, A. (1994). 'The Debate on Nominal Convergence before and after the 1992 Crisis', in A. Steinherr (ed.), *30 Years of European Monetary Integration from the Werner Plan to EMU*, Harrow: Longman, 184–91

Glick, R. and Hutchison, M. (1993). 'Fiscal Policy in Monetary Unions: Implications for Europe', *Open Economies Review*, 4: 39–65

Grilli, V., Masciandaro, D. and Tabellini, G. (1991). 'Political and Monetary Institutions and Public Financial Policies in the Industrial Countries,' *Economic Policy*, 13: 341–92

Gros, D. (1996). 'Towards Economic and Monetary Union: Problems and Prospects'. *CEPS Paper*, 65

Hughes Hallett, A. and McAdam, P. (1996). 'Fiscal Deficit Reduction in Line with the Maastricht Criteria for Monetary Union: An Empirical Analysis'. *CEPR Discussion Paper*, 1351

IMF (1995). *World Economic Outlook*, Washington, DC: International Monetary Fund (May)

(1997). *World Economic Outlook*, Washington, DC: International Monetary Fund (October)

Jensen, H. (1996). 'The Advantage of International Fiscal Cooperation under Alternative Monetary Regimes', *European Journal of Political Economy*, 12: 485–504

(1997). 'Credibility of Optimal Monetary Delegation', *American Economic Review*, 87: 911–20

Kletzer, K. M. (1997). 'Macroeconomic Stabilization with a Common Currency: Does European Monetary Unification create a need for Fiscal Insurance or Federalism', *ZEI Policy Paper*, B97-04, Zentrum für Europäische Integrationsforschung

Lamfalussy, A. (1997). 'Securing the Benefits of EMU', In *Deutsche Bundesbank: Auszüge aud Presseartikeln* 14: 4–7

Lane, T. (1993). 'Market Discipline', *IMF Staff Papers*, 40: 53–88

Levine, P. and Pearlman, J. (1992). 'Fiscal and Monetary Policy under EMU: Credible Inflation Targets or Unpleasant Monetary Arithmetic?', *CEPR Discussion Paper*, 701

Lohmann, S. (1996). 'Quis Custodiet Ipsos Custodes? Necessary Conditions for Price Stability in Europe', In H. Siebert (ed.), *Monetary Policy in an Integrated World Economy*, Tübingen: Mohr (Paul Siebeck): 139–60

Masson, P. (1996). 'Fiscal Dimensions of EMU', *Economic Journal*, 106: 996–1004

McCallum, B. (1995). 'Two Fallacies Concerning Central-bank Independence', *American Economic Review, Papers and Proceedings*, 85: 207–11

McKinnon, R. I. (1994). 'A Common Monetary Standard or a Common Currency for Europe? Fiscal Lessons from the United States', *Scottish Journal of Political Economy*, (November): 337–57

Mélitz, J. and Vori, S. (1992). 'National Insurance Against Unevenly Distributed Shocks'. *CEPR Discussion Paper*, 697

Mourmouras, I. and Su, D.-M. (1995). 'Central Bank Independence, Policy Reforms and the Credibility of Public Debt Stabilizations', *European Journal of Political Economy*, 11: 189–204

Olson, M. (1965). *The Logic of Collective Action*, Cambridge, Mass: Harvard University Press

Pisani-Ferry, J. (1996). 'Fiscal Policy under EMU'. *CEPII Newsletter*, 6, 2nd semester, Paris: 1–2

Rogoff, K. (1985a). 'The Optimal Degree of Commitment to an Intermediate Monetary Target'. *Quarterly Journal of Economics*, 100: 1169–90

(1985b). 'Can International Monetary Policy Coordination be Counterproductive?', *Journal of International Economics*, 18: 199–217

Roubini, N. and Sachs, J. (1989). 'Political and Economic Determinants of Budget Deficits in the Industrial Democracies', *European Economic Review*, 33: 903-38

Sargent, T. and Wallace, N. (1981). 'Some Unpleasant Monetarist Arithmetic', *Quarterly Review*, Federal Reserve Bank of Minneapolis (Fall): 1–17

Sørensen, B. E. and Yosha, O. (1998). 'International Risk-sharing and European Monetary Unification', *Journal of International Economics*, 45: 211–38

Thygesen, N. (1996). 'Should Budgetary Policies be Coordinated Further in EMU – and is that Feasible?', *Banca Nazionale del Lavoro Quarterly Review*, 196, Special Issue: 5–32

von Hagen, J. and Hammond, G. (1995). 'Regional Insurance Against Asymmetric Shocks: An Empirical Study for the European Community', *CEPR Discussion Paper*, 1170

von Hagen, J. and Harden, I. (1994). 'National Budget Processes and Fiscal Performance', *European Economy, Reports and Studies*, 3: 311–408

Walsh, C. (1995). 'Optimal Contracts for Central Bankers', *American Economic Review* 85: 150–67

Werner, P., *et al.* (1970). *Report to the Council and the Commission on the Realization by Steps of Economic and Monetary Union in the Community* (the Werner Report, Supplement to Bulletin II – 1970 of the European Communities, Brussels

Winckler, G., Hochreiter, E. and Brandner, P. (1997). 'Deficits, Debt and European Monetary Union: Some Unpleasant Fiscal Arithmetic', in G. Calvo and M. King (eds.), *The Debt Burden and its Consequences for Monetary Policy*, London: Macmillan

Winkler, B. (1996). 'Towards a Strategic View on EMU: A Critical Survey', *Journal of Public Policy*, 16: 1–28

(1997a). 'Of Sticks and Carrots: Incentives and the Maastricht Road to EMU', *EUI Working Paper*, ECO 97/2, European University Institute, Florence

(1997b). 'Coordinating European Monetary Union', *EUI Working Paper*, ECO 97/10, European University Institute, Florence

Woodford, M. (1995). 'Price Level Determinacy without Control of a Monetary Aggregate'. *Carnegie–Rochester Conference Series on Public Policy*

(1996). 'Control of the Public Debt: A Requirement for Price Stability?', Princeton University (February) mimeo

8 The Stability and Growth Pact in a model with politically induced deficit biases

Roel M. W. J. Beetsma

Introduction

The 'Stability and Growth Pact' (SGP or Stability Pact), which was agreed at the Amsterdam Summit in June 1997, is intended to strengthen the Excessive Deficits Procedure (EDP) once European Monetary Union (EMU) has come into existence, by making more precise the EDP time schedule as well as the sanctions in the case of violations of the deficit criterion. More specifically, if the European Council of Finance Ministers (ECOFIN) concludes that a country has an excessive deficit and that it fails to adopt the appropriate measures to correct it, it will be required to submit a non-interest-bearing deposit. The deposit will become a fine if the country persists in running an excessive deficits. The minimum fine is 0.2 per cent of GDP and increases by 0.1 per cent for each percentage point that the deficits are above the 3 per cent level, up to a maximum of 0.5 per cent of GDP. Any sanctions will be waived if real GDP falls by more than 2 per cent in a year. A fall of GDP of between 0.75 per cent and 2 per cent may or may not lead to sanctions, depending on whether the country can convince the other member states that the excessive deficits are caused by factors beyond its control. The EDP and the SGP are described in more detail in Artis and Winkler (1997) and Gros and Thygesen (1998).

The EMU entry conditions on debts and deficits – and, more recently, the SGP – have been severely criticized by commentators from the academic world (see, for example, Bean, 1992; De Grauwe, 1992; and

I am very grateful for helpful suggestions from the editors of the book, Paul de Grauwe, Philipp Hartmann, Lex Hoogduin, Henrik Jensen, Torsten Persson, Michael Steinbeisser, Claes Wihlborg and seminar participants at the Catholic University of Leuven, the Centre for Financial Studies (Frankfurt University), the EPRU Workshop on 'Fiscal Aspects of Monetary Integration', the EMI, the IIES (Stockholm University) and the Sveriges Riksbank. The usual disclaimer applies. I thank the Nederlandse Organisatie voor Wetenschappelijk Onderzoek (Grant No 400-70-015/11-3) for financial support. Part of this chapter was written at the IIES, which I thank for its hospitality.

Buiter, Corsetti and Roubini, 1993). First, the 60 per cent restriction on the debt/GDP ratio and the 3 per cent restriction on the deficit GDP ratio are often considered to be arbitrary.[1] The definition of debt, with debt being measured as gross consolidated public sector debt, has also been criticized for not taking into account the claims of the public sector on the private sector, nor any real assets that the public sector holds (for example, Calmfors *et al.*, 1997: 134). Second, it is often argued that capital markets could do the same job in disciplining governments. However, it is unclear how good markets are at assessing and pricing differences in riskiness. Markets often react abruptly and may suddenly cut off all credit. Whether or not such a reaction is rational, it may be damaging for the stability of the financial system.[2] A third criticism, which holds more specifically for the SGP, is that any potential sanctions will be imposed only after a long procedure involving many steps and negotiations. This provides a leeway to escape the sanctions and may have adverse effects on the incentive to undertake budgetary reform (see Buiter and Sibert, 1997).

The usefulness of any type of budgetary restriction motivated by EMU rests on two conditions. One is that there is some channel through which an individual country's budgetary policies affect the other EMU countries. The other is that these spillovers are strengthened (in a welfare-reducing way) by monetary unification.

There is a variety of potential spillovers from budgetary policies in EMU, either directly or through the policy responses of the European Central Bank (ECB). Here I mention only those that are potentially most important. One way in which an increase in some country's public debt may affect other countries is through an increase in the world real interest rate (see, for example the models of Chang, 1990; Canzoneri and Diba, 1991). This increases the cost for the other countries of issuing public debt. It is unclear how important this effect is empirically. It seems unlikely that the policies of a small or even a middle-sized country can have much of an effect on the world real interest rate. A joint expansion of the public debt throughout Europe may have a significant effect on the real interest rate, though. If public debt is perfectly substitutable then these effects are not altered by monetary unification and EMU as such would not justify the adoption of budgetary restrictions. In as far as investors are not risk-neutral, EMU may strengthen the interest rate spillovers because the substitutability of the public debt of its members increases (for example, through the elimination of exchange rate risk or

---

[1] Although these norms appear to be quite arbitrary, they are simple and as such serve a potentially useful role in disciplining governments, as Willett (1999) argues.

[2] The rationale for budgetary restrictions in the model we present below, does *not* rely on the potential failure of capital markets in assessing the riskiness of the public debt.

because of economic shocks becoming more similar). In response to an increase in a country's debt, investors would be willing to keep the other countries' debt in their portfolios (and thus forgo diversification gains) only if they were compensated by a sufficient rise in the interest rate on this debt.

A second spillover effect is based on the standard Mundell–Fleming argument that fiscal policy is more effective under fixed than under floating exchange rates. By forming a monetary union, the effects of a unilateral fiscal expansion on employment are no longer offset by exchange rate appreciations *vis-à-vis* the other EMU participants. Given that most of the international trade of EMU members will be among themselves, the employment effects of a fiscal expansion could be relatively large and therefore very tempting for governments, especially just before elections. Fiscal expansions put an upward pressure on prices and force the ECB to tighten monetary policy; this has a contractionary effect on all the economies in the union.

Our focus will be on a third type of spillover that arises directly from the fact that a country's debt policies affect the common monetary policy of the ECB, if the ECB is not quite as independent as it is supposed to be. Although the Maastricht Treaty guarantees the ECB's independence on paper, this does not necessarily guarantee the same degree of independence in practice. This is exactly what many people in countries with a tradition of monetary stability fear; these fears have been strengthened by the (failed) French attempts to set up a political council to act as a counterweight to the ECB (the Euro-X Council, see also chapter 7 in this volume) and by the many tricks that countries have used to reduce their deficits in order to be in the first wave of EMU entrants. If the ECB is only partially independent from the governments of the union participants, it may be tempted to raise inflation in order to reduce the real value of the outstanding public debt. Hence, because it affects the common inflation rate, an individual country's debt policy will lead to spillovers on other countries. Moreover, given that the effect of a unilateral debt increase on future inflation is weaker in a union than with national monetary policy making, debt accumulation will be higher.

The mechanism just described suggests that monetary unification creates a role for restrictions on fiscal policy. To make this more precise, I explore the role of a stability pact in a model adapted from Beetsma and Uhlig (1999). There, we construct a political–economic model of centralized monetary policy making and decentralized fiscal policy making by governments which are myopic because they can be voted out of office. The latter aspect of the model is based on earlier work by Alesina and Tabellini (1990), Tabellini and Alesina (1990) and Cukierman, Edwards and Tabellini (1992). Given their finite stay in office, policy makers are often compelled into taking a rather short-term point of view; in particular, it often looks attractive to raise additional debt to pay for expenditures, which benefit in particular the constituency of the party in power, and then leave it to successors to worry about repaying that debt. This leads to debts which are excessive from a social perspective.[3]

However, the policy maker's incentives to over-issue debt are at least to some extent kept in check by the prospect of higher future inflation. Because the ECB bases its policies on the average public indebtedness of EMU members, the inflation reduction resulting from a unilateral reduction in debt will be smaller in EMU than with national monetary policy making. The incentive to restrain debt for the purpose of lower future inflation is therefore weakened by monetary unification and, hence, the debt bias will be exacerbated. In such a situation, it may be useful to have a Stability Pact which imposes sanctions on budgetary laxity. In particular, I show that by imposing a fine which is increasing in the size of the debt, the additional debt accumulation caused by monetary unification can be corrected. However, in the presence of idiosyncratic shocks, such a pact may exacerbate the budgetary problems of a country hit by a bad shock and, as a result, the cross-country dispersion in debt levels are magnified. This is precisely one of the commonly voiced objections against the Stability Pact. To deal with this problem it is necessary that the severity of the sanctions be adjusted for the exogenous shocks that hit the economies of the union participants. In fact, one can show that with sufficient adjustment a pact can be made to act as an insurance mechanism, while still preserving its role in reducing the debt bias.

While in the basic version of the model all countries are (*ex ante*) identical, we make the analysis more realistic by allowing for asymmetries among countries. In particular, we explore the effects of differences in initial debt, differences in economic and political structure, and differences in the relative size of countries – and, therefore, in their influence on the ECB. With differences in initial debt we obtain the interesting result that all participants in the union are better off under a pact that appropriately punishes excessive deficits. In the presence of asymmetries in economic and political structure, governments differ in their desire for public spending. More disciplined governments may be worse off participating in a monetary union, which suggests that they are more in favour of a strict pact. Finally, if countries differ in their relative size, smaller countries would need to be to punished more severely for a given increase in their

---

[3.] For empirical work on the relation between length of government tenure and public debt accumulation in OECD countries, see Roubini and Sachs (1989).

debt. The reason is that a smaller country internalizes the effect of its policies on the common inflation rate to a lesser extent and hence has a stronger tendency to over-accumulate debt.

The literature on budgetary restrictions is growing rapidly. Closest in spirit to this chapter is the work by Chari and Kehoe (1997) who explore the need for debt restrictions in a two-country model of monetary union. Only if the central bank is not able to commit are debt restrictions needed. The reason is that the union members do not fully internalize the welfare effects of an increase in nominal debt on the common union-wide inflation rate. Giovannetti, Marimon and Teles (1997) extend the model of Chari and Kehoe (1997) into various directions. In particular, they allow for differences in initial debt levels and, therefore, differences in the most-preferred monetary policy across countries. A major difference with our model is that in our model the debt bias arises from a political distortion which is exacerbated by monetary unification. Even more importantly, our model also allows for stochastic shocks and gradual sanctions for excessive debts rather than rigid targets or ceilings on the public debt. Agell, Calmfors and Jonsson (1996) analyse a model in which membership of EMU may increase fiscal deficits, which leads them to argue in favour of restricting fiscal policy.

The next section presents and solves the model, and I then discuss its main results. In particular, I explore how the incentive to run excessive deficits or debts can be affected by introducing a stability pact. I also show how the pact could act as a cross-country insurance mechanism (without compromising its ability to reduce average debts) if the severity of the sanctions is reduced in response to adverse shocks. I then explore the effects of asymmetries among countries, and address some of the potential problems of the Stability Pact in practice, in particular its enforcement and the moral hazard problems that would arise if the severity of sanctions depended on countries' economic situation. This section also discusses how extending the modelling horizon might shed light on the distinction between sanctions based on excessive debts and on excessive deficits. The final section concludes.

The model

This section presents a simple, two-period model of monetary and fiscal policy interaction in a monetary union. The model is an adapted version of the basic model in Beetsma and Uhlig (1999). Monetary policy is conducted at the central level by the ECB, while fiscal policy is selected at the national level. In the absence of regulating constraints other than the need to repay the debt eventually, governments will issue too much debt if at the end of this period they may be replaced by another government with different spending preferences.

Preferences and constraints

EMU is formed by n countries which are assumed to be identical in both their economic and political structure and their preferences. The special case of $n = 1$ corresponds to monetary policy making at the national level.

Consider some participating country i $(i = 1, \ldots, n)$. Society i's expected utility is given by

$$U_{Si}(.) = u(f_{1i} + g_{1i}) + E[f_{2i} + g_{2i} - \pi^2/(2\phi)] \qquad (8.1)$$

where $f_{ti} \geq 0$ and $g_{ti} \geq 0$ is spending on public goods F and G, respectively, in period t $(t = 1, 2)$ and π is the common, union-wide inflation rate, which is determined in the second period. Parameter ϕ is the inverse of the degree of inflation aversion. $E[.]$ denotes the expectations operator. This utility function can be thought of as a social welfare function which aggregates the preferences of all agents in society. The function $u(.)$ is twice continuously differentiable with $u'(.) > 0$ and $u''(.) < 0$. For convenience, I assume that $u(0) = 0$ and that $u'(1) = 1$. Furthermore, I assume that $u'(2) < p$, where p is introduced below. There is no discounting.

The political process is modelled following Alesina and Tabellini (1990). In each country there are two political parties, F and G, which are selected to run the government by an election with random outcome. Party F cares only about public good F, while party G cares only about public good G. Hence, the utilities of parties F and G are given by, respectively:

$$U_{Fi}(.) = u(f_{1i}) + E[f_{2i} - \pi^2/(2\phi)], \qquad (8.2)$$

$$U_{Gi}(.) = u(g_{1i}) + E[g_{2i} - \pi^2/(2\phi)]. \qquad (8.3)$$

Without loss of generality I assume that in each country party F is in power in period 1. It will be re-elected at the end of the first period with an exogenous probability of p, where $0 < p < 1$.

Each government receives an exogenous endowment income of one unit in each period. Moreover, if we assume that initial debt is zero and that all debt is paid off in the second period, the budget constraints of the governments (or resource constraints of the economy) in period 1 and 2 are given respectively by:

$$f_{1i} + g_{1i} = 1 + b_i + \varepsilon_i - \psi_1(b_i - \bar{b}_i) + \left(\frac{1}{n-1}\right) \sum_{j=1, j \neq i}^{n} \psi_1(b_j - \bar{b}_j),$$

(8.4)

$$f_{2i} + g_{2i} = 1 - b_i[1 + \pi^e - \pi] - \psi_2(b_i - \bar{b}_i)$$

$$+ \left(\frac{1}{n-1}\right) \sum_{j=1, j \neq i}^{n} \psi_2(b_j - \bar{b}_j)$$

(8.5)

where b_i is the amount of debt issued by the period 1 government and traded on the world capital market (there are no restrictions on capital mobility). For convenience, I have assumed that the *ex ante* world real interest rate is zero. All debt is assumed to be nominal.[4] Hence, for risk-neutral agents to be willing to hold government bonds, the nominal interest rate, π^e, includes a mark-up equal to the expected inflation rate. The *ex post* real interest rate is given by $\pi^e - \pi$. Finally, ε_i is a mean-zero, finite-variance shock to first-period resources. It may capture a wide range of unexpected effects, such as changes in world market prices of export goods, natural disasters, etc.

Countries may sign a stability pact to punish budgetary profligacy. Because I have assumed zero initial debt and a two-period modelling horizon, it is not possible in this stylized setup to distinguish between debts and deficits. To fix the terminology, I shall refer to fines/sanctions as being based on excessive debts. The fines are given by the next-to-last terms in (8.4) and (8.5). In particular, a stability pact specifies that if the government of country i accumulates an amount of debt different from its so-called reference level, $\bar{b}_i$ it pays a fine of $\psi_1(b_i - \bar{b}_i)$ in period 1 and of $\psi_2(b_i - \bar{b}_i)$ in period 2.[5] Hence, I allow for fines both in the period in which the debt is issued as well as in the period that the debt is repaid. Note that fines may be negative. The linear structure of the fines keeps the analysis tractable.[6] Hence, the model delivers meaningful predictions

---

4. This reflects standard practice, at least for OECD countries. To keep the analysis tractable, we do not explicitly model the factors that lead to nominal debt being optimal. One reason to have nominal debt is that it acts as an instrument for hedging the real value of the government's resource (see Bohn, 1988; Calvo and Guidotti, 1993). An unfavourable shock to the budget would require an inflation surprise which reduces real debt servicing costs, while a favourable shock requires unexpectedly low inflation.

5. We assume that $\psi_1 < 1$ and $\psi_2 > -1$: that way, increases in b_i will always result in an increase in the period 1 budget and (for $\pi^e = \pi$) in a decrease in the period 2 budget, if all other countries leave their debt level unchanged.

6. Because fines are capped at 0.5 percent of GDP in practice, at high deficit levels the SCP will no longer provide an incentive to keep the deficit in check. However, it seems unlikely that such high deficit levels arise purely from fiscal profligacy. Raising fines further under such circumstances may be counterproductive and cause debt runs.

only if, in equilibrium, b_i is above $\bar{b}_i$. This will be the case if the reference debt level is set on average at the debt level that prevails in the absence of EMU. I assume that any penalty payment by a country is equally distributed among the other $n - 1$ countries. These rebates, captured by the last terms in (8.4) and (8.5), ensure that countries have an interest in the *ex post* enforcement of the punishment of other countries. It is easy to see that the sum of the fines and the rebates over all countries equals zero.

One of the commonly voiced objections against the SGP is that it may punish a government for excessive deficits that arise from factors that are beyond its own control. I therefore allow for the possibility that the reference debt levels differ across countries. In particular, they will be given by:

$$\bar{b}_i = \bar{b} - \delta\varepsilon_i. \tag{8.6}$$

In other words the reference debt level is 'indexed' to the shock. In particular, by setting $\delta > 0$, a bad shock ($\varepsilon_i < 0$) increases the reference debt level and thus reduces the fine to be paid by country i. Note that this indexation requires shocks to be observable.

While fiscal policy is conducted at the national level, monetary policy is chosen by the ECB, which selects the common, union-wide inflation rate in period 2. In the absence of political pressure (that is, under complete independence), its objective would be to maximize $-\pi^2/(2\phi)$, where ϕ reflects how severely the central banker is punished for deviations from price stability. Such an objective function would reflect the spirit of the Maastricht Treaty, which gives the ECB a mandate for price stability. I allow, however, for the possibility that the ECB is not completely independent. In particular, the ECB attaches a relative weight λ ($0 \leq \lambda \leq 1$) to its objective under complete independence and a relative weight $1 - \lambda$ to an equally weighted average of the objectives of the period 2 governments in each of the individual countries. Ignoring an irrelevant proportionality factor, the ECB's objective function is given by:

$$U_{ECB} = -\frac{\pi^2}{2\alpha} + \frac{1}{n} \sum_{i=1}^{n} \left[1 - b_i(1 + \pi^e - \pi) - \psi_2(b_i - \bar{b}) \right.$$

$$\left. + \left(\frac{1}{n-1}\right) \sum_{j=1,j\neq i}^{n} \psi_2(b_j - \bar{b}) \right]$$

$$= 1 - \frac{\pi^2}{2\alpha} - (1 + \pi^e - \pi)\tilde{b}, \text{ where } \alpha \equiv \phi(1 - \lambda). \tag{8.7}$$

Here, and in the sequel, a tilde above a variable denotes a cross-country average. Hence,

$$\tilde{b} \equiv \frac{1}{n} \sum_{j=1}^{n} b_j.$$

$\lambda = 1$ or, equivalently, $\alpha = 0$ corresponds to an extremely independent ECB, while $\lambda = 0$ or $\alpha = \phi$ corresponds to an extremely dependent ECB. If $0 < \lambda < 1$ or $0 < \alpha < \phi$, the ECB is partially independent and, therefore, more 'conservative' than the representative agent in the union (that is, the ECB attaches a larger relative weight to price stability – see Rogoff, 1985).

Although the Maastricht Treaty requires the ECB to be completely independent, in reality one could well imagine countries trying to influence its policies through the appointment of its Board Members or simply by putting sheer political pressure on the bank. I therefore allow for the possibility that the ECB is partially independent. Moreover, it is interesting to explore how debt accumulation and the stability pact are affected by the degree of independence of the ECB.

The solution of the model

The timing is as follows. First, a stability pact is signed. This involves the choice of the parameters $\bar{b}$, δ and ψ_1 and ψ_2. Then, the shock ε_i hits the government budget constraint of country i. Third, governments issue debt and period 1 fines are paid. Finally, inflation is determined by the ECB, debts are repaid and period 2 fines are paid. The model is solved through backward induction.

I assume that the ECB is not able to commit to its announcements and, therefore, takes inflation expectations as given when maximizing (8.7) over π. This yields:

$$\pi = \alpha \tilde{b}.$$

Hence, inflation rises proportionately in the average level of debt, $\tilde{b}$, in the union. An increase in $\tilde{b}$ strengthens the incentive to wipe out at least part of its real value once inflation expectations are given. In equilibrium, this incentive is anticipated and reflected in an increase in the nominal interest rate.

In period 2 all resources are spent on the public good preferred by the party that is in office. From the perspective of period 2 governments, when they select their debt levels, inflation expectations still need to be determined. They will adjust one-for-one with any effects of debt policy on future realized inflation. Hence, $\pi^e = \pi$ from the viewpoint of the governments when they choose their debt levels. Therefore, the period 1 government maximizes the objective function:

$$u(f_{1i}) + pf_{2i} - \frac{\alpha^2}{2\phi}\left(\frac{1}{n}\sum_{j=1}^{n} b_j\right)^2,$$

where f_{1i} and f_{2i} are given by the right-hand sides of (8.4) and (8.5), respectively, having imposed that $\pi^e = \pi$. The first-order condition for the government of country i is:

$$u'(f_{1i})(1 - \psi_1) = p(1 + \psi_2) + \frac{\alpha^2}{\phi n}\tilde{b}. \tag{8.8}$$

The equilibrium debt levels can now be obtained in two steps. First, I derive the average debt level in the union. In the second step I solve for the individual debt levels. As for the first step, note that the right-hand side of (8.8) is the same for each government. Hence, f_{1i} is the same for all i and, therefore,

$$f_{1i} = \frac{1}{n}\sum_{j=1}^{n} f_{1j} = 1 + \tilde{b} + \tilde{\varepsilon}, \text{ where } \tilde{\varepsilon} \equiv \frac{1}{n}\sum_{i=1}^{n}\varepsilon_i. \tag{8.9}$$

Hence, the average union debt level is determined by:

$$u'(1 + \tilde{b} + \tilde{\varepsilon})(1 - \psi_1) = p(1 + \psi_2) + \frac{\alpha^2}{\phi n}\tilde{b}. \tag{8.10}$$

Equation (8.10) can be solved for $\tilde{b}$ if we specify a functional form for $u(.)$. Note that $\tilde{b}$ does not depend on δ.

The second step is to derive the individual countries' debt levels. Conjecture that the solution is given by:

$$b_i = \tilde{b} + \gamma(\tilde{\varepsilon} - \varepsilon_i), \text{ for all } i. \tag{8.11}$$

Substituting (8.6) and (8.11) into the right-hand side of (8.4), one can write:

$$f_{1i} = 1 + \tilde{b} + \tilde{\varepsilon} + (\tilde{\varepsilon} - \varepsilon_i)\left\{\gamma\left[1 - \psi_1\left(\frac{n}{n-1}\right)\right]\right.$$
$$\left. + \delta\psi_1\left(\frac{n}{n-1}\right) - 1\right\}. \tag{8.12}$$

Finally, using (8.9) and (8.12), one obtains the following solution for debt in country i:

$$b_i = \tilde{b} + \hat{\gamma}(\tilde{\varepsilon} - \varepsilon_i), \text{ where } \hat{\gamma} \equiv \frac{1 - \psi_1\left(\dfrac{n}{n-1}\right)\delta}{1 - \psi_1\left(\dfrac{n}{n-1}\right)}. \tag{8.13}$$

Before continuing, it may be useful to explicitly define a special case which will be referred to at various occasions in the ensuing text. By 'autonomy', I denote the situation in which a stability pact is absent (i.e. $\psi_1 = \psi_2 = 0$) and in which countries select monetary policy at the national level (i.e. $n = 1$). If country i is autonomous, b_i is determined by:

$$u'(1 + b_i + \varepsilon_i) = p + \frac{\alpha^2}{\phi}b_i.$$

Analysis of the equilibrium

In this section I analyse the equilibrium solution derived above in more detail. In particular, I will distinguish between the case in which shocks are equal for all countries and the case in which each country experiences an idiosyncratic shock.

Common shocks only

Let $\varepsilon_i = \tilde{\varepsilon}$ for all i. The equilibrium debt level for each country is the value of $\tilde{b}$ which solves (8.10). It is easy to check that, in the absence of a stability pact (i.e. $\psi_1 = \psi_2 = 0$) debt will be too high (compared to the socially optimal level) if and only if $p < 1$ (cf. Alesina and Tabellini, 1990).[7] The incentive to over-accumulate debt arises as follows. Because the ruling political party may lose power, any resources that it leaves for the future may be spent by its successor on the public good that is not valued by its constituency. This causes the period 1 government to divert resources away from period 2 towards period 1; in other words, the ruling party behaves as if it is myopic. This effect is stronger the lower is p. Note that a more favourable shock in period 1 (a higher $\tilde{\varepsilon}$) reduces the amount of debt, because governments try to smooth resources over time (despite the fact that they may act as if being myopic).

[7.] A social planner maximizes (8.1), subject to (8.4) and (8.5) (with $\psi_1 = \psi_2 = 0$ imposed), and under the assumption that it can commit to zero inflation. This yields $b_i = 0$, if $\tilde{\varepsilon} = 0$.

An increase in central bank independence (a lower α) or an increase in the number of EMU participants (an increase in n) both lead to an increase in the (expected) equilibrium debt level. These effects are described in more detail in Beetsma and Uhlig (1999, proposition 3). Although each government has an incentive to over-accumulate debt, this incentive is to some extent at least kept in check by the prospect of higher future inflation if debt is higher. An increase in central bank independence guarantees lower future inflation on the outset and thus gives governments less of an incentive to keep their debt position in check. The extreme case of a completely independent central bank ($\alpha = 0$) guarantees zero inflation[8] and thus yields the highest debt level.[9] An increase in n implies that the inflationary consequences of a unilateral increase in debt are smaller (because inflation is attuned to the average union debt level). Given that all individual EMU participants perceive this benefit of a unilateral debt increase, they all expand their debt positions, which results in higher inflation.

These findings are an example of the more general result that in a model with multiple distortions removing one distortion may actually make matters worse. In the present model there are two distortions: a political one in the form of uncertainty about the re-election of the current government (i.e. $p < 1$) and the absence of commitment in monetary policy-making. Removing the latter distortion worsens the effects of the political distortion.

Finally, consider the effects of a stability pact on debt accumulation. An increase in ψ_1 or ψ_2 raises the marginal cost of issuing debt, thereby raising the cost of period 1 relative to period 2 government consumption. As (8.10) shows, this leads to a substitution away from present towards future government consumption, thus reducing debt accumulation.

Idiosyncratic shocks

Assume now that each country is hit by an idiosyncratic shock which is uncorrelated with the other shocks in EMU. Hence, the second term on

---

[8.] This case is equivalent to an ECB commitment to a zero inflation rate. The result that discretion in monetary policy making may lead to less debt accumulation can be found in other models as well. See, for example, Jensen (1994); van der Ploeg (1995); Beetsma and Bovenberg (1997); Obstfeld (1997).

[9.] The model implicitly assumes that real base money holdings are very small and, therefore, abstracts from seigniorage revenues owing to inflation eroding real money holdings. This seems to be a reasonable assumption for countries participating in EMU. If seigniorage played an important role, then a reduction in inflation might actually lead to higher debt (cf. Sargent and Wallace, 1981).

the right-hand side of (8.13) is no longer zero. I assume that

$$0 < \psi_1 < \frac{n-1}{n} \text{ and } \delta < 1.$$

Hence, $\hat{\gamma} > 0$ so that a country hit by a relatively bad shock ($\varepsilon_i < \tilde{\varepsilon}$) will choose a higher-than-average debt level.

The results of this subsection are summarized in the following proposition:

Proposition 3.1: Assume that

$$0 < \psi_1 < \frac{n-1}{n} \text{ and } \delta < 1.$$

(a) Suppose that $\delta = 0$. An increase in period 1 punishment for higher debt, ψ_1, increases the debt dispersion, as measured by $\hat{\gamma}$, for given realizations of the shocks.
(b) A higher degree of indexation, δ, of the reference debt level reduces the debt dispersion for given realizations of the shocks and for given ψ_1.
(c) An appropriate choice of δ eliminates the idiosyncratic components in the amounts of government spending in both period 1 and period 2. More specifically, this is the case if we set

$$\delta = \hat{\delta} \equiv \frac{1 + \psi_2\left(\dfrac{n}{n-1}\right)}{(\psi_1 + \psi_2)\left(\dfrac{n}{n-1}\right)}. \tag{8.14}$$

Proposition 3.1(a) states that the effect of a shock on the public debt may be amplified by a stability pact. This result confirms one of the commonly voiced objections against the SGP: the SGP will make matters worse for countries whose public finances are in a bad shape already. The intuition for this result is as follows: suppose that $\varepsilon_i < \tilde{\varepsilon}$. Hence, the government of country i has relatively few resources in period 1 and, therefore, wants to issue more debt than its EMU partners. This requires making a net transfer to the other countries and results in even fewer resources compared to them. The government of country i tries to make up for this loss by borrowing even more. As proposition 3.1(b) shows, a higher degree of indexation of the reference debt level to the shock mitigates this problem. Although the relative cost of period 1 public spending in terms of period 2 spending is unaffected, an increase in δ reduces the net fine, thereby exerting a stabilizing effect on resources in period 1 and thus on debt. In fact, by making δ sufficiently large, in particular by setting $\delta = \hat{\delta}$ (see proposition 3.1(c)), the increase in the reference debt level induced by a bad shock results in a negative fine which completely offsets the direct effects of the shock on country i's resources.[10] To see this, first note from (8.9) that period 1 public spending does not depend on the idiosyncratic component of the shock, $\tilde{\varepsilon} - \varepsilon_i$. Secondly, imposing $\pi^e = \pi$, (8.5) can be rewritten as

$$f_{2i} + g_{2i} = 1 - \tilde{b} + (\tilde{\varepsilon} - \varepsilon_i)\left\{\delta\psi_2\left(\frac{n}{n-1}\right) - \gamma\left[1 + \psi_2\left(\frac{n}{n-1}\right)\right]\right\}.$$

The final term drops out if we substitute $\hat{\gamma}$ (see (8.13)) and $\hat{\delta}$ (8.14) for γ and δ, respectively.

The optimal stability pact

How are the parameters of the stability pact determined? The answer to this question depends on who signs it. Usually, it is the participating countries' governments who bargain over issues at the EU level and the resulting agreement has then to be ratified by the national legislature or by a referendum. In the current analysis, I therefore assume that the period 1 governments sign the pact. This leads us to the following proposition:

Proposition 3.2: With EMU ($n > 1$), the optimal SGP from the governments' point of view is to set

$$\psi_1 = \frac{n-1}{n} = -\psi_2.$$

Proof: The optimal pact maximizes the expectation of V_{Fi}, where

$$V_{Fi} = u(1 + \tilde{b} + \tilde{\varepsilon}) + p\left\{1 - \tilde{b} + (\tilde{\varepsilon} - \varepsilon_i)\right.$$
$$\left. \times \left[\delta\psi_2\frac{n}{n-1} - \hat{\gamma}\left(1 + \psi_2\frac{n}{n-1}\right)\right]\right\} - \frac{\alpha^2}{2\phi}\tilde{b}^2,$$

and where $\tilde{b}$ is determined by (8.10). The expectation of this expression reduces further to

$$E\left[u(1 + \tilde{b} + \tilde{\varepsilon}) + p\left(1 - \tilde{b}\right) - \frac{\alpha^2}{2\phi}\tilde{b}^2\right].$$

For any given realization, $\tilde{\varepsilon}$, the term in the square brackets is maximized for $\tilde{b}$ given by

$$u'(1 + \tilde{b} + \tilde{\varepsilon}) = p + \frac{\alpha^2}{\phi}\tilde{b}. \tag{8.15}$$

---

[10] In particular, note that $\hat{\delta} > 1$.

Substituting $\psi_1 = n - 1/n = -\psi_2$, (8.10) reduces to (8.15), for all possible realizations of $\tilde{\varepsilon}$. ∎

Although there are many possible combinations of ψ_1 and ψ_2 which correct the expected rise in the debt bias resulting from monetary unification (see also Beetsma and Uhlig, 1999), governments are not indifferent as regards which of these combinations they should adopt. They also care about how the pact will affect their response to unexpected shocks. In particular, because all the idiosyncratic uncertainty is shifted towards period 2 (see (8.9)), they will take into account only the effect on their response to the common shock component, $\tilde{\varepsilon}$. The optimal pact requires a huge penalty for excessive debt in period 1 and a huge subsidy for excessive debt in period 2.[11] Note that the first-order condition for debt under this arrangement reduces to the first-order condition for debt chosen by an autonomous country hit by a shock of size $\tilde{\varepsilon}$.

Because all the idiosyncratic uncertainty is shifted towards the second period and because governments are risk-neutral with respect to period 2 spending, they are indifferent about the degree, δ, to which the reference debt level is indexed to the shock. This would no longer be the case if they were risk-averse with respect to period 2 spending. Presumably, the optimal pact would then have to make an appropriate trade-off among the following three objectives: (1) correcting the expected increase in the debt bias caused by monetary unification, (2) providing the correct response to the common shock component, $\tilde{\varepsilon}$, and (3) eliminating the idiosyncratic uncertainties.

Differences among EMU participants

Up to now it was assumed that countries were (*ex ante*) identical in all respects; hence, their governments were unanimous in the choice of their preferred pact. In practice, the countries that started to participate in EMU differ in a variety of ways, for example in terms of economic and political structure and in terms of initial debt when EMU started off. *A priori*, this suggests that their attitudes towards a stability pact may be quite different. This is illustrated by the fact that the idea of a stability pact, originally proposed by Germany, was only very reluctantly accepted by France. The original proposal, which envisaged automatic sanctions for violators of the EDP was watered down to the current version of the

---

[11.] Actually, for the proposed punishment schedule, the debt level is indeterminate: the punishment (reward) in period 1 exactly compensates for direct effect of setting b_i above (below) b, while the reward (punishment) in period 2 exactly compensates for the direct effect of setting b_i below (above) b.

SGP, which imposes sanctions only after a rather long sequence of steps involving negotiations with the violators.

In this section, I investigate (at a rather informal level) how asymmetries among union participants may affect a stability pact and countries' desire to participate in a monetary union combined with a pact.

Differences in initial debt

Perhaps the most important difference in initial conditions at the start of EMU concerns the dispersion in initial debt levels. Italy and Belgium have debt/GDP ratios of over 100 per cent, while Germany's public debt is close to the 60 per cent reference level in the Maastricht Treaty. Such differences in initial debt may lead to countries putting different degrees of pressure on the ECB to raise inflation. For this reason, a country with low initial debt may be reluctant to take part in a union which also involves countries with high initial debt levels. However, I will demonstrate below that, if we take monetary unification as given, all governments can be strictly better off with a stability pact that punishes changes in debt (i.e. deficits).

For simplicity, I now abstract from the presence of shocks. Then, with differences in initial debt levels, the period 1 government budget constraint has to be replaced by:

$$f_{1i} + g_{1i} = 1 + b_i - b_{0i} - \psi_1(b_i - \bar{b}_i) + \left(\frac{1}{n-1}\right) \sum_{j=1, j \neq i}^{n} \psi_1(b_j - \bar{b}_j),$$

(8.16)

which still allows for differences in the reference debt level.

The main result of this subsection is contained in the following proposition:

Proposition 4.1: Let the reference debt levels be given by the initial debt levels – i.e. $\bar{b}_i = b_{0i}$, $\forall i$. The most preferred pact of each government is given by any combination ψ_1, ψ_2 such that

$$\frac{p(1 + \psi_2)}{1 - \psi_1} + \frac{\alpha^2}{\phi n(1 - \psi_1)} \tilde{b}^* = p + \frac{\alpha^2}{\phi} \tilde{b}^*,$$

(8.17)

where $\tilde{b}^*$ is implicitly defined by:

$$u'(1 + \tilde{b}^* - \tilde{b}_0) = p + \frac{\alpha^2}{\phi} \tilde{b}^*.$$

Proof: The first-order condition for government i's debt choice can be written as:

$$u'(f_{1i}) = \frac{p(1 + \psi_2)}{1 - \psi_1} + \frac{\alpha^2}{\phi n(1 - \psi_1)} \tilde{b}. \tag{8.18}$$

Hence, $f_{1i} = \bar{f}_1 = 1 + \tilde{b} - \tilde{b}_0$, $\forall i$. Substituting $\bar{b}_i = b_{0i}$, $\forall i$, the right-hand side of (8.16) can be written as:

$$1 + b_i - b_{0i} - \frac{n}{n-1} \psi_1 (\tilde{b} - \tilde{b}_0 - b_i + b_{0i}).$$

This should be equal to $1 + \tilde{b} - \tilde{b}_0$. Hence,

$$b_i = \tilde{b} - \tilde{b}_0 + b_{0i}.$$

Hence, using $\bar{b}_i = b_{0i}$, $\forall i$, in its period 2 budget constraint, government i's indirect utility can be written as a strictly concave function of $\tilde{b}$:

$$u(1 + \tilde{b} - \tilde{b}_0) + p\left(1 - \tilde{b} + \tilde{b}_0 - b_{0i}\right) - \frac{\alpha^2}{2\phi} \tilde{b}^2 \tag{8.19}$$

where $\tilde{b}$ solves (8.18) with $f_{1i} = 1 + \tilde{b} - \tilde{b}_0$. Expression (8.19) is maximized for $\tilde{b} = \tilde{b}^*$ implictly defined by

$$u'(1 + \tilde{b}^* - \tilde{b}_0) = p + \frac{\alpha^2}{\phi} \tilde{b}^*. \tag{8.20}$$

Hence, any pact ψ_1, ψ_2 that implies $\tilde{b} = \tilde{b}^*$ is considered optimal (by each of the governments). Combining (8.18) with (8.19), the latter condition can be written as:

$$u'(1 + \tilde{b} - \tilde{b}_0) = p + \frac{\alpha^2}{\phi} \tilde{b}^* + \frac{\alpha^2}{\phi n(1 - \psi_1)} (\tilde{b} - \tilde{b}^*).$$

This equation in $\tilde{b}$ has a unique solution and, by (8.20), it is given by $\tilde{b}^*$. To finish the proof, note that in the absence of a pact (i.e. $\psi_1 = \psi_2 = 0$), average debt will be strictly higher than $\tilde{b}^*$. ∎

While in the basic model with zero initial debt levels one cannot distinguish between sanctions based on debts or deficits, we can do so now and proposition (4.1) tells us that governments would unanimously agree on a pact with sanctions based on deficits.[12] This feature of the pact corresponds to the SGP as it has been designed in practice.

Differences in economic and political structure

EMU participants will differ also in terms of economic structure. Examples are differences in the degree of labour market flexibility, the government's need for resources and the tax system. While such differences in economic structure would be relatively hard to capture formally within the context of the current model, they may account for differences in the degree of inflation aversion (ϕ^{-1}) across countries. Another asymmetry among countries concerns differences in political stability, or the frequency with which parties are ousted from government. Although our model treats the political process in a very stylized way, these differences could be captured by allowing for different values of p across countries.[13] With differences in ϕ and p, the first-order condition for government i becomes:

$$u'(f_{1i})(1 - \psi_1) = p_i(1 + \psi_2) + \frac{\alpha^2}{\phi_i n} \tilde{b}$$

where α, which captures the (inverse of) the degree of inflation aversion of the ECB is treated as a given constant. Clearly, if the likelihood of being responsible for the future repayment of the debt is higher (i.e. p_i is higher) or if the degree of inflation aversion is higher (i.e. ϕ_i is lower), government i selects a lower level of public debt. For this reason, debt positions will in general differ across union members. Given that inflation is attuned to the average union debt level, countries which are politically very stable or relatively inflation averse might be reluctant to join a monetary union, because inflation would be higher than under autonomy. One would

---

[12.] Conceptually, the distinction between debt- and deficit-based sanctions vanishes if we allow for differences in the reference debt levels and reference debt levels happen to be equal to previous debt levels. However, here and in the following, 'debt-based sanctions' refer, for example, to punishment schedules in which the reference debt levels differ because of differences in shocks hitting the union participants. Another example of debt-based sanctions is when reference debt levels reflect differences in initial debt levels, but are kept constant over time or converge to some common union-wide level over time (see below, when I discuss the implications of extending the time horizon of the basic model).

[13.] Parameter p is then interpreted in a broader sense than merely being the probability that in a two-party system the governing party loses office. In the case of coalition governments, it would correspond most closely to the probability that a party will no longer be part of the government after the election.

expect these countries to be relatively more supportive of a stability pact with strict sanctions.[14]

Differences in size and influence on the ECB

The appendix (p. 211) presents a version of the model in which countries differ in size and, therefore, in their influence on the ECB's policies. The model abstracts from the presence of shocks. It is shown that in order to eliminate the exacerbation of the debt bias which arises from monetary unification, it is necessary to differentiate the stability pact parameters across countries. In particular, it is shown that ψ_{2i} should be larger, the relatively smaller is country i. The intuition is that large countries internalize to a larger extent the adverse inflationary effects of their debt policies on the union-wide inflation rate.[15] Because the proposed arrangement implies the same debt levels as under autonomy (while the autonomy debt levels are the same across countries) it leaves all countries indifferent between autonomy and monetary unification. Whether countries would be able to agree on a pact, given that monetary unification will take place, may depend on how different countries are in size. The government of a country which is negligible in size takes future inflation as given and runs a debt policy as if the central bank were able to commit to a zero inflation rate. Under the restriction that the parameters ψ_1 and ψ_2 and the reference debt levels be equal across countries, such a country would never agree to a pact which punishes increases in debt.

Further extensions

This section addresses some of the issues which have been ignored so far, but which nevertheless are important for further analysis of the SGP. In particular, I discuss the potential problems with the enforcement of the pact, the moral hazard problems that would arise if the severity of the sanctions depends on the (reported) economic situation of countries and,

---

14. Note that, to some extent these countries are compensated for the potentially higher union inflation rate if they receive net transfers through the pact from other countries which run higher than average debt levels.

   It would be interesting to investigate whether countries could agree on a pact which is Pareto-improving, *given* that monetary unification takes place. This seems to be a non-trivial problem and is therefore not pursued further. It seems reasonable to conjecture that such a pact can be found only if the differences in ϕ and p are not too large.

15. This argument, however, ignores the fact that a large country poses a larger systemic risk if its debt becomes unsustainable. This would require more severe sanctions for large countries running excessive deficits.

finally, I elaborate on whether debt-based sanctions would have been preferable to deficit-based sanctions.

Enforcement problems with the SGP

The most important obstacles for the SGP to act as a deterrent against budgetary laxity are the perceived enforcement problems. In this chapter, a stability pact has been modelled according to the original German proposal, which envisaged automatic sanctions for violators of the EDP. In practice, however, the SGP involves a sequence of discretionary steps before a country is actually fined for its budgetary profligacy. Although it reduces the likelihood that countries would be punished for excessive deficits caused by factors which are beyond their own control, this has several adverse implications. First, it enhances the chance that truly undisciplined countries escape sanctions. Secondly, the procedure is drawn out over a substantial time period; sanctions may as a consequence fall on the successor of the government that is responsible for the budgetary mismanagement. Thirdly, countries that are willing to continue with the procedure may be a target for retaliation in other areas of EU policy making. Finally, the fact that sanctions materialize after substantial bargaining may induce governments to forgo budgetary reform if they perceive that, through bargaining, they can escape part of the sanctions. Moreover, as Buiter and Sibert (1997) argue, if a less restrained fiscal policy has relatively large negative international spillovers, a country's bargaining power increases by not making any reforms, because a breakdown of the bargaining process would lead to greater damage for the other countries.

In reality, what would probably motivate countries to keep their finances under control is the peer pressure from other EMU participants and the political embarrassment if the EDP is set in motion. Effective enforcement of the SGP will to a large extent be determined by the specific sequence in which problem cases emerge. If the first candidate for a fine is a small country, sanctions stand a good chance of being enforced and the SGP is enabled to build up credibility. If the first candidate is a large country, there may be a good chance that sanctions will not be enforced.

Moral hazard problems

In practice, the SGP allows for a crude (and indirect) adjustment of the sanctions to the shocks that hit the economy. Sanctions are not applied if the economy has shrunk by over 2 per cent in a year. If the economy shrinks by between 0.75 per cent and 2 per cent this constitutes a 'grey area' in which the EDP may or may not be set in motion. The crudeness of such a scheme suggests that it is very difficult to verify which part of an excessive deficits is caused by 'bad luck' and which by sheer budgetary mismanagement. If shocks were perfectly observable, a mechanism which indexes the reference debt (or deficit) level to exogenous shocks (as I analysed above) could in principle, be set up. If shocks are not perfectly observable, the severity of sanctions will presumably rely on the information provided by governments. Even if governments provide the correct information about the economic situation in their countries, it is not clear what they could have done to mitigate the adverse movements in their economic situation. Hence, linking sanctions to the (reported) economic situation in a country may induce moral hazard: governments' incentive to reduce fiscal profligacy is weakened, because the fine associated with a given excessive deficit will be reduced in response to a worse economic situation.

A longer modelling horizon: sanctions based on excessive debts or deficits?

The assumptions underlying our basic model did not permit us to distinguish between debt- and deficit-based sanctions. However, one way to distinguish between these two was discussed when we allowed for differences in initial debt. Another way would be to extend the modelling horizon. The main argument in favour of deficit-based sanctions is that they help to avoid current governments being punished for bad policies conducted by their predecessors (at least, if the lag between observing an excessive deficit and imposing a sanction is not too long). An argument in favour of debt-based sanctions is that public indebtedness provides a better measure for credibility problems and hence for the potential pressure on the central bank to relax its monetary policy. In addition, sanctions based on excessive debts reward policies that are on average prudent, but allow for temporary increases in deficits if budgetary conditions are sufficiently problematic. This may be quite important for countries with a large government sector, such as Sweden and Finland. Although the deficits of these countries are not necessarily higher on average than those of other countries, they are more volatile and therefore run a higher risk of falling in the range where sanctions would apply.[16] A final argument in favour of debt-based sanctions is that deficit-based sanctions become effective only after some time and are lifted as soon as the excessive deficits have been corrected. A sequence of temporarily high

---

[16.] Sanctions based on debt might motivate countries to constrain the use of debt so as to build up a 'buffer' against unexpectedly bad shocks.

and temporarily moderate deficits might go unchecked by any sanctions while still giving rise to an upward trend in the public debt.

Conclusion

Although the SGP has led to heated debates among economists, there is relatively little work that analyses it in a more formal way. This chapter has provided such an attempt. The model that I presented above shows how monetary unification and (rather surprisingly) a more independent central bank may lead to more debt accumulation, because the effect of a unilateral increase in debt on future inflation becomes smaller. I have explored how sanctions might be structured so as to offset the exacerbation of the debt bias arising from monetary unification. I have also analysed how a pact may be used to provide insurance against the idiosyncratic shock components, while still inducing countries to keep their public finances in shape by increasing the marginal cost of issuing debt. Using the pact as an insurance mechanism requires that the exogenous shocks hitting the economies are observable. If they are not, a pact that adjusts sanctions for the economic situation of a country may induce moral hazard. In particular, a government may forgo measures which enhance budgetary discipline and economic efficiency (and which, typically, are politically costly) because it knows that it will be compensated in the form of weaker sanctions for a given excessive deficit.

To highlight the intuition behind the main results, the basic model was deliberately kept simple. In particular, countries were assumed to be identical *ex ante*. In practice, however, there will be substantial differences among the EMU participants. At a rather informal level I have discussed the impact of differences in initial debt, differences in the economic and political structure of countries and differences in their relative influence on the ECB. Although with differences in initial debt it was possible to design a pact which made all countries better off, by and large, the results seem to suggest that it is more difficult for countries to agree on a pact if the differences among them are larger. If they manage to agree on a pact, it is more likely to be a pact that is weak in disciplining governments. This reflects the bargaining power of less disciplined governments, when they have the possibility to veto an arrangement. This might explain why the original German proposal, which envisaged automatic sanctions for violations of the EDP, was watered down to the current SGP, which imposes sanctions only after a relatively long sequence of steps involving negotiations with violators and voting about whether to continue with the EDP.

A number of issues, some of which have been discussed informally here, need to be investigated in a more systematic way. Examples are the potential enforcement problems associated with the SGP, the distinction between debt- and deficit-based sanctions and a more detailed modelling of the political process leading to excessive deficits.[17] A more detailed analysis would also explore how the current results are affected if we explicitly model private sector decisions and introduce taxes to finance public spending.[18]

Appendix

This appendix shows how the parameters of the stability pact need to be differentiated across countries, if they differ in size and influence on the ECB, so as to correct the debt bias arising from monetary unification.

For convenience, I assume that $\varepsilon_i = 0$, $\forall i$, and that the reference debt levels are the same for all countries. However, I do allow for differences in ψ_1 and ψ_2 across countries. It is instructive to restate the governments' budget constraints in terms aggregates for each country. Let the size of country i in terms of its population be K_i. Each individual receives an endowment income of one unit in each period, which is then fully taxed away by its government. All resource flows are population weighted. Hence, the period 1 budget constraint of government i can be written as:

$$F_{1i} + G_{1i} = K_i + B_i - \psi_{1i} K_i (b_i - \bar{b})$$

$$+ \sum_{j=1, j \neq i}^{n} \left(\frac{w_i}{1 - w_j} \right) \psi 0_{1j} K_j (b_j - \bar{b})$$

where F_{1i} (G_{1i}) is aggregate spending on public good F (G) and B_i is aggregate debt. Further, $w_i \equiv K_i / K^s$, $K^s \equiv \sum_{j=1}^{n} K_j$ (union-wide income) and $b_i \equiv B_i / K_i$ (the debt/GDP ratio). The aggregate fine paid by country i is $\psi_{1i} K_i (b_i - \bar{b})$. The final term in the equation captures the rebates of the fines paid by the other countries, where the share of the total rebate received by country i is given by its relative weight in the set of countries that remain after j has been excluded. It is easy to see that the sum of all fines and rebates over all countries equals zero.

---

[17] See Persson and Tabellini (1998) for an overview of the literature that shows how different political processes may lead to excessive deficits.

[18] Huizinga and Nielsen (1997) investigate how the availability of tax instruments affects the need for international agreement on borrowing restrictions.

The period 1 government budget constraint can be rewritten further as:

$$F_{1i} + G_{1i} = K_i \left[1 + b_i - \psi_{1i}(b_i - \bar{b}) \right.$$

$$+ \sum_{j=1, j \neq i}^{n} \left(\frac{w_i}{1 - w_j} \right) \psi_{1j} \frac{K_j}{K_i} (b_j - \bar{b}) \right]$$

$$= K_i \left[1 + b_i - \psi_{1i}(b_i - \bar{b}) + \sum_{j=1, j \neq i}^{n} \left(\frac{w_j}{1 - w_j} \right) \psi_{1j}(b_j - \bar{b}) \right],$$

and hence, in *per capita* terms as:

$$f_{1i} + g_{1i} = 1 + b_i - \psi_{1i}(b_i - \bar{b}) + \sum_{j=1, j \neq i}^{n} \left(\frac{w_j}{1 - w_j} \right) \psi_{1j}(b_j - \bar{b}).$$

The intuition for the final term can now also be seen as follows: The total fine paid by country j is $\psi_{1j} K_j (b_j - \bar{b})$. Each individual in the union *minus* country j receives an equal share of this fine. Hence, each of these individuals receives a rebate of

$$\psi_{1j} \left[K_j / (K^s - K_j) \right] (b_j - \bar{b}) = \psi_{1j} \left[(K_j/K^s)/(1 - (K_j/K^s)) \right] (b_j - \bar{b})$$

$$= \psi_{1j} \left[w_j/(1 - w_j) \right] (b_j - \bar{b}).$$

Likewise, one can rewrite the period 2 aggregate government budget constraint as:

$$F_{2i} + G_{2i} = K_i - B_i(1 + \pi^e - \pi) - \psi_{2i} K_i (b_i - \bar{b})$$

$$+ \sum_{j=1, j \neq i}^{n} \left(\frac{w_i}{1 - w_j} \right) \psi_{2j} K_j (b_j - \bar{b})$$

$$= K_i \left[1 - b_i(1 + \pi^e - \pi) - \psi_{2i}(b_i - \bar{b}) \right.$$

$$+ \sum_{j=1, j \neq i}^{n} \left(\frac{w_j}{1 - w_j} \right) \psi_{2j}(b_j - \bar{b}) \right],$$

which, in *per capita* terms, reads as:

$$f_{2i} + g_{2i} = 1 - b_i(1 + \pi^e - \pi) - \psi_{2i}(b_i - \bar{b})$$

$$+ \sum_{j=1, j \neq i}^{n} \left(\frac{w_j}{1 - w_j} \right) \psi_{2j}(b_j - \bar{b}).$$

The relative influence of countries on the ECB's objective function is equal to their relative size. The ECB's objective function then becomes:

$$U_{ECB} = \lambda \left[-\frac{\pi^2}{2\phi} \right] + (1 - \lambda) \sum_{i=1}^{n} \frac{1}{K^s}$$

$$\times \left\{ [K_i - B_i(1 + \pi^e - \pi)] - K_i \left[\frac{\pi^2}{2\phi} \right] \right\}$$

$$= (1 - \lambda) \left\{ -\frac{\pi^2}{2\alpha} + \sum_{i=1}^{n} w_i[1 - b_i(1 + \pi^e - \pi)] \right\}.$$

The second term in the top line of this equation is an equally weighted average of the period 2 preferences of all individuals in the union. The individuals are grouped country by country.

The first-order condition of the ECB yields for inflation:

$$\pi = \alpha \tilde{b}^W, \text{ where } \tilde{b}^W \equiv \sum_{j=1}^{n} w_j b_j.$$

The indirect utility of government i as a function of b_i is:

$$u(f_{1i}) + pf_{2i} - \frac{\alpha^2}{2\phi} \left(\sum_{j=1}^{n} w_j b_j \right)^2,$$

where f_{1i} and f_{2i} are given by the right-hand sides of the *per-capita* government budget constraints. The first-order condition for government i is:

$$u'(f_{1i})(1 - \psi_{1i}) = p(1 + \psi_{2i}) + \frac{\alpha^2}{\phi} w_i \tilde{b}^W.$$

For convenience, assume that $\psi_{1i} = 0$, $\forall i$. I want to show that there exists a set of period 2 punishment parameters that supports an equilibrium in which all countries issue the amount of debt they would issue under autonomy. Moreover, the smaller the country, the larger the punishment parameters need to be.

Hence, I need to find a combination ψ_{2i}, $i = 1, \ldots, n$, such that all countries choose a debt level equal to b^A (the amount of debt issued under *A*utonomy), where b^A is implicitly defined by:

$$u'(1 + b^A) = p + \frac{\alpha^2}{\phi} b^A.$$

Hence, the ψ_{2i} are implicitly defined by:

$$u'(1 + b^A) = p(1 + \psi_{2i}) + \frac{\alpha^2}{\phi} w_i b^A,$$

or, combining the latter two equations, the ψ_{2i} are implicitly defined by:

$$p + \frac{\alpha^2}{\phi} b^A = p(1 + \psi_{2i}) + \frac{\alpha^2}{\phi} w_i b^A.$$

Solving this equation yields:

$$\psi_{2i} = \frac{1}{p} \frac{\alpha^2}{\phi} (1 - w_i) b^A.$$

Hence, ψ_{2i} should be decreasing in the relative weight of the country i. The intuition is that, the larger a country, the more it internalizes the effect of a unilateral debt increase on the common inflation rate. A larger country therefore has a stronger incentive to keep its debt in check.

References

Agell, J., Calmfors, L. and Jonsson, G. (1996). 'Fiscal Policy when Monetary Policy is "Tied to the Mast,"' *European Economic Review*, 40, 1413–40

Alesina, A. and Tabellini, G. (1990), 'A Positive Theory of Fiscal Deficits and Government Debt,' *Review of Economic Studies*, 57: 403–14

Artis, M. and Winkler, B. (1997), 'The Stability Pact: Safeguarding the Credibility of the European Central Bank', *CEPR Discussion Paper*, 1688

Bean, C. R. (1992), 'Economic and Monetary Union in Europe,' *Journal of Economic Perspectives*, 6: 31–52

Beetsma, R. and Bovenberg, L. (1997). 'Central Bank Independence and Public Debt Policy,' *Journal of Economic Dynamics and Control*, 21: 873–94

Beetsma, R. and Uhlig, H. (1999), 'An Analysis of the Stability and Growth Pact', *Economic Journal*, forthcoming.

Bohn, H. (1988). 'Why Do We Have Nominal Government Debt?', *Journal of Monetary Economics*, 21: 121–40

Buiter, W. and Sibert, A. (1997). 'Transition Issues for the European Monetary Union,' University of Cambridge and Birkbeck College, mimeo

Calmfors, L. *et al.*, (1997), *EMU – A Swedish Perspective*, Dordrecht: Kluwer Academic

Calvo, G. and Guidotti, P. (1993). 'On the Flexibility of Monetary Policy: The Case of the Optimal Inflation Tax', *Review of Economic Studies*, 60: 667–87

Canzoneri, M. B. and Diba, B. T. (1991). 'Fiscal Deficits, Financial Integration, and a Central Bank for Europe', *Journal of Japanese and International Economics*, 5: 381–403

Chang, R. (1990). 'International Coordination of Fiscal Deficits', *Journal of Monetary Economics*, 25: 347–66

Chari, V. V. and Kehoe, P. J. (1997), 'On the Need for Fiscal Constraints in a Monetary Union', Federal Reserve Bank of Minneapolis. mimeo

Cukierman, A., Edwards, S. and Tabellini, G. (1992). 'Seignorage and Political Instability', *American Economic Review*, 82: 537–55

De Grauwe, P. (1992). *The Economics of Monetary Integration*, 2nd edn., Oxford: Oxford University Press

Giovannetti, G., Marimon, R. and Teles, R. (1997). 'If You Do What You Should Not: Policy Commitments in a Delayed EMU', Florence: European University Institute, mimeo

Gros, D. and Thygesen, N. (1998). 'The Relationship between Economic and Monetary Integration', in D. Gros and N. Thygesen (eds.) *European Monetary Integration*, revised edn., New York: St Martin's Press

Huizinga, H. and Nielsen, S. B. (1997). 'Higher Government Debt: Boon or Bane?' Tilburg University and Copenhagen Business School, mimeo

Jensen, H. (1994), 'Loss of Monetary Discretion in a Simple Dynamic Policy Game', *Journal of Economic Dynamics and Control*, 18: 763–79

Obstfeld, M. (1997), 'Dynamic Seigniorage Theory: An Exploration', *Macroeconomic Dynamics*, 1: 588–614

Persson, T. and Tabellini, G. (1998), 'Political Economics and Macroeconomic Policy,' in J. B. Taylor,and M. Woodford, (eds.), *Handbook of Macroeconomics*, Amsterdam: Elsevier Science Publishers

Ploeg, F. van der (1995). 'Political Economy of Monetary and Budgetary Policy', *International Economic Review*, 36: 427–39

Rogoff, K. (1985). 'The Optimal Degree of Commitment to an Intermediate Monetary Target', *Quarterly Journal of Economics,* 100: 1169–89

Roubini, N. and Sachs, J. D. (1989). 'Political and Economic Determinants of Budget Deficits in the Industrial Economies', *European Economic Review,* 33: 903–38

Sargent, T. and Wallace, N. (1981). 'Some Unpleasant Monetarist Arithmetic', *Federal Reserve Bank of Minneapolis Quarterly Review*, 5: 1–17

Tabellini, G. and Alesina, A. (1990). 'Voting on the Budget Deficit', *American Economic Review*, 80: 37–49

Willett, T. D. (1999). 'A Political Economy Analysis of the Maastricht and Stability Pact Fiscal Criteria', chapter 3 in this volume.

9 Implications of the Stability and Growth Pact: why the growth element is important

Andrew Hughes Hallett and Peter McAdam

Introduction

This chapter argues that one cost of the large-scale fiscal retrenchments implied by the fiscal provisions of Europe's emerging monetary union will be a loss of investment and output capacity. That clearly implies lower levels of actual output than otherwise, and a reduced capacity to create jobs.

This type of argument is in contrast to the short-term losses in output which have been the focus of previous work – for example Giavazzi and Pagano (1990, 1995); Vines *et al.* (1997); von Hagen and Lutz (1996); Hughes Hallett and McAdam (1998). In fact, to concentrate exclusively on the short-run costs might be rather unhelpful (especially if they are small) because, as Nordhaus (1994: 170) points out, the key variable is going to be *potential* output: 'since the whole point of the deficit-reduction programme is to increase investment and thereby increase the rate of growth of potential and actual output'. No-one has focussed on that part of the problem, or on the potential conflict between short-run benefits and long-run costs.

There is a second point to make. The benefits of economic stabilization and consolidation are often over-stated because the potential interactions between fiscal and monetary policy interventions are ignored. The costs of non-cooperation behaviour between those two instruments can be rather high, and they need to be taken into account. Nordhaus, for example, reckons that non-cooperative deficit reductions will inevitably lead to higher unemployment in the short run in order to induce the central bank to play its part in the reduction process (an independent central

McAdam thanks the ESRC's GEI programme for financial support during the time that this chapter was being prepared. We thank both David Vines and Svend E. Hougaard Jensen for a wealth of comments and suggestions.

bank's reaction function being independent of its preferences for fiscal policy). As a result, output and consumption are likely to stay below trend for a decade or more, reinforced by a natural 'immiserizing' effect on saving because low nominal interest rates will create a capital outflow from the adjusting country. Hence some of the increased savings will be invested abroad; but, because marginal propensities to import are less than one, the expenditure effects of that adjustment will not be large enough to recoup the original reductions in consumption.

Evidently what is at stake here is the role of the policy *mix* during a deficit reduction. That can be crucial. The reason is that the policy mix will change naturally, even if the central bank does nothing, because interest rates, prices and the external exchange rate will respond endogenously to the shifting pressures of demand and financing requirements. If we constrain fiscal or monetary policies, we lose the ability to adjust that policy mix to get the outcomes we want. That matters, not only because of the impact on output levels and price stability but also because we have two targets in a deficit ratio – the deficit itself in the numerator and GNP in the denominator. So we need two instruments – fiscal contractions to reduce the deficit and monetary relaxations to prevent the denominator falling at the same time (Hughes Hallett and Ma, 1997). But the key point is that the changes in monetary conditions may be either nominal or real. The former might involve a relaxation in nominal interest rates (or the money supply) to sustain GNP levels; or a currency depreciation (with wage restraints); or a deregulation of the labour market. But we can equally well get a relaxation because prices fall relative to trend, expanding the real value of money and assets. And prices will fall; first because of the reduced pressure of demand as deficits fall, and second because reduced deficits (now and in the future) bring the government's budget constraint back into balance. This is an illustration of Woodford's (1995) model of fiscal solvency in reverse, in which the removal of excessive deficits makes prices fall relative to trend. But if prices fall enough, then real interest rates will rise even if nominal rates are falling. That will kill investment, and hence any additions to output capacity. Rising real interest rate effects could easily delay or prevent a recovery in output and employment, *even if* nominal interest rates do fall, because the Stability Pact will be at its strongest in a recession when interest rates are low. The problem therefore lies in the pro-cyclical fiscal contractions necessary to avoid the Stability Pact's sanctions in the downturn.

That means those who argue that the purpose of the Stability Pact is to shield the independence of the European Central Bank (ECB), and the credibility of its policies, from less disciplined fiscal policies (for example, Artis and Winkler, 1998) are correct in logic, but have missed an important point. Not only does constraining our ability to vary the policy mix constrain our ability to absorb shocks; it also destroys our ability to get precisely those longer-term benefits (i.e. more investment and higher output potential) which those deficit reductions were designed to achieve. Consequently those who believe that the advantage of lower deficits are greater credibility and lower (nominal) interest rates are also only half right. If the reductions are large enough for real interest rates to rise significantly, then the long-term deflationary impacts on investment and output may outweigh the short-term 'credibility' effects on nominal interest rates. It is all a matter of size and intertemporal substitution.

Thus the challenge facing policy makers is to design a package of policies which offsets the pro-cyclical deflationary bias in the Stability Pact – since, if they do not, output losses and price deflations can lead to real interest rates exceeding real growth rates. That would risk making debt ratios get steadily larger – i.e. risking an 'instability pact' which imposes fiscal discipline in the short run, but destroys it in the long run. We find the only way out of this dilemma is to maintain growth rates through a careful coordination of fiscal and monetary policies.

The simulation framework

The model

The introduction of the Stability Pact, as a mechanism to limit the excessive use of fiscal policy, is an inevitable consequence of applying a single monetary policy to a group of incompletely converged economies. In such cases a 'one-size-fits-all' monetary policy (Eichengreen, 1997) is bound to be unsuitable for some of the participants. And to the extent that they are still free to use their own fiscal policies, governments will want to use them to regain the level of performance they had before the union was formed.

To explore the implications of imposing greater discipline on fiscal policy, we use one of the standard econometric models – the IMF's MULTIMOD – which contains linked models for each of the G7 economies (Masson, Symanswi and Meredith, 1990). MULTIMOD is one of the most widely used and reliable of the empirical multicountry models and has a strong theoretical structure. We include a description of that structure, and the model's performance record, in appendix 9.1 (p. 250).

Conditioning information

The simulations which follow all work from a baseline composed of historical values of the model's variables, plus the IMF's own projections forward to some terminal period. In this case the projections run forward 27 years from our start date of 1996, and are identical to those used in the IMF's annual report *World Economic Outlook* for 1996 taking into account German unification. The model is solved sufficiently far ahead so as to remove any influence of the terminal conditions on our simulation results. We in fact simulate the period 1990–2023 inclusive. In those simulations the forward-looking expectations are solved to be equal to the outcome projected for the relevant future period.[1] This baseline therefore defines our information set.

To simulate EMU, each non-German country is obliged to accept a notional parity against the D-mark, and to maintain a 1 per cent band around that for the duration of the simulation (1996–2027). Thus Italy and the United Kingdom have to maintain bands of DM 0.933 ± 1 per cent per 1,000 Lira, and DM 2.43 ± 1 per cent per Pound, respectively – that is, roughly the parities observed for mid-1996. And for the purposes of this chapter, both currencies are required to stay within these narrow bands thereafter.[2] France, of course, is allowed no realignments; we retain the official parity of 3.35 ± 1 per cent Francs per DM throughout. Germany, however, retains its monetary targeting reaction function throughout. Implicitly therefore we are assuming that the ECB will follow the same kind of policy rules as did the Bundesbank.

Tax policy

MULTIMOD has an endogenous tax rate, showing that any fiscal perturbation which pulls the budget deficit away from its target value will be counteracted by a rise in average tax rates:

$$\text{tax rate} = \alpha_1[\text{def}_{-1} - \text{def}^*_{-1}] + \alpha_2\Delta[\text{def}_{-1} - \text{def}^*_{-1}] + \text{tax rate}_{-1}$$

$$(9.1)$$

where def* is the target deficit/GNP ratio, def $= D/(PY)$, and $\alpha_1, \alpha_2 > 0$.[3] Further we cut all lagged deficit terms out of this function from 1999

[1.] In addition, the solution algorithm inserts these expectations back, in one extra step, to check that they do in fact produce the same endogenous outcomes one period earlier – i.e. that the full solution is a genuine solution to the model.

[2.] The remaining 1 per cent bandwidth plays no material role in what follows. It can be narrowed to 0 per cent without changing the results. The point is that imposing a fixed parity, and vanishingly small bands without the possibility of risk premia or time-inconsistency in the monetary reactions, is to mimic a single currency exactly.

[3.] We use MULTIMOD's values of $\alpha_1 = 0.04$ and $\alpha_2 = 0.3$. This implies that a rapid expansion (contraction) of the deficit is penalized (rewarded) much more heavily than an excessive deficit level itself. MULTIMOD's original tax function was defined in terms of debt ratios, but the Stability Pact is defined in deficit ratios. Hence the change of variable.

onwards, for reasons explained on p. 226 below. Thus tax rates rise in response to excessive deficits by an amount which is equal in every country and in proportion to the amount that the deficit GNP ratio lies above its target value of 3 per cent or 1 per cent. Moreover tax rates will continue to rise so long as def > def*, even if the deficit ratio itself is falling.

That deals with the first term and serves to keep the fiscal deficit within acceptable limits. The second term implies that tax rates also rise in response to worsening deficit GNP ratios (above target). That means tax rates rise *faster*, at a given deficit level, if the deficit ratio is worsening; but they increase *slower* if that deficit ratio has already started to fall. In fact tax rates could even start to decrease if the deficit ratio starts to fall fast enough. The latter feature supplies a 'soft-landing' effect. Conversely you get extra penalties (in the form of higher tax rates) if an excessive deficit worsens still further.

Finally any changes in the tax rate will become dominated by changes in the excess deficit ratio as we get near the target ratio – that is to say, changes in the tax rate are likely to be negative as we near the target ratio, so that we glide on to our target values rather than over-shoot. This 'smooth-landing' condition captures the spirit of the Maastricht Treaty when it says that excess deficits may be allowed provided that they are 'temporary, exceptional and remain close to 3 per cent'; and provided that fiscal corrections are made 'such that the ratio has declined substantially and continuously, and has reached a level close to 3 per cent'. Indeed the faster the pace of correction, the smaller the fiscal corrections need to be. The ratio of α_2 to α_1 therefore determines the importance attached to these aspects of the Treaty.

Fiscal rules and the timetable for eliminating excessive deficits

To eliminate the discrepancy between the current state of a variable and the desired (or target) value for that variable $-z_t$ and z_t^*, say – a controlled state variable must follow a difference equation of at least pth order:

$$\text{i.e. } (I - L)^p z_t = B(L)z_{t-p} \tag{9.2}$$

where $B(L)$ is a polynominal in the lag operator and where z_t^* follows a difference equation of order $p - 1$. Hence the controlled variable must follow a scheme of order 1 higher than the target path. Since the Maastricht Treaty and the Stability Pact specify constant debt and deficit ratios (whatever their numerical values), we have $p = 1$. But our tax reaction function has $p = 2$, which implies an element of over-kill. However, that is just what we need. It means that we can reach a deficit ratio which is constant on average (at 1 per cent of GNP, say). But, by manipulating the strength of the 'overkill' term (α_2), we can also select the speed with which we achieve that goal. In other words, our tax function is the minimum specification that can satisfy not only the Stability Pact (constant deficit or debt ratios), but also the restriction that, if a country's deficit exceeds 3 per cent, then it has two years to get that deficit back to within 3 per cent of GNP before the fines become non-returnable (the time limit by which the required ratio must be achieved).

The baseline solution

In what follows we create a baseline path for each economy in which the 1996 deficits GNP ratio, with no other policy changes, are imposed on ERM countries indefinitely. This is to simulate a counterfactual representing what would happen if the fiscal authorities were to do nothing (i.e. continue with their existing policies) so that the same fiscal deficit ratios were reproduced every year from 1996 onwards. We do this, like Masson and Symansky (1996), not because we think it produces the most realistic projections of what is most likely to happen. It does not. We do it because it shows what would have to be done to reduce a fiscal deficit of a given size over a certain period of time without the aid of favourable shocks.

The 1996 deficit ratios were: 3.7 per cent (Germany), 4.2 per cent (France), 7.3 per cent (Italy) and 3.8 per cent (United Kingdom). Having imposed these deficit figures, the baseline is a straightforward simulation from 1996 to beyond 2023 in the usual way. Since the baseline implies a steady state in which the growth in nominal GDP exceeds nominal interest rates, there is no tendency for debt ratios to increase at existing primary surpluses/deficits.

The baseline paths are therefore a feasible solution to the transition to EMU, although not a particularly likely one because it ignores the Treaty's criteria for entry. Nevertheless this solution does provide the right point of comparison since it shows what would happen were no corrections to be made.

Empirical results

We start with a reference solution which projects the policies and deflation costs needed to bring Germany, Italy, France and the United Kingdom within the Maastricht Treaty's 3 per cent deficit limit by late 1999. This may be compared to a baseline path in which there are no policy changes, and therefore no fiscal corrections imposed by policy makers.

Then we consider four possible deficit reduction strategies:
(1) a Stability Pact where the deficit *target* level is 1 per cent of GNP[4]
(2) a Stability Pact where the upper limit for the deficit is still 3 per cent of GNP and fines of $\frac{1}{4}$ per cent of GNP are levied for each percentage point by which that limit is exceeded
(3) the case where structural deficits (cyclically adjusted) are targeted for reduction to an upper limit of 3 per cent: a relaxed Maastricht criterion
(4) the case where monetary policy is not allowed to adjust in response to the contractionary effects of the Stability Pact's fiscal restrictions; this is important since, in the other scenarios, output and deflation costs are kept manageable by compensating the fiscal restrictions with a monetary relaxation. We therefore have to ask what would happen if the newly independent central bank were to block this relaxation in its determination to achieve price stability.[5]

Case I: the reference solution

The fiscal criteria

Table 9.1 describes the results of the standard Maastricht Treaty scenario, where all countries are required to reduce their deficits to 3 per cent of GNP by 1999. The instruments are the tax function (9.1) and a mildly accommodating monetary policy. The results show that the necessary deficit reductions are possible in each case. Germany reduces a 4 per cent deficit in 1997 to $3\frac{1}{2}$ per cent in 1998 and $2\frac{1}{2}$ per cent in 1999, and it stays just below the 3 per cent limit thereafter. This is accompanied by small reductions in the German debt ratio from $61\frac{1}{2}$ per cent in 1998 to around 55 per cent by 2008, where it stays. These results improve on baseline figures of 3.7 per cent for the deficit, and between 62 per cent and 66 per cent for the debt ratio.

The French fiscal position proves, after a difficult start, to be a little easier. The deficit falls from 5 per cent of GNP in 1996, to 4.7 per cent in 1997 and 2.9 per cent in 1999, and then reduces very gradually to

---

[4.] Wim Duisenberg, in a speech as the President of the EMI argues that all member states have now committed themselves to achieving a budgetary position close to balance in the medium term (The Hague, 25 October 1997).

[5.] This question was posed for the Maastricht Treaty by Allsop and Vines (1996), who argued that the convergence criteria for entry into EMU would not be met without some loosening of monetary policy, or its equivalent. Interestingly our results show that this is true of the Stability Pact, too, although the amount of loosening is fairly small (interest rates lower by $\frac{1}{3}$ per cent point). Moreover, because the output losses reported below persist in a model which gives full rein to 'crowding-in', credibility and Ricardian Equivalence effects, these fiscal contractions are not expansionary.

Table 9.1. *The reference solution, 1996–2023*
A   Deficit and debt ratios

	Deficit ratios				Debt ratios			
	Germany	France	Italy	United Kingdom	Germany	France	Italy	United Kingdom
1996	3.92	4.21	7.28	3.80	60.6	62.39	114.7	60.1
1997	4.02	3.61	5.92	2.51	61.2	62.2	113.4	60.1
1998	3.52	4.67	7.39	4.57	61.7	62.6	112.3	61.6
1999	2.50	2.91	2.90	2.63	60.9	61.8	108.5	61.1
2000	2.91	2.78	2.92	2.69	60.2	60.5	102.7	60.1
2001	2.89	2.93	2.89	2.23	59.3	59.0	96.2	58.6
2002	2.84	2.85	2.88	2.43	58.5	57.5	89.7	56.9
2003	2.90	2.82	2.77	2.19	57.7	56.0	83.7	55.2
2004	2.94	2.83	2.63	2.08	57.0	54.6	78.4	53.6
2005	2.97	2.85	3.00	2.02	56.6	53.4	74.1	52.0
2006	3.01	2.84	2.94	2.32	56.3	52.4	70.6	50.8
2007	2.63	2.86	2.89	2.83	55.7	51.4	67.8	50.2
2008	2.60	2.83	2.82	2.82	55.1	50.5	65.2	49.7
2009	2.96	2.80	2.74	2.76	54.9	49.6	62.7	49.2
2010	2.94	2.77	2.67	2.72	54.7	48.7	60.3	48.8
2011	2.93	2.74	2.59	2.72	54.6	47.9	57.9	48.3
2012	2.92	2.71	2.96	2.70	54.5	47.0	55.9	47.9
2013	2.92	2.68	2.92	2.79	54.5	46.2	53.9	47.5
2014	2.91	2.65	2.88	2.77	54.5	45.4	52.1	47.2
2015	2.90	2.63	2.82	2.76	54.5	44.6	50.4	46.8
2016	2.89	2.60	2.81	2.91	54.5	43.8	48.7	46.6
2017	2.87	2.57	2.77	2.91	54.6	43.0	47.1	46.5
2018	2.86	2.54	2.75	2.91	54.6	42.2	45.5	46.4
2019	2.84	2.52	2.73	2.90	54.7	41.4	43.9	46.1
2020	2.83	2.49	2.70	2.88	54.8	40.7	42.4	45.9
2021	2.81	2.46	2.67	2.90	55.1	39.9	40.9	45.7
2022	2.80	2.43	2.66	2.89	54.8	39.2	39.5	45.6
2023	2.79	2.40	2.63	2.88	54.5	38.4	38.0	45.4

(contd.)

2.4 per cent by 2023. The French debt ratio, having started at $62\frac{1}{2}$ per cent in 1996, likewise falls slowly but surely to 38 per cent by 2023. Had these fiscal restrictions not been applied the French deficit would have fallen no further than 4.3 per cent (and 4.7 per cent in 1998), and her debt would have remained at 62–63 per cent. In the United Kingdom, the story is

Table 9.1 (*cont.*)

B Deviations from baseline

	Germany				France				Italy				United Kingdom			
	$\dot{Y}$	$\dot{P}$	RS	TX	$\dot{Y}$	$\dot{P}$	RS	TX	$\dot{Y}$	$\dot{P}$	RS	TX	$\dot{Y}$	$\dot{P}$	RS	TX
1966	−0.00	0.00	0.00	0.00	−0.01	−0.00	0.00	0.00	−0.03	−0.01	0.00	0.00	−0.01	−0.01	0.00	0.00
1997	−0.01	−0.00	−0.00	0.00	−0.02	−0.01	0.00	0.00	−0.07	−0.04	0.00	0.01	+0.02	−0.01	0.00	0.00
1998	−0.02	−0.01	−0.00	0.00	−0.04	−0.06	−0.00	0.00	−0.15	−0.19	−0.00	0.03	−0.04	−0.07	−0.00	0.01
1999	−0.41	−0.02	−0.03	6.19	−0.49	−0.28	−0.01	7.77	−1.54	−0.73	−0.01	24.40	−0.60	−0.30	−0.00	6.19
2000	−0.12	−0.21	−0.12	3.88	−0.34	−0.48	−0.05	7.12	−1.40	−1.39	−0.05	22.70	−0.27	−0.48	−0.06	4.49
2001	−0.00	−0.28	−0.18	3.45	−0.21	−0.58	−0.10	6.64	−1.14	−1.85	−0.10	21.42	−0.2	−0.50	−0.06	6.01
2002	0.02	−0.27	−0.19	3.15	−0.12	−0.57	−0.12	6.28	−0.97	−2.04	−0.12	21.66	−0.11	−0.51	−0.13	6.08
2003	0.01	−0.23	−0.17	2.90	−0.06	−0.49	−0.13	5.97	−0.81	−2.03	−0.13	20.94	−0.07	−0.43	−0.13	6.18
2004	−0.01	−0.19	−0.13	2.70	−0.04	−0.39	−0.13	5.70	−0.73	−0.89	−0.13	20.53	−0.07	−0.35	−0.13	3.61
2005	−0.04	−0.17	−0.09	2.52	−0.03	−0.30	−0.13	5.44	−0.57	−1.68	−0.13	17.66	−0.07	−0.27	−0.13	6.44
2006	−0.06	−0.16	−0.07	2.35	−0.04	−0.24	−0.12	5.19	−0.59	−1.49	−0.12	17.34	0.00	−0.20	−0.12	4.98
2007	−0.18	−0.10	−0.05	4.25	−0.06	−0.22	−0.12	4.95	−0.67	−1.40	−0.12	17.06	0.12	−0.13	−0.12	2.31
2008	−0.16	−0.13	−0.06	4.25	−0.08	−0.24	−0.12	4.95	−0.75	−1.40	−0.12	17.06	0.07	−0.07	−0.12	2.32

Year																
2009	0.01	-0.24	-0.10	2.20	-0.07	-0.27	-0.12	4.95	-0.79	-1.46	-0.12	17.06	0.04	-0.04	-0.12	2.52
2010	0.00	-0.23	-0.12	2.20	-0.08	-0.30	-0.12	4.95	-0.87	-1.58	-0.12	17.06	-0.02	-0.06	-0.12	2.71
2011	-0.02	-0.21	-0.11	2.20	-0.09	-0.34	0.12	4.95	-0.94	-1.71	-0.12	17.06	-0.05	-0.12	-0.12	2.71
2012	-0.04	-0.20	-0.10	2.20	-0.10	-0.37	-0.12	4.95	-0.85	-1.82	-0.12	14.57	-0.06	-0.18	-0.12	2.71
2013	-0.06	-0.20	-0.10	2.20	-0.11	-0.41	-0.12	4.95	-0.92	-1.92	-0.12	14.57	-0.05	-0.24	-0.12	2.32
2014	-0.07	-0.22	-0.10	2.20	-0.12	-0.45	-0.12	4.95	-1.02	-2.04	-0.12	14.57	-0.05	-0.28	-0.12	2.32
2015	-0.07	-0.23	-0.11	2.20	-0.12	-0.49	-0.12	4.95	-1.12	-2.18	-0.12	14.57	-0.05	-0.31	-0.12	2.32
2016	-0.07	-0.25	-0.12	2.20	-0.13	-0.53	-0.12	4.95	-1.21	-2.36	-0.12	14.57	-0.01	-0.32	-0.12	1.52
2017	-0.07	-0.27	-0.14	2.20	-0.13	-0.58	-0.12	4.95	-1.30	-2.55	-0.12	14.57	-0.02	-0.32	-0.12	1.52
2018	-0.06	-0.29	-0.15	2.20	-0.13	-0.60	-0.13	4.95	-1.38	-2.75	-0.13	14.57	-0.03	-0.34	-0.13	1.52
2019	-0.06	-0.30	-0.16	2.20	-0.13	-0.64	-0.13	4.95	-1.46	-2.95	-0.13	14.57	-0.05	-0.36	-0.13	1.52
2020	-0.06	-0.32	-0.17	2.20	-0.13	-0.68	-0.14	4.95	-1.53	-3.15	-0.14	14.57	-0.06	-0.40	-0.14	1.60
2021	-0.06	-0.34	0.18	2.20	-0.13	-0.71	-0.14	4.95	-1.61	-3.35	-0.14	14.47	-0.06	-0.43	-0.14	1.52
2022	-0.06	0.36	-0.19	2.20	-0.12	-0.75	-0.15	4.95	-1.69	-3.54	0.15	14.57	-0.05	-0.46	-0.15	1.52
2023	-0.06	-0.38	-0.20	2.20	-0.12	-0.79	-0.16	4.95	-1.77	-3.74	-0.16	14.57	-0.05	-0.49	-0.16	1.52

Notes:

$\dot{Y}$ = Rate of growth of GNP in constant prices (per cent p.a.).

$\dot{P}$ = Rate of growth of domestic output prices (per cent p.a.).

RS = Short-term interest rate (three-month government bonds).

TX = Average tax rate (percentage change).

essentially similar, although the earlier restrictions are not necessary. The deficit starts at 3.8 per cent, falls to $2\frac{1}{2}$ per cent by 1997, rises again in 1998, and then hovers around 2.1 per cent till 2006 when it floats back up to 2.8 per cent. The UK debt position touches 60 per cent in 1998–9, but otherwise remains comfortably inside the prescribed boundary at around 45 per cent.

Unsurprisingly, it is in Italy where we see the real improvements in fiscal discipline. Here the deficit falls from 7.3 per cent in 1996, to 5.9 per cent in 1997, back to 7.3 per cent in 1998 and then down to 2.9 per cent or lower (as required) from 1999 onwards. This has the effect of reducing Italy's very high debt ratio from 114 per cent in 1996, through 100 per cent in 2000 and 60 per cent in 2010 to 40 per cent by 2022.[6] Thus Italy can be made to satisfy the deficit criterion by 1999 and the debt criterion 10 years later – but naturally at some considerable cost to output and employment. Yet, had fiscal discipline not been imposed the deficit would have remained at 6.9 per cent from 1999, and the debt at 96 per cent of GNP. In this respect, the conditions for entering EMU have been successfully met.

Lastly, the upward fluctuations in each country's deficit reduction between 1997 and 1998 show that any changes in tax rates have to become permanent if the deficit reductions are to be permanent. We have kept (9.1) in place until 1999 to demonstrate that point. Excess deficits in 1996 mean that tax rates have to rise. But tax rates then fall again in 1997 because the amount by which deficits exceed their target values has been reduced: the second term in (9.1) becomes negative, even if the first term remains positive. And lower tax rates in 1997, in their turn, imply that deficits rise again the following year. Thus, to stop this over-shooting, tax rates have to be frozen at their new higher levels. This we do from 1999. Interestingly the fluctuations around 1997–8 match the Italian government's official projections of an overall deficit ratio of 6.7 per cent, 3.0 per cent, 4.1 per cent and 2.8 per cent in 1996, 1997, 1998 and thereafter. Our tax rate model appears to have captured this feature rather well.

Output losses

The output costs of these fiscal contractions, *compared to the baseline*, are not very large. Germany loses about 0.1 percentage points from her growth rate most years, leaving GNP perhaps 2 per cent lower

---

[6.] It is important to note that terminal conditions are imposed to produce a steady-state growth path in each country's variables in the long term. So Italy's debt *ratio* stabilizes beyond 2023, just as it does for Germany and the United Kingdom rather earlier. Notice also that these terminal conditions are set to produce equilibrium growth paths, although they do not specify what those growth rates should be.

than it would have been otherwise in 2020. For France the output losses are a little larger; perhaps 0.15 percentage points lower growth in most years, or $4\frac{1}{2}$ per cent off GNP after twenty five years. For the United Kingdom there is a somewhat sharper contraction around 1999–2000, but otherwise the growth rate typically falls by 0.05 percentage points, and GNP by less than 2 per cent (compared to trend) over twenty-five years.

It is Italy who suffers the largest output losses; around $1\frac{1}{2}$ percentage points off her growth rate during 1999–2001, and 0.9 per cent thereafter until 2013 when the losses start to rise again to 1.8 percentage points off by 2023. This gives a sense of how difficult it is to hold Italy's deficit ratio down to 3 per cent after the initial cuts. Indeed these cuts in output growth amount to 25–30 per cent off GNP after twenty-five years.[7] And all these results need to be compared to growth rates of around $2-2\frac{1}{2}$ per cent in the baseline. So the pure output losses are relatively small for France, Germany and the United Kingdom – perhaps 6 per cent or 7 per cent of the increases in national income which could have been expected have been forgone.

But, for Italy, something approaching one-half of the natural increase in national incomes has been lost to fiscal austerity.

Price deflation

Here the 'costs' of the fiscal contractions are rather larger. Prices rise roughly 0.2–0.4 per cent slower per year than they would have done in Germany and the United Kingdom. Similarly they rise between 0.4 per cent and 0.8 per cent slower in France, and between $1\frac{1}{2}$ per cent and 4 per cent slower in Italy. Against a baseline of about 2 per cent price inflation per year, this represents lower inflation in Germany and the United Kingdom and literally stable prices in France, which carries the risk of liquidity difficulties and increasing debt burdens. That is important because of the general argument that price indices will over-state the actual rate of inflation – typically by around 1 percentage points (Moulton, 1996). This can happen for several reasons. The first is that, with the introduction of new varieties or higher-quality goods, the

---

[7.] In other words, the 60 per cent increase in GNP specified in the baseline between 1998 and 2023 has been cut to just 30 per cent. It is important to realise that MULTIMOD's full capacity level of output, and natural rate of employment, are *not* constant – but will fall with the level of potential output (appendix 9.1). Notice also that these output losses, and their associated price deflations, are the result of repeated fiscal contractions (cumulating over several years and then sustained) as reflected in the successive rises in tax rates. They therefore reduce the stream of expected future earnings – and hence wealth, and consumption and investment expenditures – in each period into the future.

index can yield zero inflation only if measured prices are actually falling. Similarly, since base-year weights are updated only at discrete intervals – that is, after demand has substituted away from higher-priced goods – zero inflation is possible only if measured prices fall.

Thus price deflation may be unimportant if measured inflation is running at 2 per cent per year. But at 0 per cent – meaning that actual prices are falling 1 per cent a year – it could be crucial to liquidity and debt servicing. And that could lead to problems in the capital markets, too. If zero inflation accompanies very low interest rates (so the real rate of interest is zero) then investors may withdraw from the credit or stock markets, preferring to hold cash instead. Japan's banking crisis and recession in the 1990s is an example of just how easily zero (measured) inflation can lead to a liquidity crisis.

Against this, price disinflation would clearly be beneficial in terms of competitiveness – mainly in Germany, the United Kingdom and France. But in Italy, where it implies prices fall around $1\frac{1}{2}$–2 per cent a year over twenty years, illiquidity and bankruptcies are a more likely outcome. And taken together (output losses *plus* price deflations), the output costs of these fiscal restrictions are quite large: a 1 per cent drop in the deficit ratio in Germany costs (in the long run) about 2 per cent in lost output and 4–5 per cent points in lower output prices. That is a multiplier of 2 in real terms. For the United Kingdom and France, the costs are much the same: a 2 per cent reduction in the deficit ratio costs 4 per cent in output and 5–10 percentage points in output prices. But the costs for Italy are considerably larger: a 5 per cent fall in the deficit ratio costs 25 per cent in lost output and 50 per cent in output prices. That is a multiplier of 5.

Real interest rates

How much monetary relaxation has been generated to compensate for these fiscal contractions? The evidence for relaxation is clear enough, but the size is rather small. All four countries have shaved around 0.1–0.2 percent points off their short-run nominal interest rates. The exchange rate restriction prevents larger reductions.[8] Hence we have a conflict between Germany and the United Kingdom, on the one side, who need little relaxation since they do not have to cut their deficits by very much, and France and Italy, on the other, who need more monetary accommodation but cannot get it because of the exchange rate restriction. This will always be the case in a union where some have to make large deficit cuts, but have to adjust to a single monetary policy set by others

[8.] Note that the monetary policy rules have not changed. But deflation means that the demand for money eases while the money supply targets remain unchanged. Interest rates have consequently to fall to re-establish equilibrium in the money markets.

who do not have to make such cuts. Moreover the external exchange rate cannot be used either, without violating the monetary targets of those who need make no adjustments, and hence of Europe as a whole. Thus, given the supremacy of price stability, the only way left to get a supporting monetary relaxation and revive activity is to deflate prices locally. This reveals a painful conflict between the fiscal criteria and monetary policy, especially for Italy.

It is important to note that this same mechanism (small reductions in interest rates, *plus* larger deflations in prices) will imply rising *real* interest rates. In the event they rise rather little in Germany and the United Kingdom (just 0.2 percentage points) and only modestly in France (0.6 per cent). But in Italy they rise by up to $3\frac{1}{2}$ percentage points, implying a huge increase in the real cost of capital. Rises on that scale must damage investment expenditures and output capacity, and hence prevent Italy profiting from the recovery elsewhere in Europe when it comes. That is the real cost of the Stability Pact's fiscal restrictions.

Tax increases

Finally, the political cost of these deficit reductions may well be larger than the output or deflation costs. In Germany, the average tax rate has had to rise by 6 per cent in 1999, falling back to just $2\frac{1}{2}$–$4\frac{1}{2}$ per cent higher than otherwise during 2000–8. That means a 30 per cent average tax rate would have to rise to 32 per cent at worst, which is not too serious.

For the United Kingdom the figures are essentially similar, except that the peak rise in tax rates lasts longer. For France the peak rise is nearly 8 per cent (1999), and tax rates then remain 5 per cent higher than in the baseline for the rest of the simulation. But Italy has more serious problems. Her deficit reductions require a 24 per cent increase in average tax rates in 1999 (e.g. from 30 per cent to 38 per cent), and they remain 15 per cent above baseline (e.g. at 35 per cent) for the rest of the simulation. If this can be interpreted as the Italian government's 'tax for Europe', then not only does it represent a very large increase, but it also has to be permanent. That raises the prospect of further distortions to output capacity and investment.

The supply-side responses

The most striking result, and one to be repeated in stronger form in table 9.3 (pp. 232–33), is the sharp increase in the *real* rates of interest in those countries with large excess deficits – principally Italy, but to some extent in France, too. This is significant because table 9.1 showed a cumulative output loss of around 20 per cent in Italy, and a corresponding

Table 9.2. *Investment, capacity and utilization losses, 1996–2033 (reference solution)*

	Real interest rates (percentage points)				Investment losses (per cent)			
	Germany	France	Italy	United Kingdom	Germany	France	Italy	United Kingdom
1996	0.00	0.00	0.01	0.00	0.00	0.00	0.00	0.00
1997	0.00	0.01	0.04	0.01	−0.00	0.00	0.00	0.00
1998	0.01	0.06	0.19	0.07	0.00	−0.00	−0.00	−0.01
1999	0.01	0.27	0.72	0.29	−0.01	−0.00	−0.00	−0.01
2000	0.09	0.43	1.34	0.42	−0.00	−0.00	−0.00	−0.00
2001	0.10	0.48	1.75	0.46	0.00	−0.01	−0.01	−0.00
2005	0.08	0.17	1.55	0.24	−0.00	0.00	0.00	−0.00
2010	0.11	0.18	1.46	−0.06	−0.47	−0.18	−0.77	−0.31
2015	0.12	0.37	2.06	0.19	−0.93	−1.92	−1.76	−2.30
2023	0.18	0.63	3.58	0.33	−0.49	−0.33	−2.52	−2.58

	Output capacity losses (per cent)				Utilization losses (per cent)			
	Germany	France	Italy	United Kingdom	Germany	France	Italy	United Kingdom
1996	−0.00	0.00	0.00	−0.00	−0.02	−0.07	−0.16	−0.06
1997	−0.00	0.00	0.00	−0.00	−0.02	−0.06	−0.24	−0.08
1998	−0.00	0.00	0.00	−0.00	−0.01	−0.46	−0.29	−0.53
1999	−0.00	0.00	0.00	−0.00	−0.12	−0.32	−1.59	−0.53
2000	−0.00	−0.00	0.00	−0.00	−0.12	−0.17	−1.40	−0.26
2001	−0.01	−0.00	−0.00	−0.01	−0.02	−0.08	−1.06	−0.03
2005	−0.01	−0.00	−0.00	−0.01	−0.10	−0.06	−0.74	0.02
2010	−0.01	−0.01	−0.03	−0.01	−0.10	−0.19	−1.29	−0.07
2015	−0.07	−0.23	−0.27	−0.15	−0.14	−0.25	−1.67	−0.07
2020	−0.11	−0.48	−0.59	−0.25	−0.18	−0.30	−2.26	−0.01
2023	−0.12	−0.62	−0.76	−0.30	−0.22	−0.33	−2.67	0.03

cumulative deflation of 40 per cent in prices compared to base. Other countries do not suffer the same price deflation, so why does Italy's output not recover with a boom driven by her emerging relative price advantage?

The answer lies in the large increase in real interest rates which is also sustained throughout the simulation period. We have seen that Italian real

Table 9.2 (*cont.*)

	Exports (percentage change from baseline)				Imports (change from baseline)			
	Germany	France	Italy	United Kingdom	Germany	France	Italy	United Kingdom
1996	−0.03	−0.04	−0.01	0.05	−0.07	−0.10	−0.33	−0.08
1997	−0.03	−0.05	0.02	−0.06	−0.12	−0.13	−1.49	−0.10
1998	−0.01	−0.04	0.13	−0.02	−0.11	−0.12	−0.61	−0.07
1999	−0.26	−0.39	−0.01	−0.43	−0.82	−1.15	−3.55	−0.78
2000	0.00	−0.03	0.60	0.05	−0.33	−0.38	−1.81	−0.23
2001	0.08	0.08	0.96	0.33	−0.04	−0.04	−0.91	−0.05
2005	−0.01	0.01	1.15	0.24	0.01	−0.18	−0.91	−0.07
2010	−0.02	−0.01	1.33	0.16	0.01	0.14	−0.84	−0.05
2015	−0.02	−0.01	1.82	0.21	0.14	−0.11	−0.73	−0.02
2020	−0.02	−0.00	2.42	0.33	0.41	−0.07	−0.60	0.06
2023	−0.01	−0.00	2.79	0.37	0.64	−0.04	−0.53	0.09

interest rates rose by $1\frac{1}{2}$ percentage points in the year 2000, increasing to $3\frac{1}{2}$ per cent by 2020. This of course reduces investment and consumption expenditures, both of which are negative in the real cost of capital (affecting asset values in the case of consumption). As a result, output and output capacity is severely damaged. In fact table 9.2 shows that Italian investment expenditures fall by up to $2\frac{1}{2}$ per cent each year from 2001 onwards (roughly double her output losses), and that output capacity is lower by up to 1 per cent each year over the same period, instead of increasing as in other countries. France suffers the same fate although the losses are smaller.

Consequently, while it is true that Italy does reduce relative prices and increase competitiveness, she is unable to do so by enough to generate a recovery. Instead, while increases in competitiveness lead to higher output through improvements in the trade account – the underlying figures show that exports rise $2\frac{1}{2}$ per cent above base, while imports fall 1 per cent – they are more than offset by the fall in investment and consumption expenditures following the rise in real interest rates. So in place of an output recovery, we get a supply-side collapse and a loss in output.

The source of this investment – output collapse is the 'liquidity trap' in which nominal interest rates cannot fall, because of the single currency constraint, while prices are being deflated. The worst thing we can do, if

Table 9.3. *Reducing actual deficits to 1 per cent, 1996–2020*

	Deficit ratios				Debt ratios			
	Germany	France	Italy	United Kingdom	Germany	France	Italy	United Kingdom
1996	3.93	4.44	7.36	3.84	60.6	62.6	115.5	60.3
1997	4.03	3.64	6.01	2.53	61.3	62.5	114.8	61.3
1998	3.51	4.68	7.50	4.58	61.8	63.0	114.3	62.0
1999	0.95	0.98	0.85	1.00	59.7	60.7	110.3	60.4
2000	0.87	0.88	0.88	0.63	57.0	57.7	103.0	57.5
2001	0.71	0.91	0.86	0.42	54.2	54.2	94.6	55.0
2005	0.64	0.57	0.55	0.60	44.2	41.0	64.0	41.3
2010	0.89	0.28	0.54	0.71	36.0	28.3	42.7	31.2
2015	0.89	0.96	0.54	0.42	31.9	19.9	26.8	23.2
2020	0.73	0.81	0.46	0.93	29.1	13.8	12.9	17.4

	$\dot{Y}$				$\dot{P}$			
	Germany	France	Italy	United Kingdom	Germany	France	Italy	United Kingdom
1996	−0.07	−0.13	−0.34	−1.14	−0.01	−0.14	−0.31	−0.16
1997	−0.07	−0.15	−0.48	−0.15	−0.03	−0.28	−0.62	−0.29
1998	−0.03	−0.13	−0.55	−0.08	−0.12	−0.53	−1.24	−0.52
1999	−0.76	−0.97	−2.62	−1.09	−0.17	−1.12	−2.59	−1.08
2000	−0.32	−0.60	−2.18	−0.48	−0.55	−1.67	−4.08	−1.54
2001	−0.03	−0.25	−1.52	+0.04	−0.81	−1.95	−5.01	−1.63
2005	−0.10	+0.07	−0.65	+0.25	−0.56	−1.11	−4.63	−0.29
2010	+0.08	−0.09	−1.08	+0.14	−0.76	−1.32	−4.66	0.59
2015	−0.03	+0.12	−1.41	+0.20	−0.84	−1.55	−6.81	−1.02
2020	+0.09	+0.28	−1.53	+0.73	−1.19	2.33	−9.23	−0.75

we want to avoid destroying capacity permanently, is to thus try to reduce deficits in a slump, and to try to reduce them in one country when the others don't need to do so, since nominal interest rates cannot fall at the same time. But, in fact, the Stability Pact would have us do both those things.

Interestingly it appears that the classical Gold Standard – the nearest comparable regime with tight monetary discipline and nationally determined fiscal policies – was also characterized by divergent economies. Moreover it appears that growth and price level dynamics were also the

Table 9.3 (*cont.*)

	RS				TX			
	Germany	France	Italy	United Kingdom	Germany	France	Italy	United Kingdom
1996	−0.02	−0.02	−0.01	−0.02	0.03	0.03	0.08	0.04
1997	−0.03	−0.05	−0.05	−0.05	0.02	0.03	0.10	0.04
1998	−0.08	−0.11	−0.11	−0.11	−0.00	−0.00	0.08	0.02
1999	−0.17	−0.20	−0.21	−0.20	13.67	17.63	37.24	13.74
2000	−0.37	−0.34	−0.35	−0.35	13.03	16.05	34.66	13.20
1201	−0.55	−0.46	−0.46	−0.46	12.55	15.53	32.40	12.74
2005	−0.38	−0.39	−0.39	−0.40	11.14	14.23	29.68	11.47
2010	−0.39	−0.33	−0.33	−0.33	8.34	13.70	26.53	8.69
2015	−0.42	−0.41	−0.41	−0.41	7.52	8.45	24.53	8.69
2020	−0.62	−0.61	−0.61	−0.61	7.11	8.01	23.53	4.71

Notes: $\dot{Y}$, $\dot{P}$, RX and TX as in table 9.1. Note that the bottom four panels of this and tables 9.4–9.7 are all measured as deviations from the baseline path.

main driving force for fiscal adjustment in that period, producing mild deflation for all participants, but low growth and high real interest rates affecting some countries more than others. It was only when money supplies were increased again (post-1895) that real interest rates fell and growth resumed, and that convergence and economic expansion reappeared (Flandreau, 1998). That is exactly the same story as here.

Case II: the Stability Pact

The deficit limit set at 1 per cent of GNP

Table 9.3 shows what would happen if one element of the Stability Pact were implemented – that which says the budget deficit should average no more than 1 per cent of GNP. Reaching that objective appears to be no problem; each country manages it from 1999, with some over-shooting in the period 2000–10 when the deficits fall to about 0.5 per cent of GNP.[9]

[9.] It would be more appropriate to set the correct target deficit ratio for each country such that the probability of exceeding 3 per cent was held to some small value. However we do not know what those targets should be. So we impose 1 per cent instead, which seems to be a commonly accepted target value (Duisenberg, 1997). That solution generates sustained primary surpluses: with nominal interest rates at 5 per cent, a 60 per cent deficit ratio would generate interest payments of 3 per cent of GNP – larger than the actual deficits in table 9.3.

All are therefore obliged to run primary surpluses; and, as a result, public sector debts are reduced. The German debt ratio falls to 30 per cent by 2020; the French to 15 per cent, the Italian to 13 per cent and the UK to 17 per cent. In other words, both table 9.1 and table 9.3 produce steady-state solutions which are consistent with the Maastricht criteria: 5 per cent nominal growth with 3 per cent deficits and 60 per cent debt ratios in table 9.1, or 1 per cent deficits and 20 per cent debt ratios in table 9.3.

The Stability Pact's objectives can thus be reached, but at some cost in additional price deflation and higher taxes (rather than output losses). In fact, for Germany, output growth is reduced by 0.8 percentage points in 1999, 0.3 per cent in 2000 and 0.1 per cent each year until 2009. But output then rises above baseline a little (up by 0.1 per cent). France has similar but stronger output losses: a 1.0 percentage point loss in 1999, 0.6 per cent in 2000, and 0.1 per cent to 2010. Thereafter growth is increased by up to 0.5 percentage points in 2022–3. The United Kingdom is similar: output growth is reduced by 1 per cent in 1999, but rises above baseline by 0.3–0.7 per cent from 2003–23. Only in Italy are there sustained losses in output compared to the baseline: 2.6 per cent off in 1999 (producing an overall recession for the first time), 2.2 per cent off in 2000, 1.5 per cent in 2001 and $1-1\frac{1}{2}$ per cent each year after that.

In this case the extra deflation in the United Kingdom, France and Germany is compensated by larger monetary relaxations than in table 9.1 – but, more importantly, by the real income effects of the larger price deflations in table 9.3. In fact, these two effects combined are now strong enough to stimulate output after 2010, rather than to contract it. Moreover the price deflations are stronger than in table 9.1, and disproportionately so. Price inflation runs a steady $\frac{1}{2}$–1 per cent to 1 per cent lower each year in Germany and the United Kingdom, and $1\frac{1}{2}$ per cent–2 per cent in France. This leaves output prices and inflation considerably lower in all three countries – prices grow at 1 per cent in the United Kingdom and Germany, but are literally stable in France. Similarly, prices are stable in Italy over the years 1998–2000, but they actually fall by 2 per cent each year over the years 2000–10, and accelerate to fall at a rate rising from 4 per cent each year to 8 per cent each year by 2020. The Stability Pact may therefore make liquidity tight in Germany and the United Kingdom, but the potential for a liquidity crunch is much higher in France and Italy.

The lesson here is that 'large' enough fiscal contractions can indeed prove expansionary for output, but only after about fifteen years and only through lower interest rates and price deflation. These results are entirely consistent with the literature which suggests that real monetary expansions (whether nominal or by price reductions) are not neutral in the long term when there are real balance effects present.[10] In other words, these much discussed 'non-Keynesian effects' come about only through real balance effects, driven by some relaxation in the policy mix. They do not come through greater credibility, Ricardian Equivalence, or 'crowding-in' effects (all three of which are present in our model, too).[11]

On the cost side, the increases in tax rates are now twice as large as in table 9.1. Germany's increase is 13 per cent at the peak and 7 per cent in the long run, with 13 per cent and 4 per cent in the United Kingdom, 17 per cent and 7 per cent in France, but 37 per cent (falling to 23 per cent) in Italy. Similarly, real interest rates now rise by up to $\frac{1}{2}$ per cent in Germany, $1\frac{1}{2}$ per cent in France and a massive $8\frac{1}{2}$ per cent in Italy. It seems unlikely that Italy, at least, could survive these extra costs, and the liquidity pressures and the loss of capacity which are implied. Indeed it seems inevitable that monetization or some realignments would come into force before we ever reached such a scenario.

A Stability Pact with fines

Our second Stability Pact simulation examines the impact of introducing fines payable by those governments who violate the 3 per cent limit for the deficit ratios. In order to study the effect of this innovation on economic performance and on the fiscal discipline achieved, we impose fines on a Maastricht-type regime with a 3 per cent deficit target, not within a Stability Pact with a 1 per cent target. This allows us to assess the impact of each part of the stability pact separately, although in practice any such pact will have both components.

A second difficulty is that we now have to switch away from a tax function like (9.1) to an expenditure-cutting exercise. The reason is that if we impose such a tax function we will automatically force a solution with deficits below 3 per cent – see the reference solution in table 9.1A. Fines would then never be used and we would learn nothing. But if we do not impose the tax function, policy makers will make no effort to reduce their deficits and the fines will be imposed for no purpose; they will simply add to the baseline deficit. Consequently we set $\alpha_1 = \alpha_2 = 0$ and introduce an expenditure-cutting rule in which each country makes a cut of 1 per cent of GNP to government expenditures in 1996, and a further cut of 1 per cent of GNP each year after that until the 3 per cent threshold is

---

[10.] Spaventa (1987); Marini and van der Ploeg (1988).
[11.] Contrast Giavazzi and Pagano (1990, 1995). On the other hand, we do not account for the theoretical prediction that 'expansionary fiscal contractions', if they occur, would lead to higher unemployment and hence to rising deficits (Barry and Devereaux, 1995).

Table 9.4. *Expenditure cuts with fines, 1996–2020 (a stability pact)*

	Deficit ratios				Debt ratios			
	Germany	France	Italy	United Kingdom	Germany	France	Italy	United Kingdom
1996	4.00	4.34	7.63	3.85	60.6	63.0	117.5	59.8
1997	4.10	3.75	6.24	2.56	61.2	62.9	116.3	60.7
1998	3.60	4.80	7.67	4.57	61.7	63.5	115.0	61.3
1999	3.29	4.06	7.16	3.46	61.7	63.9	114.0	61.9
2000	3.27	3.85	6.97	3.17	61.3	62.7	110.9	61.6
2001	3.13	3.97	6.68	3.02	60.7	63.0	106.8	60.6
2005	3.03	3.77	6.25	3.07	57.8	59.4	92.2	56.5
2010	3.15	3.91	6.04	3.19	56.7	57.6	86.1	54.6
2015	3.22	4.05	5.83	3.27	56.9	57.1	81.5	53.2
2020	3.32	4.30	5.65	3.42	58.2	57.6	76.9	53.0

	$\dot{Y}$				$\dot{P}$			
	Germany	France	Italy	United Kingdom	Germany	France	Italy	United Kingdom
1996	−0.06	−0.18	−0.25	0.01	0.68	0.03	−0.96	0.81
1997	−0.03	−0.18	−0.19	0.03	0.80	0.01	−0.96	0.88
1998	+0.04	−0.15	−0.07	0.11	0.84	−0.18	−1.09	0.80
1999	−0.66	−0.83	−0.87	−0.72	1.00	0.72	−1.54	0.39
2000	−0.35	−0.65	−0.53	−0.36	0.68	−1.36	−2.01	−0.02
2001	−0.07	−0.40	−0.11	0.18	0.41	−1.82	−2.19	−0.18
2005	+0.14	−0.00	−0.58	−0.19	−0.48	−1.44	−0.08	−0.92
2010	+0.22	−0.31	−0.49	−0.11	−0.56	−1.50	2.36	−0.79
2015	+0.28	−0.38	−0.88	−0.06	−0.66	−2.31	3.96	−0.89
2020	+0.32	−0.81	1.11	−0.04	−0.85	−2.99	6.59	−0.56

reached. The accumulated cuts are maintained thereafter. On top of this we add fines, for those who exceed the 3 per cent limit, as follows:

$$\text{def}_t^* = \text{def}_t + f_t \tag{9.3}$$

where
$$f_t = \begin{cases} 0.0025\,Y_t(\text{def}_t - 0.03) & \text{if } \text{def}_t \geq 0.03 \text{ and } t \geq 1999 \\ 0 & \text{otherwise.} \end{cases}$$

def_t is the deficit/GNP ratio in period t, and def_t^* is the target deficit

Table 9.4 (*cont.*)

	RS				TX			
	Germany	France	Italy	United Kingdom	Germany	France	Italy	United Kingdom
1996	0.28	0.24	0.28	0.24	0.23	0.29	0.72	0.15
1997	0.34	0.25	0.28	0.25	0.28	0.34	0.78	0.17
1998	0.37	0.25	0.28	0.25	0.29	0.36	0.80	0.16
1999	0.37	0.24	0.27	0.24	−0.46	−0.38	0.49	−0.52
2000	0.21	0.17	0.18	0.17	−0.70	−0.58	0.25	−0.76
2001	0.01	0.05	0.06	0.053	−0.95	−0.75	−0.08	−1.01
2005	−0.04	−0.00	−0.00	−1.71	−1.45	−1.10	−1.10	−1.69
2010	0.11	0.11	0.11	−2.27	−1.87	−1.93	−1.93	−2.23
2015	0.16	0.15	0.15	−2.81	−2.20	−2.92	−2.92	−2.80
2020	0.24	0.24	0.24	−3.19	−2.24	−3.87	−3.87	−3.04

Note: $\dot{Y}$, $\dot{P}$, RX and TX as in table 9.1.
Note that $\dot{Y}$, $\dot{P}$, RX and TX are all measured as deviations from the baseline.

ratio (including fines). Thus the fine is $\frac{1}{4}$ per cent of GNP for each percentage point that the deficit exceeds 3 per cent.

An alternative procedure would have been to subtract the fine from the current expenditure. But that implies the expenditures in any budgetary over-run can be switched off instantly. Both for reasons of pre-commitment, and because expenditure changes on that scale would almost certainly need prior parliamentary approval, that seems unlikely. So we stick with (9.3).[12] The results are shown in table 9.4.

From table 9.4 we can see that, despite a regime of quite savage cumulative fiscal cuts, imposing fines does nothing to ensure fiscal discipline. We already knew that in practice, apart from a temporary reduction in the deficit ratio, expenditure cuts alone are unable to provide a permanent

---

[12.] This discussion reveals that there is also a problem in deciding how the Stability Pact's fines should be levied. Clearly, they must not be allowed to increase borrowing. They might therefore be implemented with a lag, except that they would then depress expenditure when the necessary fiscal corrections had already been undertaken – increasing the output losses yet further. That is unhelpful, and policy makers, knowing that fines will be extracted next period, would have an extra incentive not to cut expenditures this period so that the larger than planned cuts next period turn out to be of the desired size. Neither option makes sense since we have either no effect or over-kill. So, if expenditures cannot be expected to adjust to accommodate the fines, we will actually have to make taxes adjust instead – which does make sense since one-off expenditure cuts cannot remove excessive deficits permanently anyway, even if sustained, since the resulting contractions will reduce tax revenues at the same time.

improvement in deficit ratios (see Hughes Hallett and McAdam, 1998). Adding fines on top of the expenditure cuts should not therefore be expected to make any material difference.[13] And that is what we see here. Germany squeaks inside the 3 per cent limit in 2002–5, but her deficit ratio drifts up steadily after that without ever regaining the 3 per cent limit. Similarly France converges towards 3 per cent until 2003, but never makes it, and then drifts steadily away from 3 per cent. Italy likewise moves slowly towards 3 per cent, but has got only as far as 5.5 per cent by the year 2023; and the United Kingdom briefly touches 3 per cent in 2001, hovers there and then drifts away again after 2006. So fiscal discipline is not achieved, despite massive expenditure cuts and fines as large as 1 per cent of GNP each year for Italy in the 1999–2001 period, or $\frac{1}{4}$ per cent each year for France.

It is not fair to say that *no* discipline has been achieved in this scenario since Germany, Italy and the United Kingdom finish up with deficit ratios at 0.3 per cent, 1.4 per cent and 0.3 per cent below their baseline values, respectively. But France has them 0.2 per cent higher, and no one has falling deficits. So there is not enough discipline to eliminate the excess deficits. On the other hand there are also fewer output losses. All four countries suffer small losses in output between 1995 and 2001, but only France suffers any deflation or losses thereafter. The other three actually enjoy small increases in output above baseline and a little extra inflation from 2002 onwards. However, in reality, this result is just an artefact of our simulation since, in order to switch to expenditure cuts, we have had to return taxes to their baseline. Consequently as soon as expenditure cuts get deficits below their baseline values, taxes start to fall and output rises to improve revenues and the deficit. This explains why taxes actually fall in this case; whereas, in reality, you would expect them to rise in response to the deficit increases caused by the fines.

In fact when we reran this simulation without any expenditure cuts and the same neutral tax function, in order to get a clearer picture of the pure fines effect, we found taxes did rise by 1 per cent in Italy and $\frac{1}{4}$ per cent elsewhere – and output fell, leaving the deficit ratios even *higher* than in the baseline. That confirmed our three main findings:

(1) Fines do not provide any significant incentive to reduce excessive deficit ratios.
(2) Fines do not bring the deficit ratios down to 3 per cent within two years; hence they are not returnable fines (except for Germany in 2000–1).

[13] Again this is because the expenditure cuts are approximately linear with a multiplier of one on national income, and hence of zero on the deficit ratio; and hence, with incomes falling in tandem with the cuts, revenues must fall thereafter, with the result that the deficit itself will then start to expand again.

(3) Fines leave tax rates permanently higher than otherwise – that is, fines are passed on directly to the consumer, an innocent party, instead of being absorbed by the guilty party. Therefore, if fines do anything, it will be to trigger a political backlash. Knowing that to be the case, policy makers will not believe that their colleagues will actually risk the political cost of raising additional taxes to pay the fines, especially if firms are likely to move to lower tax areas. That robs fines of any value as a threat mechanism. Indeed it is not obvious that large deficits actually caused any difficulties in Italy, France or Germany in the 1990s. But raising taxes to reduce those deficits certainly did.

On the use of taxation

We have argued that expenditure cuts are an inefficient way of reducing deficit ratios permanently. In practice, governments have found the same thing; large expenditure cuts in the mid-1990s made little impression on the deficit ratios of Germany, Italy and France, and were gradually replaced by tax rises. And it is easy to see why. If expenditure cuts reduce aggregate expenditures, national income will fall, with the result that tax revenues will fall next period, increasing the deficit ratio again. That implies we should expect to see repeated applications of the Stability Pact if expenditure controls are used.

Taxation, however, is different. Most tax systems are progressive, and tax revenues (as opposed to tax rates) increase more than proportionately with the level of activity. Consequently if there is any underlying growth, post-tax incomes will not fall in proportion if tax rates rise – and the deficit ratio will not fall as much as it would have done under an equal-sized expenditure cut. Indeed, theory shows exactly that: optimal tax rates are not constant around the cycle, if deficit- and output-smoothing are important (Anderson and Dogonowski, 1998).

In reality, however, the fiscal authorities may enjoy greater flexibility. Since our model fails to distinguish between different types of taxation (direct, indirect, corporate, on wealth, etc.) – or between different types of expenditure cuts – it may be that the distribution of tax increases over different instruments matters; or that changing the relative importance of different public expenditure components can make expenditure cuts effective. There is some evidence that shifts towards indirect taxation and cuts in welfare payments may be more useful than increases in direct taxation or other expenditure cuts (see Bartolini, Razin and Symansky, 1995; Jensen, 1997). In other words, composition matters (Perotti, 1996). Our model sheds no light on these issues – only on the average impacts.

Case III: targeting structural rather than cylical deficits

One popular idea is that the Stability Pact should apply only to an economy's structural deficit – that is, to the cyclically adjusted deficit ratio rather than to the fluctuations around the cycle (see Eichengreen, 1997). This idea gained popularity as it became more difficult for many countries actually to reach the 3 per cent deficit limit for entering EMU on time. More generally: if the European economies were in recession, a softening of the Stability Pact's convergence criteria would be in order if it could be done in such a way that the actual deficit did not violate the specified limits in 'normal' circumstances.

A more serious – or at least a less self-serving – reason for considering a softening of the deficit criterion is that it allows the authorities a little more short-run room for manoeuvre with fiscal policy – and to intervene more strongly in recessions in particular. This definition of the Stability Pact therefore meets one of the main criticisms of the original version highlighted by Allsop and Vines (1996) – that the Stability Pact could exaggerate the cycle with an asymmetric (downward) deflationary bias. In correcting that bias, there would be less upward pressure on real interest rates and downward pressure on investment and output capacity.

A third reason for considering this change to structural deficits is that, strictly speaking, many countries have probably failed to meet the 3 per cent deficit criterion for entering EMU on their current policies. Instead they have resorted to a variety of accounting 'tricks' to produce deficit figures which match the 3 per cent limit by 1997 – 'one-off' payments such as the sale of France Télécom's pension liabilities in France, or annexing the assets of the national lottery in Belgium, or revising national income statistics to account for 'hidden' economy activities in Italy, and sales of publicly owned assets or classifying payments for losses in public sector firms as 'investment' (Germany), and so on. Any of these changes would produce a smaller deficit figure than the true deficit in a given year. Our next simulation can therefore be interpreted as showing the likely consequences of having massaged the figures in this way, in order to make it appear that the conditions for entering EMU have been satisfied when reality implies something different.

In this chapter, we calculate structural deficits as follows:

$$sd_t = def_t - cd_t \tag{9.3}$$

where sd_t = structural deficit as a proportion of GNP, def_t = the model's actual deficit ratio as before, and cd_t = the cyclical deficit. We compute the cyclical component in the current deficit as

$$cd_t = \gamma_0 + \gamma_1(cu_t - cu_t^*) \qquad \gamma_0 = 0 \tag{9.4}$$

where cu_t = the models measure of capacity utilization (endogenous to the model, and derived from the difference between supply-driven potential output and actual output from the demand side). At full capacity utilization, $cu_t^* = 100$. Hence, at full capacity utilization, the cyclical deficit goes to zero. Below that, $cu_t < 100$ and the cyclical deficit is positive, and vice versa if $cu_t > 100$. The parameters γ_0 and γ_1 are computed using actual data for cd_t, taken from the IMF's *World Economic Outlook* for 1996, fitted to data for the years 1990–6, and then projected on to 2001 such that the baseline structural deficit fits the baseline deficits from 2002 onwards – that is, we expect cyclical balance ($cd_t = 0$), in the absence of shocks, after 2002. And, for fiscal policy, we revert to our normal tax function (9.1) without specific expenditure cuts or fines.

The results of this simulation show some differences from table 9.1 in the early years, but they are not large (table 9.5). Germany has a deficit of just over 3 per cent until 2004 (as opposed to 2.9 per cent). France has one of 4.7 per cent and 3.3 per cent in 1998 and 1999 (up 0.3 percentage points), but 2.8 per cent thereafter. The United Kingdom has deficits essentially unchanged at 4.5 per cent and 3.0 per cent in 1998 and 1999, but some 0.3 percentage points higher thereafter with the result that the 3 per cent limit is breached from 2014 onwards.

Major changes, however, appear in the Italian deficits. Here the reductions are broadly similar to the 'hard criterion' case for 1996–8; but are smaller thereafter, with the result the deficit ratio does not get below 3 per cent until 2003 (instead of 1999). In fact it cycles around 3.4 per cent for 1999–2002, runs at 2.8 per cent for 2003–4, rises to just over 3 per cent until 2007, falls to 2.8 per cent for 2008–11, and then runs at 3.4 – 3.7 per cent thereafter. Strict fiscal discipline, as defined by the 3 per cent limit in actual deficits, has therefore been lost.

On the other hand, softening the deficit criterion does not increase debt burdens much. For Germany there is an extra 0.5–1.0 per cent on the debt ratio for 10 years, but that does not bring cause any additional violations of the 60 per cent limit. For France and the United Kingdom there is no perceptible difference: the 60 per cent limits are still reached in 2001. Even the problem case (Italy) shows no material differences: the debt ratio runs perhaps $1\frac{1}{2}$ per cent higher, but still gets inside the 60 per cent limit by 2010.

On the cost side, output losses in Germany, France and the United Kingdom are slightly larger in the long run, but they are a little smaller in the crucial 1999–2008 period. But for Italy, they are smaller throughout – improving the Italian growth rate by 0.3 per cent each year to 2004.

Price deflations, also, are significantly smaller than when targets for the overall deficit are strictly enforced. They are halved in Germany, virtually

Table 9.5. *Reducing structural deficits to 3 per cent, 1996–2020*

	Deficit ratios				Debt ratios			
	Germany	France	Italy	United Kingdom	Germany	France	Italy	United Kingdom
1996	3.91	4.20	7.27	3.80	60.6	62.4	114.6	60.1
1997	4.01	3.60	5.90	2.50	61.2	62.2	113.3	60.9
1998	3.51	4.67	7.34	4.55	61.6	62.6	112.0	61.5
1999	3.99	3.29	3.70	3.04	62.2	62.0	108.4	61.3
2000	3.01	2.80	3.22	2.90	61.6	60.8	103.0	60.6
2001	3.02	2.98	3.22	2.47	60.9	59.4	96.8	59.4
2005	2.63	2.92	3.10	2.30	57.7	54.0	75.7	53.7
2010	2.95	2.82	3.73	2.97	55.0	49.4	61.8	50.3
2015	2.93	2.68	3.29	3.05	54.8	45.3	52.7	49.1
2020	2.87	2.56	3.64	3.02	55.2	41.5	47.2	48.3

	$\dot{Y}$				$\dot{P}$			
	Germany	France	Italy	United Kingdom	Germany	France	Italy	United Kingdom
1996	−0.00	−0.00	−0.00	−0.00	+0.00	+0.00	0.00	0.00
1997	−0.00	−0.00	−0.01	−0.00	−0.00	−0.00	−0.00	−0.00
1998	+0.00	−0.01	−0.05	−0.01	−0.00	−0.00	−0.05	−0.02
1999	−0.06	−0.33	−1.12	−0.37	−0.10	−0.10	−0.37	−0.13
2000	−0.24	−0.38	−1.30	−0.30	−0.40	−0.04	−0.87	−0.28
2001	−0.16	−0.29	−1.12	−0.28	−0.13	−0.13	−1.24	−1.27
2005	−0.15	−0.10	−0.72	−0.15	−0.08	−0.28	−1.29	−0.27
2010	+0.04	−0.12	−0.89	+0.01	−0.17	−0.23	−1.16	−0.10
2015	−0.09	−0.19	−1.01	−0.11	0.13	−0.36	−1.40	−0.21
2020	−0.09	−0.23	−1.31	−0.16	−0.17	−0.51	−1.98	−0.33

removed in the United Kingdom and France, and reduced from 2–3 per cent to 1–2 per cent each year in Italy. That effectively rules out price falls overall, and hence largely removes the risk of liquidity crises or the investment and output capacity destruction which was such a feature of tables 9.2 and 9.3. In fact, real interest rates now rise by less than 2 per cent; half the rate in table 9.2. The result is a much better recovery in investment. That confirms the deflationary bias in the Stability Pact as presently constituted.

Table 9.5 (*cont.*)

	RS				TX			
	Germany	France	Italy	United Kingdom	Germany	France	Italy	United Kingdom
1996	−0.00	0.00	0.00	0.00	0.00	0.00	0.00	0.00
1997	−0.00	0.00	0.00	0.00	0.00	0.00	0.00	0.00
1998	−0.03	−0.00	−0.00	−0.00	−0.00	0.00	0.00	0.00
1999	−0.04	−0.00	−0.00	−0.00	−0.01	0.06	0.19	0.04
2000	−0.08	−0.00	−0.00	−0.00	0.04	0.07	0.21	3.7
2001	−0.12	−0.01	−0.01	−0.01	0.03	0.07	0.20	5.5
2005	−0.09	−0.05	−0.05	−0.05	0.05	0.05	0.17	0.06
2010	0.10	−0.06	−0.06	−0.06	0.02	0.05	0.17	0.02
2015	−0.07	−0.06	−0.06	−0.06	0.02	0.05	0.12	0.02
2020	0.12	−0.07	−0.07	−0.07	0.02	0.05	0.10	0.02

Note: $\dot{Y}$, $\dot{P}$, RX and TX as in table 9.1.
Note that $\dot{Y}$, $\dot{P}$, RX and TX are all measured as deviations from the baseline.

Another important change is that tax rate hikes are no longer needed. The 6 per cent (falling to $2\frac{1}{2}$ per cent) rise in German tax rates has vanished altogether. Similarly in France the 8 per cent (falling to 5 per cent) rise in tax rates is removed. The United Kingdom is the same. And even in Italy where tax rates had risen by 24 per cent (falling to 15 per cent), the tax rate hikes have been virtually dispensed with. In other words, the great advantage of softening the Maastricht criteria is that, by relaxing the formal criterion by only a small amount (or, equivalently, by allowing the figures to be massaged by a small amount), we have been able to reach the deficit criterion more or less everywhere simply by increasing the underlying growth rates instead of hitting the offending economies with massive tax increases.[14] The prospect of tax distortions is therefore removed.

Hence what we have uncovered is a trade-off between fiscal discipline and the loss of output capacity. There is a second trade-off between discipline and cash flow (or the risk of a liquidity collapse). The ease with which we can resolve those dilemmas with a mild softening of the fiscal criteria shows just how close to being counterproductive the Stability Pact's disciplinary measures actually are – and, conversely, how easily

---

[14.] It is important to realize that it is higher output growth which has delivered these results: output losses have been halved compared to the strict form of the stability pact in tables 9.1–9.3.

indiscipline can be put right by growth and a suitable policy mix. By contrast, the slower growth and higher interest rates of the strict Stability Pact has actually generated higher debt ratios. So fiscal discipline can generate lower deficit ratios, but at the cost of higher debt burdens. Indeed, too savage a reduction of fiscal deficits can, paradoxically, generate an explosive growth in debt (see appendix 9.2, p. 251). This happens whenever the fiscal contractions are sufficient to raise real interest rate above the growth rate of national output.[15] Paradoxically, therefore, too tight a monetary policy, for the sake of achieving credibility, could easily worsen the debt position and lead to a loss in credibility – credibility being a reflection of the market's assessment of a government's ability to pay off, or at least service, its debt. Similarly, too aggressive an implementation of the Stability Pact, for the sake of ensuring that fiscal policy could not undermine the credibility of a tighter Europe-wide monetary policy, might actually worsen debt and the credibility of that monetary policy. This result is in contrast with Artis and Winkler (1998), or Beetsma and Uhlig (1998), who assume that deficit reductions are synonymous with debt reductions – whereas appendix 9.2 shows that they may not be synonymous in countries with weak growth or high debt ratios.

Obviously the chances of a counterproductive Stability Pact, and a loss in credibility, are larger if the larger members of the union are all subject to the its restrictions at the same time. Conversely, the risk of such problems will be that much lower if the central bank can be persuaded to relax its monetary policy as the Stability Pact bites. In other words, the coordination of fiscal policies is crucially important – that is coordination both among themselves and with monetary policy, to get the right policy *mix*. The danger is that the Stability Pact may restrict that coordination and the choice of policy mix.

The importance of the policy mix: deficit reductions with a fixed monetary policy

In order to emphasize the last point – that greater budgetary discipline can, if uncompensated elsewhere, lead to a loss of control over debt and deficits – we have rerun both the reference solution and the 1 per cent Stability Pact with monetary policy fixed at baseline values. Since the degree of monetary relaxation was relatively small in those solutions, the loss in discipline over debt is also fairly small. But the point is nevertheless made that increasingly severe fiscal restrictions can destroy

---

[15.]   Hughes Hallett and McAdam (1997) have a formal demonstration of this.

Table 9.6. *Fixed monetary policy and 3 per cent deficit limit, 1996–2020*

	Deficit ratios				Debt ratios			
	Germany	France	Italy	United Kingdom	Germany	France	Italy	United Kingdom
1996	3.92	4.20	7.28	3.80	60.6	62.4	114.7	60.1
1997	4.02	3.60	5.91	2.50	61.2	62.2	113.4	60.9
1998	3.52	4.68	7.38	4.57	61.7	62.6	112.3	61.6
1999	2.51	2.91	2.91	2.64	61.0	61.8	108.6	61.2
2000	2.95	2.80	2.95	2.71	60.3	60.6	102.8	60.2
2001	2.96	2.97	2.94	2.37	59.6	59.1	96.4	58.7
2005	3.04	2.91	3.09	2.09	57.0	53.8	74.6	52.4
2010	3.01	2.84	2.76	2.79	55.3	49.3	61.1	49.4
2015	2.97	2.70	2.92	2.84	55.2	45.3	51.4	47.6
2020	2.93	2.56	2.81	2.98	55.8	41.5	43.6	46.9

	$\dot{Y}$				$\dot{P}$			
	Germany	France	Italy	United Kingdom	Germany	France	Italy	United Kingdom
1996	−0.01	−0.01	−0.04	−0.01	0.00	−0.00	−0.01	−0.00
1997	−0.02	−0.02	−0.08	−0.03	−0.00	−0.04	−0.04	−0.01
1998	−0.04	−0.05	−0.16	−0.05	−0.03	−0.19	−0.19	−0.08
1999	−0.46	−0.51	−1.57	−0.62	−0.08	−0.73	−0.72	−0.30
2000	−0.21	−0.38	−1.44	−0.31	−0.32	−1.41	−1.41	−0.50
2001	−0.11	−0.26	−1.21	−0.27	−0.44	−1.89	−1.89	−0.59
2005	−0.08	−0.09	−0.65	−0.15	−0.24	−0.37	−1.77	−0.37
2010	−0.05	−0.15	−0.97	−0.10	−0.31	−0.36	−1.65	−1.15
2015	−0.13	−0.19	−1.22	−0.14	−0.31	−0.54	−2.26	−0.40
2020	−0.14	−0.20	−1.65	−0.17	−0.44	−0.72	−3.22	−0.49

(*cont.*)

the very discipline it was set up to create, by imposing an inferior policy mix.

In fact, a fixed monetary policy, in the case of a 3 per cent deficit limit, brings some increases in the German debt ratio (table 9.6): up by $\frac{1}{2}$ per cent on average, 0.2 per cent in 1999, and by 1.1 per cent in 2023. Similarly the German deficit ratio is also slightly higher, so that it breaches the 3 per cent limit in 2004–6 and again in 2009–10. In France the debt ratio also

Table 9.6 (*cont.*)

	RS				TX			
	Germany	France	Italy	United Kingdom	Germany	France	Italy	United Kingdom
1996	0	0	0	0	0.00	0.00	0.00	0.00
1997	0	0	0	0	0.00	0.01	0.02	0.01
1998	0	0	0	0	0.01	0.01	0.04	0.02
1999	0	0	0	0	6.66	7.78	24.42	6.20
2000	0	0	0	0	3.88	7.12	22.73	4.50
2001	0	0	0	0	3.45	6.64	21.51	6.01
2005	0	0	0	0	2.52	5.45	17.66	5.44
2010	0	0	0	0	2.21	4.95	17.06	2.72
2015	0	0	0	0	2.21	4.95	14.47	1.52
2020	0	0	0	0	2.21	4.95	14.57	1.52

Note: $\dot{Y}$, $\dot{P}$, RX and TX as in table 9.1.
Note that $\dot{Y}$, $\dot{P}$, RX and TX are all measured as deviations from the baseline.

rises by 0.4 per cent on average, rising to 1 per cent in 2023, although the deficit ratio is unchanged. In the United Kingdom likewise, the debt ratio rises 0.4 per cent on average and 1.2 per cent by 2023, while the deficit ratio is unchanged. The debt ratio rises the most in Italy: by 0.6 per cent on average and by 1.5 per cent by 2023, while the deficit ratio also rises enough to breach the 3 per cent limit in 2005 and 2012–13. Hence everyone's fiscal position has deteriorated because removing the support of a monetary policy relaxation has increased the output losses, lowering both the debt and deficit ratio's denominators and reducing tax revenues at the same time.

In the German, French and UK cases these output losses are doubled or more – although they correspond to just 0.2 per cent or so off the growth rate each year (1999–2000 excepted). In Italy the increase in output losses is rather smaller, although the price deflation has been increased a bit – implying bigger falls in output prices. There is also some extra price deflation in the United Kingdom, Germany and France, too, but it too is only small. Interestingly there are *no* increases in the tax rates anywhere, which demonstrates that these restrictions in monetary policy really do translate into losses in fiscal discipline.

Naturally we get more dramatic changes if we run the same exercise with the Stability Pact's 1 per cent target value for the deficit ratio

Table 9.7. *Fixed monetary policy in a Stability Pact, 1996–2020*
(*1 per cent deficit target*)

	Deficit ratios				Debt ratios			
	Germany	France	Italy	United Kingdom	Germany	France	Italy	United Kingdom
1996	3.93	4.24	7.34	3.84	60.7	62.6	115.3	60.3
1997	4.05	3.66	6.03	2.56	61.4	62.5	114.6	61.3
1998	3.56	4.74	7.56	4.56	62.0	63.2	114.4	62.2
1999	1.02	1.06	0.97	1.10	60.3	61.1	110.6	60.9
2000	1.07	1.07	1.16	0.86	58.0	58.0	58.3	103.8
2001	0.98	1.17	1.25	0.71	55.5	55.3	95.9	55.3
2005	0.88	0.83	0.93	0.87	46.0	42.8	66.7	43.5
2010	1.01	0.48	0.83	0.95	38.2	30.5	45.9	33.9
2015	1.14	1.18	0.82	0.72	34.6	22.6	30.6	26.6
2020	1.09	1.09	0.81	1.35	32.6	17.1	17.5	21.8

	$\dot{Y}$				$\dot{P}$			
	Germany	France	Italy	United Kingdom	Germany	France	Italy	United Kingdom
1996	−0.09	−0.12	−0.29	−0.15	−0.03	−0.11	−0.22	−0.13
1997	−0.15	−0.20	−0.48	−0.23	−0.09	−0.25	−0.51	−0.29
1998	−0.21	−0.26	−0.66	−0.28	−0.31	−0.56	−1.13	−0.62
1999	−1.08	−1.22	−2.87	−1.43	−0.59	−1.23	−2.52	−1.32
2000	−0.72	−0.93	−2.55	−0.92	−1.92	−1.91	−4.09	−1.97
2001	−0.45	−0.64	−1.99	−0.45	−1.61	−2.32	−5.20	−2.24
2005	−0.31	−0.25	−1.07	−0.06	−1.13	−1.70	−4.94	−1.15
2010	−0.21	0.39	−1.48	−0.20	−1.14	−1.58	−4.68	−1.12
2015	−0.36	−0.25	1.92	−0.27	−1.28	−1.73	−6.54	−1.61
2020	−0.35	−0.28	−2.33	−0.03	−1.78	−2.62	−8.89	−1.76

(*cont.*)

(table 9.7). This time the German debt ratio rises by 2 percentage points on average and 4 per cent by 2023. The German deficit ratio is also higher, and fails to remain below the 1 per cent target after 2010 (in contrast to the case with monetary relaxation). For France, the story is almost exactly the same, and the UK's fiscal discipline is damaged by even more. There, the debt ratio rises 5 percentage points by 2023 and the deficit ratio breaches 1 per cent after 2017. In Italy the loss of fiscal discipline is focused mainly

Table 9.7 (*cont.*)

	RS				TX			
	Germany	France	Italy	United Kingdom	Germany	France	Italy	United Kingdom
1996	0	0	0	0	0.03	0.03	0.08	0.04
1997	0	0	0	0	0.04	0.06	0.14	0.07
1998	0	0	0	0	0.05	0.07	0.19	0.10
1999	0	0	0	0	13.84	17.82	37.51	13.95
2000	0	0	0	0	13.03	16.05	34.64	13.20
2001	0	0	0	0	17.13	15.53	32.40	12.74
2005	0	0	0	0	8.34	14.24	29.68	10.40
2010	0	0	0	0	7.52	13.70	26.52	8.69
2015	0	0	0	0	7.52	8.45	24.53	8.69
2020	0	0	0	0	7.11	7.58	23.04	4.71

Note: $\dot{Y}$, $\dot{P}$, RX and TX as in table 9.1.
Note that $\dot{Y}$, $\dot{P}$, RX and TX are all measured as deviations from the baseline.

on the debt ratio which is likewise 5 per cent higher by 2023, while the deficit ratio stays below its 1 per cent target.

These results are driven by larger losses in output than in the corresponding flexible monetary policy case. In this exercise, no country gets output gains in the second half of the simulation period, as they did in table 9.3. Moreover the losses are now four or five times larger than in the reference solution. Price deflation is also a little bit larger than in the standard Stability Pact, but not by much. On the other hand, the tax rate rises are unchanged; so the loss in fiscal discipline really is driven by the contraction effects which are no longer offset by monetary relaxation or extra credibility.

Conclusions

(1) Stricter policies for reducing deficit ratios do indeed lead to lower deficits, but also to losses in output, price deflations and higher rates of taxation. Such a strategy risks a reduction in investment, output capacity and a loss of control over the debt accumulation process if the deflations are strong enough. It appears that a 1 per cent deficit limit might, in present circumstances, be strong enough – but a 3 per cent limit would not.

(2) Our results show that permanent deficit reductions depend on introducing permanent tax increases. Expenditure changes will not do because, in the short term, they reduce the budget and national incomes in nearly equal proportions. In the longer term falling incomes mean lower revenues, which means the deficit ratio will start to rise again. Any reductions in the deficit ratio achieved by this route will thus be temporary.

(3) Points (1) and (2) together suggest that the most effective strategy is to boost growth. That will raise the deficit ratio's denominator, while increasing revenues disproportionately through the non-linearity of the tax system. That of course conflicts with Alesina and Perotti (1995), who point out that countries which raise taxation tend to raise expenditures again and so fail to reduce their deficits. If that is true then, once fiscal discipline has been accepted at a political level, it will have to be maintained by a political sanction, not an economic one, if the Maastricht 'no-bail-out' clause is to remain credible. We assume instead that the political case for fiscal discipline has been made, because imposing budgetary constraints to block a political bias in favour of higher spending, without removing the incentives which created those biases in the first place, risks creating a frustration within the decision making process that will lead to pressures for politicians to dump the whole system.

(4) Another possible outcome is that strict fiscal constraints will, by adding to the losses in output capacity and employment (as we saw in Italy), act as a spur to labour market reform. However that sanction also cuts both ways. The inability to react to rising unemployment, because of the Stability Pact's restrictions, will further add to the deficit and add more to the problem. Fiscal inflexibility may therefore be the underlying weakness of EMU, and could even encourage the wrong kind of market reforms where rising unemployment leads to pressure for higher benefits and shorter working hours (as in France).

(5) Our results also conflict with Masson and Symansky (1996), who argue that expenditure-cutting is preferable because it causes smaller distortions than raising taxes. Distortions would not matter if the tax rises were temporary (and they do fall back in our case, but not all the way to base). But this point is relevant only if expenditure cuts can get the deficit ratios down and keep them down – but we find that they cannot. Instead, the way to deal with tax distortions is to soften the Stability Pact's criteria.

(6) Fines on those who violate the specified deficit limits have very little impact on economic performance or the deficit-reduction process.

Moreover, given the precommitted nature of fiscal expenditures and their inefficiency as a means of reducing deficits, fines tend to add to the deficit and would have to be passed on to the private sector in higher taxes. As a political sanction they therefore have very little credibility.

(7) The results in tables 9.1, 9.3 and 9.4 show that fiscal consolidation has to be done with all countries acting in concert. The question is how to persuade those who do not need to consolidate to help those who do. The Stability Pact lacks any incentive mechanism to prevent the kind of investment and output collapse we saw when one country has to adjust, subject to a monetary policy set by others who do not.

Appendix 9.1   *The econometric model*

MULTIMOD is an annual model. It explains the main expenditure categories and production flows in each country, from which employment, investment, prices, interest rates and exchange rates are determined. Financial markets, trade flows, and capital movements (including loans and interest payments) are included. Trade is divided into three markets: oil, primary commodities and manufactured goods. The oil market contains an exogenous real price, demand driven by activity levels in each country and supplies that clear the market. Perfectly flexible prices clear the commodity markets, where demand is driven by activity levels and supply by prices and a predetermined capacity. Manufactured goods are produced and traded everywhere. Aggregate demand is then built up from consumption (based on current and expected future earnings and asset values – that is, human wealth, which is positive in incomes but negative in prices and interest rates); investment (based on market evaluations of firms' current and future earnings, which is likewise positive in revenues but negative in interest rates); trade; and the net fiscal position. Both consumption and investment therefore adjust positively to earnings, but negatively to rising prices or interest rates. This determines output in the short run. Note that since assets incorporate the stock of capital and government bonds, as well as net foreign assets, human capital will be constrained to cover discounted future tax liabilities. The model therefore embodies *strong* Ricardian Equivalence. That said, potential output is determined by a production function so that capacity utilization (the ratio of actual to potential output) can vary. Domestic output prices are subject to a Phillips curve, so there is no absolute output constraint. In fact, prices change by an amount depending on both the remaining spare capacity and the state of the labour markets. Prices are therefore partly sticky and partly forward-looking, depending on wage contracts, international competitiveness and capacity utilization.

Various policy reaction functions are assumed. In the monetary sector, non-EMU exchange rates are determined by open interest parities and the *expected* depreciations consistent with a complete model solution. The non-German European exchange rates, however, are obliged to stay within a 1 per cent band around preassigned parity values. Monetary policy, for ERM members, therefore consists of forcing interest rates to follow a reaction function that targets the given DM parity and maintains the currency within its narrow band. For other countries, and for Germany, a preassigned monetary growth rate is targeted; with interest rates set to gradually reduce the gap between actual and targeted money growth. In effect that implies, near enough, a monetary union with a fixed set of monetary rules (in all simulations but the last) since everyone has the same target of growth of the money supply and there are no risk premia on interest rates.

Similarly, tax rates adjust to gradually eliminate the gap between actual and targeted levels for the deficit/GNP ratio over time, subject to an intertemporal budget constraint. Fiscal expenditures are therefore also partly exogenous and partly endogenized. Both fiscal and monetary policy rules remain fixed in all simulations. A full description of MULTIMOD's properties and simulation characteristics is given in Masson, Symanski, and Meridith (1990, 1991), and comparisons with other models in Bryant, Hooper and Mann (1993). Hughes Hallett and Ma (1993) review a number of sensitivity tests of the model's simulation properties.

Appendix 9.2 *Conflicts between the Maastricht and Stability Pact criteria*

If fiscal cuts are at least net contractionary in the short run, the new debt ratio may be written as:

$$\frac{d_t}{y_t} = \frac{d_{t-1}}{y_{t-1} + \Delta y_t} + \frac{pd_t + rd_{t-1}}{y_{t-1} + \Delta y_t} \qquad (9A.1)$$

where pd_t = the primary deficit, r = the interest rate and $\Delta y_i < 0$ as a result of the fiscal cuts. Hence $d_{t-1}/(y_{t-1} + \Delta y_t)$ can easily rise faster in (9A.1) than the subsequent term falls, if d_{t-1} is large enough in the higher-debt countries. This can happen even when we have created an overall surplus $(pd_t + rd_{t-1} < 0)$ or a primary surplus $(pd_t < 0)$. Indeed, the new ratio will *certainly* rise if $pd_t > 0$ or if $rd_{t-1} \geq pd_t$. That means that deficit and debt ratios may easily move in opposite directions, and the satisfaction of one does not always imply progress towards satisfying the other. Hence a savage deficit reduction, causing a significant contraction in y_t, can easily lead to a rapid escalation in debt burdens – especially if underlying growth is weak and interest rates high.

References

Alesina, A. and Perotti, R. (1995). 'Fiscal Expansions and Adjustments in OECD Countries', *Economic Policy*, 21: 207–40

Allsopp, C. and Vines, D. (1996). 'Fiscal Policy and EMU', *NIESR Working Paper*, 158: 91–107

Allsopp, C., McKibbin, W. and Vines D. C. (1997). 'Fiscal Consolidation in Europe: Some Empirical Issues', chapter 11 in this volume

Andersen, T. and Dogonowsi, R. (1998). 'EMU and Budget Norms' chapter 4 in this volume

Artis, M. and Winkler, B. (1998). 'The Stability Pact: Safeguarding the Credibility of the European Central Bank', *NIESR Economic Review*, 160: 87–98

Barry, F. and Devereaux, M. (1995). 'The Expansionary Fiscal Contraction Hypothesis: A Neo-Keynesian Analysis', *Oxford Economic Papers*, 47: 249–64

Bartolini, L., Razin, A. and Symansky, S. (1995). 'G-7 Restructuring in the 1990s: Macroeconomic Effects', *Economic Policy*, 20: 111–46

Beetsma, R. and Uhlig, H. (1997). 'An Analysis of the "Stability Pact"', *CEPR Discussion Paper*, 1669

Bryant, R., Hooper, P. and Mann, C. (1993). 'Evaluating Policy Regimes: New Research in Empirical Macroeconomics', Washington, DC: Brookings Institution

Duisenberg, W. (1997). 'Monetary Policy and Competitiveness', speech to the European Meeting of the Trilateral Commission, The Hague, (25 October)

Flandreau, M., Le Cacheux, J. and Zumer, F. (1998). 'Stability Without a Pact? Lessons from the European Gold Standard 1880–1914', *CEPR Discussion Paper*, 1872

Giavazzi, F. and Pagano, M (1990). 'Can Severe Fiscal Contractions be Expansionary? Tales of Two Small European Economies', *NBER Macroeconomics Annual*, Cambridge, Mass. and London: MIT Press: 75–116

(1995). 'Non-Keynesian Effects of Fiscal Policy Changes: International Evidence and the Swedish Experience', *CEPR Discussion Paper*, 1284

Hughes Hallett, A. and Ma, Y. (1993). 'Real Adjustment in a Union of Incompletely Converged Economies: An Example from East and West Germany', *CEPR Discussion Paper*, 623

Hughes Hallett, A. and Ma, Y. (1997). 'The Dynamics of Debt Deflation in a Monetary Union', *Journal of International and Comparative Economics*, 5: 1–29

Hughes Hallett, A. and McAdam, P. (1997). 'Four Essays and a Funeral: Budgetary Arithmetic under the Maastricht Treaty', *CEPR Discussion Paper*, 1505

(1998). 'Fiscal Deficit Reductions in Line with the Maastricht Criteria for Monetary Union: An Empirical Analysis', in J. Frieden, D. Gros and E. Jones (eds.), *Towards European Monetary Union: Problems and Prospects*, Denver, Colo., Rowman Littlefield

Jensen, S. E. H. (1997). 'Debt Reduction, Wage Formation and Intergenerational Welfare', in D. P. Broer and J. Lassila (eds.) *Pension Policies and Public Debt in Dynamic CGE Models*, Heidelberg: Physica-Verlag

Marini, G. and van der Ploeg, F. (1988). 'Monetary and Fiscal Policy in an Optimising Model with Capital Accumulation and Finite Lives', *Economic Journal*, 98: 772–86

Masson, P. and Symansky, S. (1996). 'Achieving the Maastricht Fiscal Criteria: Simulations of the Macroeconomic Effects', Washington, DC: International Monetary Fund, mimeo

Masson, P., Symansky, S. and Meredith, G. (1990). 'MULTIMOD Mark II: A Revised and Extended Model', *IMF Occasional Paper*, 71, Washington, DC: International Monetary Fund

(1991) 'Changes to MULTIMOD since the July 1990 IMF *Occasional Paper*, 71: Current Model, MULTIAP', Washington, DC: International Monetary Fund (July), mimeo

Moulton, B. R. (1996). 'Bias in the Consumer Price Index: What is the Evidence?', *Journal of Economic Perspectives*, 10: 159–77

Nordhaus, W. (1994). 'Policy Games: Coordination and Independence in Monetary and Fiscal Policies', *Brookings Papers on Economic Activity*, 25, 2: 139–216

Perotti, R. (1996). 'Fiscal Consolidation: Composition Matters', *American Economic Review*, 86: 105–10

Spaventa, L. (1987). 'The Growth in Public Debt: Sustainability, Fiscal Rules and Monetary Rules', *IMF Staff Papers*, 34: 374–99

von Hagen, J. and Lutz, S. (1996). 'Fiscal and Monetary Policies on the Way to EMU', *Open Economies Review*, 7: 299–326

Woodford, M. (1995). 'Price Level Determinancy without Control of a Monetary Aggregate', *Carnegie-Rochester Conference Series, on Public Policy*

Discussion

Claas Wihlborg

Chapters 7–9 in part III, by Artis and Winkler, Beetsma, and Hughes Hallett and McAdam, raise a number of issues about the reasons for, and the consequences of, a stability pact that sets limits on public sector deficits of countries participating in the European Monetary Union (EMU). Chapters 7 and 8 also analyse the optimal design of a stability pact. Hughes Hallett and McAdam in chapter 9 are particularly concerned about the long-term consequences of the Stability Pact. Whether the chapters succeed in analysing the existing pact is not entirely clear, because it is not known how it will be implemented.

Effectiveness of the Stability Pact

For the sake of modelling, it is necessary to assume that the EU Stability Pact (SGP) will have 'bite', rather than being a 'paper tiger', in Artis and Winkler's words. There are good reasons, however, to doubt that any country will ever pay fines for excessive deficits as specified in the SGP, even if the budget deficits in some countries, by any reasonable definition, exceed the preset limits. If governments believe that the probability of ever having to pay fines is minimal, then the Stability Pact would affect fiscal policy behaviour only if excessive deficits were associated with political stigma.

One reason to doubt that the SGP will impose effective constraints on deficits is that governments seem to be willing to manipulate deficit figures – as several did to satisfy the convergence criteria for participation in the EMU. A second reason to doubt the SGP's effectiveness is the forbearance shown Belgium and Italy, in particular, with respect to the EMU convergence criteria for national debt levels as a percentage of GDP. Once it became clear that the criterion level would never be achieved while the political will to form EMU existed, the criterion for membership then became that 'a credible effort' to reduce the debt levels must be shown.

254

The flexibility shown with respect to the EMU convergence criteria may very well have been wise on economic grounds, since there is little evidence that debt levels across the EU countries are related to inflation performances and central banks' credibility. Similarly, it can be argued that there is no strong link between a country's budget deficit or accumulated deficits and the political pressure exerted by the country's government on the board of the European Central Bank (ECB).

The question arises: what role does the Stability Pact play if it is not expected to be effective? The simple answer may be that Germany in particular needed to have the SGP to make the EMU more politically acceptable; the SGP may thus have already achieved its main purpose.

The scepticism regarding the future effectiveness of the SGP does not mean that there is no reason to have such a pact among EMU countries. The chapters by Artis and Winkler and by Beetsma point to two conditions under which a stability pact might indeed be welfare-improving. One is that the political process within each country tends to result in greater deficits than desired under existing economic conditions. The second is that EMU exacerbates this tendency. Both these chapters develop arguments why these conditions are likely to hold. Artis and Winkler, in particular, review the rich menu of arguments presented in the literature. The second condition for a stability pact to be desirable (i.e. that EMU exacerbates the tendency for greater than desired deficits) may actually be stated too strongly. Even if EMU does not exacerbate the deficit tendency, it is possible that the existence of EMU makes it politically and institutionally feasible to enter a pact that would be desirable with or without EMU.

Even if it can be concluded that a stability pact constraining individual countries' public sector deficits is indeed desirable, it does not necessarily follow that the existing SGP is a desirable one. Artis and Winkler, as well as Beetsma, analyse the incentive properties of the SGP and derive principles for optimal design. It is by no means clear that the existing pact is welfare-improving. Hughes Hallett and McAdam, in chapter 9, raise a very different argument against the SGP. They simulate output and investment behaviour and discuss, in particular, the consequences of the transition from initial levels of deficits to levels that are sustainable under the SGP. If one is to believe their analysis, the consequences of the pact for economic growth in particular, are (and have been) very serious indeed.

In the following, I will focus on the analyses of the SGP as an incentive device in Artis and Winkler and Beetsma. A few notes on the simulation exercise in Hughes Hallett and McAdam are made to begin with.

Simulating long-term effects

Hughes Hallett and McAdam paint a bleak picture of the Stability Pact and the associated fiscal retrenchment. An important aspect of their chapter is that the authors focus on long-term consequences of current retrenchments. For this reason, real interest rates and investments are key variables. The results of the simulation exercise, apart from the growth effects, are interesting and should be a cause for concern. For example, it indicates that permanent deficit reductions require permanent tax increases, expenditure-cutting will not do. Another result is that fines on those who violate deficit limits have little impact on economic performance and deficit reduction, the fines may thus have low credibility as a political sanction. A third result is that fiscal consolidation has to be done with all countries acting in concert, but the SGP lacks any incentive device that may persuade those with small deficits to contribute to the fiscal consolidation.

The main question that arises with respect to these results is the question of the exact mechanisms that cause them. Are the results robust to changes in controversial assumptions of the simulation model? The simulation is performed using the IMF's MULTIMOD econometric model, assumptions with respect to expectations-formation and tax-policy adjustment under the SGP are added. Expectations are essentially specified so as to be neutral by making them equal to the projected outcome for various future periods.

All large-scale econometric models rely on a specific combination of assumed rigidities and adjustment mechanisms. The exact specification of included and (implicitly) excluded adjustment mechanisms is especially important when simulating over the long term, as in this chapter. There is one aspect of the results that makes me particularly concerned that an excess of rigidities is incorporated in the simulation. Countries with large initial fiscal deficits (such as, for example, Italy) face a dramatic rise in real interest rates and consequently a sharp decline in investments. This dramatic rise in the cost of capital in some countries is caused by a deflationary process combined with nominal interest rates that are locked-in by the fixed exchange rates.

The question that arises is: whose and what cost of capital matters for investments in, say, Italy? Even if the real interest rate for Italians rises, it is not obvious that the real interest rate for Germans, or Americans, considering investments in Italy, also rises. If the deflationary process refers to consumer prices and deviations from purchasing power parity (PPP), as well as the 'law of one price', are possible, then the result of the contraction may be that Italians invest less everywhere while Germans and non-EMU firms invest relatively more in Italy.

If the deflationary process refers to producer prices for Italian goods, then the contractionary effect on investments would depend on how factor costs develop relative to output prices in Italy.

The Stability Pact as an incentive device

Artis and Winkler, as well as Beetsma, analyse whether a Stability Pact affects the incentives of EMU members to modify their fiscal policy behaviour. Artis and Winkler present a model leading to results that correspond to what I believe would be common intuition. Beetsma, on the other hand, arrives at results that are partly counterintuitive. One reason for this difference is that Beetsma incorporates a political process that leads to highly myopic behaviour.

In Artis and Winkler's chapter, the government faces increasing costs of pursuing fiscal rigour, while there are expected benefits of avoiding fines. There is uncertainty about economic conditions affecting the budget situation. Important parameters are the fine, the cost of the fiscal effort to avoid fines, the productivity of the fiscal effort with respect to deficit reduction and the nature of the shocks.

Since under uncertainty, a government will equate the marginal costs of fiscal adjustment with the marginal benefit of the risk of incurring penalties, the government will aim at a deficit providing a 'cushion' between the target deficit and the 'penalty deficit'. The countries with less fiscal discipline in the model – the countries facing high costs of adjusting deficits – would thus aim for relatively large cushions. This would imply that these countries would have smaller average deficits. This result raises the question of what is meant by 'fiscal discipline'. In the model, fiscal discipline is related to costs of changes in the deficit. If fiscal discipline is thought of as low costs of holding the deficit down, then we would expect the less disciplined governments to have higher average deficits.

If the Stability Pact provides incentives as modelled, then there is no trade-off between budget discipline and stabilization. However, if governments are myopic and wait for shocks to occur before trying to adjust the deficit, then the Stability Pact would induce pro-cyclical behaviour. The possibility that such behaviour arises under the SGP may increase if countries with high costs of adjusting the deficits are also those with high cost of keeping the average deficit at a low level.

Myopic behaviour is modelled explicitly in Beetsma's chapter. An incumbent government faces the probability of losing the next election. If so, the next government will provide services that do not enter the incumbent government's utility function. The costs of shifting the burden of payment for the current deficit to the future government is thus lower the higher the probability that the incumbent will lose the election. One country's deficit affects other EMU members through the costs of additional inflation that may be induced by the sum of the EMU members' deficits. Each country is a 'free rider' in the sense that the inflation effects of one country's deficits depend upon that country's contribution to the total deficit.

An important aspect of the model is that the only cost of a deficit is the cost of future inflation. Costs and benefits of fiscal adjustment are more general, but also less specified, in Artis and Winkler.

One counterintuitive result in Beetsma is that if the central bank for the EMU is completely independent of political influences, and it focuses solely on its inflation target, then the incentives to run deficits are particularly large. The reason is that a deficit will not affect inflation under these circumstances. The enforcement mechanism for keeping deficits low thus depends upon the central bank's being non-independent of the fiscal authorities of the member states.

It is common to argue that fiscal discipline would be induced within EMU by the country-specific real interest rate effect of accumulated national deficits. Under strict Ricardian Equivalence, as in the Beetsma model, there is no real interest rate effect, however. This assumption is certainly controversial. The surprising result of Beetsma's analysis is that the case for a stability pact is particularly strong if the ECB is credible and politically independent. The common argument for a stability pact is that the central bank is likely to be subject to political pressure to monetize deficits.

The political mechanism in the Beetsma model is also controversial. It causes myopia in a simple and elegant way but no reason is given why there is a certain probability of losing the election. Consider, for example, the possibility that an increase in government spending favouring the incumbent party's supporters would increase the probability of losing the election. The incentive to create deficits at the expense of the other party would then be reduced.

Conclusions

I find Beetsma's model intriguing, interesting, and well specified. It certainly raises questions about the conventional wisdom on the merits of central bank independence. The generality of assumptions about the political process and the costs of deficits are not entirely convincing, however.

Artis and Winkler, specifying a very intuitive model of the incentive effects of a stability pact, almost convince me that the penalties for excessive deficits will not function the way their formal model predicts. The case for government myopia leading to pro-cyclical effects of the SGP seems rather strong. Hopefully these effects will not be as strong and long-lasting as those indicated by the simulations of Hughes Hallett and McAdam. If they are correct to only a limited extent, then I hope I am correct in believing that the Stability Pact is ineffective and designed primarily to alleviate current German fears with respect to EMU.

Part IV

Asymmetric business cycles and fiscal linkages in Europe

10 The costs of EMU and economic convergence

U. Michael Bergman and Michael M. Hutchison

Introduction

The desirability of entry into a monetary union rests in large part on the perceived benefits and costs. The benefits of monetary unification and the establishment of a single currency area (SCA) are generally identified as lower transactions costs associated with the elimination of national currencies, increased credibility of participating governments' commitment to price stability and greater efficiency of resource allocation through the elimination of exchange rate-related uncertainty.[1]

The main costs of a SCA, on the other hand, are giving up an independent exchange rate policy and, more broadly, losing the option of following an independent monetary policy. Losing monetary policy would in principle place a greater burden on fiscal policies for output stabilization purposes. When labour is relatively immobile, and wages and prices are rigid, nationally independent demand management policies (monetary and fiscal) play an important stabilization role. Moreover, this option is especially important if countries are facing asymmetric shocks, in which case exchange rate adjustments and separate monetary policies could help to stabilize nation-specific aggregate fluctuations.[2] More generally,

We thank Jonathan Rubin, Tom Willett, seminar participants at EPRU at the Copenhagen Business School and Lund University and, especially, Andrew Hughes Hallett for helpful comments.

[1.] Eichengreen (1992) uses these categories in discussing the potential benefits of a European monetary union. He concludes that, in principle, the benefits are small, meaning that maintenance of firmly fixed exchange rates between distinct national currencies would reap most of the benefits. However, he suggests that the special circumstances allowing governments to commit to fixed exchange rates are not present in Europe today. The *One Market, One Money* report by the Commission of the European Communities (1990) is more optimistic over the benefits of monetary union.

[2.] See De Grauwe (1992) for a comprehensive non-technical discussion of the economics of monetary unification and a critique of the optimum currency area (OCA) literature. Fratianni and von Hagen (1992) systematically investigate issues of a European monetary union using a three-country game-theoretic model. They employ model simulations to determine the welfare effects of various disturbances. See Wihlborg and Willett (1991) for a comprehensive discussion of OCA literature.

countries with strong trade and financial ties are usually identified as good candidates for monetary union. Since even idiosyncratic shocks in this case would be rapidly transmitted to other member countries, they effectively become 'common' shocks.[3] The early literature suggests that an important criterion for the desirability of joining monetary union would be that countries face similar types of disturbances and have similar economic structures (Mundell, 1961; McKinnon, 1963; Kenen, 1969; Tower and Willett, 1970).

A large literature attempts to evaluate empirically the relative costs and benefits of European Monetary Union (EMU) and which countries appear to be ideal candidates for membership. Recent contributions include Artis and Zhang (1996, 1997a, 1997b); Bayoumi and Eichengreen (1993a, 1993b, 1994); Bergman (1996a); Demertzis, Hughes Hallett and Rummel (1997a, 1997b); Bergman, Hutchison and Cheung (1997); Whitt (1993). This literature attempts to measure economic 'disturbances' and economic structures from historical data to infer which European countries are similar enough to warrant entry into EMU. Countries are often divided into two major groupings: 'core' EU with highly similar economic disturbances and structures, and 'periphery' countries with asymmetric shocks and structures. Countries identified as core members are expected to benefit from joining EMU – the similarity in shocks and economic structures will allow a common union-wide monetary policy to be followed without sacrificing national macroeconomic stabilization objectives or placing a large burden on national fiscal policy to fill the stabilization role. On the other hand, countries identified as in the periphery are not expected to gain from immediate entry into EMU.

This chapter presents a critique of the traditional measures used to operationalize the theory of optimal currency areas and supports our arguments with empirical evidence from thirteen European countries. We argue that the costs and benefits of participating in a new monetary union may not be inferred from historical data, and that some frequently used measures of economic disturbances are not the appropriate indicators to judge the desirability of a currency union.

There are three main points supporting our argument. First, a new currency area in Europe will represent a significant structural break, making it difficult to base future policy on the basis of historical statistical relationships. A consistent long-run goal of the EU has been to foster closer economic ties among its members and this process will

---

[3.] By contrast, a small degree of linkage with other countries would tend to 'bottle up' idiosyncratic disturbances, making their impact on the domestic economy relatively large. Linkage allows the transmission of disturbances, partly absorbing the effect on the domestic economy.

most likely influence economic structures and the nature of business cycles in Europe. Secondly, most of the evidence supporting the existence of a core group of EU countries with similar economic disturbances is based predominantly on the existence of similar 'permanent' disturbances to real activity (i.e. shocks leaving a permanent imprint on the level of economic activity, unemployment and so on). However, in general, economic theory is ambiguous about whether a monetary union or a system of pegged or flexible exchange rates would be preferable (in terms of stabilizing the economy or economic welfare) in the face of asymmetric permanent disturbances to the real economy. Thirdly, most existing studies do not clearly distinguish between similarity of disturbances across countries and economic structures. In particular, it is not clear in existing work whether core countries actually have similar fundamental disturbances (common disturbances) or that shocks emanating in one country are quickly transmitted to trading partners. This is an important distinction, but often neglected.

Our objectives in this chapter are two-fold: develop the critique of the existing empirical literature on currency unions more fully, and empirically investigate whether the issues we raise have practical import. Our empirical work, designed to shed light on whether the problems identified are important in economic terms, is based on estimation of a structural vector auto-regression (VAR) model – standard in this literature – with cointegration restrictions to identify the linkages of each country in the sample with Germany and to identify the fundamental disturbances. Our sample consists of thirteen European countries, varying significantly in terms of trade and financial linkages with the EU, economic structures, exchange rate regime, time of EU membership, and political willingness to join EMU.

The chapter is organized in the following manner. The next section explains in more detail the problems of drawing inferences about the desirability of joining EMU from the existing empirical literature. We then present the empirical model and a description of the methodology applied to identify the structural shocks. We present the empirical results, discussed in the context of the literature critique, and the final section concludes the paper.

Can the desirability of EMU membership be inferred from the symmetry of economic disturbances?

Existing empirical literature

A large literature attempts to evaluate empirically the relative costs and benefits of EMU and which countries appear to be ideal candidates for membership. Recent contributions include Artis and Zhang (1996, 1997a, 1997b); Bayoumi and Eichengreen (1993a, 1993b, 1994); Bergman (1996a); Bergman, Hutchison and Cheung (1997); Demertzis, Hughes Hallett and Rummel (1997a, 1997b); Whitt (1993). Bayoumi and Eichengreen (1993a), for example, identify fundamental demand and supply disturbances for a number of European countries, and correlate these disturbances with those in Germany.[4] They identify a 'core' group of countries (Germany, France, Belgium, Luxembourg, the Netherlands and Denmark) and a 'periphery' group (the United Kingdom, Italy, Ireland, Greece, Portugal and Spain); Sweden's classification is ambiguous.[5] They find that the core countries have much higher supply and demand shock correlations with Germany than either the periphery group or a control group of countries (the United States, Japan, Canada, Australia, New Zealand and Iceland). This difference between groups is particularly noteworthy for supply shocks: the core countries have smaller and more highly correlated supply disturbances than the other two groups. Bayoumi and Eichengreen (1993a) are cautious in drawing definite conclusions, but note (1993a: 223, 224) that their results are 'consonant with arguments that have been advanced for a two-speed monetary union' [and that] for the time being, Germany and its immediate EC neighbours (the EC core) come much closer than the Community as a whole to representing a workable monetary union along American lines.

Whitt (1993), however, follows a similar empirical approach but finds less evidence for a core group prepared for EMU. Demertzis, Hughes Hallett and Rummel (1997a, 1997b) extend the work of Bayoumi and Eichengreen in several directions, including the addition of a third disturbance (demand, supply and monetary shocks) and the identification of aggregate shocks by constructing weighted averages of various country groupings: the EU core (France, Germany, Benelux, Denmark and Austria), EU periphery (remaining eight EU members) and others (a control group consisting of Canada, Switzerland, Japan, New Zealand, Australia and the United States). Each country's or group's disturbances are estimated separately, and evidence on the symmetry of disturbances is

---

[4.] This study, and most in the literature, focuses on Germany as the 'centre' country from which the symmetry of business cycles and economic linkages are measured. An alternative would be to aggregate economies or disturbances into regional groupings as do Demertzis, Hughes Hallett and Rummel (1997b).

[5.] Supply and demand disturbances are derived from the time series of domestic output and inflation and identifying demand stocks as those having only temporary effects on real output. The shocks for each country are estimated independently of other countries. The imposition of the long-run neutrality restriction to identify structural time series models was first used by Blanchard and Quah (1989). See Hutchison and Walsh (1992); Bergman (1996b) for a discussion of this methodology.

provided by correlations among the disturbances. They find that symmetries in the core are only marginally stronger than the periphery.

Artis and Zhang (1997a) find that world business cycles became more group–specific after 1979, with the German cycle linking a group of European countries stronger than the US cycle. They used monthly data on industrial production for a sample of 15 countries over the period from January 1961 to December 1993, with a sample split in March 1979. A European cycle was identified in the latter period on the basis of the relatively high cross-correlations of the cyclical components of industrial production of the countries participating in the European Exchange Rate Mechanism (ERM) with Germany. Countries outside the ERM had weaker cyclical ties to Germany. This finding, in contrast to Canova and Dellas (1993), appears to be robust to methods employed to detrend industrial production. Artis and Zhang (1997b) extend their earlier work on industrial production cross-correlations between the focus countries and Germany to cross–correlations in real exchange rates, real interest rates, exports and imports. They also use a technique to measure the cohesion or joint movement of these variables in each European country vis-à-vis Germany in a systematic manner (i.e. cluster analysis), again identifying a European core group consisting of Belgium, Germany, France, the Netherlands and Austria.

Problems in drawing policy implications from empirical work

There are several reasons to be cautious in drawing policy implications about the desirability of joining a common currency area on the basis of the degree of symmetry of economic disturbances. The first point, noted by a number of writers (for example, Bayoumi and Eichengreen, 1996), is a version of the Lucas Critique: a new currency area in Europe will represent a significant structural break, making it difficult to base future policy on the basis of historical statistical relationships. In particular, in drawing implications about the suitability of countries to join EMU, it is standard practice to assume that underlying economic disturbances and their transmission across European countries are invariant over time and across economic regimes (exchange rate, financial and trade). There are good reasons, however, to believe that the pattern of disturbances and transmission of disturbances across European countries are likely to change substantially over time in response to the EMU project and the Single Market programme. Attempts to identify a core group of countries ready for monetary union based on past structures, linkages and symmetry of disturbances may be misleading during periods of rapid economic change.

Countries frequently identified as core EU members are characterized mainly by economic dependence on German shocks, which mirrors their strong trade and financial linkages with Germany. As a major objective of the EU is economic integration, one would anticipate that the linkages of the new EU members with Germany should strengthen over time, in turn increasing the desirability of monetary union as conventionally measured. Attempts to identify a core group of countries ready for monetary union based on past structure, linkages and symmetry of disturbances may thus be misleading during periods of rapid economic change.

Fundamental disturbances may also be affected by monetary union. Demand shocks are likely to become more symmetric among countries joining EMU since a common monetary policy will be imposed, fiscal coordination will be given greater importance, and the Stability Pact (SGP) will impose restrictions on how far fiscal stances can deviate (Begg, 1997). Greater trade integration may also lead to closer relationship among countries' business cycles (Frankel and Rose, 1996).The Frankel and Rose result does not appear sensitive to alternative methods of detrending output, by contrast with Canova and Dellas (1993), or the measure of bilateral trade intensity. Krugman's (1991) analysis suggests that supply shocks may also change substantially within the EMU context. In his view, however, EMU will probably induce greater industrial specialization which would turn industry-specific supply shocks into country-specific (idiosyncratic) shocks.

Secondly, it is noteworthy that most of the support for a two-speed Europe – i.e. the argument that only a subset of European countries appears ready for monetary union – is based upon the observation that the estimated permanent disturbances to real economy activity are more highly correlated across EU core countries than among the EU periphery. Bayoumi and Eichengreen (1993a: 212), for example, find that the core–periphery distinction is much stronger for these permanent shocks (interpreted as supply-side or real shocks) than for transitory shocks (interpreted as demand shocks). The problem with this interpretation, however, is that economic theory does not unambiguously predict that a flexible exchange rate (or pegged rate) regime would necessarily be preferable over a monetary union for countries with highly asymmetric permanent disturbances to the real economy. A robust result of standard Mundell–Fleming models, and modern extensions of these models taking into account micro-foundations and welfare criteria (for example, Buiter and Kletzer, 1997), is that a flexible exchange rate regime would normally be preferable for two countries facing highly asymmetric transitory shocks to economic activity (e.g. asymmetric business cycles). However, this result does not carry over to permanent shocks.

Thirdly, there is reason to believe that most existing studies over-estimate the degree of correlation among fundamental disturbances across countries. This is because the correlation coefficients usually reflect both fundamental disturbances and economic structure. The core-country disturbances identified by Bayoumi and Eichengreen, for example, may be highly correlated with German shocks either because of symmetry in their fundamental disturbances or because German disturbances are being transmitted to these economies. The former is the traditional indicator, while the latter captures the degree of economic linkage between countries, which in turn depends on the exchange rate regime and other factors (see Hutchison and Walsh, 1992). For example, most models predict that a German monetary shock will have the strongest output effect (positive) on those economies maintaining rigid pegs to the D-mark and having strong trade links with Germany. In this case, German monetary shocks will induce higher output correlations between Germany and the EMS countries than between Germany and non-EMS member states.

In this context, it is not surprising that Artis and Zhang (1997a, 1997b) find that countries in the ERM have higher correlations among business cycles (and other economic indicators) than those outside the ERM. Close exchange rate ties with Germany also helps to explain the core countries identified by Bayoumi and Eichengreen. In principle, both the degree of economic linkage as well as the symmetry of disturbances are important criteria for judging the desirability of monetary union. Separating these two components is important, however, since a main objective of the EU is to increase economic integration (financial, goods and labour) among member states. This implies that the core–periphery distinction may change markedly if economic linkages rather than commonality of disturbances are most important.

Empirical strategy

All of the issues raised above are important in principle but, in the context of the problem at hand, may not be particularly problematic from a practical statistical or economic point of view. To address the practical import of these issues, we specify and estimate a structural VAR model for thirteen European countries: four original members of the EU (Belgium, Germany, Luxembourg and the Netherlands), two joining in 1973 (Denmark and Ireland), one joining in 1981 (Greece), two joining in 1986 (Spain and Portugal), three joining in 1995 (Austria, Finland and Sweden), and one deciding to remain outside the EU altogether (Norway). We follow most of the existing literature by focusing on Germany as the key currency country in the EU, but differ from most other work by estimating models which explicitly incorporate structural linkages with Germany.

We seek to (1) explicitly measure how closely these countries are tied to Germany; (2) determine whether these ties are related to economic structure (e.g., exchange rate regime, capital mobility and trade integration); (3) determine how the transmission of shocks, their magnitude and the patterns observed with Germany differ by the period of time countries have been EEC/EC/EU members; and (4) check the robustness of the results to changes in model specification, sample periods, and assumptions about the stationarity of variables. The overall objective is to evaluate, on the basis of common shocks and structural linkages, how robust this methodology is in picking which countries appear to make a natural OCA grouping.

Our empirical work uses VAR models with cointegration restrictions to identify the linkages of each country in the sample with Germany and to identify the fundamental disturbances. A strength of this approach is that it allows us to distinguish between permanent shocks having long-lasting effects (for example, productivity or supply-side shocks) and transitory shocks having only short-term effects (for example, demand shocks). We identify four independent disturbances – domestic and German permanent and transitory shocks. We also add oil prices to the model (treating oil shocks as exogenous) to capture potentially large structural differences in energy production and dependence between the Netherlands and Norway (large natural gas and oil producers), on the one hand, and the other countries in the sample, on the other. The country-specific disturbances (permanent and transitory shocks) are therefore measured net of oil and German influences. Using these estimates we are able to measure the degree of structural linkage with Germany and the nature of fundamental disturbances.

Empirical analysis

Methodology

Let us assume that the joint behaviour of the multivariate process, x_t – comprising German industrial production, y_t^g, German inflation, Δp_t^g, focus-country industrial production, y_t^j where $j =$ Austria, Belgium, Denmark, Finland, Greece, Ireland, Luxembourg, Norway, the Netherlands, Portugal, Spain and Sweden and focus-country inflation, Δp_t^j – can be represented by a VAR process with Gaussian errors. We will also assume that these endogenous variables are affected by the change in the oil price, z_t, which is determined outside the system. All variables are in logarithms. The standard VAR model is written as:

$$x_t = \mu + \sum_{k=1}^{p} A^{(k)} x_{t-k} + \sum_{k=1}^{p} B^{(k)} z_{t-k} + \varepsilon_t \qquad (10.1)$$

where the vector μ is a constant, A and B are 4×4 and 4×1 matrices, respectively, and ε_t is a four-dimensional error vector. The initial values $x_0, \ldots, x_{1-p}$ and $z_0, \ldots, z_{1-p}$ are taken as fixed. In addition we assume that x_t is non-stationary whereas the exogenous variable, the change in oil prices, is assumed to be stationary. Under these assumptions, the VAR in (10.1) can be written, using Granger's representation theorem, in a vector moving average (VMA) form (see Engle and Granger, 1987),

$$\Delta x_t = C(1)\mu + C(L)\varepsilon_t + C(L)B(L)z_t$$

where $C(L)$ and $B(L)$ are lag polynomials. The structural VMA model (disregarding deterministic terms and exogenous variables) linking the structural disturbances (supply and demand shocks) of interest to the observed variables may be written as:

$$\Delta x_t = R(L)\upsilon_t \qquad (10.2)$$

where υ_t is a vector of structural shocks, $E[\upsilon_t \upsilon_t'] = I$ where I is an identity matrix and $R(L)$ is a matrix polynomial. We assume that our system of variables are affected by German and focus-country permanent and transitory shocks. In particular, we let $\upsilon_t = [\varphi_t^g \ \varphi_t^j \ \psi_t^j \ \psi_t^g]'$ where φ denotes permanent and ψ transitory shocks. Following the much of the literature in this area, we interpret 'permanent shocks' as supply disturbances and 'transitory shocks' as demand disturbances.

Our problem now is how to recover the structural shocks in (10.2) from conventional estimates of the VAR in (10.1). A useful approach is to let $R(L) = C(L)\Gamma^{-1}$ where the matrix Γ translates and identifies the structural shocks υ_t from estimates of the residuals ε_t, (i.e. $\upsilon_t = \Gamma \varepsilon_t$). In the next section, we discuss how the Γ matrix can be constructed.

Identification

After estimating the model in (10.1), some additional identifying restrictions on the estimated disturbance terms are necessary to calculate the structural shocks, impulse response functions and variance decompositions. Such identifying restrictions have taken a variety of forms in the recent literature. One approach achieves identification by imposing *a priori* restrictions on the contemporaneous interactions among the variables in the system. These restrictions normally take the form of exclusion restrictions following a recursive structure popularized by Sims (1980).

Another approach introduced by Blanchard and Quah (1989) is to impose long-run restrictions on the impulse-response pattern. This approach achieves identification by dividing the shocks into two groups – those having only transitory effects on the variables in the system and those having permanent effects on at least one variable. Typically, permanent shocks are associated as supply shocks whereas transitory shocks are viewed as demand shocks.

A third approach, which we will use below, is to base identification on a common trends model following King *et al.* (1991); Warne (1993); Quah (1994). Within this approach, knowledge about the cointegration space allows us to identify both permanent and transitory shocks. In our model we have assumed that focus-country and German inflation is stationary and that output levels are non-stationary but not cointegrated such that there are two cointegration vectors and, thus, two common trends in the data.[6] For example, in a simple bivariate system, consider two variables sharing a random-walk trend term (one common trend). By definition, these two variables must be cointegrated since the two trend cancel out in a bivariate regression, leaving a stationary residual term. In our four-variable system, two (one) cointegrating vectors implies two (three) common trends.

Within this framework, the system may be exactly identified by two additional restrictions. One restriction is needed to distinguish between the two supply shocks and one to similarly disentangle the two demand shocks. To identify the supply shocks, we assume that focus-country supply shocks cannot affect German industrial production in the long run. Although not strictly true, this identifying assumption seems reasonable since the twelve countries we examine can be regarded as small open economies relative the German economy. This restriction, including the implicit assumption that demand shocks leave only transitory imprints on the variables, implies that the long–run system linking the two supply shocks to the observable variables can be written as

$$
\begin{bmatrix} y_t^g \\ y_t^j \\ \Delta p_t^g \\ \Delta p_t^j \end{bmatrix} = \begin{bmatrix} 1 & 0 \\ \gamma_{21} & 1 \\ 0 & 0 \\ 0 & 0 \end{bmatrix} \begin{bmatrix} \tau_t^g \\ \tau_t^j \end{bmatrix}
$$

[6.] In a note available from the authors we discuss in some detail how, in the general case, the two permanent and the two transitory shocks are identified using estimates of our model.

where the parameter γ_{21} is freely estimated and measures the long-run effect from German supply shocks on the focus country, and τ_t^g and τ_t^j are the foreign and domestic common trends, respectively.[7] With no further restrictions it is possible to identify the two supply shocks affecting our system.

The two demand shocks can be identified using a procedure discussed in detail by Warne (1993) and Quah (1994). They propose an identification scheme similar to the standard Choleski-based identification suggested by Sims (1980), discussed above. The individual effects of the two demand shocks are distinguished by assuming that a certain innovation does not exert a contemporaneous impact on one selected variable. In our particular application, we assume that focus-country demand shocks have no period-effect on German inflation. We could, of course, add additional restrictions such as also restricting the period-response of German industrial production. In this case, our system would be over-identified. We choose not to add over-identifying restrictions, however.

Since some of the shocks in v_t give only short-run effects on the variables, certain coefficients in $R(1)$ (see (10.2)) must be zero. In our model, with two transitory shocks (demand shocks), this implies that the last two columns of $R(1)$ are zero. The first two columns contain the factor loadings of the common trends – i.e. a measure of the long-run impact on certain variables from the two supply shocks. Moreover, our assumption that the focus-country permanent shock has no long-run effect on Germany implies that the second element in the first row of $R(1)$ is zero.

We have now the necessary tools to examine the influence of German and focus-country disturbances on each country and investigate the properties of the estimated structural shocks. This is the focus of the next section.

Empirical results

Data

The data set consists of monthly observations on industrial production and inflation measured by the consumer price index (CPI) for Austria, Belgium, Denmark, Finland, Germany, Greece, Ireland, Luxembourg, the Netherlands, Norway, Portugal, Spain and Sweden. We employ industrial production data as the measure of output, rather than the broader

---

[7] Note that we have normalized the effects from the supply shocks such that a 1 per cent positive German supply shock leads to a 1 per cent rise in the level of German industrial production in the long run. This normalization makes it easier to compare estimates of the different countries below.

GDP measure, since it is available monthly. All data are obtained from OECD Main Economic Indicators except industrial production in Denmark (compiled by Danmarks Nationalbank).[8] The crude petroleum prices in dollars are obtained from the Citibase data base, converted into D-marks (at the spot exchange rate) and real values (deflated by German CPI). All variables are expressed in natural logarithms. We examine two non-overlapping subperiods: the Bretton Woods era from 1960:1–1970:12 and the post-Bretton Woods period from 1974:1–1995:12.[9]

These European economies represent a large variation in terms of their trade and exchange rate linkages with Germany, industrial structures and length of membership in the EU and the ERM. With the (possible) exception of Spain, however, all of these countries are small economies relative to Germany. This group fits the small-country assumption reasonably well, and at the same time offers a wide range of sample variation in order to test our hypothesis that the symmetry of economic disturbances with Germany should depend on the focus countries' membership in the EU, exchange rate policy, trade patterns and industrial structures.

For example, we would expect that the size and magnitude of estimated correlations of the fundamental disturbances with other European countries, and the transmission of German shocks to each country, would depend on the degree of economic integration with Germany. Economic integration – trade and financial – may in turn depend on the period of membership in the EU and the ERM, among other considerations. In this context, five countries of our sample (Belgium, France, Germany, Luxembourg and the Netherlands) were among the original members of the EU; two joined the EU in 1973 (Denmark and Ireland); one joined in 1981 (Greece); two joined in 1986 (Portugal and Spain); and three joined in 1995 (Austria, Finland and Sweden); and one country in the sample has chosen to remain outside the EU (Norway). ERM membership among these countries has also varied considerably. During the early sample period (Bretton Woods), we would therefore expect to observe differences in how shocks from Germany are transmitted to Belgium, Luxembourg and the Netherlands compared to the other non-EU members. For the latter sample period (post-Bretton Woods), the group of long-standing

[8] We thank Ninette Pilegaard Hansen at the Economic Policy Research Unit at the Copenhagen Business School for providing the Danish data.
[9] Any decision on the sample time period is somewhat arbitrary. We choose a common sample split for all countries, providing adequate data points in each subsample, where the latter period reflects (the beginning of) the expansion of the EU from the five core members to the current membership. One alternative might be to change the sample period for each country depending on its entry into the EU. Another alternative might be to choose a common sample split depending on the creation of the ERM in 1979 or the 'hard' ERM in 1984.

EU members is extended to include Denmark and Ireland, and we would also expect this distinction to be reflected in how disturbances are transmitted. Other factors, such as Austria's strong historical ties to Germany, are also likely to play an important role.

Model estimates

In this section we estimate the structural VAR model (with six lags) given in equation (10.1) for each country separately, identify the system along the lines described above, and extract the four structural shocks. We begin by determining the lag length of the VAR[10] and testing the restrictions imposed in our identification procedure above – i.e. that there are two cointegration vectors in the data and that inflation in both Germany and the focus country is stationary. Table 10.1 reports the results from using the so-called Johansen approach of testing for cointegration (i.e. likelihood-ratio (LR) trace tests, Johansen, 1991; Johansen and Juselius, 1990). One potential problem with our model is that we have added a (stationary) exogenous variable and this will affect the asymptotic distribution of the trace tests. However, using the standard critical values for a model with linear trends, the LR trace tests suggest at least two cointegrating vectors for almost all countries. For the Bretton Woods period, the tests suggest one vector for Finland, Norway and Sweden and three vectors for Austria whereas for the latter sample, our tests indicate three vectors for Greece and four vectors (all variables are stationary) for Ireland. Given the inherent difficulty in determining the number of cointegration vectors when sample sizes are limited, we proceed on the assumption that two cointegration vectors exist for all of the countries.[11]

We then test whether industrial production and inflation are stationary using an LR test conditional on the assumption that there are two cointegration vectors in the data. The results from these tests are summarized in table 10.2. These test statistics suggest that we often can reject the null hypothesis that the data series are stationary. In general, the *p*-values of

[10.] Residual tests on the VAR model were undertaken (tests for autocorrelation and ARCH) to guide in the choice of lag length. These tests suggest that our model with six lags is reasonably well specified; the test statistics do not change dramatically when adding more lags. These results are available on request from the authors.

[11.] We choose to use the same empirical specification for each model in order to compare the results across time and across countries in a systematic way. Assuming a different number of cointegrating vectors for each model has important economic implications for the interpretation of structural shocks and does not allow easy comparison across models. Given the underlying uncertainty in determining the 'true' number of cointegrating vectors from a limited number of sample observations, we rely here on both the Johansen cointegration test results and some judgement on the underlying structure of the economy.

Table 10.1. *LR trace-tests for cointegration*

| | Bretton Woods | | | |
	$r = 0$	$r = 1$	$r = 2$	$r = 3$
AUS	125.32$^+$	51.60$^+$	15.90$^+$	0.84
BEL	108.50$^+$	44.67$^+$	9.11	0.31
FIN	86.71$^+$	23.82	9.85	0.13
GRE	102.54$^+$	38.72$^+$	6.27	0.02
LUX	109.83$^+$	39.08$^+$	10.80	5.05
NDL	124.80$^+$	50.69$^+$	9.78	3.99
NOR	85.51$^+$	25.61	3.63	0.00
POR	119.00$^+$	47.01$^+$	7.24	0.00
SPA	87.19$^+$	36.87$^+$	6.86	0.02
SWE	84.74$^+$	25.88	5.09	0.12
	Post-Bretton Woods			
AUS	112.99$^+$	46.35$^+$	9.81	0.02
BEL	104.96$^+$	35.50$^+$	11.12	0.99
DEN	109.19$^+$	39.29$^+$	6.65	0.70
FIN	85.23$^+$	39.12$^+$	3.59	0.11
GRE	109.58$^+$	45.83$^+$	20.08$^+$	2.08
IRL	84.59$^+$	43.77$^+$	16.51$^+$	4.12$^+$
LUX	84.31$^+$	32.69$^+$	11.93	0.15
NDL	99.27$^+$	27.81$^+$	11.81	1.50
NOR	96.78$^+$	32.11$^+$	10.14	0.00
POR	95.01$^+$	48.85$^+$	7.29	1.95
SPA	79.40$^+$	29.56$^+$	9.24	0.71
SWE	101.96$^+$	43.43$^+$	3.89	0.24

Notes: Tests are performed within the unrestricted dynamic simultaneous equations model given in (10.1) using six lags.
$^+$denotes significance at the 10 per cent level.

tests of the null that industrial production is stationary is lower than for testing if inflation is stationary. Our interpretation is that our assumptions made in the context of the discussion of identification are rejected in many cases. These mixed results are resolved by estimating two separate structural models. The first imposes the restriction that both German and focus-country inflation are stationary (our base model) whereas the second assumes that inflation is non-stationary. In this latter model, we form two cointegration vectors that include all four variables and

Table 10.2. *Tests for stationarity*

	Bretton Woods			
	$y^f \sim I(0)$	$y^d \sim I(0)$	$\Delta p^f \sim I(0)$	$\Delta p^d \sim I(0)$
AUS	30.22*	32.08*	10.44*	0.54
BEL	34.35*	34.17*	0.74	11.23*
FIN	12.83*	13.57*	2.30	1.44
GRE	32.25*	32.31*	4.81[+]	0.70
LUX	22.82*	22.66*	7.20*	3.55
NDL	35.68*	35.55*	9.33*	1.89
NOR	21.98*	21.86*	2.12	4.09
POR	39.70*	39.27*	4.74[+]	6.28*
SPA	27.44*	26.01*	3.29	10.18*
SWE	20.30*	19.66*	0.81	4.52
	Post-Bretton Woods			
AUS	35.51*	36.34*	5.09[+]	12.95*
BEL	22.93*	23.39*	3.38	12.96*
DEN	31.27*	31.29*	25.09*	22.24*
FIN	34.77*	35.37*	9.74*	25.53*
GRE	20.92*	8.81*	2.71	10.54*
IRL	22.18*	19.78*	2.41	12.45*
LUX	19.44*	20.44*	4.83[+]	9.35*
NDL	13.28*	14.22*	0.59	3.59
NOR	21.40*	21.72*	7.16*	15.82*
POR	39.39*	38.42*	8.54*	19.07*
SPA	19.39*	19.23*	2.31	13.73*
SWE	37.03*	38.99*	5.03[+]	13.35*

Notes: The LR-test statistic is χ^2-distributed with two degrees of freedom.
Tests are performed within the unrestricted dynamic simultaneous equations model given in (10.1) using six lags and assuming that the cointegration rank is 2. *denotes significance at the 5 per cent level, [+]at the 10 per cent level.

apply our identifying restrictions discussed above.[12] Below we report the base-model results – i.e. assuming that inflation is stationary. Results for this alternative structural model are discussed below but not reported. They are available from the authors upon request.

[12] Note that our identifying restrictions discussed above are not affected by the fact that all variables are contained in the cointegration space.

Importance of German shocks

To examine the effect of German supply and demand shocks on smaller European economies under the two sample periods, we compute the impulse responses of focus-country output to German shocks and their relative importance. In particular, we examine the influence of a standardized supply shock and demand shock on the evolution of focus–country output over time holding other factors constant.[13] While the impulse-response analysis provides information on the effects of standardized German supply and demand shocks during the sample periods, it does not take the actual variability of focus-country output into consideration. Whether German shocks played a larger or smaller role in determining output fluctuations in the small European economies depends on the strength of the linkages as well as the importance of the disturbances emanating in Germany. This is investigated through variance decompositions.

Impulse responses

German supply shocks should be interpreted as productivity developments and other factors that are standardized to effectively cause a 1 per cent permanent rise in German output. Figure 10.1 shows the output response for each country to a one-unit German supply shock during the early sample period (solid line) and recent sample period (dashed line). In every case except for Greece and Portugal, the output response to a German supply shock is greater in the recent sample period (post-Bretton Woods) than in the earlier sample period (Bretton Woods). This difference is substantial in Austria, Belgium, Luxembourg and the Netherlands – countries highly integrated with Germany via their long-standing membership in the EU (Belgium, Luxembourg and the Netherlands) or for historical reasons (Austria) and having the strongest exchange rate link. (Denmark and Ireland are also long-standing EU members, but data is not available to make a comparison with the earlier episode.)

Perhaps most interesting for our purposes, however, is that these same EU core members – Austria, Belgium, Denmark, Luxembourg and the Netherlands – are much more influenced by German supply shocks than are the other European countries. In the recent sample period, long-run output in these five countries each increased by over 0.73 per cent in response to a one-unit German supply shock. These countries are most exposed to supply shocks emanating from Germany because of the economic structure

[13.] We normalize the system such that a 1 per cent supply shock leads to a 1 per cent permanent change in German output.

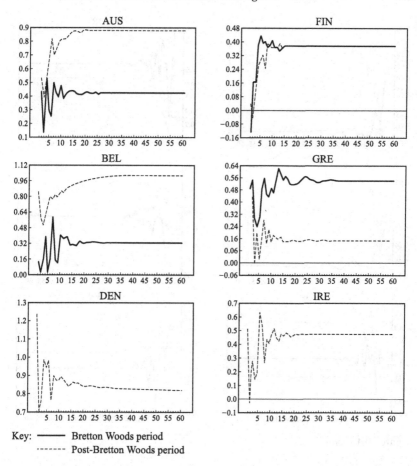

Figure 10.1 Impulse responses of domestic output to German demand shocks

linking their economies, which in turn leads to a strong transmission mechanism.

The evidence on German demand shocks is more difficult to interpret than the supply shocks. Demand shocks are identified as having only short- and medium-run effects on focus-country (and German) output, and the dynamics in most cases are complicated. The effects of German demand shocks on focus–country output is shown in figure 10.2 for the earlier and recent sample periods. Although considerable short-run variation is evident, the transmission of the German demand shock is generally positive in ten countries: Austria, Belgium, Denmark (after the first five months), Finland, Ireland, Luxembourg, the Netherlands, Norway,

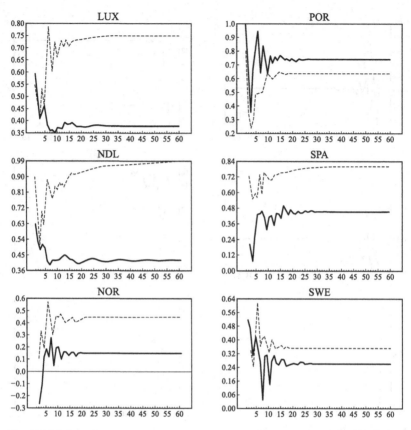

Figure 10.1 (*cont.*)

Portugal and Spain. The effect on output in Greece and Sweden is mixed in the sense that the initial positive impact from the German demand shock is subsequently followed by negative impulses in several periods.

We also calculated the impulse responses of focus-country output to German supply and demand shocks under the alternative model where inflation is assumed to be nonstationary (results available upon request). Comparisons with our baseline model reveal only minor differences. The model specification in this instance does not qualitatively influence the main results.

Variance decompositions
Another way of measuring the importance of Germany for the output of the smaller European economies is to decompose the percentage

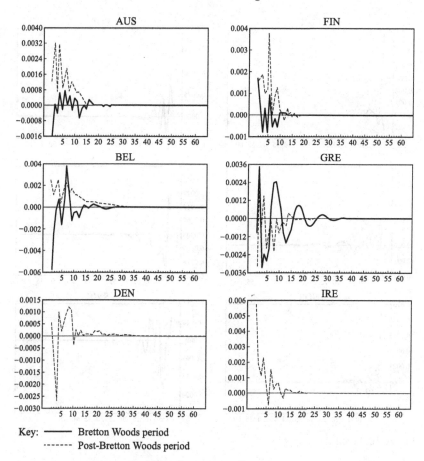

Key: ——— Bretton Woods period
------- Post-Bretton Woods period

Figure 10.2 Impulse responses of domestic output to German demand shocks

of the focus-country's output forecast error variance at different horizons to that part attributable to German supply shocks, German demand shocks, and other disturbances. These variance decompositions are shown in table 10.3.

A significant portion of the output (forecast error) variances of the core EU members – Austria, Belgium, Denmark, Luxembourg and the Netherlands – are explained by German disturbances, mainly emanating from supply-side shocks. German shocks explain 30 per cent or more of the six-month-ahead output variance for these countries, with Belgium at the high end (65 per cent). Over the longer horizon, the percentage of total variance explained rises, with a range from 45 per cent (Denmark) to 75

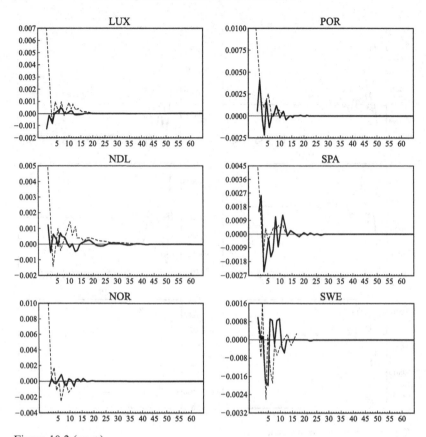

Figure 10.2 (*cont.*)

per cent (Austria and Belgium). It is also interesting that German shocks are very important for Spain and Portugal. These countries joined the EU in 1986.

Comparing the estimates from earlier and recent sample periods also reveals that the long–run influence from German shocks mainly increases in the core EU countries. For Austria and Belgium, the six-month-ahead output variance also increases. Output variance explained by German shocks also increases in Norway and Spain in both the short and long run. By contrast, a short-run and long-run decrease in the relative influence of Germany is noted in some of the periphery EU countries (i.e. Finland, Greece, Portugal and Sweden).

An interesting feature of table 10.3 is the small percentage of output variance explained by German demand disturbances, defined as those

Table 10.3. *Output variance explained by German supply (GES) and demand shocks (GED) and focus-country supply (DS) and demand shocks (DD), inflation is stationary*

		Bretton Woods				Post-Bretton Woods			
		GES	GED	DS	DD	GES	GED	DS	DD
AUS	1	16.3	0.2	82.3	1.2	22.8	0.6	76.1	0.5
	6	32.6	1.4	65.2	0.8	52.2	1.5	43.5	2.8
	12	41.3	1.3	56.8	0.5	62.6	0.8	35.0	1.6
	24	46.4	0.7	52.5	0.3	69.7	0.3	29.2	0.7
	36	48.2	0.5	51.1	0.2	71.9	0.2	27.5	0.4
	∞	52.1	0.0	47.9	0.0	75.5	0.0	24.4	0.0
BEL	1	1.2	7.2	89.6	2.1	24.5	19.3	53.9	2.3
	6	4.4	5.8	88.2	1.6	47.7	18.5	31.5	2.3
	12	11.6	4.2	82.2	4.2	57.0	13.9	27.3	1.6
	24	15.8	2.6	80.4	1.2	65.5	8.2	25.3	0.9
	36	17.7	1.9	79.5	0.9	68.9	5.4	25.0	0.6
	∞	22.8	0.0	77.2	0.0	74.9	0.0	25.1	0.0
DEN	1					21.3	6.1	71.2	1.4
	6					33.0	7.4	58.0	1.6
	12					35.4	5.4	57.9	1.2
	24					39.0	3.3	57.0	0.7
	36					40.7	2.3	56.6	0.5
	∞					44.9	0.0	55.1	0.0
FIN	1	1.6	30.4	66.4	1.6	0.6	29.1	69.0	1.3
	6	14.8	18.7	65.6	0.8	3.7	22.1	71.6	2.6
	12	19.3	10.1	70.1	0.5	6.7	15.8	76.0	1.5
	24	20.5	5.0	74.2	0.2	9.4	9.1	80.7	0.8
	36	20.9	3.3	75.6	0.1	10.3	6.1	83.1	0.5
	∞	21.7	0.0	78.3	0.0	12.0	0.0	88.0	0.0
GRE	1	13.4	13.6	72.7	0.2	5.1	18.1	72.3	4.5
	6	18.0	9.3	69.3	3.4	6.2	11.9	77.9	4.0
	12	24.3	7.0	66.1	2.6	5.6	8.1	83.1	3.2
	24	31.5	3.7	63.2	1.5	4.0	4.8	89.3	1.9
	36	34.0	2.5	62.4	1.0	3.2	3.4	92.0	1.3
	∞	39.2	0.0	60.8	0.0	1.3	0.0	98.7	0.0
IRL	1					4.0	0.0	93.6	2.3
	6					6.2	0.7	91.4	1.7
	12					8.6	0.6	89.8	0.9
	24					10.2	0.3	88.9	0.5
	36					10.8	0.2	88.6	0.3
	∞					12.1	0.0	87.9	0.0

Table 10.3 (*cont.*)

		Bretton Woods				Post-Bretton Woods			
		GES	*GED*	*DS*	*DD*	*GES*	*GED*	*DS*	*DD*
LUX	1	49.1	3.2	45.7	1.9	9.1	0.7	79.9	10.2
	6	57.4	1.1	40.7	0.8	30.4	1.3	62.6	5.6
	12	55.4	0.7	43.4	0.5	45.1	1.1	50.7	3.1
	24	55.3	0.4	44.0	0.3	54.0	0.7	43.8	1.6
	36	53.3	0.3	44.2	0.2	57.2	0.4	41.2	1.1
	∞	55.1	0.0	44.9	0.0	63.9	0.0	36.1	0.0
NDL	1	52.9	1.3	44.4	1.4	14.3	20.9	60.5	4.2
	6	62.8	2.6	33.8	0.7	37.2	16.7	43.6	2.5
	12	59.3	1.9	38.3	0.5	50.7	13.1	34.6	1.6
	24	57.4	1.1	41.2	0.3	60.6	7.8	30.7	0.8
	36	56.8	0.8	42.3	0.2	64.7	5.2	29.6	0.5
	∞	55.2	0.0	44.8	0.0	72.1	0.0	27.9	0.0
NOR	1	3.4	0.0	96.5	0.1	0.1	10.4	81.4	8.0
	6	6.1	0.9	92.8	0.2	4.7	11.3	78.6	5.4
	12	6.7	1.1	92.0	0.2	7.4	8.9	80.1	3.6
	24	7.0	0.7	92.1	0.1	11.1	5.8	80.9	2.2
	36	7.2	0.5	92.2	0.1	13.4	4.1	80.9	1.5
	∞	7.6	0.0	92.4	0.0	20.3	0.0	79.7	0.0
POR	1	22.5	0.2	77.3	0.0	10.5	26.5	52.9	11.0
	6	38.7	0.7	59.1	1.5	14.3	15.9	62.7	7.1
	12	43.6	0.5	54.9	0.9	19.1	9.1	67.8	4.0
	24	48.5	0.3	50.7	0.5	23.0	4.4	70.7	1.9
	36	50.2	0.2	49.2	0.4	24.4	2.8	71.4	1.2
	∞	54.1	0.0	45.9	0.0	27.2	0.0	72.8	0.0
SPA	1	1.6	2.5	94.2	1.7	8.4	4.1	82.3	5.2
	6	8.7	3.0	86.6	1.7	29.9	4.8	62.6	2.7
	12	13.1	1.7	84.1	1.1	36.9	4.5	56.9	1.6
	24	16.4	0.8	82.2	0.6	43.0	3.3	52.7	0.9
	36	17.5	0.6	81.5	0.4	45.8	2.5	51.1	0.6
	∞	19.8	0.0	80.2	0.0	53.0	0.0	47.0	0.0
SWE	1	13.3	0.0	86.3	0.3	3.1	24.6	71.9	0.4
	6	28.7	1.8	68.2	1.2	11.7	16.0	71.2	1.1
	12	28.7	1.3	68.8	1.2	12.7	8.7	77.8	0.7
	24	29.6	0.8	68.8	0.8	12.6	4.6	82.3	0.4
	36	30.1	0.6	68.7	0.6	12.6	3.2	84.0	0.3
	∞	31.3	0.0	68.7	0.0	12.4	0.0	87.6	0.0

shocks having only transitory effects on output. By construction and definition, German demand shocks do not influence the forecast error variance of output in the long-run. But it is noteworthy that German supply shocks also dominate (over German demand shocks) the short- to medium-term output variance. German demand shocks play a small role even in those cases where a substantial part of the one-month-ahead forecast error variance in output is explained by aggregate German disturbances (supply and demand).

Similar to the impulse-response functions, the variance decompositions are also largely unaffected in the alternative model specification allowing for a non-stationary inflation rate.

Conclusion

In this chapter, we argue that only limited information on the costs and benefits of participating in a new monetary union may be inferred from historical economic linkages among the countries. Losing national monetary policy as an instrument for stabilization purposes is traditionally seen as a primary cost of EMU, and an important argument for a more activist fiscal policy (at either the national or the EU level). However, since a major objective of the EU is to foster stronger economic ties among members, one would expect that this process would itself reinforce a European-wide business cycle and increase the degree of compatibility for a common currency area. In these circumstances, the cost of losing the monetary instrument – and need for more activist fiscal policies – may not be as large as some studies based on historical relationships have indicated.

That European economic structures change in response to important policy developments such as EMU has been suggested by many authors (for example, Frankel and Rose, 1996, 1997). Our work suggests that economic structures have already changed: economic linkages among the small European countries and Germany have increased markedly over the past twenty years. Greater trade and financial integration in Europe has led to more interdependence in the region, and more dependence on the German economy. We also find that the core group identified by Bayoumi and Eichengreen (1993a, 1993b) is noteworthy by their strong trade and financial linkages with Germany. This leads to a rapid and powerful transmission of German shocks to the economies of the core group, which in turn may be misleadingly interpreted as 'common' disturbances.

Attempts to identify a core group of countries ready for monetary union based on past structures, linkages and symmetry of disturbances may be misleading during periods of rapid economic change. It is not clear that fiscal policy, at either the national or the EU level, will come under increasing pressure to fulfil the stabilization role formerly played by independent monetary policy.

References

Artis, M. J. and Zhang, W. (1996). 'Business Cycles, Exchange Rate Regimes and the ERM: Is There A European Business Cycle?', *EUI Working Papers*, RSC 96/55

(1997a). 'International Business Cycles and the ERM: Is There A European Business Cycle?', *Internaitonal Journal of Finance and Economics*, 2: 1–16

(1997b). 'On Identifying the Core of EMU: An Exploration of Some Empirical Criteria', *CEPR Working Paper*, 1689

Bayoumi, T. and Eichengreen, B. (1993a). 'Is there a Conflict Between EC Enlargement and European Monetary Unification?', *Greek Economic Review*, 15: 131–54

(1993b). 'Shocking Aspects of European Monetary Unification', in F. Torres and F. Giavazzi (eds.), *Adjustment and Growth in the European Monetary Union*, Cambridge: Cambridge University Press: 153–229

(1994). 'Macroeconomic Adjustment under Bretton Woods and the Post-Bretton Woods Float: An Impulse-response Analysis', *Economic Journal*, 104: 813–27

(1996). 'Operationalizing the Theory of Optimum Currency Areas', *CEPR Working Paper*, 1484

Begg, D. (1997). 'The Design of EMU', *IMF Working Paper*, WP 97/99

Bergman, M. (1996a). 'Do Monetary Unions Make Economic Sense? Evidence from the Scandavian Currency Union 1873-1913,' *SNS Occasional Paper*, 77

(1996b). 'International Evidence on the Sources of Macroeconomic Fluctuations', *European Economic Review*. 40: 1237–58

Bergman, M., Hutchison, M. M. and Cheung, Y.-W. (1997). 'Should the Nordic Countries Join A European Monetary Union? An Empirical Analysis,' *EPRU Working Paper Series*, 1997–21

Blanchard, O. J. and Quah, D. (1989). 'The Dynamic Effects of Aggregate Demand and Supply Disturbances,' *American Economic Review*, 79: 655–73

Buiter, W. H. and Kletzer, K. M. (1997). *Monetary Union and the Role of Automatic Stabilizers*, Boston, Dordrecht and London: Kluwer Academic

Canova, F. and Dellas, H. (1993). 'Trade Interdependence and the Internaitonal Business Cycle,' *Journal of International Economics*, 34: 23–47

De Grauwe, P. (1992). *The Economics of Monetary Integration* 2nd edn., Oxford: Oxford University Press

Demertzis, M., Hughes Hallett, A. and Rummel, O. (1997a). *Is a Two-speed System in Europe the Answer to Conflict Between the German and Anglo-Saxon Models of Monetary Control?*, New York: Elsevier Scientific

(1997b). *Is the European Union a Natural Currency Area, or is it Held Together by Policy Makers?* Cambridge: Cambridge University Press

Eighengreen, B. (1992). 'Should the Maastricht Treaty Be Saved?', *Princeton Studies in International Finance*, 74

Engle, R. F. and Granger, C. W. J. (1987). 'Co-integration and Error Correction: Representation, Estimating and Testing,' *Econometrica*, 55: 251–76

European Commission (1990). 'One Market, One Money', *European Economy*, 44

Frankel, J. A. and Rose, A. K. (1996). 'The Endogeneity of the Optimum Currency Area Criteria', *CEPR Discussion Paper*, 1473

Frankel, J. A. and Rose, A. K. (1997). 'Is EMU More Justifiable Ex Post Than Ex Ante?', *European Economic Review*, 41: 753–60

Fratianni, M. and von Hagen, J. (1992). *The European Monetary System and European Monetary Union*, Boulder, Colo.: Westview Press

Hutchison, M. M. and Walsh, C. (1992). 'Empirical Evidence on the Insulation Properties of Fixed and Flexible Exchange Rates: The Japanese Experience', *Journal of International Economics*, 32: 241–63

Johanson, S. (1991). 'Estimation and Hypothesis Testing of Cointegration Vectors in Gaussian Vector Autoregressive Models', *Econometrica*, 59: 1551–80

Johansen, S. and Juselius, K. (1990). 'Maximum Likelihood Estimation and Inference on Cointegration – With Applications to the Demand for Money', *Oxford Bulletin of Economics and Statistics*, 52: 169–210

Kenen, P. (1969). 'The Theory of Optimum Currency Areas: An Eclectic View,' in R. A. Mundell and A. Swoboda (eds.), *Monetary Problems in the International Economy*, Chicago: University of Chicago Press

King, R. G., Plosser, C. I., Stock, J. H. and Watson, M. W. (1991). 'Stochastic Trends and Economic Fluctuations', *American Economic Review*, 81: 819–40

Krugman, P. (1991). *Geography and Trade*, Cambridge, Mass. and London: MIT Press and Louvain: Louvain University Press, Gaston Eyskens Lecture Series

McKinnon, R. (1963). 'Optimum Currency Areas', *American Economic Review*, 53: 717–25

Mundell, R. A. (1961). 'A Theory of Optimum Currency Areas', *American Economic Review*, 51: 657–65

Quah, D. (1994). 'Identifying Vector Autoregressions', in *FIEF Studies in Labor Markets and Economic Policy, 5*, Oxford: Clarendon Press

Sims, C. A. (1980). 'Macroeconomics and Reality', *Econometrica*, 48: 1–48

Tower, E. and Willett, T. D. (1970). 'The Theory of Optimum Currency Areas and Exchange Rate Flexibility', *Special Papers in International Economics*, 11, Princeton: Princeton University Press

Warne, A. (1993). 'A Common Trends Model: Identification, Estimation and Asymptotics', Institute for International Economic Studies, University of Stockholm, *Seminar Paper*, 555

Whitt, J. (1993). 'European Monetary Union: Evidence from Structural VARS', paper presented to the Federal Reserve Committee on International Economic Analysis (October)

Wihlborg, C. and Willett, T. D. (1991). 'Optimum Currency Areas Revisited on the Transition Path to a Currency Union', in C. Wihlborg, M. Fratianni, and T. D. Willett (eds.), *Financial Regulation and Monetary Arrangements after 1992. Contributions to Economic Analysis, 204*, Amsterdam: North-Holland

11   Fiscal consolidation in Europe: some empirical issues

Christopher Allsopp, Warwick McKibbin and David Vines

Introduction

European countries have been, simultaneously, engaged in a massive fiscal consolidation and an attempt to build a monetary union. This chapter explores the proposition that, in a monetary union, a coordinated approach to such fiscal consolidation will be necessary.

The chapter explores the circumstances under which fiscal consolidation in a European monetary union (EMU) has the features of a prisoner's dilemma, and it produces empirical evidence to show that these circumstances may actually pertain, using simulations on the McKibbin–Sachs Global Economic model (MSG2).

The chapter thus produces a convincing argument for an understanding of the 'Stability and Growth Pact' (SGP hereafter Stability Pact) as a solution to a collective action problem. The Maastricht fiscal convergence criteria have often been seen, not very convincingly, as intended to exclude those countries from the projected monetary union whose governments were pursuing policies that would make their countries insolvent.[1] It is instead argued here that the Maastricht criteria result from the generally shared objective of fiscal restraint and consolidation in Europe, and the recognition that such consolidation in a monetary union would be more costly for individual countries – in terms of lost output – without cooperation.[2] The Stability Pact has similar rules for the continuing operation of EMU, we believe for similar reasons.

We are grateful for comments on earlier versions of this chapter made at seminars at Oxford University and the Australian National University, and by participants at a workshop on 'Fiscal Aspects of Monetary Integration' Trouville, Denmark, on 15–16 August 1997). We are glad to acknowledge financial support from the Foreign and Commonwealth Office.

[1.] These arguments are reviewed in Allsopp and Vines (1996). The difficulty with them is that the problem which they identify is too extreme – the likelihood of actual insolvency by European sovereign governments is very small since they possess the power to tax.

[2.] This is an argument which we initially explored in Allsopp and Vines (1996) and Allsopp, Davies and Vines (1995).

The chapter also sounds a strong note of caution. It is shown that – if European short-term interest rates, the European exchange rate, and the long-term real European interest rate do not fall enough – collective Europe-wide consolidation will not cause lower output losses for participant countries but higher ones, as output falls are transmitted from country to country. It turns out that the empirical evidence on these key responses is not strong, and we believe that more work on this question is of fundamental importance.

The chapter is organized as follows. In the next section, background issues are explained; we then explain the form of the possible 'prisoner's dilemma'. We then present simulations which illustrate these ideas on the MSG2 model. We then discuss the implications of the simulations for the prisoner's dilemma issue, discuss our note of caution, and in the final section conclude. An appendix (p. 309) contains a simple 'consensus' analytical macroeconomic model for Europe, and we use this model to enunciate three propositions which formalize the key part of our argument.

The issue of fiscal consolidation

The problem of deficits and debt in Europe

It is no exaggeration to say that Europe has been facing a fiscal crisis. For the group of fifteen EU countries combined, gross government debt in relation to GDP has more or less doubled over the past fifteen years from about 40 per cent in 1980 to about 78 per cent in 1996. Over the same period, the average public sector deficit was 4 per cent of GDP, always exceeding (except briefly in 1989) the Maastricht convergence limit of 3 per cent of GDP (see figure 11.1). There are, of course, some quali-fications.[3] However, the trend of debt[4] appeared inexorable. It rose with only a pause in the late 1980s' boom period, which was widely regarded as unsustainable.

The Maastricht limits – tough though they seemed – were regarded by many commentators as not tight enough for the medium term. International organizations such as the IMF and the OECD pointed to the need for more ambitious targets for restraint (for example, IMF,

[3.] The deficit figures for the group are affected by the very high numbers for Italy and Greece. Nevertheless it is true that only a few small countries will have found the Maastricht limits at all easy to meet. Another qualification is that, in the past, inflation was high and this distorts the deficit figure upwards because of the neglect of the 'inflation tax' in conventional national accounting procedures; that is however, no longer the case.

[4.] Note that a concern for debt ratios rather than deficits in effect involves adjusting for both inflation and growth.

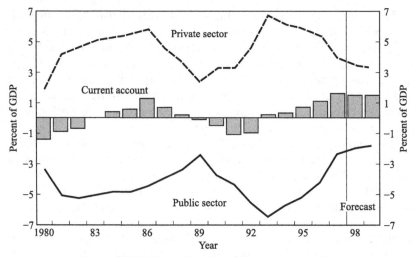

Source: OECD; Forecast from Oxford Economic Forecasting.

Figure 11.1   European sectoral balances, 1980–1998

1996). Within Europe, the Stability Pact (agreed at Amsterdam in 1997) is intended to limit deficits to a *maximum* of 3 per cent (after that, fines are envisaged if the deficit persists). Even more importantly, countries participating in EMU are committed to aim for average budget deficits, over the cycle, of zero or surplus. It is widely recognized that, if any room for fiscal manoeuvre over the cycle is to be built in, the target for average deficits must be considerably lower than 3 per cent. At a minimum,[5] the necessary margin appears to be about 3 per cent of GDP, justifying the zero deficit target (see Buti, 1998). On any plausible estimation, such a target for the medium term would produce a trend decline in debt ratios.[6]

But such a target, if it is to be met, requires further fiscal consolidation over and above that which has already occurred. Even though European countries on average met the Maastricht target of 3 per cent for 1997, there is still a substantial amount of consolidation to go. The illustrative figure – 2 per cent – which we use for the simulation exercises reported below roughly corresponds to estimates of the structural deficit in the reference year 1997.

[5] This is a ballpark figure widely quoted by many commentators. It comes from a casual examination of the movement of the budget deficit over the cycle.

[6] The Maastricht targets are arbitrary, but at least they do have some consistency. At a debt ratio of 60 per cent and with nominal GDP growing at 5 per cent per annum, the equilibrium deficit would be 3 per cent. Zero deficits on average would imply a falling debt ratio. It has yet to be explained why acceptance of this would be desirable for particular countries, especially those with low debt ratios.

The magnitude of the fiscal adjustment that Europe is attempting should not be under-estimated. The average structural – or cyclically adjusted – deficit over the past fifteen years has been about 4.3 per cent of GDP. Thus, to meet the objectives of the Stability Pact would require a sustained change of over 4 per cent of GDP. Such a change is an entirely reasonable objective. However, it is not a small change and will involve, of necessity, not just changes in the public sector but also major adjustments within the private sector.

Some accounting

To illustrate the nature of the adjustment that must follow a fiscal consolidation, it is useful to examine a set of accounting identities that hold within any economy or region. These identities can be considered in terms of stock and flow relationships.

For any economic area, the sectoral financial balances (B_i) must add to zero. Thus, for an individual country,

$$B_g + B_p = -B_f$$

here, g, p, and f refer to government, private sector and foreign sector, respectively; note that $-B_f$ is the current account of the balance of payments.

The balance of the private sector can be broken down as

$$B_p = (S_p - I_p)$$

where S_p is private sector savings, including business savings, I_p is private investment.

The equivalent stock identities relate total private sector financial wealth W_p to claims on the capital stock, K, *plus* net claims on foreigners, F, and claims on the government B, where B is government debt. The identity is:

$$W_p = K + B + F.$$

However, in looking at behaviour, it is useful to express private sector wealth as

$$W_p = K + \lambda B + F.$$

In this, λ is the degree to which government debt is considered as wealth by private sector agents. In the Ricardian limit ($\lambda = 0$) there is no issue with B crowding-out capital stocks, because for every change in the fiscal deficit, households internalize the tax implications and adjust consumption accordingly. Empirically the hypothesis that $\lambda = 0$ is rejected. But the closer is λ to zero, the easier is the job of fiscal consolidation since lower government debt would imply lower future taxes and lower savings. (This issue is of importance in the discussion below.) The figure for external assets does not disappear because it represents claims on foreigners which are not balanced by future tax liabilities. The stock–flow identities relate the sectoral balance of any sector to the accumulation of financial assets by that sector.

The counterpart to the fiscal objectives

The accounting identities are immediately useful in showing what other changes must go with a successful implementation of the fiscal strategy.

Looking first at the *flow* (sectoral balance) identities, these express the fact that a successful cut in the public sector deficit (a rise in B_g) must be matched by either an improvement in the balance of payments or by a fall in the private sector's surplus. For a given balance of payments position, the adjustment in the private sector balance could occur either by a reduction in savings or by an increase in investment.

The *stock* identities show that a fall in the amount of government debt (the bond stock for simplicity) implies a fall in the private sector's holdings of financial wealth unless there is an increase in (claims on) the capital stock (owing, for example, to an increase in the capital stock) or an increase in private sector's holdings of foreign assets.

The *stock-flow* identities relate the change in a sector's assets to its sectoral balance. For example, if the flow counterpart to a public sector deficit reduction were a balance of payments surplus, this shows that the private sector's holdings of government bonds are being replaced over time by increased holdings of overseas assets. If it were a fall in the private sector's surplus, brought about by increased private sector investment (savings unchanged), the counterpart would be an increase in the private sector's holdings of claims on capital (equity, for example).

Economic mechanisms and the output costs of consolidation

As noted, for any economy, a cut in the budget deficit will necessarily have a flow counterpart – in an improvement in the balance of payments, in reduced private savings or in an increase in private investment.

In the short run in which wages and prices are sticky, *and failing other responses*, such counterparts will be brought about by the Keynesian process of falling incomes and output. In the extreme, income and output will fall until the initial fiscal consolidation is balanced by: (1) a fall in private sector savings, (2) a fall in imports and (3) a fall in public sector savings owing to a fall in tax revenues. It is the output fall associated with this Keynesian process that is identified in this chapter with the costs of consolidation. The central question is: what other responses are to be expected so that the economy's reliance on this Keynesian method of equilibration is rendered small, or even superfluous?

Looking first at the balance of payments, this will improve if the real exchange rate depreciates, as a result of competitiveness effects on imports and exports. Such a (flow) improvement in the current account will replace over time the private sector's holdings of government bonds by foreign assets. Effects on investment could eventuate through changes in the real interest rate and through changes in competitiveness. Lower private sector holdings of public sector assets can lead to an increased demand for (claims on) private sector assets and hence to a larger equilibrium capital stock, through the mechanism of lower real long-term interest rates. (There are some difficulties with this if real interest rates are determined at the international level). In practice, most investment functions, even if based on Tobin's Q and thus sensitive to long-term interest rates and stock market prices, suggest lagged responses and accelerator-type reactions. This means that, if there is a tendency for output to fall, short-term investment responses could work in the wrong direction, intensifying this tendency. This is an area where the degree of forward-lookingness in the model of economic responses will make a very important difference. The more that long-term interest rates, stock market prices and the exchange rate move appropriately in the short term, the more likely it is that investment will rise.

Turning to savings, one could appeal to the operation of Ricardian Equivalence. For example, higher present taxes implying lower future taxes would, in the Ricardian limit, have no effect on current consumption; in flow terms, private savings would simply fall to match the improvement in the budget deficit (in stock terms, a reduction in the supply of government bonds would be 'matched' by reduced demand for assets to hold). Similarly, cuts in public expenditure (the consolidation instrument assumed for the simulations) would be matched by rises in current consumption. This may be an extreme view, because the vast body of empirical evidence suggests that many economic agents are liquidity-constrained.[7] Furthermore there are a number of forces which may limit any rise in consumption following lower public spending. If, as seems increasingly probable, fiscal consolidation in Europe is seen as associated with the likelihood of decreased health and welfare provision in the future,

---

[7.] In the forward-looking MSG2 model used below, about 70 per cent of the economy is regarded as liquidity-constrained, with Ricardian Equivalence applying to the other 30 per cent. McKibbin and Wilcoxen (1998) demonstrate that even if individuals are not liquidity-constrained, the economy as a whole may be liquidity-constrained if there are adjustment costs in physical capital accumulation.

lifecycle-type considerations could suggest increased rather than reduced incentives to save.

This brief discussion has suggested where to look for the counterpart changes to a fiscal consolidation that would prevent output from falling. Given private sector financial behaviour, the most plausible and obvious counterpart change is in the balance of payments. Underlying savings behaviour may be quite hard to change – though the possibility of large wealth effects should not be ruled out. In policy terms, the most attractive counterpart change would be a sustained rise in investment, leading to growth in output capacity.

Fiscal consolidation as a prisoner's dilemma

Channels of influence

We now show how the above arguments lead to the view that the output costs of consolidation can be less if all consolidate together than if consolidation is done separately. A formal version of the argument may be found in the appendix.[8] There are two separate channels, both of which are a consequence of short-run nominal rigidities.

(1) Membership of a monetary union imposes constraints on monetary policy. A single country acting on its own within a monetary union cannot accompany its own fiscal consolidation with a 'matching' easing of monetary policy because monetary policy is set union-wide. In the short run in which wages and prices are sticky the consequence of this will be a tendency towards a Keynesian process of falling incomes and output and employment. By contrast, if all countries in a monetary union were to consolidate collectively, then all could induce an easing of monetary conditions, union-wide, and unemployment costs caused by nominal rigidities could be reduced.

(2) The second channel is to do with the effect of fiscal consolidation on the long-term real interest rate, quite independently of the way monetary policy operates within a monetary union. Consolidation by any one country produces some lowering of long-term real interest rates throughout the union. To the extent that consumption and investment are forward-looking, this increases short-run aggregate demand and so reduces the above-mentioned output costs of consolidation. But collective consolidation increases the reduction in the long-term interest rate for the whole area and so further reduces the output

---

[8.] A slightly different version of the formal argument may also be found in Allsopp, McKibbin and Vines (1998).

costs. Collective consolidation causes smaller output losses than consolidation done alone if these two effects are strong enough to outweigh the negative effects on home output of foreign fiscal consolidation, working directly through the import leakage. Of course, the risk involved in collective consolidation is that these two effects are weak and so collective consolidation causes higher output losses than those which result from separate consolidation, as falls are transmitted from one country to another through the import leakage.

The incentive structures associated with consolidation in a monetary union are thus quite different from what happens in a floating exchange rate regime. Indeed, when exchange rates are floating, consolidation by an individual country might lead to *smaller* output losses than would result from a consolidation by a group of countries. It is true that the second of the two channels discussed above, coming from the effects on long-term real interest rates (which operates independently of the monetary regime) continues to point towards a prisoner's dilemma. But under floating exchange rates any given easing of monetary conditions in a single country acting on its own will actually lead to a *bigger* dampening of output losses than would result from the same easing of monetary conditions by a group of countries. This is because a single country is more open than is a group of countries, so that the currency depreciation following the easing of monetary conditions would cause a larger net-exports response, and so more damping of output falls.

Representation as a prisoner's dilemma

Suppose that each country in a monetary union has decided that it wishes to achieve fiscal consolidation by cutting government expenditure. The alternatives that we will consider are: 'Cut' or 'No cut'. A prisoner's dilemma structure could result if the pay-offs were such that (1) if all countries played Cut then the output costs would be small so that consolidation would be pursued, but that (2) if an individual country played Cut but the other country played No cut then the output costs would be so large as to make the consolidation unattractive.

We can present a simple intuitive representation of these ideas using a symmetrical two-country framework. Entries in the pay-off matrix in table 11.1 represent output costs. In each entry, the first item represents output costs for the home country and the second output costs for the foreign country.

A prisoner's dilemma structure can arise if the output costs resulting from collective consolidation, C, are smaller than the output

Table 11.1. *Output losses per unit cut in G*

	No foreign cut	Foreign cut
No home cut	0, 0	*B, A*
Home cut	*A, B*	*C, C*

costs, *A*, which result if one country consolidates but the other does not.[9]

It is our conjecture that, for the reasons explained above, there might well be a prisoner's dilemma in a monetary union that would not be present under floating exchange rates.

This is an empirical question, and so we now turn to an empirical investigation of this issue using the MSG model.

Simulating fiscal consolidation with the MSG2 model

Design of our empirical experiments

We simulate the effects of a fiscal consolidation of 2 per cent of GDP, brought about by a one-off, unphased reduction in government expenditure. To clarify the effects we suppose that this contraction is embarked upon in one year, calendar 1999. This consolidation is then supposed to be gradually phased out, over a period of forty years. The idea is that this is consolidation which happens sooner rather than later – i.e. that would have happened eventually, but very slowly – and what we are comparing in the simulation is the effect of doing it sooner rather than later, rather than comparing the effect of doing it permanently rather than never. This consolidation is done, either in France alone or for the whole of Europe, depending on the simulation.

We suppose that any resulting changes in debt interest because of the reduction in public debt are cancelled by means of variations in a 'lump-sum' tax which have no supply-side consequences. (This is a standard method of simulation for the MSG2 model and prevents unstable implosion of debt as a result of reduced interest payments on a reduced debt.) The effect of this assumption, together with the phasing-out

[9] We note that if the effects of consolidation on output are additive, then $B = C - A$. If A is large relative to C then B will actually be negative – i.e. that there will be output gains to reneging on cooperation. A prisoner's dilemma also requires that these output gains to reneging would be large enough to outweigh the loss of the benefits of consolidation which such reneging would bring.

assumption explained above, is that the consolidation causes public debt to fall to a new lower equilibrium level.

The money supply is held constant in all countries when operating under floating exchange rates, or in EMU, the European money supply is held constant. We simulate consolidation in three different ways. First, as a benchmark, we display the effects of consolidation by one country, France, on its own, when all European countries have freely floating exchange rates. Second, we display the effects of consolidation by one country, France, on its own, when all European countries are in EMU. Third we simulate the effect of all European countries consolidating together in EMU (which we believe will be virtually identical to the effect of them all consolidating together when all have freely floating exchange rates). Outcomes are displayed only for France for ease of understanding and comparison.

The MSG2 model

The MSG model was developed by Warwick McKibbin and Jeffrey Sachs, in two distinct stages. The first model, called MSG, formed the basis of a number of papers by the authors in the mid-1980s. This model is also the version which participated in the international model comparison project reported in Bryant *et al.* (1988). This earlier model was a macroeconomic model of the world economy with rational expectations in the foreign exchange market. The parameters were essentially reduced-form parameters calibrated to the estimates of existing macroeconometric models. This model was then completely reconstructed beginning in 1986, following the approach taken by CGE modellers which focuses on individual optimization by economic agents. This new model, called MSG2, is reported in McKibbin and Sachs (1991). The MSG2 model, like CGE models, is based more firmly on micro-foundations than the standard macroeconometric model. But it is also dynamic: it is described by its authors as a dynamic general equilibrium model of a multiregion world economy. Explicit intertemporal optimization of agents forms the basis of structural behavioural equations: in contrast to static CGE models, time and dynamics are of fundamental importance. In addition, as in all macroeconomic models, there is an explicit treatment of the holding of financial assets including money.

In order to be able to fit macro time-series data the behaviour of agents is modified to allow for short-run deviations from optimal behaviour caused by either myopia or by restrictions on the ability of households and firms to borrow at the risk-free bond rate on government debt. Deviations from intertemporal optimizing behaviour take the form of rules of thumb which are consistent with an optimizing agent that does not update predictions based on new information about future events. These rules of thumb are chosen to generate the same steady-state behaviour as optimizing agents. Actual behaviour is assumed to be a weighted average of the optimising and rule of thumb assumption. For example, aggregate consumption is a weighted average of consumption based on wealth and consumption based on current disposable income. The other key modification to the standard market-clearing assumption in CGE models is the allowance for short-run nominal wage rigidity in different countries. As a result, the model has a mix of Keynesian and Classical properties.

The version of the model used in the current chapter consists of the following country blocs: the United States, Japan, Germany, the United Kingdom, France, Italy, the Rest of the EMS (denoted *REMS*),[10] Canada, the Rest of the OECD (denoted *ROECD*),[11] non-oil developing countries (denoted *LDCs*),[12] oil-exporting countries (denoted *OPEC*),[13] and eastern European economies including the Commonwealth of Independent States.[14] The model is of moderate size (about four dozen behavioural equations per country region).

The main features of the model are as follows.

(1) Both the demand and the supply features of the main economies are explicitly featured (which is a reason why it is an attractive vehicle for a much fuller treatment of the questions at hand than the simple demand model set out in the previous section).

(2) Demand equations are based on a combination of intertemporal optimizing behaviour and liquidity-constrained behaviour (which means that there are income feedbacks of the kind identified in the IS curve above). There are explicit demand equations for both exports and imports which depend on foreign demand and relative prices in the manner presented above.

(3) Prices adjust rapidly to equate the supply of and demand for both assets and produced goods, but wages adjust sluggishly to imbalance between the supply of and demand for labour. This gives the model something of the flex-output character of our simple fix-price model above, *but only in the short run.*

---

[10] This group consists of Belgium, Denmark, Ireland and Luxembourg.
[11] This group consists of Australia, Austria, Finland, Iceland, Norway, Spain, Sweden, Switzerland and New Zealand.
[12] Non-oil developing countries are based on the grouping in IMF, *Direction of Trade Statistics* (1996).
[13] Oil exporting countries are based on the grouping in IMF, *Direction of Trade Statistics* (1996).
[14] These countries are Bulgaria, Czechoslovakia, Eastern Germany, Hungary, Poland, Romania, Yugoslavia and the USSR.

(4) The supply side takes explicit account both of the effect of exchange rate change on the costs of imports and thus on prices. It also explicitly considers the intertemporal effects of the accumulation of physical capital and also of the use of intermediate capital goods inputs (whose role in international trade is explicitly modelled).

(5) Major flows such as private physical investment and public physical investment, fiscal deficits, and current account imbalances cumulate into stocks of capital (and equity), infrastructure capital, government debt and net external debt, and as a result the level and composition of national wealth changes over time.

(6) Wealth adjustment determines stock equilibrium in the long run but also feeds back into short-run conditions through the effect of asset proportions on prices in forward-looking share markets, bond markets and foreign exchange markets.

(7) Asset markets are linked globally through the high international mobility of capital.

The careful attention to micro-foundations in the model and its empirical basis makes it particularly suited to checking the usefulness and empirical relevance of the linkages discussed above.

Simulations using the MSG2 model

> *(1): Consolidation in a single country (France) under floating exchange rates*

We will take this experiment as our benchmark (see Figures 11.2 and 11.3).

Output falls in year 1 by about a quarter of the fiscal cut – i.e. the short-run output multiplier is only about 0.25. That the short-run multiplier should be so small should come as no surprise under a regime of floating exchange rates, with nominal wage stickiness. In the short run the nominal (and real) exchange rate depreciates by about 8 per cent and the trade balance improves by about 1.5 per cent of GDP (i.e. by three-quarters of the fiscal cut). Investment falls a little because output is depressed, even though the short-term nominal interest rate falls (and even though the short-term real interest rate falls even more than the nominal rate); and consumption initially falls too, because output falls. There is an initial burst of inflation – because of the currency depreciation – and this is why the short-term real interest rate falls more than the short-term nominal rate, but this quickly dies away.

In these results, the effects of lower long-term real interest rates appear to have little influence. The medium- to long-run outlook (i.e. out to the full 45 years shown and beyond) is one in which nominal and real interest

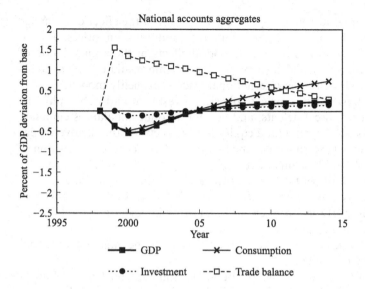

Figure 11.2   France fiscal adjustment – Europe-wide flexible exchange rates: national accounts aggregates, 1995–2015

rates, Europe-wide, are very slightly lower, because of the French conso-lidation, and thus in which there is a very slightly higher level of capital and output. (France does contribute something to the European sum.) But these effects are not very large. In the long run, the adjustment comes about primarily through changes in consumption. Fiscal consolidation leads to lower external indebtedness, the real exchange rate appreciates and the terms of trade are improved because of the need for less foreign debt service, and so consumption can be higher.

In the transition to the long run the critical role is played by the recovery of consumption. This is brought about by rising real income as a result of the real exchange rate appreciation, and consumers' forward looking expectations of this. Notice that such a strategy is in a sense a 'beggar-thy-neighbour' strategy. All of the budgetary improvement will be brought about by an improved trade balance *vis-à-vis* other European countries and the rest of the world.

(2): Consolidation in a single country (France) within EMU

Fiscal consolidation under EMU is expected to look different, for two reasons, both discussed in the theoretical appendix. First, since inter-est rates are now determined Europe-wide, it is not possible independently

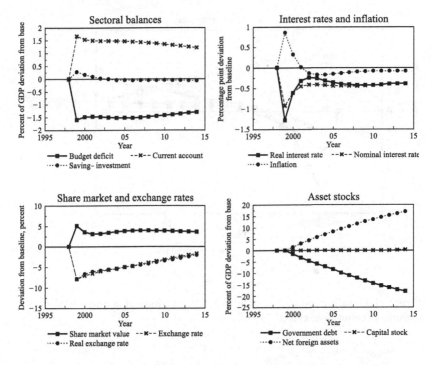

Figure 11.3 France fiscal adjustment – Europe-wide flexible exchange rates: sectoral balances, interest rates and inflation, share market and exchange rates, asset stocks, 1995–2015

to cut interest rates simultaneously with fiscal tightening, so adjustment to fiscal consolidation by stimulating interest-sensitive expenditures is not possible. Second, since the real exchange rate of this country *vis-à-vis* the rest of Europe cannot be easily depreciated in the short run, adjustment to fiscal consolidation through an expansion in exports *to the rest of Europe* also becomes more difficult.[15]

Referring to figures 11.4 and 11.5, it is clear that output now falls in year 1 by slightly more than the full extent of the fiscal cut – i.e. the short-run output multiplier is just over unity. That the short-run multiplier should be so large should come as no surprise under fixed exchange rates, because

[15.] This is nothing more than the familiar problem that it not possible to have the trilogy of integrated capital markets, fixed exchange rates and independent monetary policy. With a low degree of capital mobility it would be possible to undertake fiscal consolidation, retain a pegged exchange rate and at the same time cut interest rates so as to lessen, at least partly, the development of unemployment and the emergence of a trade surplus at the expense of other countries.

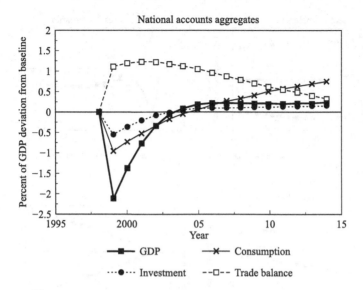

Figure 11.4   Impact on France of a French fiscal contraction under EMU:
national accounts aggregates, 1995–2015

of the absence of the damping effects discussed above. In the short run
both consumption and investment fall significantly, because output is
depressed, and also because, with nominal interest rates hardly falling
and prices falling because of the slump, the real interest rate actually
rises. (This is just the Walters Critique of fixed exchange rate regimes.)
The trade balance improves, because of the fall in output and also because
the fall in the nominal interest rate is not completely negligible since
France has some size in Europe.

The theoretical analysis of the appendix suggests to us that the Europe-
wide effects of this simulation should be more or less identical to those of
the previous simulation, since the same shock has been applied and all that
differs between the two is intra-European monetary arrangements. This is
confirmed by noting that – as in the previous simulation – these are short-
run results in which the effects of lower long-term real interest rates appear
to have little influence. As in the previous simulation, the medium-to-long-
run outlook (i.e. out to the full 45 years of the simulation, beyond the
length of time shown) is one in which nominal and real interest rates,
Europe-wide, are very slightly lower, because of the French consolidation,
and thus in which there is a very slightly higher level of capital and output.
But these effects are not large.

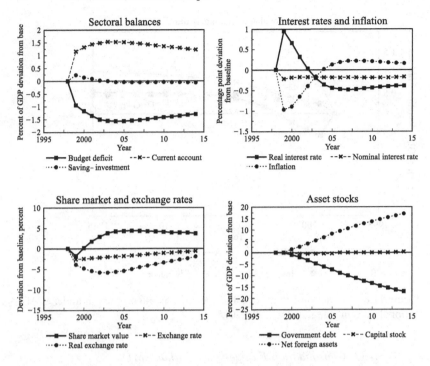

Figure 11.5   Impact on France of a French fiscal contraction under EMU: sectoral balances, interest rates and inflation, share market and exchange rates, asset stocks, 1995–2015

Notice in addition that by about fifteen years out, *all* of the differences between the two experiments have essentially disappeared. Although our theoretical analysis was not set up to demonstrate this, such an outcome is what we would expect. One would expect that effects of intra-European monetary arrangements would wash out after a decade and a half.

Notice that such a strategy is – as in the previous case – in a sense a 'beggar-thy-neighbour' strategy. Just as previously, essentially all of the budgetary improvement will be brought about an improved trade balance *vis-à-vis* both other European countries and the rest of the world.

We have shown that the effect of fixed exchange rates is to make fiscal consolidation by a single country much more costly in terms of the short-run loss of output. We have thus illustrated empirically the first major argument of this chapter.

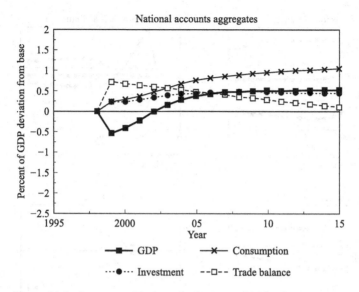

Figure 11.6   Impact on France of a Europe-wide fiscal contraction under EMU: national accounts aggregates, 1995–2015

(3): Consolidation Europe-wide (within EMU)

We will now consider the same time-profile consolidation (a cut in government expenditure by 2 per cent of GDP) Europe-wide. We have undertaken this under the assumption of EMU, but believe that since the shock applied is symmetrical almost identical results would obtain under floating exchange rates. (In the theoretical model, intra-European monetary arrangements were of no consequence at all; in empirical work, they will matter only to the extent of asymmetries in economic structures.) From now on we will speak as if they *are* identical.

Referring to figures 11.6 and 11.7, output now falls in year 1 by about a quarter of the fiscal cut – i.e. the short-run output multiplier is only about 0.25 (exactly the same as in the France-only case) , and output immediately starts recovering, so that the cumulative output loss is much less than in the France-only case. That the short-run multiplier should be so small when we fiscally consolidate for Europe as a whole requires comment. As suggested by the theoretical analysis, consolidation elsewhere will be dragging down French output because other European countries will be importing less from France. Furthermore, even although the French nominal (and real) exchange rate now depreciates by the very large figure of more than 12 per cent (c.f. 8 per cent in simulation (1)) the trade balance improves by about 0.75 per cent of GDP (c.f. 1.75 per cent in simulation (2)).

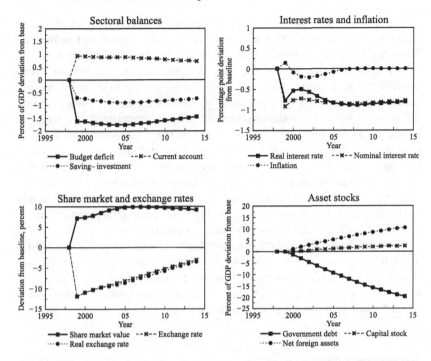

Figure 11.7   Impact on France of a Europe-wide fiscal contraction under EMU: sectoral balances, interest rates and inflation, share market and exchange rates, asset stocks, 1995–2015

This discrepancy occurs because Europe is less open, something to which to which the earlier theoretical analysis also drew to our attention. The explanation lies in the behaviour of investment and consumption. Investment now *rises*, even though the fall in output is identical to that in simulation (1), and even though the short-term fall in the nominal interest rate is identical to that in simulation (2) (as we might expect with European monetary policy now being conducted in the same manner as French monetary policy was in simulation (1), in response to essentially identical output changes[16]), a point which is reinforced by noting that the short-term real interest rate falls by less than it did in simulation (1) (because imported inflation is much less as a result of other European countries depreciating along with France). Consumption rises, too, even though output falls.

[16.] Although there is more inflation in France in simulation (1) this is imported – it results from the currency depreciation – and does not matter for the demand for money which depends on output and on output prices not consumer prices.

The reason is that these are short-run results in which the effects of lower long-term real interest rates appear to have a very significant influence. The simulation is one in which all the way from the short to the medium to the long run (i.e. out to the full 45 years shown and beyond) real interest rates, Europe-wide, are nearly one per centage point lower, because the Europe-wide consolidation has lowered the global demand for savings. Investment thus booms, absorbing approximately a quarter of the fiscal cut for a significant length of time. Consumption booms, too, because the investment leads to higher capital and output, and thus to higher income. Consumers discount this back to the present (at the lower real interest rate) to give higher human wealth now. This is why consumption rises immediately. Notice that such a strategy is very much not a 'beggar-thy-neighbour' strategy. Half of the budgetary improvement is reflected in increased investment *minus* saving.

We have shown that the effect of a collective fiscal consolidation can be a much lower level of output loss than if this consolidation is done by one country acting on its own under floating, if the effects of long-term real interest rates are large enough. We have thus illustrated empirically the second main proposition of this chapter.

The prisoner's dilemma issue

Empirical implications

Our empirical simulations of the MSG2 model have given us information on the empirical counterpart of the home-country entries in the bottom row of the pay-off matrix in table 11.1. We have seen that, in the MSG2 model, home output loss is *slightly larger* under floating when the home country acts alone as compared with when the foreign country cuts as well as the home country. Nevertheless, the differences in the output losses in the simulations are not large. Thus, under floating exchange rates, consolidation could have a prisoner's dilemma structure, but this is not likely: consolidation which is desirable collectively is probably also desirable individually.

Our empirical simulations of the MSG2 model have also given us information on the empirical counterpart of the home-country entries of the table 11.1 matrix under EMU. In particular, we have seen that, in the MSG2 model, home output loss is *very much larger* under EMU when the home country acts alone as compared with when the foreign country cuts as well as the home country. Thus, under EMU, consolidation could well have a prisoner's dilemma structure: consolidation which is desirable collectively may well be difficult to achieve without cooperation.

The Maastricht criteria and the Stability Pact: a 'solution' to the coordination problem for deficit reduction?

If European policy authorities actually want to cut the fiscal deficit but are not indifferent to the unemployment consequences, then our analysis suggests that they do indeed face a coordination problem under EMU. We believe that the Maastricht criteria, and the Stability Pact, can be seen as a response to this coordination difficulty by enforcing the cooperative solution between the fiscal authorities.

We see the actual quantitative numbers – deficits down to 3 per cent on entry as a result of the Maastricht criteria and heading down towards 1 per cent as a result of the Stability Pact – as, in some sense, the actual outcome of some process of game-theoretic reasoning by Europe's leaders. They see – we argue – this prisoner's dilemma. They see the prospect of an integrated Europe-wide fiscal and monetary package, with the kind of contours that we have displayed in the simulations – in particular, with a fall in short-term interest rates, the exchange rate and long-term interest rates, and an associated improvement in the trade balance and investment. Such Europe-wide fiscal consolidation, with a floating euro and a sensible Europe-wide monetary policy, does not look too difficult. Fiscal co-ordination allows Europe as a whole to carry out fiscal consolidation in a manner that is even easier than if this were done by a single country with an independent monetary policy and a floating exchange rate.[17]

Cautions, and the need for further work

Our argument has been buttressed by evidence from MSG2 model. But this is not without difficulty.

The MSG2 model is a forward-looking model whose jump variables adjust to place the trajectories on a path towards a new equilibrium. This is a path along which the spot depreciation in the exchange rate reflects both the expected change in the long-run equilibrium exchange rate and

---

[17.] Notice, of course, that such a strategy has world implications. Some – perhaps a large part – of Europe's budgetary improvement would be brought about by the effects of exchange rate depreciation on the trade balance. Such effects will be directly at the expense of a worsened trade balance, and worsened budgetary position, of other countries in the rest of the world. But the rest of the world would also experience lower real interest rates. We do not examine game-theoretic interactions with the rest of the world here.

all future deviations of home from foreign interest rate, and in which the spot fall in the long-term real interest rate reflects both the long-run equilibrium real interest rate and any deviations of the short-term real interest rate from this rate.

The following questions have not been addressed:

(1) Will the fall in interest rates which results be large enough?
(2) Will the large currency depreciation shown in the MSG2 simulations be forthcoming?
(3) Will the necessary investment response be forthcoming in response to lower equilibrium real interest rates?
(4) Will the forward-looking consumption response be forthcoming in response to lower equilibrium real interest rates?

The answers to all of these questions may, in fact, be 'no'. However there is evidence in Gagnon, Masson and McKibbin (1996) that this model and the two other expectation-driven models surveyed in that paper, performed well in their *ex ante* predictions of the effects of German unification. Nonetheless, there is reason for caution.

- First of all, is there any evidence that a fledgling European Central Bank (ECB), keen to establish its credibility, will cut interest rates as required to help stem output falls, even by the small amount shown in these simulations?
- Secondly, will the ECU fall by the large amount shown in the MSG2 simulations? Note that the forward-looking exchange rate behaviour in this part of the model is necessarily assumed rather than being well grounded in evidence.
- Thirdly, and fundamentally, will the rise in investment be forthcoming? In the MSG model the demand for investment comes from a Cobb–Douglas production function, which means that a 100 basis-points change in the real interest rate causes a very large change in the desired capital stock; and the relevant real interest rate is the rationally foreseen real interest rate. We should note that available empirical evidence suggests that the response of investment to interest rate changes in most European countries may actually be relatively small (although it is difficult to measure the expected real interest rate required for empirical testing) – considerably smaller than in the US case. Furthermore, to obtain the required rise in investment will be fundamentally dependent on growth expectations – or, more broadly, confidence effects – which may be problematic.
- Finally, will the rise in consumption be forthcoming? Even though in the MSG2 model the majority of consumers are liquidity-constrained, nevertheless the forward-lookingness is doing a lot of the work in causing consumption to rise.

If the answers to these questions are 'no', then Proposition 3 from our simple theoretical model shows that the effect of a fiscal consolidation, Europe-wide, will not be to solve a coordination problem but to create an even larger output loss.

Because the answers to all of these questions appear so problematic, and because the issue is so important, it seems essential to explore the sensitivity of our results to the underlying assumptions. Such work is underway at present, using the Oxford Economic Forecasting World Model; preliminary results suggest that, if the outcomes are to be robust, the fiscal consolidation may need to be accompanied by a preemptive cut in interest rates.

Time will tell which set of modelling results is closer to reality. However with a divergence of views as embodied in these models it is important for policy-makers to be ready to adjust quickly as evidence of the mechanisms embodied in each model becomes more apparent.

Conclusions

This chapter has explored the circumstances under which fiscal consolidation in a European monetary union has the features of a prisoner's dilemma and has produced empirical evidence to show that these circumstances may actually pertain. It has thus produced a convincing argument for an understanding of the Stability Pact as a perceived solution to a collective-action problem. Our theoretical argument has been buttressed by evidence from the MSG2 model. Nevertheless the argument is not without its weakness – concerning the required falls in short-term interest rates, the exchange rate and long-term interest rates, and whether the trade balance and investment really would pick up as required.

Appendix   *The output costs of fiscal consolidation in EMU: inter-country spillovers*

A two-country short-run European model

In this appendix, we sketch a simple model in which the factors determining the output costs of consolidation, which were considered informally in the text of the chapter, are formally identified. The model is designed to illustrate how these output costs of consolidation are influenced by the spillovers between countries within EMU.

It is a model of a two-country 'European' economy, constructed and solved in such a way as to highlight spillovers. The model is short-run, in that prices are fixed and output is demand-determined. All variables are treated as differences from a pre-shock equilibrium, so a value of zero simply means 'no change'. All shocks are treated as temporary, and there is no explicit treatment of adjustment dynamics, although these play an important part in the simulations reported in the text.

For convenience we now define the symbols which we will use in what follows. Starred variables, where they appear, are those for the foreign European country. Variables for the rest of the world ('the United States') are all set to zero.

y level of domestic final production, measured in proportional deviations from its initial level

y^* level of final production within the foreign European economy, again measured in proportional deviations from its initial level

r domestic nominal interest rate, measured in percentage points

r^* nominal interest rate in the foreign European economy, measured in percentage points

e nominal exchange rate of the domestic economy *vis-à-vis* the US dollar, defined as the domestic currency price of dollars, so that an increase in e denotes a real depreciation, and measured as percentage deviations from initial level

e^* nominal exchange rate of the foreign European economy *vis-à-vis* the US, defined according to the same convention, and measured in the same way as e

v long-term real interest rate.

g a fiscal shock to domestic demand.

The IS curves for the home and the foreign country

Home output is determined by demand, according to an open-economy IS curve.

$$y = \sigma e + \delta(e - e^*) - \gamma r - \mu y + \eta y^* - \xi v + \lambda g. \qquad (11A.1)$$

The first two terms are competitiveness effects. These come in two parts, the first depending on competitiveness *vis-à-vis* the US, e, and the second depending on competitiveness *vis-à-vis* the foreign European country, $e - e^*$. The coefficients on these two competitiveness terms will depend on the price elasticity of demand for exports, on the openness of the economy, and on the relative importance of intra-European trade vs. non-European trade, but the details of this need not concern us here.

The next term shows the effects on demand of domestic interest rates. The import leakage is denoted by μy, and the term ηy^* shows the effects of higher activity in the foreign European country on the demand for home-country output. The term ξv represents the effect of the long-term real interest rate on investment, and on the discounting of human and non-human wealth and thus on consumption. The final term shows a shock to domestic demand coming from home fiscal consolidation.

We write a similar IS curve for the foreign country.

$$y^* = \sigma e^* + \delta(e^* - e) - \gamma r^* - \mu y^* + \eta y - \xi v^* + \lambda g^* \qquad (11A.2)$$

Monetary policy and exchange rates

We will examine the effects of two different types of monetary policy.

Floating exchange rates in each European economy

$$r = \beta y \qquad (11A.3)$$

$$e = -\theta r \qquad (11A.4)$$

where β, $\theta > 0$.

One interpretation of (11A.3) is that it shows the conduct of monetary policy under a floating exchange rate regime with a fixed money supply, implying that the interest rate falls whenever the nominal income falls (which in a fixed-price model means whenever output falls) This is the setup which we impose in the simulations below of the MSG2 model. The coefficient of response which we use, 1.66, is equal to the inverse of the interest rate semi-elasticity in the demand for money, which is equal to 0.6.

An alternative interpretation of this rule is that it is an explicit interest rate rule, in which the nominal interest rate is lowered whenever nominal income is below target. Such a nominal income rule is a special case of the general class of Bryant-Henderson-McKibbin–Taylor (BHMT) rules[18] (see Henderson and McKibbin in Bryant, 1993 and Taylor, 1994).

Equation (11A.4) shows the size of exchange rate appreciation caused by a gap between the home interest rate, r, and the US interest rate (which does not change and so is zero) In a simple Mundell–Fleming model with

---

[18.] The coefficient which Taylor (1994) uses, of around 1.5, is almost exactly equal to that which we have taken from inverting the demand for money in the MSG2 model. But more recent versions of the BHMT rule such as those analysed by Henderson and McKibbin in Bryant (1993) have a smaller coefficient, of 0.5, and apply this not to the proportional deviation of nominal income from base (i.e. to the log of output plus log of the *price level*), but to the deviation from base of the sum of the log of output and the log of *inflation*. None of these important, but finer, points matter for the analysis of this chapter.

perfect capital mobility and static exchange rate expectations, this effect would be infinitely large, i.e. $\theta \to$ infinity (it means that, whatever the monetary policy under operation, home interest rates can not end up different from US interest rates). But we wish for something more in the spirit of a simple Dornbusch model, in which a gap between home and foreign interest rates is possible and we represent this by a value of θ of less than infinity: we suppose that the interest rate differential is offset by an expectation that the exchange rate will gradually return to its equilibrium level.[19]

We add similar equations for the foreign country

$$r^* = \beta y^* \tag{11A.5}$$

$$e^* = -\theta r^*. \tag{11A.6}$$

European Monetary Union

In the EMU regime, interest rates are the same in both countries. They are set by a European Central Bank (ECB). This bank follows an interest rate rule of exactly the kind displayed in (11.3) and (11.4) for Europe as a whole. One interpretation is simply that the ECB fixes the European money supply, and this is how we implement the rule in our simulations below. The other interpretation is that the ECB follows *exactly* the same BHMT rule for Europe as would be followed by an individual European central bank.[20]

$$r = \beta(y + y^*)/2 \tag{11A.7}$$

$$r^* = \beta(y + y^*)/2. \tag{11A.8}$$

In this EMU, the euro floats *vis-à-vis* the rest of the world. European exchange rates are one and the same. We suppose, reasonably, that the connection between the exchange rate and the interest rate at the European level is the same as it was for each of its component parts under floating.[21] The exchange rate equations for Europe thus become

$$e = -\theta r \tag{11A.9}$$

$$e^* = e. \tag{11A.10}$$

[19.] In our setup in which all shocks are temporary this equilibrium will be equal to the old value.

[20.] Division by 2 is necessary because of choice of units: interest rates rise, Europe-wide, by the same amount as they would in the single-economy case if European output is, *on average*, above base by the same amount as it was in the single economy.

[21.] This finesses the (second-order) point that the macroeconomic behaviour of Europe as a whole is slightly different from that of its constituent economies.

Henceforth, in the EMU case we will simply refer to r as the European interest rate and e as the European exchange rate.

The long-term real interest rate

We argue that – independently of monetary regime, the long-term real interest rate is determined Europe-wide so as to equalize the demand for and the supply of savings obtaining when resources are fully utilized. We then argue, in a shorthand fashion, that this real interest rate will be lower the lower is the *sum* of government expenditure, Europe-wide[22]

$$v = \alpha(g + g^*).\qquad(11A.11)$$

To save on parameters we define $\psi = 2\xi\alpha$.

Solving

By utilizing the simple sums-and-differences approach due to Aoki (1981)[23] we may write the above two-country model in an intermediate form that helps with understanding the results that follow. We first add the equations for the home and the foreign country, to obtain a model for Europe as a whole (a 'sums' model) and then subtract the equations for foreign from those for home, to obtain a model for the differences between home and foreign (a 'differences' model). There will, of course, be two ways of doing this, depending on whether there are freely floating exchange rates within Europe, or an EMU with an externally floating exchange rate.

We denote sums by the subscript s and differences by the subscript d; thus for any variable, x,

$$x_s = x + x^*,$$

and

$$x_d = x - x^*.$$

Thus

$$x = (x_s + x_d)/2.$$

---

[22] In full long-term equilibrium with integrated global capital markets, interest rates can only be lower Europe-wide if they are lower world-wide, but we abstract from this effect.

[23] See also Henderson and McKibbin (1993).

Sums and differences under floating

The sums model may be written as

$$y_s = \sigma e_s - \gamma r_s + (\eta - \mu)y_s + (\lambda - \psi)g_s \tag{11A.12}$$

$$r_s = \beta y_s \tag{11A.13}$$

$$e_s = -\theta r_s. \tag{11A.14}$$

Substituting (11A.12)–(11A.13) and defining $\phi = \beta(\sigma\theta + \gamma)$ gives:

$$y_s = g_s[(\lambda - \psi)/(1 + \phi + \mu - \eta)]. \tag{11A.15}$$

The differences model is

$$y_d = (\sigma + 2\delta)e_d - \gamma r_d - (\eta - \mu)y_d + \lambda g_d \tag{11A.16}$$

$$r_d = \beta y_d \tag{11A.17}$$

$$e_d = -\theta r_d, \tag{11A.18}$$

which gives

$$y_d = g_d[\lambda/(1 + \phi + 2\theta\beta\delta + \mu + \eta]. \tag{11A.19}$$

The effect on home output y of an own-fiscal change is simply $(y_s + y_d)/2$. When comparing the own-fiscal policy change with the co-ordinated-fiscal policy change it is clear that the size of the differences matters. In fact, we don't need to calculate the own-country multiplier from the sums and differences multipliers to get the intuition as to what parameters matter for the relative effects of home vs. coordinated fiscal policy changes. We can do all this from the sums and difference multipliers.

One can immediately note that, under floating, the relative size of the sums and differences multipliers are ambiguous – i.e.

$$\partial y_d/\partial g_d \gtrless \partial y_s/\partial g_s. \tag{11A.20}$$

There are two counteracting tendencies which give rise to the indeterminacy underlying result (11A.20), which come from the two important ways in which the structure of the sums model differs from the structure of the differences model.

First there are what we might call Keynesian reasons. These in turn have two components.

(1) There are *positive* income feedback effects in the sums model, and negative income feedbacks in the differences model. In the sums model foreign interaction effects augment disturbances to the IS

curves: demand shocks are 'bottled-up' within the European sum. An alternative way of putting this point is simply that the sums model is less open than a basic open-economy model would be, and so the damping due to imports is less, in particular it is $\mu - \eta$ rather than μ. In the differences model the foreign interaction effects damp disturbances to the IS curves: demand shocks are dissipated when considering intra-European differences. An alternative way of putting this point is simply that because disturbances to output are positively transmitted between European countries, the damping due to imports is now $\mu + \eta$ rather than μ. A rise in output leads to a smaller change in the differences in outputs between the countries.

(2) The damping effects of changes in competitiveness effects are *smaller* in the sums model – for Europe as a whole. This is because when output rises, and thus interest rates rise, Europe-wide, these effects operate only through the parameter σ, showing the effects of competitiveness on net exports external to Europe – this is because intra-European competitiveness effects are of no concern for the European total. By contrast, the damping effects of changes in competitiveness are *stronger* in the differences model. In that model, when output and interest rates rise in one European country relative to another, these damping effects operate not only on the differences between the countries' demands for rest of the world (US) goods but also on the differences in their demands for each other's goods, and both of these latter effects depend on the difference between the competitiveness of each country[24]).

On the other hand there are what we might call neoclassical reasons, which tend to make the sums multiplier smaller than the differences multiplier (i.e. the own-country multiplier bigger than the combined multiplier). The fall in the long-term interest rate resulting from the fiscal consolidation is a Europe-wide phenomenon. This stimulatory effect operating through the parameter ψ, does not appear in the differences model. It is thus possible for the coordinated fiscal contraction to have a smaller output effect than undertaking a fiscal contraction alone if the fall in long-term interest rates is powerful enough.

Sums and differences under EMU

The sums model for EMU is absolutely identical to that under floating, since intra-European monetary arrangements affect only intra-country

[24]. This is why there is a 2δ term in the IS equation.

differences and make no difference to Europe's aggregate behaviour.[25]
That is

$$(\partial y_s/\partial g_s)^{\text{EMU}} = (\partial y_s/\partial g_s)^{\text{FLOAT}}. \qquad (11\text{A}.21)$$

The differences model is still given by

$$y_d = (\sigma + 2\delta)e_d - \gamma r_d - (\eta - \mu)y_d + \lambda g_d. \qquad (11\text{A}.22)$$

But now we have

$$r_d = 0 \qquad (11\text{A}.23)$$

$$e_d = 0 \qquad (11\text{A}.24)$$

and so

$$y_d = g_d[\lambda/(1 + \mu + \eta)]. \qquad (11\text{A}.25)$$

This immediately enables us to write

$$(\partial y_d/\partial g_d)^{\text{EMU}} > (\partial y_d/\partial g_d)^{\text{FLOAT}}. \qquad (11\text{A}.26)$$

This result, together with the result that the 'sums' model under both
regimes is identical, implies that the effects of an own-fiscal policy change
must be larger than the effects of a coordinated-fiscal policy change in the
case of EMU compared with that under floating.

This result – that in the 'differences' model the output fall from own-
fiscal consolidation under EMU is necessarily smaller than it is under
floating – follows immediately from one critical difference between the
structure of the 'differences' model under EMU and that under floating.
This is that since all of the intra-European damping effects due to intra-
European changes in interest rates and in competitiveness are now absent,
all that remains (under both EMU and floating) is damping effects due to
the intra-European import leakages.[26]

Finally, we may also write

$$(\partial y_d/\partial g_d)^{\text{EMU}} \gtrless (\partial y_s/\partial g_s)^{\text{FLOAT}} \qquad (11\text{A}.27)$$

depending on the parameters ψ and ϕ. The counteracting tendencies which
give rise to the indeterminacy underlying this result are now rather different from those underlying result (11A.19).

[25.] While this statement is true for our model, of course it may not end up actually being true
for Europe. The ECB may not operate the same policy as would the individual countries.
[26.] What this account misses is damping effects due to relative price changes. But since, under
EMU, such relative price adjustment is driven by relative output changes, nothing is lost
qualitatively by this omission.

First, as in the previous case, there are *positive* income feedback effects in the 'sums' model, and *negative* income feedbacks in the 'differences' model. (For fuller explanation see the discussion following (11A.19).

Second there are damping effects of changes in nominal interest rates, and of the changes in competitiveness which flow from these, operating in the 'sums' model - i.e. Europe-wide – but none at all in the 'differences' model - i.e. within Europe. Thus on this score the output fall now tends to be *smaller* in the 'sums' model. Similarly, for neoclassical reasons, the effects are also smaller in the 'sums' model: the stimulatory effect of a fall in the long-term interest rate is a Europe-wide phenomenon and does not appear in the 'differences' model.

Thus if output is to fall more in the 'sums' model than in the 'differences' model under EMU we require *both* that the effect of the long-term fall in interest rates for Europe as a whole is not very large *and* that short-term interest rates do not fall by very much (and thus that the exchange rate does not change by very much).

Three propositions on the output costs of fiscal consolidation in Europe

The above analysis enables us to demonstrate the following three propositions concerning the negative output effects of fiscal consolidation.

Proposition 1: If a single country is undergoing fiscal consolidation, the output loss for that country is larger under EMU than under floating.

We have already demonstrated above that since

$$(\partial y_s / \partial g_s)^{\text{EMU}} = (\partial y_s / \partial g_s)^{\text{FLOAT}}$$

and

$$(\partial y_d / \partial g_d)^{\text{EMU}} > (\partial y_d / \partial g_d)^{\text{FLOAT}}$$

then given

$$y = (y_s + y_d)/2$$

it must be the case that

$$(\partial y / \partial g)^{\text{EMU}} > (\partial y / \partial g)^{\text{FLOAT}}.$$

The reason for this is simple. Under floating, less of the output fall occurs in the home country because of the damping effects which operate through changes in interest rates and competitiveness and which push more of the output fall onto the other country; these do not operate under EMU.

Proposition 2: In a world in which the effects of long-term interest rates, ψ, are strong then the output loss when the whole of Europe undergoes consolidation at the same time can actually be smaller than if one country alone with floating exchange rates undertakes consolidation of a similar size.

The reasoning behind the proposition is then straightforward. We know that the 'sums' multiplier for a fiscal consolidation can tend to be larger than the 'differences' multiplier because (1) the demand effects are not bottled up within one country but are bottled up Europe-wide, and (2) the floating exchange rate shock-absorber mechanism is less powerful in the 'sums' model than for the 'differences' model because under floating the consolidating country can offload some of the output fall not only on to the rest of the world but on to the other country as well by means of a relative currency depreciation. Nevertheless the ambiguity arises because these effects can be over-ruled by the effects of the fall in long-term real European interest rates, which operates in the 'sums' model only.

Proposition 3: In a world in which *both* the effects, ψ, of long-term real interest rates are weak *and* the interest rate responsiveness β is low then the output loss when the whole of Europe undergoes consolidation at the same time can actually be larger than that if one country undertakes consolidation of a similar size alone within EMU.

The reasoning behind the proposition is also straightforward. We know that the 'sums' multiplier for a fiscal consolidation can tend to be larger than the 'differences' multiplier (whether under EMU or floating) because the demand effects are not bottled up within one country but are bottled up Europe-wide. However for Europe as a whole there are interest rate or exchange rate shock-absorber mechanisms whereas these do not operate at all within the 'differences' model under EMU. Furthermore there are the damping effects of the fall in long-term real European interest rates, which operate in the 'sums' model only. Nevertheless in a world in which both the effects, ψ, of long-term real interest rates are weak and the interest rate responsiveness, β, is low, these damping effects will be low. In that case, the 'sums' multiplier will actually be bigger than the 'differences' multiplier.

References

Allsopp, C. and Vines, D. (1996). 'Fiscal Policy and EMU', *National Institute Economics Review*, 158: 91–107

Allsopp, C., Davies, G. and Vines, D. (1995). 'Regional Macroeconomic Policy, Fiscal Federalism and European Integration', *Oxford Review of Economic Policy*, 11: 126–44

Allsopp, C., McKibbin, W. and Vines, D. (1998). 'Fiscal Consolidation in Europe: Is the Stability and Growth Pact a Solution to a Prisoners' Dilemma?, Institute of Economics and Statistics, Oxford University, mimeo

Allsopp, C., Davies, G., McKibbin, W. and Vines, D. (1997). 'Monetary and Fiscal Stabilisation of Demand Shocks Within Europe', *Review of International Economics*, 5: 55–77

Aoki, M. (1981). *Dynamic Analysis of Open Economies*, New York: Academic Press

Bryant, R., Henderson, D. W., Holtham, G., Hooper, P. and Symansky, S. A. (eds.) (1988). *Empirical Macroeconomics for Interdependent Economies*, Washington, DC: Brookings Institution

Bryant, R., Hooper, P. and Mann, C. (1993). *Evaluating Policy Regimes: New Research in Empirical Economics*, Washington, DC: Brookings Institution

Buti, M., Franco, D. and Ongena, H. (1998). 'Fiscal Discipline and Flexibility in EMU: The Implementation of the Stability and Growth Pact', *Oxford Review of Economic Policy*, 14: 81–97

Eichengreen, B. (1997). *European Monetary Unification: Theory, Practice and Analysis*: Cambridge, Mass.: MIT Press

Gagnon, J., Masson, P. and McKibbin, W. (1996). 'German Unification: What Have We Learned from Multi-Country Models?', *Economic Modelling*, 13: 467–97

Henderson, D. W. and McKibbin, W. (1993). 'An Assessment of Some Basic Monetary Policy Regime Pairs: Analytical and Simulation Results from Simple Multi-region Macroeconomic Models', in R. Bryant, P. Hooper and C. Mann, (1993). *Evaluating Policy Regimes: New Research in Empirical Macroeconomics*, Washington, DC: Brookings Institution: 45–218

IMF (1996). *World Economic Outlook*, Washington, DC: International Monetary Fund

McKibbin, W. and Sachs, J. (1991). *Global Linkages*, Washington, DC: Brookings Institution

McKibbin, W. and Wilcoxen, P. (1998). 'Macroeconomic Volatility in General Equilibrium', *Discussion Paper in International Economics*, 140, Washington, DC: Brookings Institution

Taylor, J. B. (1994). *Macroeconomic Policy in a World Economy: From Econometric Design to Practical Operation*, New York: Norton

12 Could the 'ins' hurt the 'outs'? A welfare analysis of international fiscal links

Giancarlo Corsetti and Paolo Pesenti

Introduction

The fiscal convergence criteria in the Treaty of Maastricht and the fiscal rules agreed upon with the Treaty of Amsterdam have generated a considerable debate in the economic literature. Early contributions have analysed the economic rationale for imposing quantitative limits to debt and deficits as prerequisites for joining the European Monetary Union (EMU) (see, for instance, Buiter, Corsetti and Roubini, 1993). Later on, with the Stability and Growth Pact (SGP, hereafter Stability Pact), the adoption of strict policy rules as a permanent feature of the European fiscal constitution has motivated analyses of their long-run implications (see, for instance, De Grauwe, 1998; Eichengreen and Wyplosz, 1998).

While this vast body of literature has settled a number of theoretical and empirical issues, the desirability of imposing permanent quantitative fiscal rules remains quite controversial. According to the consensus view, their main economic rationale relies on a combination of the following arguments: (1) to prevent undue pressures on the European Central Bank (ECB) from countries with large debt and deficits, (2) to minimize the danger of systemic financial crises that could be triggered by debt repudiation in a country member of EMU, and (3) to offset the distortions caused by the presence of a political bias towards excessive deficits. As stressed by several authors, however, in all these cases rigid fiscal rules are not the best institutional response to the underlying problems. In addition, a number of issues remain unsolved, including the implications of fiscal rules on output and unemployment and the sustainability of alternative strategies to reduce budget deficits (spending cuts vs. tax increases, reducing public investment vs. cutting current spending).

With a few exceptions, the available analyses are based on models lacking micro-foundations – and, most crucially, tend to downplay economic

320

spillovers across countries: they focus instead on the domestic implications of domestic fiscal retrenchment. The approach commonly followed in the literature thus falls short in two important respects.

First, the lack of micro-foundations hampers the possibility of carrying out proper welfare analyses. The positive predictions of economic models regarding variables such as output, inflation, growth and interest rates need to be evaluated in terms of their implications for national or union-wide welfare. This is usually accomplished either in an informal way – based on intuitive reasoning – or by positing ad hoc social welfare functions. As is well known, the shortfall of such a methodology is that it may lead to misleading results, reflecting the arbitrary choice of the implicit or explicit welfare weights assigned to different variables.

Second, downplaying international spillovers blurs fundamental issues in the cost–benefit analysis of participating in EMU and accepting its Stability Pact. From the standpoint of a prospective member of EMU, the choice of status of 'in' or 'out' depends crucially on the fundamental interactions between the two groups. The lack of a proper framework for the analysis of international fiscal links severely limits our ability to understand the terms of this choice.

Although the literature has long suffered from a 'theoretical gap' on these issues (see, for instance, Persson and Tabellini, 1995), recent developments in open-economy macroeconomics have opened new perspectives for the study of the mechanism of international policy transmission. Such perspectives appear to be particularly promising for the analysis of Euro-related issues. The goal of this chapter is to offer a preliminary theoretical application of these new developments in the literature, focused on their fiscal dimension. Our framework builds upon the 'new open-economy macroeconomics' model, following Obstfeld and Rogoff (1995, 1996) and Corsetti and Pesenti (1997), among others. Taking as a datum the existence of strict fiscal rules that the member countries of a monetary union must satisfy, in our analysis we study the long-run welfare implications of such policy stances for both the 'ins' (the member countries themselves) and the 'outs' (considered either as the countries at the periphery of the system – say, the rest of the EU – that remain free to determine their fiscal stance or, in more general terms, the rest of the world).

A notable feature of the analytical framework proposed in this chapter is the possibility of carrying out a consistent analysis of both positive and normative aspects of the international transmission of fiscal policy. The model can be solved in closed form, thus enhancing formal tractability and simplicity while clarifying analytically the logic of welfare changes. On the negative side, to highlight the core features of the model, we focus our analysis on its fundamental properties – leaving a full exploitation of its interpretive potential to future work – and, to maintain simplicity and tractability, we abstract from a number of topics that are of crucial relevance in understanding fiscal issues in EMU. First, we look only at the long-run dimension of the problem. We therefore concentrate on spending cuts rather than other strategies towards deficit reduction. Second, we leave unspecified the preferences over public goods – public goods could also affect utility indirectly, through production efficiency – and look mainly at the impact of spending cuts on aggregate demand. Third, we (realistically) confine our analysis to public goods that are supplied domestically.

The setup of the model

The model consists of a N-country world, each country supplying goods produced by using a variety of domestic labour inputs. Agents have monopoly power in the supply of their own specific labour inputs, so that in equilibrium the output level is too low relative to its efficient standard.[1] Each national agent consumes a basket of international goods and derives utility from money holdings, the availability of a domestically supplied public good, and leisure. Preferences are assumed to be symmetric across countries only as far as consumption parameters are concerned: preferences over leisure, liquidity services and public goods can be (and in general will be) different across countries.

Preferences

Each of the N countries is specialized in the production of a traded good. In each country i, with $i = 1, 2, \ldots, N$, there is a continuum of economic agents, with population size normalized to 1. Agents in country i are indexed by j^i, with $j^i \in [0, 1]$.

The lifetime utility of agent j^i, denoted $U(j^i)$, is given by:

$$
U_t(j^i) = \sum_{\tau=t}^{\infty} \beta^{\tau-t} \left[\frac{C_\tau(j^i)^{1-\rho}}{1-\rho} + \chi^i \log \frac{M_\tau^i(j^i)}{P_\tau^i} \right.
$$

$$
\left. + V^i(G_{i,\tau}) - \frac{\kappa_i}{2} \ell_\tau(j^i)^2 \right]
\tag{12.1}
$$

---

[1] In this chapter we abstract from short-run issues, specifically the effects of fiscal policies under monopolistic competition in the presence of nominal price rigidities. For an analysis of such effects see Obstfeld and Rogoff (1996); Corsetti and Pesenti (1997).

Here β is the discount rate, equal to $(1 + \delta)^{-1}$ where δ is the rate of time preference; $1/\rho$ is the elasticity of intertemporal substitution; C is a consumption index (to be defined below); ℓ denotes the amounts of labour supplied by the agent. In providing public goods, G, the government spends exclusively on domestically produced goods; the function V is individual utility from public goods.

Financial wealth, measured in composite consumption units, is allocated among two assets – real-money holdings, M/P and an internationally traded bond, denoted B in what follows. Any national money, M^i, provides liquidity services that enter the utility function of country i's residents. The international bond is in zero net-supply world-wide:

$$\sum_{z=1}^{N} \int_{0}^{1} B_t(j^z) dj^z = 0. \tag{12.2}$$

Consumption and price indexes

The consumption index is defined as

$$C_t(j^i) \equiv \prod_{z=1}^{N} (C_{z,t}(j^i))^{\gamma_z} \quad \sum_{z=1}^{N} \gamma_z = 1 \tag{12.3}$$

where $C_z(j^i)$ is consumption of the zth good by a resident of country i.[2] Note that preferences on the N goods are identical across countries. The parameter γ_z indexes the effective macroeconomic 'size' of country z, in terms of the weight of zth goods in world consumption.

In the absence of market segmentation across countries, the consumption-based price indexes that correspond to the above specification of preferences[3] are

$$P_t^i \equiv \frac{1}{\gamma_W} \prod_{z=1}^{N} (E_z^i P_z^z)^{\gamma_z} \tag{12.4}$$

where

$$\gamma_W \equiv \prod_{z=1}^{N} \gamma_z^{\gamma_z}. \tag{12.5}$$

[2.] Throughout the model, superscripts index the country of the consumer, subscripts index the country of the producer.

[3.] The consumption-based price index, P, is defined as the minimum expenditure that is necessary to buy one unit of the composite good, C, given the local-currency prices of the N goods.

In (12.4), P_z^z is the price of the zth good in units of country z's currency, and E_z^i is the nominal exchange rate (ith currency per unit of zth currency), with $E_i^i = 1$ and $E_i^z = 1/E_z^i$. Consumption-based purchasing power parity (PPP) ($P^i = E_z^i P^z$) holds as a straightforward implication of the law of one price and the assumptions on preferences.[4]

Production and market structure

Production of national goods requires a continuum of differentiated labour inputs that are supplied by domestic agents. In each country, technology is described by a linear-homogeneous CES production function:

$$Y_{i,t} = \left(\int_0^1 \ell_t(j^i)^{\frac{\phi_i-1}{\phi_i}} \, dj^i \right)^{\frac{\phi_i}{\phi_i-1}} \qquad \phi_i > 1 \qquad (12.6)$$

where Y denotes output and the parameter ϕ is the elasticity of input substitution. Note that in a symmetric equilibrium where $\ell(j^i) = \ell_i$, output is a linear function of labour: $Y_i = \ell_i$.

While national firms act competitively, each economic agent is a monopoly supplier of one type of labour input. As agents use their market power, economic efficiency is reduced by monopolistic distortions and output is suboptimally low. The higher the degree of substitutability among inputs (the larger ϕ), the lower the market power of workers. Thus, the elasticity of input substitution ϕ is also a (decreasing) index of imperfect competition.

Profit-maximizing firms choose each type of labour according to the following labour demand schedule:

$$\ell_t(j^i) = \left(\frac{W_t(j^i)}{P_{i,t}^i} \right)^{-\phi_i} Y_{i,t} \qquad (7)$$

where $W(j^i)$ is the nominal wage rate. Acting as a monopolistic supplier of productive inputs, each agent j^i takes into account the labour demand above when maximizing her lifetime utility. The condition (12.7) implies that, in a symmetric equilibrium with $Y_i = \ell_i$, nominal wages must be equal to product prices ($W(j^i) = W_i = P_i^i$).

Individual budget constraints and optimality conditions

In country i, the individual budget constraint is

[4.] The model can be extended to encompass deviations from the law of one price and pricing-to-market. See, for instance, Betts and Devereaux (1996); Hau (1999); Chari, Kehoe and McGrattan (1997), Tille (1997).

$$P_t^i B_{t+1}(j^i) + M_t^i(j^i) = P_t^i(1 + r_t^i)B_t^i(j^i) + M_{t-1}^i(j^i) + W_t(j^i)\ell_t(j^i)$$

$$- P_t^i T_t^i(j^i) - \sum_{z=1}^{N} E_{z,t}^i P_{z,t}^z C_{z,t}^i(j^i) \qquad (12.8)$$

where B is the international bond and T non-distortionary (lump-sum) net taxes; both B and T are denominated in composite consumption units. The real rate of return on the international bond is denoted r^i. The standard transversality condition holds.[5] Note that in country i the government budget constraint is

$$\int_0^1 \frac{M_t^i(j^i) - M_{t-1}^i(j^i)}{P_t^i} \, dj^i + \int_0^1 T_t^i(j^i)dj^i$$

$$= \frac{M_t^i - M_{t-1}^i}{P_t^i} + T_t^i = \frac{P_{i,t}^i G_{i,t}}{P_t^i}. \qquad (12.9)$$

Recalling equation (12.7), the demand for labour supplied by individual j^i, agent j^i labor incomes are given by

$$W_t(j^i)\ell_t(j^i) = \ell_t(j^i)^{1-1/\phi_i} P_{i,t}^i Y_{i,t}^{\frac{1}{\phi_i}}. \qquad (12.10)$$

After substituting (12.10) into (12.8), the individual maximization problem can be written in terms of the following Lagrangian:

$$\mathcal{L}_t(j^i) = \sum_{\tau=t}^{\infty} \beta^{\tau-t}$$

$$\times \left[\frac{C_\tau(j^i)^{1-\rho}}{1-\rho} + \chi^i \log \frac{M_\tau^i(j^i)}{P_\tau^i} + V^i(G_{i,\tau}) - \frac{\kappa_i}{2} \ell_\tau(j^i)^2 \right]$$

$$+ \sum_{\tau=t}^{\infty} \beta^{\tau-t} \lambda_\tau(j^i) \left[-P_\tau^i B_{\tau+1}(j^i) + P_\tau^i(1 + r_\tau^i)B_\tau(j^i) \right.$$

$$- M_\tau^i(j^i) + M_{\tau-1}^i(j^i) + (\ell_\tau(j^i))^{1-1/\phi_i} P_{i,\tau}^i(Y_{i,\tau})^{1/\phi_i}$$

$$\left. - P_\tau^i T_\tau^i(j^i) - \sum_{z=1}^{N} E_{z,\tau}^i P_{z,\tau}^z C_{z,\tau}^i(j^i) \right] \qquad (12.11)$$

The first-order conditions with respect to $C_{z,t}(j^i)$, $B_{t+1}(j^i)$, $M_t(j^i)$, and $\ell_t(j^i)$ are, respectively,

[5] Namely,

$$\lim_{\tau \to \infty} \frac{1}{\Pi_{s=t+1}^{t+\tau}(1 + r_s^i)} \left(B(j^i)_{t+\tau+1} + \frac{M^i(j^i)_{t+\tau}}{P_{t+\tau}^i} \right) = 0.$$

$$C_t(j^i)^{1-\rho} \frac{\gamma_z}{C_{z,t}(j^i)} = \lambda_t(j^i)E^i_{z,t}P^z_{z,t} \quad z = 1, 2, \dots i, \dots N \quad (12.12)$$

$$\lambda_t(j^i)P^i_t = \beta\lambda_{t+1}(j^i)P^i_{t+1}(1 + r^i_{t+1}) \quad (12.13)$$

$$\frac{\chi_i}{M^i_t(j^i)} = \lambda_t(j^i) - \beta\lambda_{t+1}(j^i) \quad (12.14)$$

$$\ell_t(j^i) = \lambda_t(j^i)\frac{\phi_i - 1}{\kappa_i\phi_i}(\ell_t(j^i))^{-1/\phi_i}P^i_{i,t}(Y_{i,t})^{1/\phi_i} \quad (12.15)$$

Welfare and fiscal stances in a steady-state equilibrium

We now solve the model focusing on a flex-price, steady-state equilibrium in which neither country is a net debtor or creditor ($\int_0^1 B_t(j^i)dj^i = 0$) and national money stocks are constant at some level M^i. As agents are symmetric across countries, individual variables are equal to per capita variables (so that, for instance, $C_z(j^i) = \int_0^1 C_z(j^i)dj^i \equiv C^i_z$). The previous optimality conditions can thus be rewritten in terms of the following equilibrium relations.

First, from (12.12) the consumption index is characterized by:

$$P^iC^i = \sum_{z=1}^N E^i_z P^z_z C^i_z = \frac{1}{\gamma_z}E^i_z P^z_z C^i_z. \quad (12.16)$$

Second, from (12.14) equilibrium in the money market requires:

$$\frac{M^i}{P^i} = \chi_i\frac{1 + \delta}{\delta}(C^i)^\rho \quad (12.17)$$

where the long-run nominal interest rate in both countries is equal to the rate of time preference δ.[6] This is because the steady-state CPI inflation rate is zero, and (12.13) implies that the steady-state real interest rate is equal to the rate of time preference.

Third, the equilibrium condition (12.15) refers to the optimal trade-off between labour and leisure:

$$\ell_i = Y_i = \frac{\phi_i - 1}{\kappa_i\phi_i}\frac{P^i_i}{P^i}(C^i)^{-\rho} \equiv \Phi_i\frac{P^i_i}{P^i}(C^i)^{-\rho}. \quad (12.18)$$

Equation (12.18) guarantees that, at the margin, the utility cost of forgoing leisure is equal to the benefit from consumption financed with the income generated by supplying additional labour. Note that labour

---

6. In the long run, government spending is not among the determinants of the real interest rate.

supply will be higher (other things being equal) when consumption is lower or the real wage (P_i^i/P^i) is higher. Equation (12.18) also relates labour supply to a (decreasing) index of domestic market distortions, denoted by Φ. When labour inputs are very poor substitutes for each other (ϕ is close to 1), workers have a high market power and Φ is close to zero. Thus, low values of Φ correspond to low equilibrium levels of employment and output, owing to distortions associated with monopolistic competition.

Aggregating the individual budget constraints in country i, the steady-state current account relation can be written as:

$$C^i = \frac{P_i^i(Y_i - G_i)}{P^i}. \qquad (12.19)$$

In the previous expression, the steady-state consumption level is equal to output net of government spending *plus* net interest payments to the rest of the world, equal to zero since the long-run net asset position of each country is zero. The model is closed by writing the aggregate resource constraints as:

$$Y_i - G_i = \sum_{z=1}^{N} C_i^z = \frac{\gamma_i P^i}{P_i^i} \sum_{z=1}^{N} C^z. \qquad (12.20)$$

Due to the parameterization of the consumption index, the long-run aggregate equilibrium conditions in the goods markets show that real net income in each country ($P_i^i(Y_i - G_i)/P^i$) is a constant share of real-world consumption spending ($\sum_{z=1}^{N} C^z$).

To proceed, we introduce a few useful notational conventions. We first define an index of fiscal stance, g_i, as the ratio of total output to output net of spending. We can therefore write $Y_i - G_i \equiv Y_i/g_i$. Note that g_i is equal to one when government spending is zero, and it is increasing in the spending to output ratio G_i/Y_i. We also denote with the subscript W (for 'world') a geometric average of country-specific variables, using γ_i as weights. So, for example, the world fiscal stance index is defined as follows:

$$g_W \equiv \prod_{z=1}^{N} (g_z)^{\gamma_z}. \qquad (12.21)$$

Using the notation above, and following the solution strategy presented in Corsetti and Pesenti (1997), it is straightforward to show that in a steady-state equilibrium consumption and output are given by:

$$C^i = \gamma_i(\gamma_W)^{(1-\rho)/1+\rho}(\Phi_W)^{1/(1+\rho)}(g_W)^{-1/(1+\rho)} \qquad (12.22)$$

$$Y_i = (\gamma_i)^{(1-\rho)/2}(\gamma_W)^{(1-\rho)^2/2(1+\rho)}(\Phi_i)^{1/2}(\Phi_W)^{(1-\rho)/2(1+\rho)}$$
$$\times (g_i)^{1/2}(g_W)^{-(1-\rho)/2(1+\rho)} \qquad (12.23)$$

Interpreting the previous expressions, observe that national consumption levels in the long run reflect exclusively *global* macroeconomic fundamentals, either related to system-wide indexes of structural monopolistic distortions (Φ_W) or to system-wide fiscal policies (g_W). Country-specific variables (Φ_i or g_i) play no direct role in determining steady-state consumption levels, besides their contribution to the determination of the global indexes.

Country-specific variables matter, instead, in determining long-run output (and employment) levels: Y_i rises when either g_i or Φ_i increase. The impact of global variables on domestic output is more complex, as it depends on the sign of $1 - \rho$. If $1 - \rho$ is positive, a fiscal contraction world-wide or structural reforms that enhance labour market competitiveness in the system boosts domestic output, while the opposite effect prevails if $1 - \rho$ is negative. We will return on these results shortly.

Welfare effects of fiscal contractions

We can now delve into the analysis of the international transmission mechanism of fiscal policy. A properly micro-founded welfare analysis can be carried out by using (12.24) below, expressing the lifetime utility of the country i's representative agent:

$$U^i = \left(1 + \frac{1}{\delta}\right)\left[\frac{(C^i)^{1-\rho}}{1-\rho} + \chi^i \log \frac{M^i}{P^i} + V^i(G_i) - \frac{\kappa_i}{2}\,Y_i^2\right] \qquad (12.24)$$

after substituting for the equilibrium levels of the endogenous variables. The closed-form expressions provided by (12.22) and (12.23) above, together with (12.24), makes welfare analysis in our model remarkably tractable. In fact, the utility function can be rewritten as

$$
U^i = \left(1 + \frac{1}{\delta}\right)\left(1 - \frac{(1-\rho)}{2}\frac{\phi_i - 1}{\phi_i} g_i\right)
$$

$$
\times \left(\frac{(\gamma_i)^{1-\rho}(\gamma_W)^{(1-\rho)^2/(1+\rho)}(\Phi_W)^{(1-\rho)/(1+\rho)}(g_W)^{-(1-\rho)/(1+\rho)}}{1-\rho}\right)
$$

$$
+ \left[\left(1 + \frac{1}{\delta}\right)V^i(G_i)\right] + \left\{\left(1 + \frac{1}{\delta}\right)\chi^i \log\left(\chi_i \frac{1+\delta}{\delta}(C^i)^\rho\right)\right\}.
$$

$$(12.25)$$

The previous expression can be thought of as the sum of three components. The first refers to the trade-off between consumption and leisure, the second (in square brackets) captures the direct utility effects of consuming public goods, the third (in curly brackets) reflects the utility from real money holdings, and substantially reinforces the utility from consumption.

Consider first the long-run impact on domestic welfare of a domestic fiscal contraction (that is, the effects of a fall in g_i). Taking into account the effects of g_i on g_W, it is straightforward to verify that the first component of (12.25) is unambiguously negatively related to g_i. Intuitively, a fall in g_i implies that in the long run the supply of domestic labour (and output) falls by less than public spending, so that the world supply of consumption goods increases. As wages adjust downward to reflect the permanent fall in demand for domestic goods, the price of country i's goods decreases relatively to foreign goods, and country i's currency depreciates in real terms while prices fall in the world economy. Thus, country i reaches an equilibrium corresponding to higher consumption and lower output levels relative to the initial allocation.

The mechanism of transmission described so far holds regardless of the nature of public expenditure. Government spending may be purely dissipative ($V^i = 0$), or fall on public goods that increase agents' utility ($dV^i/dG_i > 0$). Trivially, when public spending is purely dissipative, the impact on domestic welfare of a fiscal contraction is unambiguously positive.[7] In our framework, steady-state levels of g_i larger than one are therefore desirable only to the extent that the government is able to raise domestic agents utility by transforming private into public goods.[8] The overall welfare impact of a domestic fiscal contraction is in this case ambiguous, as the welfare gains in terms of higher consumption must

---

[7]. When the utility of real holdings is considered as well, the positive welfare effects of higher consumption are reinforced.

[8]. Alternatively, steady-state levels of g above one could be rationalized by considering public goods (spending) as an input in production.

be assessed against the direct utility loss from lower consumption of public goods.

Consider now the effects of a fiscal contraction abroad on country i's economy (that is, the effects of a fall in g_W on U^i). In the long run, the contraction abroad appreciates country i's terms of trade and increases its real wages. The new equilibrium corresponds unambiguously to a higher level of consumption. Output, instead, can increase or fall relative to the initial equilibrium. Since the world fiscal contraction increases the availability of goods to world consumers, world demand for country i's goods falls if domestic and world goods are substitutes, and increases otherwise. From a different point of view, country i's output falls if the fall in labour supply following the increase in consumption more than offsets the positive effects of the real wage boost.

To interpret the latter result, observe that country i's output is subject to two contrasting forces: a higher world consumption tends to increase the demand of domestic goods (by a fraction $1/\rho$), while the real appreciation of the currency tends to reduce it (with unit elasticity). Thus, as observed above, a fiscal contraction abroad has a positive impact on country i's output when $\rho < 1$, and a negative effect when $\rho > 1$.

Another way of interpreting the previous result focuses on the complementarity of domestic and foreign goods in the utility function. Within the class of utility functions considered in our model, two goods are complements – that is, the marginal utility of one good increases with the consumption of the other – when the elasticity of intertemporal substitution is larger than the elasticity of intratemporal substitution, and substitutes otherwise. In our specification, the intertemporal elasticity is $1/\rho$ while the intratemporal elasticity is 1. Since world consumption of foreign goods is unambiguously higher after the fiscal contraction abroad, world demand for country i's goods (and country i's employment) increases only insofar as domestic and foreign goods are complements (when $\rho < 1$), and falls otherwise.[9]

The results above help to understand why the welfare impact on the domestic economy of a fall in spending abroad is ambiguous. Formally, taking the derivative of the welfare function with respect to g_W and disregarding liquidity effects, we obtain

$$\text{sign}\left(\frac{\partial U^i}{\partial g_W}\right) = \text{sign}\left(\frac{\phi_i - 1}{\phi_i}\frac{1 - \rho}{2}g_i - 1\right). \tag{12.26}$$

[9.] Svensson and van Wijnbergen (1989) provide an early analysis of international links in relation to intertemporal and intratemporal substitution within the context of a model with complete markets and perfect pooling.

This expression is clearly negative if $\rho > 1$, whereas a fiscal contraction abroad determines a rise in country i's consumption of both leisure and final goods. However, it can be positive if $\rho < 1$ (a necessary condition), provided that ϕ_i and g_i are sufficiently high.

The previous result hinges upon the two key features of fiscal policy transmission in the world economy. First, by depreciating the real exchange rate of the country that reduces spending, a budget cut increases purchasing power, consumption and welfare of all other national agents in the world. The spillover through this channel is unambiguously positive. Second, the increase in the demand for the private good supplied by the country that reduces spending can either increase or decrease the demand for output from the other countries, depending on whether national goods are substitutes or complements in consumption.

The international transmission of fiscal cuts is always positive when consumption goods are substitutes. Private agents in the rest of the world increase their consumption of both goods and leisure. When consumption goods are complements, however, the sign of the spillover from the second channel is ambiguous. A spending cut by one country increases demand in the rest of the world, and this may produce a situation of 'overheating' that decreases leisure down to inefficient levels.[10]

The likelihood of such a 'overheating' scenario increases when public demand for domestic goods is relatively high (g_i is large), or when the distortions in labour markets caused by monopolistic competition are low (ϕ_i is large), so that output and employment are close to their upward limit. This explains the result of (12.26).

Implications for policy and further research

The stylized model presented in this chapter stresses that the welfare impact of international fiscal policy spillovers hinges upon the following elements: first, national preferences over public goods; second, the degree of complementarity or substitutability of nationally supplied goods; third, the degree of labour (and goods) market distortions. These elements provide a stylized yet useful framework to assess the cross-border implications of the bias towards reducing spending, implicit in the fiscal rules of the EMU.

A core group of countries implementing spending cuts implies a long-run depreciation of their terms of trade (unless these cuts lead to a substantial reduction in private productivity, a possibility that we have not

---

[10.] In our framework, the 'overheating' scenario is such that the increase in foreign demand sharply raises the opportunity cost of labour in terms of forgone leisure.

allowed for in our analysis). This is good news for consumers in the 'out' countries and the rest of the world, where the terms of trade between domestic labour income and foreign goods improve. To the extent that national goods are substitutes, the consumption of leisure increases. A scenario of positive spillovers from budget cuts is favourable to a large euro area. Even if EMU fiscal rules translate into spending cuts that are inefficient according to national preferences, such country-specific welfare losses are offset by EMU-wide fiscal spillover.

A totally different outlook, however, characterizes a scenario of negative spillovers from budget cuts. Countries whose goods are complementary to the goods produced in the EMU core experience a strong demand for their products, as a result of the fiscal contraction of the 'ins'. If the economies of the 'outs' are already operating close to full capacity, the external demand boost is not good news, as the spillover effect enhances domestic overheating. In such a scenario, the fiscal contraction of the 'ins' hurts the 'outs'. Note that the likelihood of this negative spillover is higher for an 'out' country with high propensity to consume public goods (we may call it Denmark) or an 'out' country that, because of structural reforms in its labour and goods market, is able to operate close to its potential output level (we may call it England).

The possibility of a long-run negative spillover from overheating – and the conditions under which such a scenario are more likely – are one of the novel results from our analysis. Clearly, exploring the implications of these long-run fiscal spillovers for the decision to join a monetary union, as well as for the optimal design of domestic policies by the 'outs', is the next crucial step in the research agenda. In this regard, the formal tractability (and, specifically, the closed-form solution) of the contribution presented in this chapter can represent a useful starting point for welfare-based, micro-founded analyses aimed at exploring strategic equilibria and game-theoretic policy interactions among European countries, as well as between EMU and the rest of the world.

References

Betts, C. and Devereux, M. (1996). 'The Exchange Rate in a Model of Pricing-to-market', *European Economic Review*, 40: 1007–21
Buiter, W., Corsetti, G. and Roubini, N. (1993). 'Excessive Deficits: Sense and Nonsense in the Treaty of Maastricht', *Economic Policy*, 16: 57–101
Chari, V. V., Kehoe, P. J. and McGrattan, E. R. (1997). 'Monetary Shocks and Real Exchange Rates in Stocky Price Models of International Business Cycles', *NBER Working Paper*, 5876
Corsetti, G. and Pesenti, P. (1997). 'Welfare and Macroeconomic Interdependence', *NBER Working Paper*, 6307

De Grauwe, P. (1998). 'The Risk of Deflation in the Future EMU: Lessons of the 2990s', *CEPR Discussion Paper*, 1834

Eichengreen, B. and Wyplosz, C. (1998). 'The Stability Pact: More than a Minor Nuisance?', *Economic Policy*, 26: 65–104

Hau, H. (1999). 'Exchange Rate Determination: The Role of Factor Price Rigidities and Nontradeables', *Journal of International Economics*, forthcoming

Obstfeld, M. and Rogoff, K. (1995). 'Exchange Rate Dynamics Redux', *Journal of Political Economy*, 103: 624–60

(1996). *Foundations of International Macroeconomics*, Cambridge, Mass.: MIT Press

Persson, T. and Tabellini, G. (1995). 'Double-edged Incentives: Institutions and Policy Coordination', in G. Grossman and K. Rogoff (eds.), *Handbook of International Economics, III*, Amsterdam: Elsevier

Svennsson, L. E. O. and van Wijnbergen, S. (1989). 'Excess Capacity, Monopolistic Competition, and International Transmission of Monetary Disturbances', *Economic Journal*, 99: 785–805

Tille, C. (1997). 'The International and Domestic Welfare Effect of Monetary Policy under Pricing-to-Market', Federal Reserve Bank of New York, mimeo

Discussion

Paul De Grauwe

Chapters 10–12 in part IV, by Bergman and Hutchison, Allsopp, McKibbin and Vines, and Corsetti and Pesenti present a rich cocktail of policy problems that EMU will face. They all pertain to the operation of fiscal policies in EMU, discussing linkages across countries and fiscal policy as a stabilization instrument. Rather than going into a detailed analysis of each of the chapters, I want to organize my discussion around a limited number of problems, relating to the same broad issue of fiscal policies in EMU.

How reliable are calculations of optimum currency areas?

There is a massive literature on the issue of whether the EU countries form an optimum currency area (OCA). Bergman and Hutchison's chapter 10 adds another – and I must say, very interesting – study of this topic. It is also quite intriguing. One of its main conclusions is that the historic past is of little guidance in forecasting how the structure of asymmetric shocks will look in the future EMU. The reason is that EMU itself is going to affect the degree of integration and the economic structures of the EMU participants. The authors then go on to analyse the structure of the asymmetry of shocks during the last twenty years. Their findings are interesting. During this period shocks have become more symmetric among a group of EU countries mainly because the increasing dominance of Germany. Shocks that originate in Germany are quickly transmitted (and increasingly so) to the other EU countries.

The question that arises here is whether this structure of transmission of shocks will continue to exist in the future EMU. One could invoke the authors' first conclusion and claim that this structure may very well disappear in EMU. In the past twenty years, the importance of Germany has increased mainly because of its dominant position in the EMS. Since 1979 the German monetary authorities have gradually taken over the conduct of monetary policies for most of the EU countries – for example, the major shock of unification of Germany was easily transmitted to the rest of the EU because the Bundesbank reacted by pursuing restrictive monetary policies, thereby negatively affecting all EU output. As a result, shocks originating in Germany were easily transmitted to other countries.

This situation is unlikely to last in the future EMU. The ECB will set monetary policies based on the aggregate development of output and prices in euroland as a whole, and not only in Germany. As a result, the shocks that originate in Germany will no longer have the same strategic importance: they may not be of much greater importance than shocks originating in Italy, France or the Iberian peninsula. The ECB will react to these shocks to the extent that they affect the euroland aggregates; in other words, when future shocks arise in Germany the monetary authorities will be much less sensitive to these shocks than the Bundesbank was in the past. In the future EMU, it is much more likely that the dominant position Germany has taken during the last two decades will be very much reduced in scale. Germany, will continue to be important, but much less so than in the past.

The implications of this conclusion for fiscal policies are not immediately evident. In Bergman and Hutchison's view, the greater shock symmetry produced by the dominant position of Germany relieves the pressure on national fiscal policies to fulfil a national stabilization role. In the view defended here, asymmetric shocks may increase again in the future EMU; up to now 'German shocks' became common shocks thanks to the ERM transmission mechanism. In EMU, the dominant role of Germany will diminish, as will German-induced common shocks. This may then put fiscal policies as a stabilization instrument back into the front seat. Other forces, however, may go counter to this conclusion. To the extent that further economic integration leads to less shock asymmetry (see Frankel and Rose, 1996, for evidence), this pressure on fiscal policies to perform a stabilizing role would be correspondingly reduced.

The cost of a coordinated fiscal consolidation

In their chapter 11, Allsop, McKibbin and Vines use a multicountry model to evaluate the Stability Pact. Their main conclusion is that it solves a coordination failure (prisoner's dilemma). Under certain assumptions about consumption and investment behaviour their model shows that (under fixed exchange rates) a fiscal consolidation undertaken by a single country has a greater output loss than when the same consolidation is undertaken by all countries together. As a result, a coordinated fiscal contraction will be less costly in terms of lost production than an uncoordinated one. The authors are careful to stress that one has to assume rather large interest elasticities of investment demand to obtain this result, together with a few other assumptions. Nevertheless, they conclude that in a fixed exchange rate regime there is a presumption that a coordinated fiscal consolidation is less costly than an uncoordinated one. This then also provides *ex post* justification for the Maastricht approach to fiscal consolidation.

Although this is an interesting conclusion, one wonders about its general relevance. First, the model used is a sophisticated Mundell–Fleming model which, not surprisingly, predicts that a fiscal consolidation (expansion) leads to a real depreciation (appreciation) of the currency. It is unclear whether this is a result that can be trusted to be generally accepted. Certainly, much of the policy advice given by IMF economists today is based on a model that predicts that currencies appreciate when fiscal consolidation is pursued. Second, the empirical evidence sustaining the authors' conclusion is weak. They claim that there is evidence for their propositions. However, the empirical evidence is based on simulating their model. This can hardly be called an empirical test – these simulations only confirm the priors that were used to construct the model, they do not tell us whether the model has anything to do with reality.

Despite its intellectual attractiveness, the idea that a coordinated fiscal consolidation reduces the output losses compared to an uncoordinated consolidation is not firmly grounded. More important for the success of fiscal consolidation seems to be the monetary policy context in which it is pursued. The next section presents a case study contrasting the US and EU approaches to fiscal consolidation during the 1990s, illustrating the importance of the right monetary–fiscal policy mix.

Fiscal consolidation in the United States and the EU during the 1990s

In figure DIV.1 we present the trends in the government debt in the EU-11 and in the United States (we selected the 11 EU countries that started EMU in 1999). The differences between the EU-11 and the United States are quite striking. We observe a significant increase in the government debt/GDP ratio in the EU-11 during the 1990s. From approximately 55 per cent in 1990, the EU-11 government debt increased to close to 75 per cent of GDP in 1997. As a result, despite tight fiscal conditions, EMU will start with a substantially higher debt level than when the Maastricht Treaty was signed.

The United States experienced very different debt dynamics during the 1990s. After initial increases, the US government debt ratio started a decline from 1993 so that in 1997 it was barely higher than at the beginning of the 1990s. The contrast between the United States and the EU is all the more

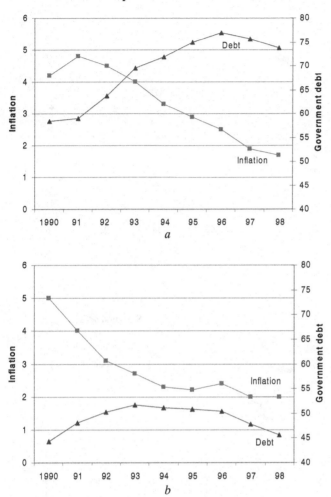

Figure DIV.1   Inflation and government debt, 1990–1998: *a* EU; *b* United States

striking since the official policies in the EU were dominated by the Maastricht requirement of deficit and debt reduction, which the EU countries accepted in the framework of a coordinated approach of fiscal consolidation.

The limited success of the EU in budget consolidation also appears from the evolution of the government budget deficits. In Figure DIV.2 we show the budget deficits in the United States and the EU during the 1990s. We compare the overall budget deficits with the structural deficits, and observe two striking phenomena. First, the US budget deficits declined steadily from 1991. This is not the case in the EU-11, where

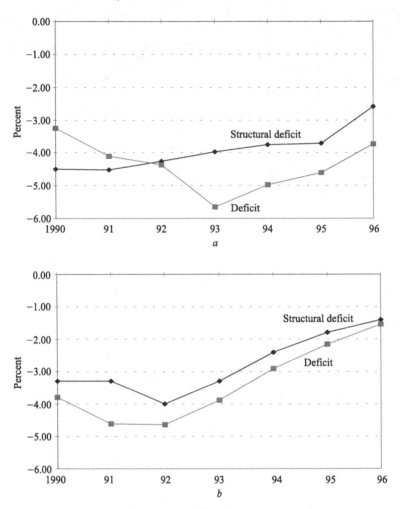

Figure DIV.2   Budget deficit and structural deficit (per cent of GDP), 1990–1996:
a EU-11; *b* United States

during the first half of the 1990s deficits increased substantially; only after 1993 do we observe a substantial improvement. The result of all this is that the budget deficits in the EU-11 returned to the level of 1990 only in 1998.

A second observation one can make from figure DIV.2 is that the tightness of fiscal policies (as measured by the structural deficits) was as strong in the EU-11 as in the United States, and yet the effectiveness of

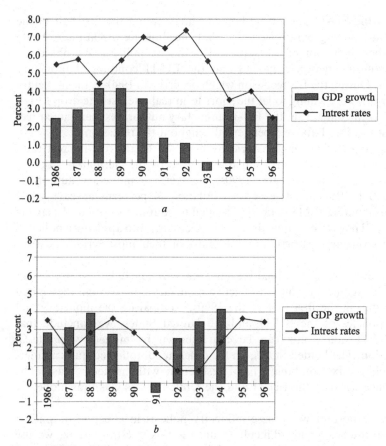

Figure DIV.3   GDP growth rates and short-term real interest rates, 1986–1996:
a EU-11; *b* United States

these policies of fiscal contraction in lowering the budget deficits was
significantly lower in the EU-11. In the US we observe that a 1 percentage
point fiscal restriction had the effect of reducing the budget deficit by
approximately 1 per cent. In the EU-11 this was certainly not the case
during the early 1990s, when despite policies of fiscal contraction deficits
continued to increase.

How can this relative lack of success of the EU in reducing budget
deficits and debts be explained? In order to answer this question, we
turn to monetary policies pursued during the first half of the 1990s.

Figure DIV.3 provides some evidence concerning the conduct of
monetary policies. We present and compare the real short-term interest

rates in the EU-11 and in the United States during the first half of the 1990s: it is now generally accepted that the short-term real interest rate is the best indicator of the stance of monetary policies. We observe a great contrast between the US and the EU-11 conduct of monetary policies. During the US recession which occurred in 1990–1, the monetary authorities were willing to let the short-term real interest rate drop to 1–2 per cent. In contrast, in the EU-11 monetary authorities maintained real interest rates well above 5 per cent throughout the recession.

This policy of keeping historically high short-term real interest rates during a recession was very much influenced by the German position in the EMS. During the early 1990s, the German monetary authorities fought a battle against 'excessive' inflation (4 per cent a year), while most of the other EMS countries decided to continue to peg to the strong D-mark. They were thereby dragged by Germany into applying a policy of strong monetary restriction in the midst of their most serious postwar recession.

Whatever the institutional reasons, one can conclude that the EU-11 followed significantly more restrictive monetary policies than the United States during the first half of the 1990s. Comparing the monetary and fiscal policies of the EU-11 and the United States, we conclude that the EU-11 policy mix can be characterized by monetary *and* fiscal restriction. The United States, on the other hand, followed quite a different policy mix, combining fiscal restriction with monetary ease. The difference between the EU-11 and the United States was thus monetary policy.

How important were these monetary policies in affecting output? It will, of course, remain difficult to answer this question. Here, we use the econometric evidence collected by Smets of the BIS (1995), who compared the transmission mechanism of monetary shocks in existing econometric models produced by central banks. The results are given in table DIV.1.

Let us now assume that the EU-11 had followed similar policies of monetary ease during its recession as did the United States. In that case the EU-11 would have allowed its short-term interest rate to drop by 4.2 percentage points compared to the observed rate. We therefore compute the loss of output in the EU-11 countries caused by the fact that these countries allowed their short-term interest rates to increase by 4.2 per cent above the US benchmark. The results are given in table DIV.2 (note that we include only the countries that appear in Smets' econometric study, 1995; the other EU-11 countries were not available). We also show the weighted average of these countries. It can be seen that the monetary

Table DIV.1. *Impact of a temporary 1 percentage point increase in short-term interest rate on GDP*

	Year			
	1	2	3	4
GER	−0.15	−0.37	−0.3	−0.07
FRA	−0.18	−0.36	−0.2	0.01
ITA	−0.32	−0.53	−0.22	−0.08
NDL	−0.1	−0.18	−0.15	−0.09
BEL	−0.03	−0.12	−0.23	−0.15
SPA	−0.05	−0.02	0.03	−0.17
AUS	−0.08	−0.14	−0.02	0.04

Note: These numbers show the effect on GDP (in per cent) of an increase in short-term interest rates of 100 basis points at the start of year 1 and maintained until the end of year 2, when the short-term interest rate returns to its initial level. *Source:* Smets (1995).

Table DIV.2. *Loss of output due to monetary tightness, 1991–1993*

	Year			
	1	2	3	4
GER	−0.64	−1.58	−1.28	−0.3
FRA	−0.77	−1.53	−0.85	0.04
ITA	−1.36	−2.26	−0.94	−0.34
NDL	−0.43	−0.77	−0.64	−0.38
BEL	−0.13	−0.51	−0.98	−0.64
SPA	−0.21	−0.09	0.13	−0.72
AUS	−0.34	−0.6	−0.09	0.17
Average	−0.72	−1.41	−0.87	−0.27

tightness applied by the EU-11 countries may, at its peak, have led to a loss of output of 1.4 per cent. We conclude that the policies of monetary restriction applied during the first half of the 1990s have probably intensified the recession to a considerable degree. They may also be responsible

Table DIV.3. *Growth rates of GDP in the EU-11 and the United States, 1981–1990 and 1991–1996*

Period	EU-11 (%)	US (%)
1981–90	2.4	2.5
1991–6	1.7	2.3

Source: European Commission, European Economy.

for the significant decline in the growth rates observed during the 1990s in the EU-11 (see table DIV.3).

The low-growth environment made possible by the European policy mix of monetary and fiscal restriction goes a long way to explain the difficulties experienced by European governments in reducing budget deficits and debt levels. Cutting budget deficits when monetary policies are restrictive is more difficult than when they are expansionary and stimulate economic activity. Similarly, the difficulties experienced by the European authorities in reducing government debt ratios can be traced to the deflationary policy mix. Not only did this policy mix reduce the decline in the deficit (the numerator in the debt ratio); in addition, the low growth of GDP to which this policy mix contributed also helped to keep the growth rate of the denominator in the debt ratio low. In fact, the policies of macroeconomic deflation ensured that the numerator continued to increase faster than the denominator, so that the debt ratio increased.[1] US policies were quite different, the budgetary restrictions combined with monetary expansion made it possible for the numerator to decline relatively fast, whereas the denominator increased more quickly than in the EU. All this made it possible for the debt GDP ratio in the United States not to deteriorate during the 1990s. In addition, this mix was also exactly right to avoid inflation increasing. As can be seen from figure DIV.1, the United States managed to reduce its inflation rate during the 1990s.

One can conclude that the nature of the monetary policies used during a process of fiscal consolidation is of great importance. The high cost of the

---

[1] A more formal analysis of this difficulty of reducing debt ratios when deflationary policies are followed can be found in Craig (1994); Demertzis, Hughes Hallett and Rummel (1996); Hochreiter (1997).

fiscal consolidation in the EU during the 1990s must have something to do with the fact that it was pursued for a long time in an environment of monetary tightness. Only after 1995–6 was monetary policy relaxed. It is, therefore, no surprise that from then on, fiscal consolidation appeared to become much easier. Whether fiscal consolidation was facilitated (i.e. less costly) because it was coordinated, as is contended by Allsop, McKibbin and Vines, remains an open question. If coordination reduced the output cost of disinflation, it must have been overwhelmed by the negative output effects of monetary tightness, which was also pursued in a coordinated manner.

The 'ins' and 'outs'

The success of the EU countries in satisfying the convergence game as mandated in the Maastricht Treaty has been quite spectacular. Few observers expected that EMU would start on time and with *all* the EU-countries that had expressed a desire to be in EMU right from the start. This success contrasts with the fears that the Maastricht convergence game would allow only a few countries to enter EMU, thereby splitting the Union apart. Similarly, the fear that the Maastricht convergence game might lead to negative selection, whereby the virtuous countries turned their back on EMU, does not seem to have happened.

One may wonder why these fears have not been realized. A first thing to note when analysing this question is the fact that the fiscal convergence criteria were interpreted in a flexible way, avoiding the most draconian budget cuts and strong fiscal spillover effects (as analysed in Corsetti and Pesenti's chapter 12). This is most obvious with the debt criterion, which one can say was not applied. We show the evidence in figure DIV.4 .

It can be seen that nine out of the eleven countries admitted to EMU had a debt/GDP ratio exceeding 60 per cent. As we all know, the Treaty allows for some flexibility. According to the Treaty, this ratio should not exceed 60 per cent. If it does, it should be 'sufficiently diminishing and approaching the reference value at a satisfactory pace' (art. 104 c). Clearly, even the flexibility of art. 104 would not have been sufficient to let so many countries in. Of the nine countries with a debt GDP ratio exceeding 60 per cent, six had seen this ratio *increase* recently, and one (Belgium) had reduced it but at a pace which will require twenty-five years to reach the magical 60 per cent. Thus, more than half of the EU-11 countries that were accepted into EMU did not satisfy one of the Maastricht convergence criteria.

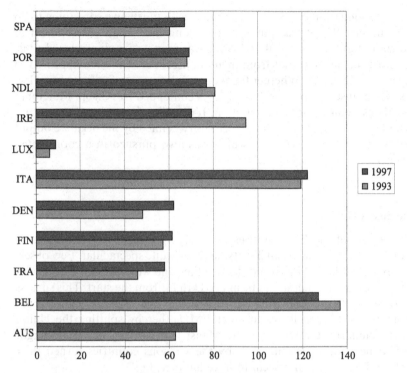

Figure DIV.4   Debt/GDP ratio in the EU-11 (per cent of GDP), 1993 and 1997

Why were the Treaty provisions not applied? The politics of the convergence criteria was such that those who were commonly believed to become 'outs' (the Southern European countries) were in a strategic position to block the start of EMU. These countries had achieved convergence in other areas (e.g. inflation and interest rates) and performed at least as well in the budgetary field as most of the core countries. In addition, the voting procedure (qualified majority) was such that they could have blocked entry of some core countries. Thus, the choice the EU-governments had was either to start EMU with all the countries who wished to join, or not to start EMU at all. The heavy political investment in the success of EMU that had been made by leaders like Helmut Kohl prevented the second scenario from happening. This created a strong political consensus to start EMU anyway, whatever the numbers showed. It was decided that the Treaty would not be an obstacle to achieving the goal of monetary unification. Whether this was a wise decision, only the future will tell.

References

Craig, R. (1994). 'Who Will Join EMU?', *International Finance Discussion Paper*, 480, Board of Governors of the Federal Reserve System

Demertzis, M., Hughes Hallett, A. and Rummel, O. (1996). 'Is a Two Speed System in Europe the Answer to the Conflict between the German and the Anglo-Saxon Models of Monetary Control?', *CEPR Discussion Paper*, 1481

European Commission (DG II) (1997). 'Economic Policy in EMU, Part B, Special Topics', *Economic Papers*, 125

Frankel, J. and Rose, A. (1996). 'The Endogeneity of the Optimum Currency Area Criteria', *NBER Discussion Paper*, 5700

Hochreiter, E. (1997). 'Disinflation, Fiscal Positions and Seigniorage. A Comparative Analysis of the EU Countries 1970-96', Österreiches National Bank (September), mimeo

Smets, F. (1995). 'Central Bank Macroeconomic Models and the Monetary Policy Transmission Mechanism', in *Financial Structure and the Monetary Policy Transmission Mechanism*, Geneva: BIS

Index